365 daily readings
from the non-Pauline books
of the New Testament

Taken from the **Geneva Bible Notes**
published by Grace Publications
Edited by Ray Tibbs

Grace
Publications

DayOne

© Day One Publications 2022

ISBN 978-1-84625-729-2

British Library Cataloguing in Publication Data available

Joint publication with Grace Publications Trust and Day One

Day One Publications
Ryelands Road, Leominster, HR6 8NZ
Telephone 01568 613 740
Toll Free 888 329 6630 (North America)
sales@dayone.co.uk
www.dayone.co.uk

Grace Publications Trust
7 Arlington Way, London EC1R 1XA
editors@gracepublications.co.uk
www.gracepublications.co.uk

Printed by 4edge Limited

PREFACE

This volume is part of a series providing a devotional commentary on all the books of the Bible. It is compiled from material previously published as daily Bible reading notes. The Geneva Bible Notes were first issued by the Grace Publications Trust in 1988. They became a quarterly publication in 1994. New sets of Notes continue to be produced and are available as individual copies or by subscription from the address below.

The aim of the Notes is to help 'ordinary' readers gain a better understanding of the Word of God and how it applies to their daily lives. Most contributors were serving or retired pastors – men experienced in 'rightly dividing the word of truth'.

The holy Scriptures are the richest jewel that Christ has left us. They are profitable for all things (2 Tim. 3:16-17). Let us therefore endeavour to search the Scriptures (John 5:39) in order to find Christ (Luke 24:27,44-45).

When reading the Scriptures the following method is recommended:

(a) **Pray:** Before turning to the portion for each day, pray that the same Spirit who wrote the Word may assist you in reading it. Pray that he might show you more of Christ (John 15:26), and pray that you might grow in the love and knowledge of Christ.

(b) **Read** the allocated portion for the day before you turn to these Notes.

In reading the Bible, do so with:

reverence: remember that God is speaking to you in every line;

seriousness: it really is a matter of life and death, of heaven and hell;

affection: warm your souls each day with the live coals from off the altar of truth – Isa. 6:6; Luke 24:32.

The Word of God is a love letter sent from God that it might delight your heart (Ps. 119:16,35,47,70,97). Prize, therefore, the written word (Job 23:12). The Word is the field where Christ, the pearl of great price, is to be found.

(c) **Study** the explanatory notes and comments in these daily Notes. If you have any queries then please see your minister, or write to the editor.

(d) **Try to memorise** at least one verse from each daily portion and meditate upon it (Ps. 1:2).

(e) **Write down** in the Notes pages anything you have found helpful.

(f) **Share** what you have discovered by writing or talking to another Christian.

(g) **Prayerfully consider** what you can do to translate what you have learned into action.

Geneva Bible Notes are distributed by DayOne with whom all trade orders should be placed. Geneva Bible Notes, DayOne, Ryelands Road, Leominster HR6 8NZ
Telephone 01568 613740 (Monday to Friday 9.00am – 5.00pm)   www.dayone.co.uk

Readings in

Acts

by Ray Tibbs

WINDOW
ON THE
WORD

Title. The title of this book was not given by the author and we must be sure that as we read it, we do not become too preoccupied with the apostles. That is not Luke's intention. Various books in Scripture are given titles according to key characters but in each one it is the acts of God which are being illustrated. It is the same with this book and Luke begins as he means to carry on, by writing of Christ (Ps. 45:1).

Author and purpose. Luke makes it clear he is writing a continuation of something he has already written (Luke 1:4). The book covers a period of about thirty years and broadly refers to the areas mentioned in 1:8. Acts is theological history – facts chosen and arranged according to a prior purpose, i.e. the development of personal faith in Christ. About 75 per cent of this book is made up of speeches and their contexts, most of which are evangelistic messages.

Registration. Acts explains both the origin of the church and its mission. It shows the effects of the death and resurrection of Jesus. It demonstrates that our faith is traceable back to that period and is not of recent origin. It continues the written record of redemption from the Old Testament, individually and corporately. It is related to the past – to the person of Christ and beyond, but also to the future in the advance of the gospel from Jerusalem to Rome and from Jews to Gentiles. It is extensive rather than intensive and provides an historical framework for the epistles. One example of its historical precision is found in its accurate use of official titles, e.g. 16:35; 17:6; 18:12; 28:7.

Vindication. Acts proves the claims for the divine origin of Christianity, amidst stories of its founder being executed as a criminal and then returning to life. Luke demonstrates Gentile sympathy and Jewish antagonism. He shows how Christ kept his promise of sending the Holy Spirit and how he governs the church through him. He also shows how the hostility of Satan is constantly exercised against it. He illustrates the harmony within the church and among the apostles.

Edification. The power of Christ was exercised in the gospel through ordinary men and brought the world into submission to himself. The obedience, courage and faithfulness of the disciples are our example in their refusal to depart from the truth or their God-given task. Their message was that salvation is found in Christ alone (4:12). He is the fulfilment of the prophetic promises. That way of salvation had been prepared by God and did not originate with men. Luke, the Gentile author, shows how the gospel was offered to all.

Acts 1:1-14   The commission and ascension of Christ

Luke makes it clear that what he writes about is a continuation of something he has already written (Luke 1:4). The book covers a period of about thirty years and broadly refers to the areas mentioned in 1:8.

The resurrected Christ (1-8). Christ presented himself alive on a number of occasions during the forty days before the ascension. One feature of this period was that he was not with the disciples all the time as he had been before. It is pointless to ask where he was between appearances but more pertinent to ask why his appearances were spasmodic. It was probably in anticipation of his ascension and despatch of the Holy Spirit. In future, while they could be assured that he was alive, they must realise he could not be with them in bodily form. During this period he gave the disciples instruction (4,8), but their grasp of where everything was leading was inevitably unclear (6). The resurrected Christ commissioned them and at the same time promised them the spiritual resources which would enable them to fulfil their commission. Since nothing could stand in his way – not Satan, sin or death – he would ensure that nothing stood in their way as they obeyed him. And so it remains.

The ascended Christ (9-14). The disciples had not witnessed his birth, death or resurrection but they saw his ascension. Having accepted the other events by faith, the sight of this confirmed the truth of them. Jesus was returning to his rightful place having completed the work God had given him to do. This is not to be regarded as a separate event, but as a necessary consequence of the others. It never took a more prominent place than the cross in their future testimony. They consistently witnessed to Christ crucified.

The reminder of the angels concerning Christ's return provides an additional motivation for the apostles to fulfil their commission. As we serve Christ, we have the same commission and hasten his coming. Our witnessing must not only be done in the light of his first coming but also of his Second Coming. And, like the disciples, how better to spend that waiting period than 'with one accord, in prayer'?

Something to think about: Has the cross of Christ become displaced from its central position in our testimony?

Something to talk about: This passage contains one of only six references to the baptism of the Holy Spirit. What do we learn from them? Matt. 3:11; Mark 1:8; Luke 3:16; John 1:33; 1 Cor. 12:13.

Something to pray about: Seek the enabling of God in your own life, but you must make sure your motives are pure (James 4:3).

Something to do: Review the Lord's teaching on the kingdom, using references such as Matt. 3:2; Mark 9:1; Luke 11:20; 17:20; John 18:36, etc.

Acts 1:15-26   The appointment of Matthias

Some say this action was mistaken because Matthias is never heard of again and Paul was God's choice. This is the first attempt by believers to make sure they kept themselves in line with what they saw to be God's requirements. No one could have anticipated the appointment of Paul. Before Pentecost, the circumstances were unique and subsequent losses from among the apostolate (for example 12:2) were not replaced.

The apostles had encountered failure in their midst (16). Even the company of those closest to Christ included an unworthy member. Paul warned the Ephesian elders that among them would be those who would be unfaithful and harmful to the church (Acts 20:30). When it happens in our own circles, we will grieve over it, try to correct the situation and endeavour to prevent its recurrence, but it should not incapacitate us. There are special dangers in leadership, and none are immune to temptation.

A faithful public testimony was preserved (19). Everyone knew how Judas died and it is likely the word spread that he had betrayed Jesus. The church took deliberate action to remove whatever stigma was attached to his loss. They did not allow the vacancy caused by the betrayal to go unnoticed. A grievous sin had been committed and whereas the major consequence of it could not be altered, deliberate action was taken to limit the damage done and remove one result of it at least.

The situation was consistent with Scripture (20). Peter showed that the Scriptures had something to say about the matter. It not only foretold the event but also showed what action should be taken because of it. Jesus knew what would happen (John 17:12) and spoke of the future in terms of the completed number (for example Matt. 19:28). We should be able to scrutinise any aspect of church life by Scripture to see the consistency.

Confidence in the office was retained (21-22). Failure by one office holder did not destroy the validity of the office itself. The qualifications for a successor were made clear. Guidelines were set out which the existing apostles already met. They were based on closeness to Christ. At the same time, the task of the successor was made clear. The qualifications for office had to match the work to be done. Only those who had been closest to Christ could give testimony to his resurrection.

The church was guided in making the appointment (23-26). The apostles took the lead in nominating those who were eligible. They were in the best position to know who was suitable, but they did not make the final decision. They sought the guidance of God, but they involved the whole community of believers. The choice was his, not theirs, but he used human means to demonstrate his choice. The means employed was an approved method to discover the will of God (Lev. 16:8; Prov. 16:33; Luke 1:9). Believing prayer and faithful action must be combined if God's will is to be done.

Acts 2:1-4   The coming of the Holy Spirit at Pentecost

This passage has been likened to Genesis 1 and Matthew 1 in importance. It brings a revelation of the third person of the Godhead in proportions previously unknown. The Holy Spirit was active before, as Christ was active before Matthew 1. Here, he enters history in an unprecedented manner and brings about the third greatest event in the history of the world – the formation of the church. There is a sense in which the work of the Father was incomplete without the work of the Son and the work of the Son was incomplete without the work of the Spirit. Each work must be seen in the light of the others. This event does not emphasise the Spirit for his own sake. We gain a clearer understanding of God, through Christ, because of the Spirit.

Today, we are the beneficiaries of all three revelations. We live in the last days because there are no more events to come on the same scale, apart from the return of Christ. The revelation of God is complete and has been preserved in the Bible. It is therefore improper to suggest that manifestations of the Spirit which took place during the period of Acts should be reproduced exactly in succeeding generations. The creation and incarnation, although isolated events, were obviously profoundly influential upon subsequent generations, but could not be repeated. So it is with Pentecost. Any contemporary claims to a return to Acts 2 erode the work of the Spirit in the same way that Roman Catholic claims about the mass erode the work of Christ.

The feast of Pentecost was fifty days after Passover and celebrated the ingathering of the first fruits of the harvest. Thus, the feast of Pentecost found its fulfilment, as had the feast of Passover. The Old Testament dispensation was passing away as the New Testament era was being established. This is a supernatural attestation to the transition, completed by the fall of Jerusalem in AD 70, showing it to be unmistakably the work of God, not men.

The sound prepared those who met for a heavenly intervention. The nearest earthly comparison was wind, an image which Jesus had used for the coming of the Spirit (John 3:8; 20:22), as well as one which had familiar Old Testament associations (for example Gen. 8:1; Exod. 14:21; Num. 11:31). The sound inside the house caused people to gather outside. They were not attracted by the tongues.

The sight of fire illustrated another feature of the Holy Spirit. Although he came with power (wind) he also came with intimacy. He met each one individually and they all knew each one had been met in the same way. Fire was traditionally associated with cleansing and the protective presence of God (Exod. 3:1-6; 19:18; Isa. 6). Both John the Baptist and Jesus specifically associated the Holy Spirit with fire (Matt. 3:11; Luke 12:49).

The speech showed they had been given a divine ability to communicate beyond their human limitations. This was the beginning of the worldwide spread of the gospel. Ten days before, they had been given a commission which at the time they were unable to fulfil (1:8). Now they could witness 'to the ends of the earth'.

Acts 2:5-13   The miracle of Pentecost

There is both a reality and a symbolism in this event. Initially it was used to attract interest and bring people from many nationalities under the sound of the gospel. But the event also showed how things would develop in future: a company of God's people extending beyond Jerusalem, with many nationalities hearing the Word of God in their own language.

God has spoken. No other god speaks. The voice of God had not been heard for about four hundred years until John the Baptist, Jesus and now these men. God gave them words and the ability to speak about himself and what he had done. The God-fearing hearers knew they were hearing about God because God himself was making it possible. From that time, God has not been silent (Heb. 1:1-2). The Holy Spirit continues the ministry of Christ. He makes God known by directing people to himself through his Word. The power, presence and truth of God had broken into the world in a remarkable way and was not going to be limited.

God speaks to everyone. God was deliberately speaking to people who lived outside Israel. God overcame national barriers, evidently intending, even at this early stage, that the truth about him should go beyond the borders of a single country. It has been said that this event reverses the tower of Babel. There, man was punished for rebellion by the imposition of many languages and dispersion. Here, all were united by the truth. However, the different languages remained and they dispersed again. Human distinctions will always remain, but there is no discrimination because of them (Col. 3:11). The truth is equally relevant to all, as they are.

God uses his own people to speak to everyone. This phenomenon is not to be regarded as normative. As we shall see, it was Peter's message which was used in the conversion of these hearers. But as a non-repeatable event, it was foundational. The 'all' of v. 1 must refer to the apostles. They had a unique position (Eph. 2:20), and are the subjects of the immediate context (1:26). If it is the 120 who are considered as the recipients of the Holy Spirit, why should they be distinguished from the rest of 500 believers (1 Cor. 15:6)? The apostles had no successors because they alone had witnessed the resurrection and had been commissioned directly by Jesus. The promise of Jesus was kept, by means of which they could serve him (Acts 2:33). But because of their pure, unadulterated message, the Holy Spirit was diffused. The truth was passed on by common means. Their experience was the impulse that created a momentum, and that momentum continued irresistibly on its course.

We are caught up in that momentum. The Holy Spirit in us is our energising influence. We fail to witness because we resist the Spirit. He illuminates our mind, revitalises our will, enlarges our heart and confirms our faith. He came in to the world to testify of Christ – through us (John 7:39; 16:13-15). The Holy Spirit continues to be active according to a certain plan, not indiscriminately. That plan is certain to be completed (2 Cor. 5:5).

Acts 2:14-21   Peter's first sermon [1]

The first part of Peter's sermon to the curious crowd was an explanation of the phenomenon they had witnessed. His explanation was not based on appearances but upon Scripture. This was the fulfilment of a prophecy made 850 years before. The men described in v. 5 were not the only ones present, for Peter addressed a wider group (14). Peter obviously spoke in a language all were familiar with.

The Holy Spirit was poured out (17-18). By using the quotation from Joel, Peter said the last days had begun. The crowd was privileged to be part of a vital chapter in the God's plan for the world. The Spirit of God had been given to Old Testament saints, but now he came:

(a) *In greater measure* – being 'poured out' in abundance, as compared with earlier limitations (for example 1 Sam. 16:14).

(b) *In wider distribution* – to all types of people, not just leaders as before (Num. 11:29).

(c) *For divine communication.* Truth was revealed to them directly and they were to pass on the same truth to others (Jer. 31:33).

The end was foretold (19-20). In addition to the increased activity of the Holy Spirit, a further indication that the last days had arrived would be by the increased disturbance of the stable features of the world. The physical elements of the world would become so seriously affected that people would start to ask why such things were happening. By this means, they would be reminded of powers greater than their own. They would be confronted with the fact that their security could not be found in anything belonging to the created order. God would warn the inhabitants of earth that its days were numbered.

Salvation was offered (21). This summary verse connects the earlier themes. The end of the world was at hand. Many signs would point to it, but at the same time there was hope. God could be called upon and known personally in a way that was previously impossible. Heaven was open and many people would speak of it with certainty, because God had shown himself to them. Those who sought God by this new access would not be disappointed and would escape the judgement that had been heralded.

In these last days, God has given us his Son, his Spirit and his Word. With such great heavenly resources available to us, how can we say this is a day of small things? What more can God give? If we feel impoverished, then we must look to ourselves for an explanation. We need to learn to think spiritually about events around us and prepare ourselves for his return. We need to show others that God is at work in his people and in this world and that there is an inseparable connection between that work and Jesus Christ.

Acts 2:22-36   Peter's first sermon [2]

The central thread in the main section of Peter's sermon is the relationship between God and Jesus of Nazareth, illustrated especially by the resurrection.

God approved him (22). God demonstrated his involvement with Jesus by giving him great power. Thus, God worked through Jesus in an unparalleled way in the sight of everyone. Jesus used the testimony of those signs to point to his identity (Matt. 11:4-5; John 10:25,37-38).

God delivered him (23). God's involvement in the life of Jesus included not only the giving of power but also the ordering of events. It was God who gave him over into the hands of men so that he would die. He could easily have prevented it, but instead he used it. Although it was man's responsibility, it was still God's intention.

God raised him (24-32). The crowd would be familiar with the life and death of Jesus, but not with his resurrection. That resurrection was proof of the relationship he had with God. God's involvement with Jesus continued uninterrupted. His death was not a setback. It was necessary so that it could be overcome and the greater power of God could be conclusively seen at work in him. Peter used part of Psalm 16 to show that this was God's plan from the beginning. David was not referring to himself in the psalm but knew that the Messiah would be one of his descendants. The Word of God confirmed the truth of the resurrection. In turn, Peter confirmed the resurrection by his own eyewitness account. Peter was saying that as Joel spoke of the coming of the Spirit which the crowd had witnessed, so David spoke of the resurrection of the Messiah which the apostles had witnessed.

God exalted him (33-36). Even the resurrection did not end God's dealings with Jesus. He had been sent from heaven and so returned there, to be reinstated with even greater glory, because he had completed his divinely appointed task. The two events, resurrection and the giving of the Spirit, are connected by the exaltation of Jesus Christ to the place of highest authority. Thus, the second event provides additional proof for the validity of the first. If you doubt the resurrection, look at the power of God – he could do it. Then look at the plan of God – he would do it. Now look at the people of God – he has done it.

The once and for all entry of the Spirit into the world introduced his extensive availability. He would be received by all who believed on Christ as Saviour and Lord. He was the one through whom the benefits of the cross would be transferred across space and time. Because we know he is already at work within us, we can seek a greater measure of his enabling. Our Spirit-filled lives should bear a radiant testimony to the power and authority of the risen Christ. That is why he has been given to us (Rom. 8:5; 2 Thess. 2:13; Heb. 9:14).

Acts 2:37-41   'Save yourselves from this corrupt generation'

Peter's sermon was used by the Holy Spirit to bring conviction of sin to his hearers (37; Heb. 4:12). The exhortation which followed is very instructive as the first example of how to help people in that position. They must:

Recognise the truth. They had been confronted with the truth about Jesus and crucially their involvement in his death – the death of their own Messiah. They had been an unwitting party to it and felt the grief and guilt of that association. They were helpless, as the situation could not be changed and were justifiably under the wrath of God. They sought deliverance from that condemnation and were ready to do whatever was necessary to escape it. Ever since then, sinners must be brought to see the same things – their personal involvement in the death of Christ, the just condemnation of God and the necessity to take action to avoid it.

Repent of their sin. More was required than the recognition of their sin. True conviction brings revulsion also – a sorrow for sinning against God and a resolution to forsake it. It was not a fear of the consequences of it, but a hatred of its nature. Baptism illustrated the desire to remove the pollution of sin and be united with the death and resurrection of Christ which procured it. The immediate result was the forgiveness of their sins – as they had turned from their sin and put their faith in Christ. God did not hold their past against them. This free gift created a new start in life. Again, the way of salvation has not changed, nor ever will.

Receive the Holy Spirit. The promised Holy Spirit, now poured out (33), would be received by others. He was a gift from heaven and would dispense other, lesser gifts and graces according to the divine purpose – some of which had been witnessed already. His entrance into the world was not limited to those original recipients, therefore. His coming to them unleashed a massive potential that would spread to others through them. Joel's prophecy had a continuous rather than an instantaneous fulfilment. Although recipients of the Spirit were instrumental in his distribution, it is clear that the promise, gift and call were all of God.

Rescue themselves. The final appeal, summarised in v. 40, invited them to be saved by means of what had already been declared. He appealed to them not to go the same way as other members of the doomed generation which surrounded them, by their inactivity. They had to reject the corrupting influence of their society with its inevitable tendency to lead them away from God. This was not salvation by works. It meant by actively receiving God's free gift, they would be saving themselves from their corrupting generation – not their sin. Then, having been separated from the world, they immediately became united with the church.

Acts 2:42-47   The character of the early church

The three hallmarks of the Christian church found here provide a general description of how the church developed, not what it was like immediately. It is something of an ideal picture, summarised in v. 42 and then expanded, rather than a permanent condition.

A learning church. Everything else followed from this first feature. Belief determines practice. We must understand before we do. The apostles held unquestioned authority as those who had been with Christ and whose ministry had since been authenticated by the Holy Spirit.

The new converts continued steadfastly to sit under this teaching. There is an element of perseverance here. That is, they did not give up, however difficult the teaching was to understand or apply. If our teachers, who pass on apostolic truth to us, need a similar commission, recognition and authentication, then we need the same persistence to learn.

A loving church. The people were committed to each other. Their spiritual union with Christ drew them together and they demonstrated their unity. They were all devoted to the whole body, without anyone hiving off into individualism. As well as a common purpose, they had a common practice. They were not under any instructions to share their goods (5:4) but it was a spontaneous demonstration of their new attitudes to God, others and to themselves and their possessions. They were concerned to care for the needy, among themselves at first, but also to visitors and unbelievers. What they had received freely, they gave freely.

A worshipping church. There were evidently two types of gatherings. Believers met informally in each other's homes and in a single, Christ-centred event, linked the breaking of bread (in which the death of Christ was remembered) with a meal (1 Cor. 11:20). Such gatherings were inevitable, given the large numbers, the lack of large buildings and the unique nature of the event. In addition however, the believers did meet formally with specific gatherings for prayer. This was a daily, public occasion for everyone at a pre-arranged time, in the temple area. Western church life has preserved neither of these occasions exactly – nor need it do so. It is the spirit of worship that must be preserved and expressed in a manner that is mutually agreed and appropriate for the circumstances of the period and place.

A growing church. This factor is recorded as a result of the previous three. This church was winsome and made its own impression upon the society around it. They were filled with a new reverence for God, and fruit of the Spirit was manifest among them. It was evident that God was with them, and people were attracted to them. Numbers grew because God blessed them with salvation, but also because 'they enjoyed the favour of all the people'.

We may need to view our church life as a whole and then undertake our evangelism, without compromise, having this factor in mind.

Acts 3:1-10   The man at the Beautiful Gate of the temple

This section continues until 4:31 and was apparently selected as an incident to illustrate some points from the previous portion before picking up the same theme again in 4:32. Peter displays some admirable qualities as a believer, not just an apostle.

A godly disposition. Peter and John were intent upon engaging in a spiritual exercise – corporate prayer. Although attendance at such times is not always a good indication of our spiritual condition, it can reveal something of the state of our heart. They went together and thereby encouraged each other – always a good thing to do. They were anticipating meeting God and their fellow believers and such a readiness to give themselves to honouring God in this way brought a greater receptivity to his constraints upon them.

An openness to others. However, they were not so intent upon getting to the prayer meeting that they failed to hear a cry for help. They allowed themselves to be distracted, not because they saw an opportunity, but because they saw a need. They knew they had the means to meet that need and were not prepared to withhold it until their return journey. Like the Lord Jesus they responded to such a request immediately and sympathetically. Even if it meant missing the meeting, they were ready to help anyone in need who asked them. Are we?

Giving what he had. It was part of the ministry of the Holy Spirit to continue the work of Jesus through his apostles. They were to speak of him, and they were to be like him. The compassionate use of his miraculous power would demonstrate how closely linked with him they were. Although we are not apostles, the ministry of the Holy Spirit is essentially the same. He is simply at work in different people in different ways in different generations, but still commending Christ to the world by means of his people. If Christmas says 'God with us' and Easter says 'God for us', then Pentecost says 'God in us'.

Pointing people to Christ. As in the sermon that followed, Peter directed the man away from himself to Christ. Peter appeared to give the man a command which was impossible for him to obey, but in fact it was a promise. 'In the name of Jesus Christ (you can) walk.' He was inviting the man to put his faith in Christ. When he did so, he turned his back on his old life and received complete healing (16). Although he held on to Peter physically, he held on to Christ by faith. Missing prayer meetings should not happen regularly, but there are times when, sensitive to the Spirit, we can respond to someone's need and find Christ is glorified.

Acts 3:11-26   Peter's second sermon

Peter began this sermon in the same way as he had when he preached at Pentecost. He began with a current event – an undeniable fact familiar to his hearers – and explained it in terms of its place in the purposes of God. He clearly showed that God's purposes were focused on Jesus Christ. He used Scripture to interpret events witnessed by his hearers.

The explanation (12-16). Peter immediately swept aside any misunderstanding that the healing came from them. They had no supernatural resources of their own. They were simply tools in the hands of God. They were used by God so that Jesus could be glorified through them. The crowd (mainly residents of Jerusalem) had been directly involved in the death of Jesus, but it was his resurrection which demonstrated his identity. Peter used exalted titles of Jesus. The 'Holy and Righteous One' speaks of someone who was set apart from others for the service of God and distinguished by his innocent, law-abiding life. The 'author of life' points to him as being the one from whom life originates. Death had no power over him.

His perfect life demonstrated he had no reason to be punished for his sin. God reversed the death penalty imposed on Jesus by the wishes of these people. They had been grievously mistaken in their assessment of Jesus. Jesus, the servant of God, has been glorified and is to be worshipped.

The obligation (17-21). Although they acted in ignorance, they were still guilty of acting against God and killing his Son. It had been prophesied, but they remained responsible for their own actions and would have to face the consequences of rejecting their long awaited Christ. Peter called upon them to recognise the gravity of their sin and turn away from it. They needed to turn to God – the very one they had so seriously offended, and cast themselves upon his mercy. If they did that, their sin would be erased and a new period of blessing would come upon them. It was guaranteed by the promises of God. The prospect of his return was mentioned with the implication that they would therefore face him again one day. Their best course of action was to turn their earlier rejection of him into wholehearted acceptance – immediately. Jesus, the Christ suffered and is to be trusted.

The confirmation (22-26). Peter concluded by saying that everything he had described had been foretold. What had happened was in keeping with what they already knew about God. He quoted Moses, Abraham and Samuel to support his contention that recent events demonstrated the truth about God and his Son. Those who refused to embrace this revelation of God in Jesus Christ could expect only justifiable punishment. The message of salvation he embodied had to be heeded. They were living in the momentous days that had been expected for so long. Such a high privilege gave added urgency to their need to embrace this gracious offer. Jesus, the prophet, has spoken and must be listened to.

Acts 4:1-22   Men who have been with Jesus

Participated in a demonstration of power. Undeniably, a miracle had taken place and, as before (3:16), an explanation was given (10). Peter did not claim to have any power of his own but declared that the power which had been used was linked with faith in Jesus Christ of Nazareth. It was clearly the work of God but it was associated with a man they had known. He had been tried by them only a few weeks before. Peter had been incapable of such action some months previously (see Matt. 17:19-20), but later, he and others had received a promise from Jesus that such things would be possible (John 14:12-14). Peter had implicit trust in the will and the ability of God to accomplish the miracle through him. Hebrews 11 reminds us of what faith in God is capable of. Although it was not always miracles that were involved, there was always a tenacious belief that God would act according to his word. Today, those who have been with Jesus can still participate in demonstrations of God's power – by faith, without their being miraculous, in church growth for example.

Proclaimed salvation of the soul. The name of Jesus had greater power than just healing the body. Peter shifted the focus to what was more important: the salvation of the soul. He showed that salvation is:

(a) *Restricted*. It comes from one source only, Jesus Christ, the incarnate Son of God (1 Tim. 2:5). There can only be one plea for anyone and everyone.

(b) *Rejected*. The author of their salvation had already been rejected by those same men. They had been grievously mistaken and were being given an opportunity to correct that mistake and accept sure ground for their future eternal security.

(c) *Required*. A positive response from them was necessary. There was no option. God had been offended and punishment awaited them. It was senseless to decline.

Today, those who have been with Jesus can still proclaim salvation for souls guilty of sin.

Presented a transformation of character. A few weeks before, Peter had been fearful of being identified with Jesus (Luke 22:54ff), but he was different now. Even after the experience of Pentecost, he had been filled with the Spirit for this specific task, as Jesus had promised (Luke 12:11-12). God had given this gift so that Peter would be changed in a way which would honour God. This change was:

(a) *Shown in boldness of speech*. Peter was prudent in his approach to the Sanhedrin and courteous in his address to them. He was very frank with his answers while being faithful to the truth.

(b) *Seen by others*. Peter's words impressed the Sanhedrin who were well versed in presenting and defending arguments. He was evidently an untrained layman who, although unschooled in rabbinic discourse, could hold his own in such an assembly without being intimidated.

(c) *Sought by others*. Rather than being cowed by the experience, when Peter returned to the rest of the believers, he proved to be an inspiration to them. They sought and received, through prayer, the very characteristic that Peter had displayed (compare vv. 13,29,31 where the same word is used).

Today, those who have been with Jesus show evidence of their transformed nature to others by words which glorify God in their manner, explanation and challenge.

Acts 4:23-31   After further threats...

They reported back. After being released, Peter and John went immediately to the church – the group with which they were most closely identified. They did not go home, to work or to the press. No doubt word of the apostles' imprisonment had spread and the church had met already. Perhaps they had met to encourage each other in the face of potential danger at this early expression of opposition. The apostles had much to share, not just because what affected one affected all but also because such events could have an influence upon the whole church. They had a real sense of belonging and knew what they said could affect others who would need support in similar situations in future.

They prayed together. The report of the apostles prompted prayer, not the creation of a policy document on what to do in the event of further persecution. It was a fervent, positive and spontaneous response to the situation, which, while either being led by one voice or reported in summary, embraced everyone. The form of address to God acknowledged his supreme authority, reflected in the use of 'slaves' when referring to themselves in v. 29, a different word from that used to refer to David (25) and Jesus (27). As the God of creation, he ruled over all things. As the God of revelation, he warned of such occurrences. As the God of history, he designed and accomplished his own plan for the good of his people in which Jesus Christ was central. They did not seek vengeance or guidance. They did not ask God to remove the threats, only take them into account. They asked for boldness to continue what had

been started, without fear, and they asked for miracles to confirm the word they would declare to demonstrate that God was with them and not with the Sanhedrin. This was united prayer, governed by the knowledge of God and his will.

They spoke boldly. Their prayer was definitely answered, but we know few details.

(a) *The building was shaken.* This was for a similar purpose to the physical phenomena recorded in 2:2-3. They indicated the reality of the active presence of God, as in Exodus 19:18 and Isaiah 6:4.

(b) *The Spirit came.* Although he was never absent, he came on particular occasions to equip his people for special acts of service. This was the third time Peter had received this filling (2:4; 4:8) and this would not have been just for the apostles. The church did not ask for this, but the gift confirmed the correctness of their petition, for they were given the means by which it would be fulfilled (Luke 11:13).

(c) *The word was spoken.* The word used does not mean preaching, but is the ordinary word for speaking. The people became ready to speak freely. They would speak with courtesy, dignity and magnanimity. They would be prudent but frank towards their hearers and would maintain a loyalty and fidelity to the truth. They would speak without fear of opposition, with a confidence and certainty in the Word of God.

Does such prayer characterise our response to the reports we hear?

Acts 4:32-37   Some characteristics of the early Christian church

They were united (32a). The church had a common affection, being devoted to each other. They also had a common purpose and were not pulling in different directions. Later, other churches had to strive for this condition (Phil. 2:2). As in any church, there were tendencies that would divide them if given the opportunity to do so, no doubt, but there was even more to unite them. God loved them and Christ had died for them. The Spirit indwelt them and one day they would dwell in heaven. In the meantime, the lost surrounded them. It takes effort to preserve unity (Eph. 4:1-6), and involves not being critical or wanting one's own way.

They testified (33). Internal harmony facilitated effective witness by the apostles. At that time they could maintain their particular commission without hindrance, but it would not always be so (6:1-2). The focal point of their testimony was the resurrection (2:32; 3:15), an event they had witnessed themselves and to which all other features of the ministry of Jesus related. The power referred to here was not in terms of delivery but effect. The grace of God honoured their message, and their labours were singularly blessed.

They shared (32b,34-37).

(a) *A radical attitude.* Having all things in common meant that everyone willingly placed their possessions at the disposal of others. They retained the right of ownership but were conspicuously unselfish. Freedom of conscience was maintained, for the action was voluntary, not commanded. The believers considered themselves to be stewards of God's provision. Other ideologies compel conformity to apparently similar principles by force or legislation.

(b) *A sacrificial action.* Occasionally, wealth was surrendered as an offering, not an obligation. By being placed under the jurisdiction of God-appointed leaders, such gifts were consecrated to God. The community did not possess the gift before it was given and nor did they after it was given. There was no separate identity between the community and the individuals who made it up. They considered God, not the donor, the community or the recipient, to be the owner. Barnabas was a positive illustration of this principle, in stark contrast to Ananias and Sapphira, who in the next chapter prove to be a negative illustration. Other ideologies are materialistic, accumulating possessions for their own sake or for the good of all to the extent that the individual is lost sight of.

(c) *An equitable principle.* Distribution was made according to need, not indiscriminately so all could receive similar or appropriate shares. The circumstance of v. 34a was the result not the intention. The proper use of God-given resources will remove need on an international scale as much as on a local scale. The personal response in the first instance was to God and then the corporate response was to need, expressed via the apostles (11:29-30). Individual preferences were voluntarily submitted to the corporate will as needs were more accurately observed and assessed by the church (1 Cor. 16:2).

In its earliest and perhaps purest days, this was the issue which distinguished the church.

Acts 5:1-11 Great fear seized the church

The early church was taught two important lessons through this shocking incident.

Sin is serious.

(a) *The nature of sin.* However much Ananias and Sapphira may have sought to deceive the church, their real sin lay in lying to God. They evidently despised him, having no sense that he would know about and condemn their action. They had not really yielded themselves or their possessions to him and retained what they had supposedly devoted to him. Retaining what was devoted to God reflects the sin of Achan (Josh. 7).

(b) *The punishment of sin.* The sin of Ananias and Sapphira was exposed, not just to Peter but to everyone and thereby achieved the very opposite of what was intended. They were shown to be the worst in the church, not the best. Their secret sin was punished publicly, immediately and unexpectedly. It was severe and clearly judgemental, having been described as the first miracle of judgement for 900 years (see 2 Kings 1:10).

(c) *The aftermath of sin.* The church was in awe of God after this (5,11). Although sin has been forgiven through Christ, God cannot be trifled with (Gal. 6:7-8). They were shown how important it is to keep a clear conscience before God who sees beyond our actions and judges the secrets of the heart. We must learn to live transparently under the eye of God (Acts 24:16). We cannot expect judgement to fall again in the same way, for it was a warning to succeeding generations, but it will certainly fall one day (1 Peter 1:17).

The church is precious.

(a) *Under threat.* Satan tried to suffocate the church at birth through the action of the Sanhedrin but failed. Here he was trying a new tactic by sowing seeds of corruption within the church, but again he failed due to the singular care God exercised over his people. Despite the apparently ideal picture of 4:32, there were imperfections and God cleansed his people by a radical action, not intended to be repeated. Luke faithfully records the failure but at the same time records the glory of God and the limitation of Satan.

(b) *Under instruction.* In this way, God showed he requires a pure church. Written guidance for the church had not yet been compiled, apart from the Old Testament, and this action was consistent with Deuteronomy 21:21. In future, such disciplinary matters would be placed within the hands of the church leadership (Matt. 18:15-20). It was intended that the church would be edified whenever such action was necessary so that even if the sinner could not be won, the church would be warned.

(c) *Under construction.* This passage contains Luke's first use of the term 'church' in Acts. It comes at a significant point when the people of God were evidently separated from others by the Holy Spirit, united by the Holy Spirit and administered by the agency of the Holy Spirit. He was the most predominant influence, both actively and passively, in a new social grouping that was neither man-made nor man centred. There is a level of individual accountability which must have corporate expression. Harbouring sin can hinder the church.

Acts 5:12-16 Signs and wonders

This transitional passage illustrates the impression the church made upon the public.

Meetings.

(a) *Regularity.* The church met habitually and purposefully (2:46). The large crowd and the teaching given would have attracted even more attention.

(b) *Respect.* Recent events had helped to establish the reputation of God's people. There was no disorder, only an evident devotion to God. The work of God in and through the believers prevented people from forming a casual attachment to the church. This was more than just another religious movement.

(c) *Growth.* Despite that reticence, the church grew as a work of God, rather than as a choice of men. People were brought to Christ and saved through the Word of God. As a result, they joined the church. That is still the normal order today, but in the these days when the presence of God among his people no longer causes onlookers to keep their distance, an informal acquaintance with the church first usually leads the way to hearing the Word of God and being convicted by it.

Miracles.

(a) *Definition.* The use of the term 'miracle' has become somewhat broader than its use in the Bible. Any amazing event, defying explanation in which the power of God is apparently involved, seems to come into this category. But usually a biblical miracle had both revelatory and redemptive significance and was not only an exercise of power. They were rare in the Old Testament, establishing divine truth and helping to secure an impact for it at significant points in history.

(b) *Characteristics.* 'Miracle' highlights the power, 'sign' highlights the meaning of an event, 'wonder' highlights an impression made by an event. They are:

(i) *Visible*, unmistakable, obvious and able to be examined, and immediate.

(ii) *Inexplicable*, for although verifiable they cannot be explained any other way.

(iii) *Awesome*, attributable to God and having a widespread impact, and complete.

(iv) *Revelatory*, instructive about the redemptive character or purpose of God.

(v) *Confirmatory*, confirming the ministry and message of the agent, and successful.

(c) *Agents.* Miracles were performed by the apostles as the unique witnesses to Jesus Christ. As far as we know, they did not perform the same variety of miracles as Jesus because theirs did not point to the worker as did his. They were related to answered prayer and testimony to Jesus (4:29-30). Later miracles (1 Cor. 12:9-10), while not performed by the apostles, may have therefore have been of lesser significance, as they bore indirect testimony to Jesus at a time when written testimony was being circulated and greater evidence of the work of the Holy Spirit was being seen in changed lives and growing churches.

(d) *Effect.* The crowd drew a crowd, and when it was known that God was among them some took advantage of the situation and brought sick friends and relatives to be healed, some from miles away. The reference to Peter's shadow gives the motivation, not the explanation. Superstition may have caused them to act that way, but not necessarily receive healing. Today, God works constantly and directly through the means which are available to all believers (2 Cor. 12:9).

Acts 5:17-26 Persecution begins

The previous encounter with the Sanhedrin (4:1-22), after a night in custody, resulted only in threats, but no punishment. Since then, the blessing upon the church had increased and, as a result, the antagonism of the religious authorities grew more intense (17). The apostles were arrested and imprisoned without charge.

Divine intervention.

(a) *Prison walls could not restrict God's activity.* Such a miraculous intervention was not often repeated on later occasions, but this early example of the care of God for his beleaguered people would bring strength to many in future. Paul's experience was quite different, but God was equally active in his incarceration, albeit in another way (Phil. 1:12-14).

(b) *The miracle was hidden from unbelievers.* The angelic release took place at night and was not witnessed by anyone else. The results were obvious and certain implications could have been made, but as with other miracles they were for the strengthening of believers and the confusion of unbelievers. Even if someone were to rise from the dead, sceptics would remain unconvinced (Luke 16:31).

(c) *Further hardship followed.* After their release, the apostles were rearrested and subsequently flogged (40). Divine intervention on one occasion does not prevent future pain. The earlier experience strengthened the believers so that they were able to manage the later experience (41).

Divine instruction.

(a) *Human commands cannot restrict God's Word.* The angel gave very clear instructions what to do upon their release – more of the same. They obeyed without delay and faced the consequences. They had no assurance that the threats would be removed or that they would be unharmed. They were encouraged to continue the vital work of teaching the truth. They were to go to the temple, not the marketplace, to people in whose lives some groundwork had already been done.

(b) *The message was unchanged.* Angels could not deliver this message themselves. They had not experienced the salvation to which it referred and could only look on in wonder (Heb. 1:4 – 2:3; 1 Peter 1:12). The apostles were told specifically not to abbreviate their message or hold anything back. This 'news' of which they spoke was spiritual and eternal, not physical and temporal. It could be known through repentance towards God and faith in Jesus Christ. It could be sustained by abiding in Christ through the power of the Holy Spirit and would only be fully realised in the world to come.

Something to think about: How can you maintain a faithful testimony in the face of antagonism to your faith in Christ?

Something to talk about: What are the most obvious forms of opposition to the gospel in this country?

Something to pray about: Pray for believers you know who are suffering for their faith.

Something to do: Find out about the persecuted church in other countries.

Acts 5:27-42 Is it of man or of God?

How do we know what is the work of God and what is not? This was a dilemma the Sanhedrin faced (38-39), and we sometimes face today.

Jesus Christ is magnified (30-32).

(a) *He was raised by God.* Resurrection was a controversial issue with some members of the Sanhedrin (17; 4:1-2), but Peter proclaimed their core belief that the resurrection of Jesus was a work of God. The same God they worshipped had the power of life and death and had foretold this resurrection, as Peter had testified before (see 2:24-28).

(b) *He was exalted by God.* From the lowest place of a despised, executed criminal God lifted him up to the very highest place: of Saviour – he who appeared to be unable to save himself; and Prince – whose crown had once been thorns and whose sceptre a reed. Human assessments of him are reversed (Isa. 53:12).

(c) *He was appointed by God.* God made him the mediator through whom the people of God would enter into the spiritual blessings promised in the covenant. They were not earned or engineered but freely given (Isa. 49:5-7).

(d) *He was witnessed to by God.* The gift of the Holy Spirit to the followers of Jesus was further testimony to God's ownership of him. The Spirit had testified to Jesus during his own earthly ministry. The apostles spoke of him with new-found boldness and worked miracles. The church continued to grow.

Opposition to Christ and his church hardens (33-40).

(a) *It is destructive (33).* When the Word of God is spoken, it confirms existing hostility.

Here, the authorities did not threaten, debate or bribe, but wanted to eliminate the church completely, because they were intent upon self-preservation.

(b) *It is passive (38).* A more moderate position was presented by Gamaliel. Although pragmatic and ultimately beneficial to the church, inactivity is not usually a sound principle. While advocating the need for discernment, a work of God invites zealous promotion and spirited defence, not neutrality.

(c) *It is restrictive (40).* The course of action finally taken by the Sanhedrin was a compromise between their original murderous intention and the inertia of Gamaliel. By beating the apostles, their bodies were hurt in the hope that it would hinder them in the pursuit of their cause. By limiting their speech, they expected their behaviour to be hampered. Some will still try to restrict the work of God by the imposition of their own will upon others.

The church is strengthened (41-42).

(a) *They rejoiced.* The apostles were not intimidated, depressed or angered by their treatment. They had no fear of men and their experience brought them closer to Christ. Although physically weaker, they were spiritually stronger.

(b) *They preached.* They ignored the command, knowing they were answerable to a higher authority. They took every opportunity they could to speak of Christ and left the consequences of their actions – both positive and negative – to God. The fear of God motivates true service for him and promotes it in others.

Acts 6:1-7 Dealing with problems in the church

The persecution recorded in chapter 4 strengthened the church rather than weakened it and so Satan attempted, to damage it internally through Ananias and Sapphira. The subsequent opposition from 5:17 again was ineffective and Satan attempted internal disruption once more.

Murmuring. There was some discontent in the Jerusalem fellowship but it was not in the open. Although the point was legitimate, the spirit was wrong as it took the form of a complaint. It was the subversive element which was dangerous, rather than the criticism itself. We must learn to guard our spirit and give attention to Philippians 2:3-5,14. The apostles went public and treated it as a church-wide matter. They called a special meeting and involved everyone in the decision-making process.

Cultural tension. The two named groups were both Jewish but from different backgrounds and had their own traditions. The original disciples, and especially the apostles, were familiar with their own community and aware of their needs. There was no deliberate neglect, but offence was taken (by new Christians) when none was intended. A multiracial church should be particularly careful about cultural sensitivities and exercise some flexibility. To quell criticism, it seems seven Hellenists were appointed, but they supervised food distribution to all. Working out Col. 3:11 is not always easy.

Poverty. This was the real problem and was later addressed on a wider scale (Rom. 15:26). Without a welfare state, and having no charities or, in some cases, families to care for them, believers were bound to care for such needy ones. It was part of their distinctive Christian testimony (1 Tim. 5:3; James 1:27), in accordance with the existing requirements of God's Word (Exod. 22:22; Isa. 1:17). In accepting the duty of care, the apostles made sure the needs of individuals were met by the whole church.

Inefficiency. Were the apostles themselves at fault for allowing the situation to develop? Whether or not the complaint was personalised, the apostles addressed the matter as if it were. They recognised the diversity of needs and gifts within the church and were willing to delegate so that suitable men could meet clearly identified needs. The apostles guided the decision-making process without imposing their will. They presented a realistic solution to the church and affirmed the result.

Commission. Some tasks were outside the God-given limits of the responsibilities of the apostles and this issue gave them the opportunity to state the nature of their calling. It would not be proper or beneficial to the church for them to depart from it. They had already been called upon to take up leadership in ways they had not expected. They were primarily witnesses, and the discipling of others that became necessary as a result of that work involved some organisation. We may need to remember that teaching and leadership are different gifts (Rom. 12:7-8) and are not always found in the same person.

Growth. Was the church too big? Growth inevitably means less contact between everyone, but the solution did not break up the church or halt growth. Instead, it proclaimed the gospel more efficiently – by word and deed. The apostles were liberated and the believers were satisfied. The church continued to grow under the gracious hand of God (9:31; 12:24; 16:5; 19:20). We must not only pray for church growth but also for the necessary grace and wisdom to handle it when it arrives.

Acts 6:8-15   Stephen: an exemplary Christian

Gifts notwithstanding, in Stephen we have a good example to follow (1 Cor. 11:1; Phil. 3:17).

A good reputation (3). Stephen had an outstanding character which had won the respect of others. His public conduct was without blame (1 Tim. 3:8). In his dealings with others, he had to be well spoken of, otherwise he would have brought the church and the Saviour into disrepute. Holiness is admired – even by unholy people. We are called upon to be separate from sinners, not superior to them. Such a character must be pursued deliberately (24:16; Prov. 22:1).

Full of the Holy Spirit (3,5,8,10; 7:55). Although the ministry of the Holy Spirit is varied, it has certain key features (John 15:26; 16:8,13). There would be a readiness and an ability to speak of Jesus. There would be a heightened power of communication which could not be gainsaid as truth was delivered with great fervour, accuracy, perception, boldness and effectiveness. Matched with an intense desire and an abandonment of self to God, this unusual measure of ability would confound any opposition.

Full of wisdom (3,10). This refers to a God-given gift upon which the Holy Spirit operated. It is a mental excellence which does not simply include a good mind – being clever – but involves the correct attitude to, and proper use of, knowledge so that it is rightly employed. It pursues the highest ends and uses only the best means to achieve them. It is described in James 3:17 and perfectly exemplified in the Lord Jesus by the manner in which he conducted himself before those who opposed him. Such a gift can be sought

(James 1:5-8), but must be demonstrated by action (James 3:13).

Full of faith (5). This is defined in Hebrews 11:1 as the acceptance as fact of what is not known to the senses. It is the conviction that things out of sight are still real. Stephen set his sights on God who had called and equipped him for special service. He knew God would help him in the defence of the truth and would bless his ministry. He would persist diligently, despite opposition, and would give it the practical expression needed (James 2:26). It is a gift already possessed by all believers but is so often unused.

Full of grace (8). This refers to a gracious disposition caused by the grace of God. It is fearless, with a bearing and conduct which are even-tempered, considerate and constructive. It is the ability to carry other gifts without ostentation and is seen in Stephen's ministry and defence. This too can be sought (Rom. 1:7), but is only given to the humble (James 4:6) and once again is illustrated in Christ (2 Cor. 8:9).

Full of power (8). 'Signs' and 'wonders' are two terms which describe the same phenomenon; the first from the point of view of intention and the second from the point of view of perception. Stephen was not an apostle, but the Lord gave gifts to whomever he pleased (see Luke 10:17; Acts 8:6) and they still affirmed the messenger as being the bearer of the apostolic message. His mighty power is still operative in and through believers, but it is no longer at their disposal in exactly the same way that it was in apostolic times, although it can be sought (Eph. 1:18-20) and known (Eph. 3:20).

Acts 7:1-29   Stephen's sermon [1]

The first charge against Stephen (6:13) was that he never stopped 'speaking against this holy place' (the temple). The Jews had excessive reverence for places and Stephen addressed this.

A place is of secondary importance.

(a) The experience of Abraham showed that people were more important than places. He was chosen while he was in a foreign land. He was sent to another country on the basis of a new relationship with God. The destination was not significant and remained undisclosed until he arrived. On arrival he was told that the land was for his descendants, rather than for himself, but the covenant was given as a sign that the promise would be kept. The first part of the promise was fulfilled as his descendants multiplied. However, their greatest growth came through hardship in a foreign land where they were nurtured for over 400 years.

(b) Although provided or permitted by God, special places brought no guarantee of faithfulness or acceptance with him (9,38-39). He provided the land and designed the tabernacle but no direct spiritual benefit was gained from them. God had moved with his people in the desert and the clearly temporary nature of the tabernacle contrasted with the permanence of God's presence with them. Even when the temple was projected, it was not established by the highly revered David, but by the lesser Solomon. David's favour was not dependent upon the temple, nor was Solomon's disfavour nullified by the temple.

(c) Stephen's listeners were proving themselves to be consistent with their forefathers by retaining the lesser and rejecting the greater. They had made an idol of the temple and clung to that while despising their Messiah. The danger of becoming too attached to physical things is almost inevitable because we are sensual creatures who are constantly battling with our newly formed spiritual nature. Many churches have been damaged by conflicts which have grown out of proportion over petty physical and practical matters.

God is not limited to a particular place.

(a) God had used various places in dealing with his people – Mesopotamia, Haran, Egypt, Midian and the Sinai desert. The call of Moses took place on 'holy ground' (33), because God was there. The new faith defended by Stephen was entirely in keeping with the widespread activity of God. It involved a universal commission which went beyond national boundaries.

(b) The purposes of God were continuing to unfold. Christianity was not a result of spontaneous growth, but of linear development. In the progressive nature of God's plan, the temple was only ever expected to be temporary and would be replaced – indeed had been so already – and Stephen was helping to prepare the way for it, after the original warnings of Jesus (Luke 21:6). He was correct to confirm its significant past but was bound to speak of its imminent demise. Previous providences and punishments presented the precedents.

(c) There would be greater blessing to follow because God was not limited to a particular place. God was present within the lives of his people – and Stephen himself was an example of that, being filled with the Holy Spirit. It was the promise of Christ (Matt. 28:20), and was taught by the apostles (1 Cor. 3:16-17; 6:19-20). Although Stephen's persecutors were resisting the witness of the Spirit, such resistance is not confined to unbelievers and we must be aware of the potential we have to turn our backs on promised blessing,

Acts 7:30-53   Stephen's sermon [2]

In his sermon, Stephen used facts with which the Council would be familiar, but he gave them a new interpretation. Jews regarded their history as the unique outworking of God's plan. Their religion and history were inextricably interwoven like those of no other nation. Stephen used this accepted principle and directed them to Christ. Old things were passing away. All was becoming new.

The second charge against Stephen (6:13) was that he spoke against the law (that is, not illegally but disrespectfully).

God gave purpose to the law. The function of the law was limited. It only had temporary significance. The law was never intended to give life or provide the basis for acceptance with God (Gal. 3:21-24).

(a) It revealed the nature of God by setting out the standards he wanted man to keep and by condemning his failure to obey it.

(b) It showed to man the reality and enormity of his sin (Rom. 7:7) and actually inflamed it – as was seen at the time of its delivery (38-41).

(c) It showed that man needed to have his sin dealt with – through salvation. God would accept man only when the law was fulfilled by perfect obedience. Salvation could only come through God's acceptance of a perfect substitute in man's place.

(d) It reveals the perfections of Jesus Christ, who was perfectly obedient to it.

The law is still in operation for the same purposes and is therefore a means of grace. By its negative application, it is a beneficial instrument because it sends us to Christ.

The Jews had a wrong attitude to the law.

(a) They were proud that it represented their special relationship with God – but they did not listen to it (51). They were unbending before it and refused to repent of their sin.

(b) They were proud of their adherence to the law, but in fact their obedience was selective and formal. They could only abide by it externally for there was no change of heart.

(c) The history of the nation revealed that they had repeatedly rejected both its message and its messengers – even their own Messiah. They had acted against the law far more than Stephen, having treated it as an end itself, rather than as a means to an end.

God is known apart from the law.

(a) God had revealed himself to Abraham and the patriarchs before the law had been given. Stephen used that exalted title because God had already shown himself to be glorious by his command (3), his gift (5), his promise (5), his justice (7) and his presence (9).

(b) God can be known and worshipped without it. It is derived from him and is therefore less than him and must never replace him (Rom. 1:20). It is highly significant, but it is not the only means of revelation. God became known gradually (Heb. 1:1), until his final revelation in Christ (Heb. 1:2). Scripture is the medium for it, providing both the record and the explanation. But we must be wary because we can become guilty of bibliolatry – the exaltation of the written word over its author.

Acts 7:54 – 8:3   Blessed are they who die in the Lord

Stephen was comforted in persecution. Stephen's sermon prompted fury as had the sermon of Peter to the same group (5:33), but it was his account of his vision which provoked them further. Perhaps there was an expectancy in his look, knowing the growing hostility of his hearers. It seems that the vision was given in anticipation of his martyrdom. It was given not just for his benefit, but to instruct future generations. Like other miraculous events which would never be repeated, even though similar circumstances would be repeated, it was intended to teach spiritual truth (4:31; 5:5,10-11). Knowing this event would be recorded, God gave the vision to reassure others who would also suffer for the testimony, that the Lord was present with them in their suffering. The promises of John 14:18-19, 15:18-21 and 16:2 were seen to be fulfilled. When we are opposed, we will find comfort in that same upward look (Rom. 8:33-39).

Stephen was confirmed in the truth. Stephen saw the very person about whom he had been speaking. He saw Jesus risen, ascended and glorified, restored to his rightful place in heaven because he had completed the work God had given him to do and his sacrifice had been accepted. Perhaps he was standing to receive Stephen or testifying to God about him (Matt. 10:32). The Son of Man was a Messianic designation (Dan. 7:13-14), and these men had heard it attributed to Jesus before (Mark 14:62). Opposition can cause us to doubt the truth, but, as here, it should have the opposite effect of deepening our conviction. Heaven is open and we can enter by faith (1 Peter 1:8-9).

Stephen was contented in death. He was submissive to his death and did not ask for deliverance by a miracle. Although he died in agony, he deliberately imitated Christ in two prayers: for himself (59; cf. Luke 23:46); and for others (60; cf. Luke 23:34). Facing imminent death can test the reality of our convictions, and he died embracing the truth he had taught, that the fate of the soul was more important than the fate of his body (Matt. 10:28). Death is not to be feared (1 Cor. 15:26,54). It is described here as sleep, from which there would be a later awakening.

Stephen contributed to the future. The loss of Stephen would have been a great shock to the church, but there are no untimely deaths with God. The value of a life is not measured in its length. God could bring great things from it. Stephen paved the way for the break with Judaism. The contrast of his testimony against his accusers showed where truth and godliness lay. His contribution to the church in Jerusalem should not be overlooked (6:7-8), nor his instrumentality in the conversion of Saul (22:20). His death was directly related to the spread of the gospel and provided a continuing testimony through Scripture. Justice will be done one day, and in the meantime there is more for us to do as we invest in the next generation (Rev. 6:9-11; 14:13).

Acts 8:1-8   The church in the world

As an enemy – opposed by the world: persecution. Stephen's sermon stood against the cherished ideas of the religious establishment – who by their reaction to it revealed that they were more closely aligned with the world than they were with the people of God (John 8:44). So, intent upon self-preservation, it sought to destroy not only Stephen but all like him. Although done in the name of God, the methods employed were violent and not at all godlike. But whatever degree of vehemence is used against the church, it remains invincible. It cannot be destroyed because the promise of Christ stands firm (Matt. 16:18). Although its external form and location may change due to the pressures applied to it, it will never disappear for God has pledged to preserve his chosen people as the manifestation of Christ to the world (1 Cor. 12:27).

As a minority – hidden throughout the world: dispersion. Escape is sometimes the wisest response to opposition (Matt. 10:23). It is not always so – for apparently the apostles at least stayed, perhaps mindful that their first calling was to Jerusalem (1:8). However, the term 'scattered' gives only the result of persecution without hinting at a reason for the dispersion. It may well have been positive. If Jerusalem proved so antagonistic to the truth, then there were many more places where the gospel could be made known, with a more favourable response, perhaps. So it was not just a matter of preservation, but extension. By remaining behind, the apostles could always be found and provide support and encouragement when necessary – as proved to be the case later in the chapter. It

is no accident that the people of God often seem so isolated in the big wide world. In such circumstances, they ought to become more dependent upon God. Opposition to the gospel is not a sign that God has deserted us. It is an opportunity to prove how close he is.

As an authority – speaking to the world: declaration. Whatever happened to them, the church was not silenced, and two forms of declaration are described. The term 'preaching' here stresses the content of what was said, rather than the style of delivery. The 'word' refers to the general truth of God – albeit centred upon Christ. The sense is how the Christians related the truth to their everyday experience as they moved around. There is a deliberate contrast to the action of Philip. The word 'proclaimed' is different and refers more to the method of delivery – like a herald. His subject matter was more specific and his ministry was accompanied by miracles – even though he was not an apostle. The truth of formal testimony was confirmed in this way, while the truth of informal testimony was confirmed by the godly lives of the 'ordinary' believers. So although some may have been given special gifts of utterance, all shared the same gospel in ways appropriate to them. Perhaps our own testimony will be strengthened when we recognise that God has put us in a particular place for that purpose – whatever means he may have used to get us there. We need to look to him for help, be spiritually minded and ready to speak, conscious that God has entrusted us with his Word – whatever method we may use to deliver it.

Acts 8:9-25   Simon Magus: deceiver or believer?

Simon: his experience. Simon was a gifted man who had magic powers which gained him a great following. But he deliberately exalted himself and people were taken in and regarded him as divine.

When he was presented with the gospel, like many others, he believed what he heard. He was baptised, publicly demonstrating his acceptance of, and commitment to, that truth. He followed Philip – and here is the first sign of a problem. He attached excessive significance to man, perhaps being impressed by his personality and gifts. He had cultivated such devotion himself, and returned it when he saw someone who was greater than him. His astonishment was another manifestation of the same disposition: giving attention to mere externals.

The arrival of the apostles provoked a return to the old ways for Simon. When he saw that the power of the Holy Spirit was apparently at their disposal, he took an opportunity to become greater than Philip. He sought the means by which he could control others without any awareness that he should have been under the control of God. Peter exposed him. His heart was not right before God. No inner change had taken place and he had not been humbled. He was still self-seeking instead of wanting to honour Christ. Worse, when challenged about his condition, he did not repent of his sin. His response was evasive, expressing only a fear of the consequences of his words.

Simon: his significance. There is something of a puzzle here. Why was the Holy Spirit not given to these believers in the first place, and then only by means of the apostles? There must be good reasons for this deviation from the normative operations of the Spirit.

Samaritans were descended from colonists sent to inhabit the region by the king of Assyria after the exile. Thus, they were not pure Jews, but of mixed race and therefore despised by the Jews, creating racial tension. They rejected much of the Old Testament, but accepted the books of Moses and were expecting the Messiah. Perhaps the Holy Spirit was deliberately withheld so that by the coming of the apostles, they knew they were an authentic part of the church. This confirmed to the apostles the nature of a true work of God. These events also showed to the Samaritans – used to putting fallible men on a pedestal – that the apostles represented a higher authority and must be given more attention than they had given even to Philip.

This incident helps us to see the real nature of saving faith. We cannot be sure, but it seems that Simon was not really saved. He had a sincere conviction that the gospel was true and gave an outward conformity to some of the norms of Christian behaviour. His understanding and commitment were evident and the general influence of the Holy Spirit could be seen in the moral influence of the truth upon him and the strength of his religious sympathies. However, it appears there was no real heart work in him. He had not denied himself nor shown any repentance before God. He remained impenitent and had not put real faith in Christ. He may have had joy, but it was only temporary (Matt. 13:20-21), and it does not purify the heart or overcome the world. The work of the Holy Spirit brings spiritual illumination (1 Cor. 2:5; 2 Cor. 4:6; Rom. 8:16) and makes Christ, as mediator, the object of our affections (John 1:12). We must receive him, not just believe in him.

Acts 8:26-40   A portrait of a seeking soul

After the contrast of Ananias and Sapphira with Barnabas (4:32 − 5:11), Luke now contrasts Simon with the Ethiopian eunuch.

He worshipped God (27). Although an important man, his position left him unsatisfied and he sought to worship the God of Israel − despite being obliged to worship his monarch as a deity. He may have been a convert to Judaism, for many people were attracted by the high moral code Judaism offered. He dedicated considerable time and expense to making the journey − a possible sign of his sincerity.

He read the Scriptures (28). Attending worship was not enough. He acquired a scroll − which usually only rabbis possessed. The extent of his thirst for God is further indicated by his desire to study it personally, straight away, despite the discomfort of the journey. He did not wait for a tutor (John 5:39).

He recognised his need (31). Although a man of ability, his intellect was of limited value and he knew it. He admitted he was spiritually blind because he did not understand what he was reading (2 Cor. 4:4). A genuine seeker will come to the Scriptures with that same humble spirit (Jer. 29:13).

He sought help (31). He invited an insignificant stranger to help him. This would not be a wise course of action for us perhaps, but in trusting Philip he may have been acknowledging the providence of God. Despite his superior status, he was not ashamed of reading and talking with God's people. A seeker will take any opportunity to learn, unaware of how God can order events for their good.

He asked questions (34). It is so important to discover the correct application of God's Word and the Ethiopian rightly asked questions of the text. He had an open mind − apparently being willing to be taught without doubt or prejudice. But when searching leads to finding, a response is necessary. Once God has been found in Christ, then learning must result in action.

He chose obedience (36). The truth had started to affect him, for it went beyond his mind and influenced his will. He wanted to translate his understanding into deeds immediately, and in those circumstances it seemed to him that the most appropriate act of obedience was baptism.

He confessed his faith (37). The Ethiopian was not travelling alone. His retinue witnessed what Philip did. Perhaps the conversation between them had been overheard. Philip would almost certainly have taken the opportunity to explain to the onlookers what was happening. Even if this verse is a later editorial addition, it is very likely that something similar was said.

He expressed his joy (39). Even after Philip's removal, the Ethiopian lost none of the joy of his salvation − because it did not depend on Philip. He knew the joy of discovering God for himself, in Christ. He knew the joy of sins forgiven and communion with Christ. He continued on his way home − not back to Jerusalem, for he had a job to do and he knew the joy of being entrusted with the gospel that needed to be transmitted to everyone.

Acts 9:1-9 Saul's conversion

In 1 Cor. 15:8, Paul included his conversion experience in his list of the resurrection appearances of Jesus. That is how it is recorded here, although later he also describes it as a vision (26:19). It was:

Unexpected and undeserved. Paul's background is well known: a religious zealot, rooting out error from Judaism by persecuting the growing sect that claimed the Messiah had already arrived. He was not ignorant of the claims of Christianity but had never met Jesus as far as we know. No-one did more harm to the early church and therefore no-one deserved the punishment of God more than Saul. Knowingly and openly antagonistic to Christianity, he was the least likely person to become a Christian (1 Tim. 1:13-15). But Saul was not in control of his own destiny, and Jesus broke into Saul's life dramatically without being invited. Although not a 'typical' conversion experience, it encourages us not to give up praying for, and witnessing to, the worst of sinners we know.

Supernatural and powerful. It was not the light of reason that suddenly impacted upon Saul's life, but the risen Christ himself. He came specifically for Saul. Others were affected by what happened, but not addressed directly. They saw the light and were fearful, but they could not hear any voice. Though preached to many people at the same time, the gospel brings light to some but darkness to others, as did the pillar of cloud (Exod. 14:19-20) and the parables of Jesus (Matt. 13:10-17).

Revealing and convicting. Jesus did not identify himself when he asked Saul the first question, because Saul did not believe Jesus had risen. His question made Saul think. Without using his title, Jesus spoke to Saul in terms he would understand. The Word of God and people of God had not convinced Saul about the truth concerning Jesus. Only a personal encounter could do that – and the keynote of that encounter was the declaration of the unity between Christ and his people. Christ must be the focus of our testimony. We must invite people to come to Christ. In a sense, the church is a means to that end.

Unsettling and transforming. The whole foundation of Saul's life was wiped out instantly and a new one laid at the same time. The new foundation was the very one he had sought to destroy in others. Jesus appeared to Saul in order to appoint him as his servant and his witness (26:16). In a moment of time Saul had experienced the glory, grace, authority and omniscience of Jesus. He had been blinded to the world by the brilliance of the light of Christ. The life he knew had come to an end and the change was so overwhelming that even the desire for food and drink was eclipsed by the mixture of joy and anguish, peace and pain. His meat and drink would be to do the will of the one who sent him. He had seen the Son; he knew the truth; his sins were forgiven; God was reconciled; heaven was secured: all of grace.

Acts 9:10-19   Ananias: my chosen instrument

He was ready to hear Christ (10). There were a few believers in Damascus, and Ananias was a man with a singular reputation (22:12). He was God-fearing and was recognised as someone who sought to live by the Word of God. When he was entrusted with a vital ministry, his response to a sudden vision was calm and submissive. Are our devotions preparing us to hear Christ to speak to us?

He was reluctant to serve Christ (11-14). Although he was prepared to hear Christ, he was not prepared for what he said. It was a puzzling commission which seemed to be, 'Give yourself into the hands of the enemy.' He had an understandable reserve, but did not refuse. He could not have known that Jesus had already prepared the way for him and he was expected. Saul had been praying and Ananias was told that his visit would be an answer to that prayer. We can sometimes question how God can expect something from us when there are certain obstacles in the way. How easy it is to respond to him according to our knowledge of a situation, rather than trust that God knows the situation better than we do.

He was reassured of the purpose of Christ (15-16). The command was repeated and Ananias was told of Saul's unique calling. He had a singular place in God's plan which would sound strange to a devout Jewish believer. Why did Jesus not send Saul to the house of Ananias? This way, Ananias had to exercise his own will power. He needed to suppress his doubt and fear and, in an act of faith, be strengthened in the process of becoming involved in Saul's life. God places us in some situations for our improvement. He orders them in a certain way so that there is a greater opportunity of usefulness.

He was resolute in obeying Christ (17-19). Reading 22:12-16 shows us that Ananias went beyond the specific command to heal Saul. Everything he did was both necessary and natural and illustrates the point that simple obedience can open up unexpected areas of service.

(a) He gave a loving greeting to his greatest enemy, demonstrating true Christian forgiveness and his acceptance of Saul as a brother in Christ.

(b) He gave testimony to his own commission from Christ and communion with him.

(c) He confirmed the reality of Saul's experience.

(d) He confirmed Saul's own commission in general terms.

(e) After a specific challenge, he baptised him.

Here is an account of an ordinary believer being used for an extraordinary task (2 Tim. 2:20-21).

Something to talk about: The phrase in the title of these notes was used of Saul, not Ananias (15). Are we justified in applying it to Ananias?

Something to do: Consider if improvements need to be made to your daily devotions so that you can become more responsive to what the Lord says to you.

Acts 9:19-30   Saul's early ministry

The conversion of Saul had a substantial effect on the church. The churches with which he was first associated – Damascus and Jerusalem – produced exactly the same responses.

He was feared (13,26). Saul's reputation was so well known that believers in both Damascus and Jerusalem found it difficult to accept the validity of his conversion. They may have thought it was a change of tactic – using deception to infiltrate the church and destroy it from inside. They could not believe the grace of God could extend to Saul. We may be hesitant about receiving strangers ourselves, fearing they will be disruptive or change the shape of the church. Early Christians were exhorted to avoid partiality (James 2:1-11) and perhaps we need to do the same by taking steps to receive all and discourage none.

He was received (19,28). Saul was not discouraged by the initial cool response he received, but continued to seek fellowship. He came to be accepted by personal recommendation. He was first befriended by sympathetic individuals and then defended by them before the rest of the church. We need to win the friendship of newcomers so that they come to trust us, and then we can be of help to them. Rather than remaining a casual acquaintance, cultivating a personal friendship with a new believer can be a very significant step forward in their spiritual growth.

He witnessed (20,29). Saul's acceptance by the church opened the way for service immediately. He soon found the opportunity, and his gift for preaching was identified and encouraged. Although a new Christian, the fact that he stood up for and with other believers showed the measure of his acceptance by them. His service was evidently Christ-centred, courageous and costly. If we are really nurturing new believers among us, it will show itself in their growing usefulness – not necessarily in preaching, but in ways that are appropriate both for them and for the church.

He was threatened (23,29). Saul's ministry produced an immediate response – hostility. Both inside and outside the synagogues, he spoke effectively about Christ, but many disagreed and remained unchanged. In Jerusalem, he would have spoken to the very ones he had sided with against Stephen. Such an amazing reversal prompted antagonism, not acceptance. We must not invite opposition by our insensitivity, but neither must we be lukewarm in our presentation of the truth. It is too important to be sidelined.

He was helped (25,30). Other believers did not desert Saul, but rallied round him. He had to be told to leave Jerusalem (22:17-21). In both cases, the church did not hold on to him, but freed him for further, more extensive ministry, so that he could serve the Lord more fully. We may feel that our own local church needs all the help it can get, but there are times when we must recognise that some are equipped to serve the wider church and we must not hold on to them selfishly.

Acts 9:31　The growth of the church

This summary verse concludes this section of Luke's narrative and reviews the situation of the whole church at that particular point in time.

The church was at peace. In those early days, Christianity had taken root in three provinces. Although made of many separate congregations, the church is referred to as a single entity and for a time was free from external interference. Saul was neither persecuting nor being persecuted. The Jews were facing their own problems with growing Roman oppression and so Christians were left to themselves, undisturbed. Although affliction can be a means of church growth, it is neither normal nor preferable. Peace is a desirable and God-given condition (1 Tim. 2:1-2), and when provided should be utilised as much as possible. If we find ourselves at peace then let us be thankful for it and pray for its continuation. Let us learn to recognise opposition in other forms and not become complacent and unguarded. If we are not facing direct attack ourselves, let us faithfully uphold those who are.

The church was edified. Peace produced strength, not decline. The foundations of the church were being put in place. The church was being consolidated through purposeful activity involving both human and divine activity.

Going on in the fear of the Lord. The church made progress because it lived in the constant knowledge that it was always under the eye of God. It held God in awe and did not live for its own sake. Leaving the old way of life behind, believers would try to avoid bringing shame upon God and sought to live in obedience to his Word. By being charitable to each other and helping the weak, they would show they were different but not distant from the rest of society. Their good reputation reflected their devotion to the Lord Jesus Christ.

Going on in the comfort of the Holy Spirit. The church was conscious of the help of God at this time of progress. A spiritual work was happening among them. It was not a matter of mere human effort. The strengthening of the church could not take place without the work of God. They were:

- Taught by him – given understanding of the Scriptures.
- United by him – they enjoyed and expressed Christian fellowship together.
- Transformed by him – lives were changed in ways which were unmistakable.
- Inspired by him – freed from this world, they looked forward to their heavenly home.
- Strengthened by him – enabled to see their way through many problems.
- Employed by him – used to give faithful witness of his saving grace to others.

The church increased. The result of edification was growth. Congregations expanded and new ones were formed. The word spread by personal testimony and church efficiency, continuing in the same way it had begun (2:41; 4:4; 6:7; 12:24; 16:5; 19:20). Although numerical growth is never to be a goal in itself, it can be the result of the deliberate cultivation of strong Christians. Only God can give the increase, and our portion is to go on in the fear of the Lord. Evangelism is a product of strength, not just a means of becoming strong.

Acts 9:32-43   The church was strengthened

Peter had travelled back to Jerusalem from Samaria (8:25), and the peace enjoyed by the church, highlighted in v. 31, facilitated an even greater freedom of travel. This eventful tour of Peter illustrates some evidences of its strength.

Visitation. Peter's visit to Lydda was at his own initiative, apparently born out of a desire for fellowship and service. It is a source of strength when others care enough to go out of their way to show an interest and offer help. His visit to Joppa was by invitation and he was flexible enough to accept it. The church at Joppa recognised the need for apostolic ministry. Distance should not be a barrier to usefulness.

Dedication. Peter found himself being used by God in unexpected ways. He had been involved in miracles of healing before (3:6) and used his God-given gift again. There is no reference to Aeneas being a believer, in marked contrast to the description of Dorcas (36). The gifts of God may be used to the benefit of unbelievers, but always in honour of Jesus Christ. As far as we know, Peter had not been used to restore anyone to life before and he prayed for guidance. Peter was so dedicated to God that he was willing to go beyond his normal sphere of Christian service. His next encounter, in Caesarea, would take him even further out of his 'comfort zone'.

Restoration. Life and health were granted by God. Sometimes, God takes away in order that he may gloriously restore so that he is honoured by the whole event. The church was strengthened by witnessing the work of God among them. There was a divine preservation of a highly commendable Christian testimony. It does not happen like that every time, of course. Nor does God work in the same way in every church. But he is bound to work among his people, even if it is not in such a spectacular way as this – if they are not harbouring sin.

Salvation. Although the churches and the events were different, the outcome was the same in both places (35,42). Testimony to the deity of Jesus Christ was enhanced in each place. There was visual evidence of the heart of the message proclaimed by his people – healing and freedom, life and usefulness. Without any adulation being given to Peter at all, the credibility of the church was strengthened.

Association. The concluding verse anticipates the coming event. A leather worker handled unclean animals and would have been avoided by strict Jews – but not Peter. Barriers were already starting to break down. The church is strengthened when it follows the example of Christ and mixes with publicans and sinners. Such loving commitment prepares the way for greater blessing.

Acts 10:1-8   Cornelius

The conversion of Cornelius is one of the most far-reaching events in the early church as 'God granted even the Gentiles repentance unto life' (11:18). How instructive that God did not use the apostle to the Gentiles (Rom. 11:13) but rather one who had a proven ministry among Jews.

A devout man (1-2). This was his defining characteristic. It was more significant than his job.

(a) *He feared God.* He had a reverence for God which would mean he would take care not to offend him.

(b) *He instructed his family.* His faith was not something he kept to himself, but he instructed others in what he considered to be important.

(c) *He gave alms.* He was unselfish and charitable, giving generously and directly to anyone in need.

(d) *He prayed often.* He did not simply pray at set times but at other times also. He maintained a constant attitude of prayer.

These characteristics were seen in him before he was saved – and they serve as a rebuke to many who are saved. By what characteristics are we known locally – our job or our testimony? Is it evident that we hold God in higher esteem than we do men? What of our home life, our prayers, our giving?

A chosen man (3-4). Cornelius received a communication from God in the form of an angel. His heart was prepared. God had been at work in his life already by making him the devout man he was. Such preparation could only happen by the enabling of God. Cornelius exercised simple faith according to the light given to him and he was about to be enlightened further. God did not choose to reveal himself to Cornelius because he was devout. God had a plan for the church at large and it involved Cornelius. The coming of the angel was the next stage in that plan which had been conceived before the world began (Eph. 1:3-6). Cornelius was surprised by the revelation he received. We should not be surprised when God reveals himself and his purposes to us. God has chosen us for himself, but our familiarity with the things of God can be so shallow that there is no rejoicing in our hearts when we hear him.

A needy man (5-6). However blessed Cornelius was, there was something missing. He was not converted. He had not heard the gospel and it was not the task of the angel to preach it. If Saul had difficulty joining the church, how much more would Cornelius? He needed to hear the truth from none other than Peter, and Peter needed special prompting to take it to him. God uses human means to reveal his truth – but sometimes he uses unlikely people to do so. Sometimes those people need extra help from God to spur them on.

An obedient man (7-8). The angel told Cornelius to summon Peter from Joppa and he did so – but only after he had shared his experience of revelation with others. God was real and had spoken to him, and he wanted others to know about it straight away. This was more than formal compliance. Obedience for Cornelius was a joyful testimony. Can we say the same?

Acts 10:9-33 The beginnings of cross-cultural mission?

This event is important, because it inaugurated a new phase of church growth, and corrected a wrong attitude (11:3). Cross-cultural mission had taken place before (8:26ff), but only through divine intervention. The risen Christ had commanded worldwide witness (1:8). Peter had obeyed that command (for example 8:25) and his ministry had been blessed (4:4). But left to itself, the church would still not take the next step, and divine intervention was necessary again.

The barrier to cross-cultural mission (9-16). The vision shows the greatest barrier to cross-cultural mission is in the heart of the messenger, not any external differences. Peter defended what he believed to be right and argued with God. A God-given distinction had been mistakenly extended by tradition and preserved in a fledgling church. Union, not association, with Gentiles had been forbidden. Church tradition was hindering the spread of the gospel. The church had to learn to distinguish between absolute truth and what issues are negotiable because they are culturally conditioned. It might be useful to analyse our church structures so that, if necessary, they can be redesigned to facilitate cross-cultural mission.

The call to cross-cultural mission (17-23). The context for cross-cultural mission was not just the commission of Christ but also the church to which Peter was accountable. Although the Jerusalem church could not give its approval in advance, subsequently (11:18; 15:14-19) it needed to affirm this development for the sake of the wider Christian community. The factors involved in Peter's call to cross-cultural mission were:

(a) *Divine revelation*. Peter was already engaged in this work in obedience to Christ. But further revelation was needed to bring the conviction that he should go into a new expression of the same work.

(b) *Divine providence*. God worked at the same time as he spoke, so that Peter could not mistake the fact that this was indeed of God. His action interpreted and expanded the vision, giving it an immediate relevance.

(c) *Personal faith*. If God is really at work, he works subjectively as well as objectively – moving us to respond positively to what he has said and done. In faith, we take steps to act upon what God has told us.

The practice of cross-cultural mission (24-33).

(a) The messenger was aware that both he and his hearers had been prepared by God.

(b) The messenger needed to correct any false ideas his hearers might have about him, in case they distorted his message (26).

(c) The messenger acknowledged the existing religious perceptions of his hearers at the outset (28).

(d) The messenger gave ready testimony to his own sin and the reality of a personal God (28).

(e) The messenger did not launch straight into the gospel, but tried to discover more about his hearers (29).

(f) The hearers were found to be reverent, attentive and expectant because of the prior work of God (33).

Acts 10:34-48   The message of peace

There is a message from God.

(a) *Originally for the Jews.* It was delivered by the prophets God sent and concerned One who would bring peace with God after generations of rebellion. The source and the content of this message were clear and already familiar to Peter's hearers.

(b) *Fulfilled in Christ.* God did not just send a message and the messengers but also the subject of the message. He came and lived an exemplary life, evidently testifying to the presence of God with him. These facts were also known to Peter's hearers and spoke of a living, personal God who communicated meaningfully with his creatures, demonstrating himself to be both powerful and faithful to his own word.

The message comes through witnesses.

(a) *In authentic history.* Peter confirmed that the events described were verifiable facts. They really happened and many eyewitnesses testified to them. But there were other significant events also. The fame of Jesus seemed to stop at his death but later events confirmed his centrality to the original message. God raised him from the dead and caused him to be seen by many. The real significance of the ministry of Jesus did not rest with his life.

(b) *Peter's personal testimony.* Witnesses to the resurrection of Jesus were far fewer than those to the life of Jesus – but Peter was one of them. It was a truth that could not be observed by everyone, but the testimony of the few who had witnessed it had to be believed. They were able to speak not only of the events but also of their meaning. Once again, God communicates through man, first the prophets, then Jesus himself; after that the apostles and now the church. In each case, the messenger is part of the message, and there is a sense in which the church is now the truth incarnate (1 Cor. 12:27).

The message is for you.

(a) *You will be judged.* Jesus Christ is more than just another man. He is Lord of all. By God's appointment, he holds the supreme place in the order of creation, which can be held by no one else (Col. 1:15-20; Rom. 10:12; 14:9). Because of that he is the Judge of all and sets the standard against which others will be measured (17:30-31; Rom. 2:16).

All human beings are sinners by nature, and although sin is expressed in various degrees and in different forms there is one condition shared by all (Num. 32:23). The Judge will condemn all who stand before him with that condition unchanged.

(b) *Forgiveness is available.* This is the message of peace – for all, not just Jews, because Jesus is Lord and Judge of all. The enmity between God and man is removed and reconciliation achieved through him. It comes through his death (Heb. 9:22). God both required it and provided it (Eph. 1:7). This truth, now made known to all, must be received before the benefits of which it speaks can be enjoyed.

Something to do: Identify the work of the different persons of the Trinity in this passage.

Acts 11:1-18 Peter explains events in Caesarea

Luke recounts Peter's report to the church in Jerusalem, and because of this the reality and significance of that crucial event in Caesarea is confirmed.

The coming of the Holy Spirit:

(a) *Proved the acceptance of the Gentiles by God.* The initial receiving of the Holy Spirit is a distinctive factor in becoming a Christian (John 3:5; Rom. 8:11). His influence cannot be replicated, and it is his work to bring repentance and faith (18; 15:7). He is sent as a gift, not summoned as a right, and is common to all believers – including Gentiles.

(b) *Demonstrated by particular gifts.* The circumstances required immediate, demonstrable proof that God had accepted them. This was a totally new group of believers. Peter and other Jewish Christians would need convincing of their equality, and so they were given the same external signs that believers received at Pentecost – which Peter would recognise. Others would be saved without the same signs but not without the same Spirit.

(c) *Did not replace human ministry.* The new believers still had to be baptised in water as an act of obedience and testimony. Also as a result, fellowship between strangers was offered and received. The presence of the Holy Spirit within his people does not eliminate the need for the provision of appropriate human support. His continued indwelling should be seen in a growing likeness to Christ (Gal. 5:25).

The unity of the church.

(a) *It is established by God.* The formation of the church is seen unmistakably as the work of God. There are four points of direct divine intervention which led to its establishment (10:3,11,19,44). Making clean the unclean can only be done by God. We cannot choose who joins the church. All we can do is try to recognise those whom God has chosen, and even if some are not quite what we might expect we must learn to accept them, knowing that God has already done so. We may need a more open heart if we are not to oppose the Spirit of God.

(b) *It is endangered by men.* It is noticeable that although the new believers praised God for their salvation, some more established believers did not. Trouble was brewing because some people had:

• the fixed viewpoint of an existing prejudice;

• insufficient information and so jumped to conclusions;

• a critical spirit – commenting negatively before Peter spoke;

• overlooked both the word and the work of God.

Sometimes a defence of the status quo can involve criticism of, and a hindrance to, a genuine work of God.

(c) *Preserved by a gracious spirit.* Peter did not attempt to defend himself (1 Peter 2:23). He gave a plain statement of the facts, without embellishment, showing how God had to deal with him first as his own attitude had been inconsistent with the spread of the gospel. He honestly reported his own reaction to events but pointed to Christ. He was guided by what he knew of God, and peace within the church was retained as it came to recognise that God had indeed been at work.

Acts 11:19-30   The church in Antioch

Luke brings three threads of his narrative together: the actions of scattered believers (8:1,4), the growing evangelisation of Gentiles (11:18), and the ministry of Saul of Tarsus (9:30).

The beginning of the church in Antioch (19-21). Antioch was the third most important city in the Roman Empire, with a strong Jewish community. Some persecuted believers settled there and began preaching the gospel, but went beyond the confines of their own community. They may have heard of the events in Caesarea. If Luke is being chronological here, the principle had been established that Gentiles could be as much a part of the Christian church as the Jews.

It was work among the Gentiles that bore fruit in Antioch, rather than work among the Jews. Through this account of blessing, Luke shows his readers that what had happened in Caesarea was not an isolated incident. Having moved out of their homeland, it is possible that for these persecuted preachers their Jewish distinctives had become less important as they established themselves in a new community. These unknown men were keen to commend Christ to anyone and everyone. They did not seek permission from the church in Jerusalem to do so. It is all too easy to limit ourselves to certain people when we proclaim the gospel. Inevitably we witness to those who are similar to ourselves, but we must not restrict our testimony to those people alone.

The growth of the church in Antioch (22-26). The response of the Jerusalem church was not to interrogate but to encourage. This is reflected in their choice of an emissary – Barnabas ('encourager'), a Cypriot like some of the founding preachers of the new church. He was not only called, but anointed for his work. Evidence of the grace of God made him glad and he encouraged the church to live a life of consistent dependence upon God. As the church grew, he selflessly sought help – not from Jerusalem, but from Saul. Their joint ministry consolidated the church and gave it a unique identity. Although possibly a nickname used by others, it is also possible that the term 'Christians' was chosen by the church itself because it meant 'anointed ones' and emphasised the difference between pagans and believers rather than believers and Jews. That would be more consistent with the events earlier in this chapter.

The service of the church in Antioch (27-30). Here is an early example of the strength of the church. They received prophets from Jerusalem and allowed them to exercise their spiritual gifts. Having heard the message from God, they acted upon it straight away. Although a corporate decision, the believers responded individually. These Gentiles recognised they were in debt to their Jewish brethren and welcomed the opportunity to assist them. The worth of Barnabas and Saul was acknowledged, but there was a large enough team of leaders to allow them to leave the church for a while.

Acts 12:1-24   Persecution and its consequences

Although he reappears in chapter 15, this chapter ends the detailed record of Peter's ministry as the majority of the remainder of the Acts presents the ministry of Paul. Four related incidents have lessons to teach us.

The persecution of the church (1-4).

(a) *It was political.* The earliest persecution had religious origins as Jewish leaders tried to eradicate what they considered to be an heretical sect. This new wave of persecution came from King Herod. Although he was the grandson of the Herod in the Christmas story, his right to the succession was not automatic and was confirmed by the Roman authorities. If he was going to win the support of the Jewish leaders, he had to demonstrate that, in some areas at least, he was on their side. So, in order to gain popularity, he persecuted the fledgling church.

(b) *It was systematic.* Herod targeted the church leadership, which Saul of Tarsus had not done. This was a strategic action supported by the right to execute – a speedy and potentially effective weapon. Perhaps the mixture of Jews and Gentiles in some gatherings bred suspicion. What could possibly unite such diverse people other than subversive plots?

The prayers of the church (5-19). We do not know exactly what the church was praying for in relation to Peter. James had been killed, a fulfilment of Mark 10:39. Presumably the church had prayed for James, but he was still killed and they had no reason to expect Peter would receive different treatment. Was the church expecting a fulfilment of John 21:18 and so praying for Peter's release? Two events could suggest they were praying, 'Your will be done.' First, the fact that Peter could sleep on what was probably expected to be the night before his execution was surely a God-given answer to prayer (6). Also, the response to Peter's arrival suggests that release was not the outcome they had anticipated. Prayer shows that man has a real place in the work of God. He will prompt and enable his people to do things that are within our power, but we must trust him to do other things which are beyond us, knowing that 'he is able to do immeasurably more than all we ask or imagine' (Eph. 3:20).

The enemy of the church (20-23). Herod was guilty, not only of persecuting the people of God but also of setting himself up in the place of God. His fate – described in more detail in secular history, was an evident act of judgement, perhaps intended to warn others against imitating such conduct and also to prevent him from doing even more harm to the church. The wicked will always get what they deserve (Ps. 1:4-5).

The growth of the church (24). Despite the concerted actions of wicked men, the truth of God continued to spread because God enabled it to do so – using the prayers and preaching of his people. At the beginning of the chapter, James was dead, Peter was in prison and Herod was triumphing. At the end of the chapter, Herod was dead, Peter was free and the Word of God was triumphing. That is the continuing pattern not just through the Acts of the Apostles, but today.

Acts 12:25 – 13:12   Antioch sends its first missionaries

Earlier church growth seemed somewhat spontaneous (8:4; 11:19), although the Jerusalem church had responded to new churches (9:32; 11:22). Here is the first account of commitment to deliberate, long distance missionary work.

Characteristics of a missionary church.

(a) *Firmly established.* The church in Antioch was founded by zealous believers who had spoken of Christ (11:19-21), perhaps seven years before. The new church then willingly received further help from outside, first from Barnabas and then from Saul (11:22-25).

(b) *Distinctive character.* Founded through cross-cultural mission, the church did not develop into a carbon copy of the church in Jerusalem. It was unfettered by Jewish tradition, was cosmopolitan in its outlook and strategic in its location. It had not faced poverty, persecution or prejudice and its distinctiveness in society was evident (11:26).

(c) *Gifted leadership.* Having received help, the church soon gave help to others (11:27-30). The church was strong enough to spare Barnabas and Saul and later welcomed them back, with John Mark (12:25). The men named in 13:1 came from a variety of backgrounds and were equipped by God with spiritual gifts which enabled them not only to serve their own church but to be of assistance elsewhere.

(d) *Devoted leadership.* The church leaders were serious about their communion with God and it was during such a time when they were seeking God that the Holy Spirit spoke and prompted them to take this radical step of constructive separation. The group did not hold back but involved themselves directly in the divine commission by further prayer and positive commendation to this new direction in ministry.

Characteristics of missionary work.

(a) *Initiative.* There was room for flexibility and personal choice within the instructions from the Holy Spirit. The 'work' was not defined and the destination was perhaps chosen by Barnabas (4:36). John Mark was not set apart by the Spirit, but went anyway, perhaps as a relative of Barnabas (Col. 4:10) in a secondary role.

(b) *Strategy.* The account reads as if the party aimed for the capital of Cyprus, as being the place with the greatest potential influence. There is no record of witnessing in Seleucia, and although they spoke in Salamis it seems they did not linger there. This was not the first time the gospel had come to Cyprus (11:19-20) and perhaps they did not want to build on other foundations (Rom. 15:20).

(c) *Opposition.* Early opposition had to be resisted. The missionaries met a false prophet who was punished immediately, prophetically, mercifully (temporarily), symbolically and victoriously for attempting to pervert the truth that had already been declared to the proconsul.

(d) *Sympathy.* Here was a man of intelligence and responsibility with an existing interest in spiritual matters. Seeing the power of God at work along with hearing the truth convinced him. The greatest testimony is when God is both seen and heard. Although this is the only recorded conversion, perhaps others followed. It is God who gives the increase.

Acts 13:13-41   Paul's sermon in Antioch

Having travelled through Cyprus, the missionaries returned to a different part of the mainland and passed on to another town named Antioch. Going first of all to Jews, as visitors to the synagogue, they were given the customary invitation to speak to the assembled company. No longer referred to as Saul, Paul seized the opportunity and we have his first recorded sermon here.

A Saviour promised (17-22).

(a) *For a chosen people.* The unique relationship between God and Israel was indisputable and recognised by surrounding nations, even though it was sometimes ignored by the people themselves. God took care of them and shaped their destiny in a way he did not do for other nations (17). These verses provide an insight into what God had done for his people. Fundamental to God's care was the provision of a Saviour who would rescue them from tyranny and oppression. For most people this expectation would be fulfilled in military or political terms and only a minority recognised that it would be fulfilled spiritually (Isa.11:1-5).

(b) *For a careless people.* God's care for the people did not come because they had loved him and were consistently obedient. The opposite was the case (18). God gave them judges but they wanted a king. They did not seek a Saviour even though they needed one. God would give them one anyway because he loved them. Careless of their spiritual condition, they were more concerned about outward appearances.

A Saviour provided (23-31).

(a) *Unacceptable.* God sent his Saviour to live among mankind. Preparation for his arrival had continued for generations but the final stage was the ministry of John the Baptist. He was his immediate forerunner and inferior to him. Upon his arrival, the Saviour went unrecognised (27), and misunderstood (28), until he was unjustly killed. The very one the people had been waiting for – the one who would truly save them and was the ultimate expression of God's love, was despised and rejected through blind, proud ingratitude.

(b) *Incorruptible.* But the Saviour had not failed in his mission. He accomplished the salvation of many. Even though he had been unacceptable to man, God accepted his work. Man does not have the final say about his salvation. God reversed man's judgement and vindicated the Saviour by raising him from the dead. The resurrection was the reward, the proof and the completion of the Saviour's work.

A Saviour presented (32-41).

(a) *A promise kept.* Man's rejection did not alter God's promise. The death of the Saviour was expected and referred to by David and Isaiah in terms of resurrection. The Saviour could save beyond the bounds of this life and a single nation. Salvation is provided for any who accept it.

(b) *A pardon granted.* The Saviour is relevant to all and comes to save from a condition shared by all – sin. Its penalty has been paid by the death of the Saviour. That awful condition has been replaced by the free bestowal of the Saviour's righteousness. We reject him at our peril.

Acts 13:42-52   The word of the Lord is honoured

The rest of the chapter recounts three consequences of Paul's sermon.

The truth was welcomed (42-44).

(a) *Awakening.* Part of the congregation that listened to Paul's message hungered after truth, and having heard it did not want it to elude them. In response to their appeal, Paul and Barnabas exhorted them to hold on to the truth they already knew – by thinking about it, believing it and acting upon it, so that nothing else would take its place in their lives.

(b) *Attraction.* It seems those devout men took the exhortation to heart and during the week they lived according to the grace of God they knew. Their lives had been observed and their words noted so that many more came to the synagogue the following Sabbath to find out for themselves what had happened. If we are living out the grace of God in our lives, it should attract others to him.

The truth was opposed (45-47).

(a) *Jealousy.* But not all the congregation gave the missionaries such a sympathetic hearing. Some of the establishment were envious of the newcomers, jealous that their message had been so well received and generated such a strong interest. Their opposition to Paul's message showed itself in abuse, not reason or debate. It is often so today.

(b) *Rejection.* Paul and Barnabas appeared to expect such a reaction and did not try to persuade their opponents but pointed out their folly. They knew that while some were open to the truth, others would never be convinced. Rejecting the Word of God meant rejecting eternal life and so they pronounced judgement upon themselves.

(c) *Concentration.* Paul and Barnabas did not withdraw from such people of their own accord. They were obeying the command of God. They were under instructions to take the gospel to the Gentiles. Having gone to their own people first, they knew that the gospel was good news for all and would not waste time among those who rejected it.

The truth was received (48-52).

(a) *Conversion.* Some who heard the word gladly were converted. The text notes that it is God who appoints some to eternal life, even though others may have responded favourably to the truth.

(b) *Circulation.* The gospel spread among the Gentiles, not just through the missionaries but through those lives which were changed by it. The truth circulated when it went beyond the walls of the synagogue.

(c) *Persecution.* Because they considered the gospel a perversion of their own beliefs and feared for their own waning influence, the envious Jews precipitated official opposition to the missionaries and they left.

(d) *Expansion.* The city fathers and the Jewish antagonists would consider themselves victorious, but the reverse was the case. Their rejection of Paul and Barnabas represented God's rejection of them. The remaining disciples were reinvigorated as God continued to work among them. God had preserved them and enabled the cause of truth to prosper as the preaching of the gospel continued to bear fruit, both near and far.

Acts 14:1-18   Turn to the living God

The mission in Iconium. Paul and Barnabas travelled about 80 miles to Iconium, where they had a similar response to their reception in Antioch. Going first to the synagogue, some hearers were convinced by the message but others were strongly opposed to it. The favourable reaction of some led to increased public speaking and the nurturing of new believers. The antagonism of others which polarised the community led to the prospect of life-threatening violence and therefore withdrawal. Once again their exit resulted in the widespread proclamation of the gospel, rather than silence.

The miracles in Iconium. Miracles were not used everywhere and the reason for their use here is given. They were not used to draw a crowd but to confirm the validity of the word already declared and received. Some form of visible testimony was added to the personal testimony of the truth. The message was clearly the priority. This did not happen at every location and we are specifically told that it was the Lord himself, not Paul and Barnabas, who chose to work in that way here.

The mistake in Lystra. The use of miracles continued in Lystra – presumably with the same purpose. But the outcome in this less sophisticated and more superstitious community was different. A local legend spoke of a previous visitation from the gods being ignored by the population with dire consequences, and they were anxious not to repeat the experience. The strong agitation Paul and Barnabas showed at their reception reflected the seriousness of the misconception the people had about the true God and they sought to correct it immediately.

The message in Lystra.

(a) *God is real*. First, the missionaries declared the true God to be real – in contrast with the empty and worthless nonentities the people worshipped. Such errors had to be deliberately repudiated and the only true God acknowledged and sought.

(b) *God is the Creator*. Everything that exists is dependent upon this one God, who brought it all into being and controls it by the free exercise of his unrivalled and wise dominion. All things – including mankind, are accountable to him for he is exalted over all.

(c) *God is revealed*. He has made abundant provision for man, which should cause him to consider its source. God's kindness is intended to lead man to repentance, but the truth about God, evident in creation and conscience, has been silenced (Romans 1:18-23).

The sermon was probably leading to Christ, but was interrupted before that climax was reached. A new dispensation had dawned in which God's personal involvement in the world had increased. Far from being the passive observer of world history, God's apparent inactivity exposes man's need of him. Man cannot find God unaided. Any such search results only in perverse deviation from the truth, rather than the discovery of it. Christianity categorically denies that all religions lead to God or that God is in all of us.

Acts 14:19-28   Workmen approved by God

Here is an interesting insight into the ministry of Paul and Barnabas. It was:

Harmful (19-20). The opposition to the message of the missionaries was so strong that some men travelled almost 100 miles to destroy it and gathered accomplices on the way (see 13:45,50; 14:5). The strength of this persecution reflected the impact of the truth. It angered and offended the Jews so much that they were not content for its advocates simply to leave their region. Nothing less than complete eradication would suffice. The truth was so damaging to their precious falsehoods that they could not allow it to circulate any longer. The sinner sees the harm the message of the cross will do to him. It will slay him – if he does not slay it first. If any offence is to be given by the gospel, let us be sure it is in the message and not in the messengers.

Faithful (21-22). Paul did not allow his near-death experience to put him off. After recovering from his stoning, he went on to the next town and did the same thing that brought the stoning upon him – he preached the gospel. Not only that, after a successful ministry there he did not stay to bask in the comfort of a growing church, but turned round and went back to the same towns which had spawned his persecutors! He was more fearful of God than he was of them. God had raised him up to preach and he would go on doing it regardless of the personal consequences. He was not only faithful to his commission from God, he was also faithful to God's people. He was more concerned for their spiritual welfare than he was for his own physical welfare. He became a living example of the message he gave (22b).

Careful (23-25). But Paul knew that such nurturing was not enough. He had to take effective action to ensure that the work they had done was not undone after they left. Therefore, elders were appointed to care for and lead the churches in the future. Recognising such men for that important task required seeking the Lord's will, setting them apart to the people and offering up of them to God. Paul and Barnabas had to delegate responsibility so the men were appointed, not elected by the church. The missionaries were in the best position to choose men who would honour God, maintain the purity of the truth, the edification of the church and the extension of the kingdom. Only when the churches were in safe hands could they move on.

Thankful (26-28). Reaching home, their first task was to report to the church what God had done during their travels. They had much for which to be thankful – many personal blessings such as life preserved and fellowship enjoyed. They would be thankful that God used them to proclaim the gospel – when new life was given to many people and new churches came into being as a result. In particular, they would be thankful that salvation was not restricted to one nationality as many Gentiles were brought into the church. For what are you thankful?

Acts 15:1-11   The Council of Jerusalem

A dispute arose in the church at Antioch which was fundamental to Christianity. It was referred to the church at Jerusalem because it remained the seat of apostolic authority. The issue was the nature of salvation. Peter's address covered:

The communication of salvation (7). Salvation comes as part of a process. In order to believe, one must first hear. In order to be heard, the gospel must first be preached. In order to be preached, the gospel must be entrusted to the preacher. In order to preach, the preacher must be sent (Rom.10:13-15a). There are two strands in the plan of God which are brought together in order for him to grant salvation: his plan for the speaker and his plan for the hearer. Peter traces this plan in relation to the Gentiles. They came to believe having heard Peter, who was clearly sent by God (ch.10). Peter appeals to the obvious work of God in the past in which Gentiles were saved with no reference to circumcision. God chooses not only who will be saved but also the means through which they will be presented with the gospel.

The working of salvation (9). The preacher has no power or right to do any more than that. It is God who works in the heart of the hearer. All hearts are the same – whether Jew or Gentile. External differences do not reflect any internal differences. Both are equally sinful and are saved in the same way. God works within them, cleansing their hearts. Both must put their faith in Christ having turned from their sin. Self-trust must be renounced and give way to a desire for, and expectancy of, God's help. Then there must be a recognition of, and total confidence in, God's provision and promise.

The demonstration of salvation (8). God knew whether or not those Gentiles had exercised genuine faith. They had, and he bore witness to the fact by sending the Holy Spirit in a manifestation that had been seen in other new believers. Gentiles were not inferior Christians. They received the same heavenly gift as Jews (10:44-48). The genuine nature of their conversion could not be disputed because the evidence did not depend on Peter's account but on the testimony of God. God did not make any more requirements of the Gentiles before the reality of their faith was made public. The indwelling Holy Spirit is still God's testimony in the life of the believer (1 John 4:13), even though the manifestation of his presence may not take exactly the same form as it did then.

The denial of salvation (10). Peter says that the immediate salvation of Gentiles is in keeping with the revealed will of God. His policy, activity and testimony all declare it. Why go against what he has already made clear and enslave again those whom God has made free? The law has its place. Christians are to be law-abiding, but it must not be an additional burden imposed by men as a prerequisite for salvation.

The provision of salvation (11). Jew and Gentile have both received salvation through the same means – the grace of Christ. The favours of his death are freely given to all who come to him in faith. Making this qualification about the law denies this gracious gift by requiring it to be earned.

Acts 15:12-21   God visited the Gentiles

After Paul and Barnabas had spoken about the way God had authenticated their work among Gentiles, James concluded the discussion.

Gentiles are called (14-18):

(a) *By God's grace.* God had taken the initiative with the Gentiles. They were ignorant of him and careless but he came to those who were not his people when they did not deserve it.

(b) *To God's glory.* God did this so that his glory might be revealed in them. Not all Gentiles were chosen. God is glorified in his loving choice of some, but he is as much glorified in his just condemnation of others. None had any right to his mercy and choosing some rather than none is a glorious act of grace.

(c) *In God's Word.* The Scriptures foretold the choice of the Gentiles. The house of David had been restored, not only so that Jews could find salvation but also so that Gentiles would know where God was to be found. The salvation of Gentiles was spoken of as the work of God before it began (Isa.49:6).

(d) *In God's plan.* The salvation of Gentiles was not an afterthought by God. He knew what he was going to do from the very beginning. The rejection of Christ by the Jews was a vital part in the salvation of the world (10:33). God was glorified in the rejection of his Son because his mercy was more evident (John 13:31).

Gentiles are counselled (19-21). Having established the equality of Jews and Gentiles in terms of salvation, James applies that truth to the issue at stake. Since God had treated Jews as Jews and Gentiles as Gentiles, everyone had to do the same. There were exhortations to:

(a) *Refrain.* Jews should refrain from trying to impose Jewish rites on Gentiles, and Gentiles should refrain from the more offensive Gentile customs. Both should be aware of the need to conform to God's standards, not man's, and recognise that it would inevitably mean a change of habit. Gentiles had the freedom in Christ not to submit to Jewish rites, but that freedom was not unlimited. Salvation from the guilt and penalty of sin does not leave the way open to continue in it (Gal.5:13). All sin was to be put away as offensive to God, but some things must be stopped because they are offensive to others. Although perhaps not sinful in themselves, they could have the effect of causing others to sin if carelessly and relentlessly pursued.

(b) *Respect (21).* Behind the appeal to refrain is the motive of respect – love. If you have a relationship with God, you desire to please him and want to show your love for him by your obedience, and so you do not sin. If you have a relationship with other believers, the same thing applies. In your desire to please them and to show your love for them you do nothing that will cause offence (1 Cor.8:9). This verse refers to tradition-bound Jews and says as they are being exhorted to respect your Gentileness, so you must respect their Jewishness. The Christian rarely has as much liberty in practice as he does in principle because the Christian law of liberty is always conditioned by the law of love and the susceptibilities of the weaker brethren.

Acts 15:22-35   Rejoicing in consolation

The council decision involved:

(a) *Correction (24)*. The council cleared away any misunderstanding by disassociating themselves from the visitors to Antioch. This statement rebuked those who did not represent them.

(b) *Commendation (25-27)*. Genuine representatives were sent from among the leadership who were respected and responsible. They would confirm and explain the contents of the letter and prevent misunderstanding. Also, Paul and Barnabas were openly commended and their work acknowledged.

(c) *Submission (28)*. Judas and Silas were 'apostles' sent by the Jerusalem church, as its representatives and with its authority. The message they carried came with the authority of the Holy Spirit. There had been a harmony over this decision which was recognised as the work of God. A potential rift had been healed and unity created and promoted through this message. All must submit to the Holy Spirit – Antioch and Jerusalem.

(d) *Consideration (29)*. The tone of the message was representative of its content. The church did not issue a strong command but a recommendation. The church in Jerusalem had no right to burden others either with customs – what other churches were doing, or with traditions – for although having some purpose, the law was essentially a thing of the past.

The results of the decision were:

(a) *Rejoicing (31)*. The outcome was very positive with the only 'burdens' being:

(i) *Charity* – Christian love rejoices in doing what it can to serve others – even willing to have liberty limited for the good of others;

(ii) *Responsibility* – any mutual association involves the common acceptance of agreed terms of fellowship, which means that personal freedom must sometimes be surrendered as a demonstration of the priority of responsibility to others.

(b) Service (32). The visitors were given every opportunity to exercise their gifts in a new church, as a result of their commendation. See also 11:22,25,27.

(c) *Unity (33)*. The whole situation had strengthened links which already existed between the churches. The commendation of the church in Antioch showed the church in Jerusalem that their message had been accepted. The churches had equal status. One church had appeared to disturb another. Judas and Silas not only delivered the message but restored fellowship also.

(d) *Maintenance (35)*. The work of God continued unhindered. Disputes distract, and their resolution means the restoration of normality. The heart of the work of the church revolves around the dissemination of the Word, and any hindrance to that must be removed to ensure it is faithfully declared and displayed.

Acts 15:36 – 16:8   Disagreements

With others (36-41). Paul and Barnabas planned to revisit churches founded as a result of their earlier work. Disharmony arose over the choice of suitable personnel (see 13:13). Note:

(a) Paul and Barnabas were more than friends. Their disagreement did not seem to affect their relationship, only their work. There is no suggestion that their friendship suffered.

(b) Although their relationship was important, the work was more important. If fellowship cannot be maintained in the face of differences of opinion, then ways must be found for gospel work to continue.

(c) God can bring good out of disagreement. Two journeys were made instead of one and perhaps John Mark's association with Barnabas was instrumental in his restoration (2 Tim. 4:11). If disagreements occur we must humbly ask God to bless them to our good and his glory.

Within self (16:1-4)? It might seem that Paul was contradicting himself here, for after standing against circumcision he now appeared to give in to it. But this did not reflect any conflict within himself. Paul's contention was that circumcision was not a qualification for salvation. Timothy was already saved. The circumcision was not for the good of Timothy, but for others. Paul knew that if Timothy was going to accompany him, he would encounter all sorts of opinions. Circumcision would help to authenticate his Jewish background while leaving his Gentile background unaffected. By circumcision, Timothy could be all things to all men and an offence to none. Consider:

(a) Have we thought through the practical implications of our belief system? We may think we are sure of what we believe, but can we defend it consistently to those who disagree with us?

(b) We must learn to anticipate the reactions of both believers and unbelievers to our views. We cannot disregard the opinions of others in trying to establish our own. Weaker brethren should be taken into account without any compromise on our part. An apparent lack of consistency is easier to dispel than a real lack of love.

With God (5-8). Paul and Silas were evidently out of step with the mind of God at this point. How can we avoid disagreeing with God when we are doing his work?

(a) Don't take it for granted that you know what God wants you to do. Don't rely on your own feelings, preferences or plans. God can use them, but they are not an infallible guide. We must seek the mind of God through his Word. Paul and Silas were prevented by command not circumstance. See 8:29; 10:19; 13:2. We must look for clearer guidance from what God says, for what God does – circumstance, is not usually enough on its own.

(b) However, circumstances can play a part. The Holy Spirit did not tell Paul and Silas where to go. They continued until they could go no further. They were obedient to the word they had been given. Sometimes we must press on in faith until the blessing of God confirms we have gone the way of his choosing.

Acts 16:9-15   The conversion of Lydia

Preparation for conversion.

(a) *Providence*. Paul and Silas had been prevented by the Holy Spirit from preaching in the area they had expected to go. They were then directed in a vision to go into Europe. The combination of these remarkable features of guidance redirected them to a place they otherwise would not have gone to. Knowing only which region they should go to, they chose to visit the capital city first. Once they were there, they sought out those who were most likely to be sympathetic to their message.

(b) *Background*. The description of Lydia suggests she was not Jewish by birth but was a proselyte who had rejected paganism and embraced Judaism. She was religious and attended a place of prayer, but that was not enough. In that situation she was more likely to hear God and pay attention to what was said. Some people are ready to be invited to church, but not everyone.

The experience of conversion.

(a) *The message*. Although the details are absent, clearly Paul would have spoken about Christ. The presentation was not necessarily a formal sermon.

(b) *The Lord*. Paul could only open up the truth but could not open up a heart. Lydia could change her religion but she could not change her heart. Each was as powerless as the other in this respect, but both became aware of a greater power than their own as Lydia showed a certain receptivity.

(c) *The response*. Lydia was not demonstrating a superficial interest or mere curiosity arising from habit or sentiment. An acceptance, trust and commitment arose from humble penitence – a settled surrender to someone far greater than anyone she had known before.

The outcome of conversion.

(a) *Baptism*. This may have happened immediately, but it certainly happened soon. It was an act of obedience and Lydia accepted it as something which was required of her. An unbaptised Christian is a disobedient Christian and therefore a bad example to others. It was an act of testimony in which she made a public statement of what had happened to her. An unbaptised Christian is a secret disciple, which is a contradiction in terms as such a person cannot follow Christ properly if he is not observed doing so.

(b) *Good works*.

(i) *Lydia desired Christian fellowship*. She sought increased association with other Christian believers. Christians need each other and are not intended to live in isolation.

(ii) *Lydia sought some form of Christian service*. She wanted to do something which would further the cause of Christ. She was not content to let others continue the work unaided.

(iii) *Lydia opened her home*. She gave up her privacy and sacrificed her possessions by putting them at the disposal of others. Her selfless use of time, energy and property was the way she could be used to help others. She considered that such action was a necessary part of the Christian life and was proof of her devotion to Christ.

Acts 16:16-24   Servants of the Most High God

Going to prayer (16). The place of prayer continued to be just that – even though Lydia's house was perhaps available for such gatherings. No doubt prayer was made there also, but this reference shows that prayer was both regular and public. Assuming it was the same place referred to in v. 13, it was a place for evangelism as well as worship. Do you have a place of prayer? If you have a church building, it serves that purpose, but Satan will try to hinder your attendance. Sometimes it requires perseverance to make sure we get there. Although we can pray anywhere, God seems to honour the place where his people meet together to address themselves to him. 'My house shall be called a house of prayer' (Isa. 56:7). It can be helpful to find a place of prayer of our own, to which we go regularly for our private devotions. It may be nothing more than a particular chair in a particular room, but the discipline of setting aside such a place and going there regularly can be a blessing in itself.

Showing salvation (17). Servants are often identified by their task, and the evil spirit spoke the truth about these men. The public testimony given about them was not that they prayed, did good deeds or established churches but that they showed the way of salvation. Other activities followed, but that was central. We may not be apostles, but as servants of God our basic task is no different. We will not go about it in the same way as the apostles, but witnessing is our first duty

– to which many other things are related. This preliminary encounter had far-reaching consequences, as we shall see.

Overcoming evil (18). Paul cast out the evil spirit from the girl because it dismayed him to see her under its control. He knew that in Christ he had authority over it. Also, it was affecting his own ministry adversely because although what the spirit said was true, it was being expressed by one who was publicly associated with pagan superstition. Paul could not accept that testimony because it came from one who was obviously evil. If he did accept it, he would be implying there was no difference between what he and she stood for. Gospel truth is still in danger of being entangled with and discredited by lying spirits who appear to be disciples. The pure gospel is to be declared and defended by the purer life.

Bearing affliction (19-24). Although we have looked at other matters, the majority of this account is taken up with the unfolding of events which prepared the way for what happened next. Satan appeared to take his revenge and Paul and Silas were unjustly accused, badly beaten and imprisoned. The charges were false and their treatment was excessively severe, but they bore it bravely and silently and, later, joyfully. Some form of affliction is the lot of every faithful servant of God. We should expect it (John 15:18-20), but we have a good example to follow when it comes (1 Peter 2:18-24).

Acts 16:25-40   Christian conduct in adversity

Testimony (25-26). Paul and Silas were not downcast at what had happened to them. Despite the injustice, they were still in God's care. He had called them to Macedonia (9) and used them there (14). They could praise God for his presence and pray for his help. They did so boldly so that others knew of their faith and therefore their God. As they bore testimony to him, so God bore testimony to them and set them free. If we are in adversity that is not the result of our own sin, we can give testimony to God also with the expectation that although he may not free us from it, he will use us in it.

Honesty (27-29). Although the new situation was to the advantage of Paul and Silas, they did not rush away but stayed to find out what help they could be to others. They did not help others to escape because that would involve them in evading justice. They did not consider the jailer their enemy or persecutor but acted honourably towards him as well as the prisoners. God does not usually overturn an injustice for the comfort of his own people. When our circumstances change suddenly and we find ourselves in an unexpectedly advantageous position, it can be difficult to maintain our integrity and act in ways which will help others and honour God.

Authority (30-32). The jailer was convinced that Paul and Silas were two special men. Their testimony to God, the earthquake and their subsequent conduct showed him that they were men of God – a God who was evidently worth knowing. These men had access to his power and protection. After leading them out for the sake of safety, he asked that all-important question. He was probably an old soldier – a man under authority. He knew when he was in the presence of his superiors and the course of action he had to take. Our faith in God can give us a certain authority even in adversity, not so that we lord it over others but so that they see and seek our Lord.

Sanctity (35-39). Although their adversity had ended, Paul would not go out free until those who had imprisoned him acted justly. He wanted a public declaration of their innocence and an admission that they had been mistreated. To have left immediately would have given rise to gossip and speculation as to their guilt. Paul wanted to make sure that righteousness was held up to public view. The jailer made exactly the same point in his baptism: he was not what people had thought him to be, and made a public declaration of a righteousness that was not his own.

Charity (33-34,40). Charity is one of the marks of the Christian. The jailer washed and fed Paul and Silas, not as prisoners, but as brothers in Christ – their new relationship which took precedence over others. Paul and Silas returned to their brethren to show they were safe and well. In so doing those who had gone through adversity were the ones to help others. By the increase and demonstration of love for each other, adversity draws people together. The innate love among Christians needs sharing not stifling.

Acts 17:1-15   The gospel arrives in Thessalonica and Berea

Events unfolded in a similar and familiar way in Thessalonica and Berea.

The Scriptures (2,11).

(a) *God's Word.* Holy Scriptures already existed and were regarded as messages from God not man. Paul demonstrated in both towns they were incomplete and that the Christ of whom he spoke was their fulfilment. He knew he spoke God's truth without error under the direction of the Holy Spirit.

(b) *God's authority.* The delivery of God's Word was not entrusted to all men indiscriminately. God had authorised Paul to declare it and he was answerable to God for his stewardship. But that authority also determined the way he delivered it. He spoke with boldness because he had a greater fear of God than man. He spoke with urgency because he knew how much the message was needed by his hearers and he would not let opposition silence him.

Some believed (4,12).

(a) *The word received.* God's Word has a spiritual power that ordinary speech and writing do not have. Beyond the persuasive influence of rhetoric or eloquence, God's Word breaks down barriers of ignorance, prejudice, self-confidence and other forms of sin. Because it is living and powerful, it enters the mind and heart and is able to make all kinds of people wise unto salvation.

(b) *The word changed.* Once the word has been received and believed, under the influence of the Spirit it continues to be effective. Once someone is convinced that Christ is their Saviour, it works with life-transforming power. Sometimes instantaneously and sometimes over a longer period, thoughts, habits, beliefs, attitudes and interests, all begin to change. In turning us from self-serving to serving God, the ways of God replace the ways of the world.

Some opposed (5,13).

(a) *It was expected.* The forces of opposition did not simply disagree with Paul's interpretation, but considered it dangerous enough to require expulsion (6-7). Paul expected it, not only because the same thing had happened in Philippi, Lystra, Iconium and Antioch, but mainly because Jesus had predicted it (John 15:19-21). Hardship is inevitable for anyone who publicly declares God's truth, because it stands against all that the world holds dear.

(b) *It was edifying.* Despite appearances, the effects of the opposition were not all negative. In Luke 21:12-19, Jesus taught that it can help build up faith, giving further opportunity for testimony (13), trust (15) and then triumph (19); it would strengthen ties with Christ and his people (17). The ability to survive such treatment and continue unhindered presents a fine example.

Sent away (10,14).

(a) *Growth.* Paul did not leave in disgrace or disharmony, but for his own good. He knew his departure would be best for the cause of Christ. The church had a task and a testimony of its own to establish. Silas and Timothy were left there.

(b) *Affection.* Paul's absence increased his concern for these new churches as his subsequent letters show. He exercised loving care for them from a distance and gave written, and then practical, assurance of it by sending Timothy later (1 Thess. 3:6).

Acts 17:16-34   The unknown God

Paul tells the Athenians about the true God and shows how that truth leads to Jesus Christ. The gospel begins with the doctrine of God. Creation involves the cross, and salvation is incomplete without judgement.

He can be known (23). Human beings naturally want to worship something, but sin compels them to worship only what they can see, hear or touch. Plenty of people worship a god they do not know (John 4:22). Although invisible, God is knowable, but not through idols. The true God has made himself known to all and given mankind the capacity to know him (Eccles. 3:11). But that revelation and the ability to receive it are perverted or rejected (Rom. 1:18-23).

He has created (24). The thought of a single, supreme deity would be new to these people. Every other deity was immediately dwarfed by such a concept, as each one only represented different aspects of life. There can only be one infinite being. He would be limited if there were others, and therefore not infinite. Unity in the design of creation as a single non-contradictory system points to one, designing intelligence.

He sustains (25). His greatness and transcendence suggest that he cannot be manipulated or placated like other deities. The one who sustains all life can hardly need sustaining himself by inferior beings. He is not absent from his creation, but actively and personally involved in its maintenance.

He governs (26). The God of nature is also the God of history. He has planned who should live and where they should live. He has done this with everybody ever since the world began. The human race has a unity, a dignity and a destiny because of God.

He is accessible (27-29). The purpose behind his allocation of time and territory is that he should be sought and known by mankind. He has made us and he wants us to know that we are his. So although he is of unequalled magnitude, he is also intimately personal and immanent. Paul quotes pagan poets to show that their conclusions have a glimmer of truth and point to the true God. Idolatry points in the opposite direction. Gods who need idols to represent them are not worthy of the name.

He is merciful (30). Paul's God is merciful. He is willing to overlook the fact that up to that time the Athenians were wilfully ignorant of him. Without approving, he understands, but they need to know that there is more to this God than mercy.

He commands (30). Because they are God's offspring and are dependent on him, because he has revealed himself and rules them, they are accountable to him. He has authority over them to require certain things of them. He insists they turn from their foolish, empty idols and humble themselves before him.

He will judge (31). God is within his rights to expect allegiance and acquiescence from his creation and to test whether it is forthcoming. The standard of judgement he will apply is Jesus. His resurrection proves his identity and authority. Rejection of him is rejection of God. The prospect of judgement was alien to these thinkers, but the day had been set and they must respond to it as they could no longer claim ignorance.

Acts 18:1-17   The Lord spoke to Paul

In the words of Jesus here, there are two commands in v. 9 and three promises in v. 10.

Persist. The familiar pattern emerged in Corinth that Paul had experienced in Antioch, Iconium, Thessalonica and Berea. Preaching to Jews first of all, his message was soon rejected and so he preached among the Gentiles with some success. However, Jewish opposition persisted and he became anxious for himself and the vulnerable new church. Fear and weariness are not unknown among the Lord's servants and they can hinder their ministries. The Lord himself told Paul to continue his ministry in the city. He was not to give in to his fears. 'Do not be afraid.'

Proclaim. He was not to move on, but nor was he to remain silent. Jesus told Paul to continue his work openly. Has fear silenced you at home, at work or in your neighbourhood? The Lord still commands his people to persist with their witness and proclaim his Word in ways appropriate to their circumstances. The world continues to need the gospel message. Let our ministry continue, openly and boldly. 'Do not be silent.'

Presence. The first promise was of his continuing presence. Jesus did not say, 'I will be with you,' but, 'I am with you.' The vision reminded Paul of the unchanging reality of the presence of Christ. Nothing has changed. The Lord is not only with the greatest saint but also with the newest believer. His presence is instrumental in removing our fear. We know that we are not alone, and the never failing nearness of our Saviour gives us courage to continue. Also, the presence of the Lord gives us the assurance that we will know what to say or do when the time comes. We can have peace and confidence knowing he is there to prompt us and to use us. 'I am with you.'

Protection. Jesus confirmed Paul's suspicions that there would be opposition, but it would be limited. Having commanded him to speak, the Lord would make it possible for him to do so. Although not spared persecution, it would not adversely affect his testimony. If the Lord calls us to serve him, he will prepare the way for us to do it. God is active among both the speakers and the hearers. He will restrain the wicked. Satan cannot hinder God's eternal work. 'No one will harm you.'

Prosperity. Jesus reassured Paul that his preaching would be effective and that he would know fruit for his labours. The word that Jesus enabled Paul to speak would take root in the hearts of those Jesus knew were his (2 Tim. 2:19). The Lord is not going to do so much to send out his word only to let it fail at the last moment (Isa. 55:11). His purpose may not always be salvation (Isa. 6:9-10), but blessing is promised here. The Lord works in people's hearts in ways we can know nothing about. Sometimes, it is only later that we can see how they and we were prepared for a particular encounter. 'I have many people in this city.'

Read Paul's reflections on these events in 1 Corinthians 2:1-5.

Acts 18:18-28 The conduct of Christians

Towards law-abiding citizens: challenge, not compromise. It can be puzzling to see Paul as a Christian continuing some Jewish practices (18; 16:3; 17:2) while teaching that such things were not essential to Christianity. Normally for Jews, race and religion could not be separated, but Paul and many other Jews had ceased to be Jewish by faith, but remained Jewish by birth. He felt his national identity very strongly and he continued to mix with others as long as he could, knowing that his pedigree would at least gain him a hearing (Phil. 3:5-6).

As a religious Jew he had been under the bondage of the law. As a Jewish Christian, his relationship to the law had changed. His righteousness did not depend on personal obedience to it but on Christ. Now, he had control over the law, rather than the law having control over him. The law still represented God's standards, but Paul used it as a challenge to those who advocated that conformity to it would secure acceptance with God. Paul used the law as a way into his own community (1 Cor. 9:20), but at the same time declaring that the Christ, Jesus, had won him peace with God by his obedience to the law and his sacrificial death.

Most people around us claim to be law-abiding citizens. As Christians we ought to be seen to be law-abiding and at the same time make clear that our 'goodness' does not make us Christians. We live that way because we are Christians, obeying the laws of the land because God requires it of us.

Towards Christians: careful not careless. Paul exercised a very wide influence in his ministry, but in his desire to break new ground he did not neglect the 'old ground'. He was careful to do what he could to strength and nurture the newer Christians. He left Aquila and Priscilla in Ephesus, Luke in Philippi and Timothy and Silas in Berea. Some of his own journeys served that purpose (23). He was also aware that he had a measure of responsibility to those churches with which he had had meaningful fellowship in the past. He did not drop the relationships he had established with the churches in Antioch and Jerusalem. For some Christians, circumstances change greatly throughout life, and individuals and churches which were once important to us are replaced by others. We may not be in a position to visit them, but a letter, a call, a gift and certainly a prayer can show the loving concern that Christians ought to have for old acquaintances who have now passed beyond our immediate circle.

Towards unbalanced teachers: correct not criticise. Aquila and Priscilla identified in Apollos an unbalanced teacher, not a false teacher, and that is an important distinction. What Apollos said was accurate, but he did not say enough. He was ignorant, and his teaching was incomplete as a result, but that was different from being wrong. Their approach to him is significant. They spoke to him privately rather than addressing him publicly. They saw his strengths and weaknesses and encouraged him to continue in a work for which he was clearly equipped. He had a teachable spirit and being corrected did not curtail his fervency. Many believers are satisfied with accuracy today, when more accuracy is required. In these days we can all cultivate a deeper familiarity with the things of God, so that we can help any Apollos who might appear among us.

Acts 19:1-10   Receiving the Holy Spirit

The baptism of John. It seems these disciples were what we might call 'nominal Christians'. They had left traditional Judaism and were on the threshold of Christianity. Their baptism had been one of repentance – a turning away from a former way of life with abhorrence, and was the beginning of reformation. It was a necessary starting point, but not the finishing point. They had not turned to God and accepted the provision he had made for them. They had not found forgiveness. They may well have heard about Christ, but had no experience of him. Becoming a Christian involves a change of heart which only God can accomplish by the power of the Holy Spirit. It is much more than a change of mind, when one set of beliefs and practices is rejected and another set adopted in their place.

The baptism of Jesus. This is an unusual situation as it is the only recorded instance of re-baptism, but it shows the necessity of believers' baptism. The truth about Christ was presented and received and baptism was the necessary consequence of that acceptance. We see here that it is possible to be baptised in ignorance when all the facts are not known, and although done with the best intentions it is invalid. Baptism is a testimony to a new life and a declaration of allegiance to the one who has given it. To a lesser extent there is an element of initiation into a group of people who share a common faith in Christ and are united in their pursuit of living in a way which will honour him.

The reception of the Holy Spirit. Their baptism was not dependent upon a verbal declaration. Paul did not ask them for their testimony. Their reply might have suggested a change in their lives and a new desire to follow Christ. Paul's question related to the subjective nature of their faith, not its external features. Evidence for the work of the Holy Spirit must be seen, for it was promised by Christ (John 7:38-39; 14:16-17) and confirmed by the apostles (Rom. 8:9; Eph. 1:13-14; Acts 2:38; 5:32; 1 John 3:24). It is the new birth which brings about a change in life, not our own efforts (John 3:5; Eph. 3:17).

The demonstration of the Holy Spirit. The rightness of this re-baptism was immediately confirmed by the evident gift of the Holy Spirit. This unusual occurrence, at variance with the normal operations of the Holy Spirit, can be explained as a means of authenticating the messenger in an unusual situation during this transitory period in the revelation of Jesus Christ. The coming of the Holy Spirit upon these men removed the self-trust of their earlier religious life. They were equipped with supernatural gifts and could not preserve the illusion that they could sustain their faith unaided. Gifts were given so that God would be glorified, not man. As a result, Paul had a group of believers around him who were equipped to serve and desired to be obedient. Under his leadership, instead of settling down into a comfortable holy huddle, they went far and wide proclaiming the gospel.

Acts 19:8-22 The word of the Lord spread widely and grew in power

The word of the Lord was proclaimed (8-10). Paul naturally took the gospel message to the synagogue first because he was a Jew and Jesus was the Jewish Messiah. But once again there was a negative reaction of stubborn unbelief and abuse. Such strong opposition resulted in a tactical withdrawal, for to continue in those circumstances would have been counterproductive. This separation served as:

(i) a testimony against unbelief,

(ii) protection for believers against further antagonism,

(iii) an opportunity to nurture believers by the unopposed declaration of the truth and closer fellowship,

(iv) an opportunity to establish a centre from which the gospel could be spread.

The word of the Lord was endorsed (11-12). This almost incidental reference to miracles was not referred to by Paul in his summary of his time in Ephesus (20:18-21). Their mention shows they were both outstanding and relevant. This was a superstitious city where God condescended to show his power in terms the people would understand. They demonstrated genuine benevolence and give no sanction to relics. They authenticated the messenger and his message, pointing to the even greater miracle of new birth. If such miracles became normative their purpose would be lost.

The word of the Lord was defended (13-16). The success of this aspect of Paul's ministry provoked an attempt to counterfeit it. Satan can sometimes deceive people by appearing to work against himself and draw them into his power. It is a warning not to take up the name of the Lord for ourselves falsely. It can harm others and it brings punishment upon ourselves. He is too great to be trifled with in this way – the Son of God, the Saviour of mankind and the victor over Satan. There is none more powerful and exalted.

The word of the Lord was magnified (17-20). The name of Christ was honoured by:

(i) *Fear.* There was respectful recognition of his greatness. For some that meant distancing themselves from him, but for others it meant submitting themselves to him.

(ii) *Reformation.* Lives were changed as new believers rejected their former ways. The degree of seriousness with which they addressed their sinful past was seen in a public display of their open antagonism to what they had previously valued.

(iii) *Report.* News spread rapidly of what had happened and why. The truth of the gospel was illustrated. The Word of God was seen to be living and able to prevail over all opposition – sin, Satan and death, both within personal lives and in whole communities.

The word of the Lord was despatched (21-22). Paul's decision seems to have been influenced by:

(i) *A thriving church in Ephesus.* He could leave, and know the church would grow and spread the gospel (20; 20:17).

(ii) *The needs of other churches.* He had retraced his steps before (15:41; 18:22-23) and wanted to do so again.

(iii) *the needs of the Jerusalem church.* 1 Corinthians 16:1-8 might fit in here.

(iv) *The needs of the unevangelised* – especially Rome (Rom. 15:22-33; 1:9-13).

Acts 19:23-41 Christianity creates a disturbance

This passage highlights some of the unique features of Christianity.

Christianity is a lone religion (26). Christianity is often bracketed with Judaism and Islam as one of the great monotheistic faiths. But any common ground is illusory because they do not accept the centrality of Jesus Christ as the full and final personal manifestation of God. All other religions are discredited; by Scripture (for example Ps.115:2-8), by reason – the lesser (man) cannot create the greater (god), and by experience – bringing little temporal and no eternal benefit to their adherents. False religion in its many forms brings the same result, bondage and damnation. All other faiths are false.

Christianity is a living religion (27). Christianity is not primarily an agent for social change, moral reform or religious expression. Those factors are the secondary results of the prime feature of Christianity which is the impartation of divine life to humanity. Its power is seen in the change brought to the individual – new birth, recreation (John 10:10; 5:26; 1 John 5:11-12). The claims of other religions are far inferior. Take for example the religion of Artemis. Her divine majesty was only bestowed by men, while that of Christ was his by right. He is God incarnate. Her temple, not only discredited, is in ruins, where the temple of Christ thrives (1 Cor. 3:16; 6:19). Her followers, although numerous then, no longer exist, whereas the followers of Christ, while few at the time, continue to increase. The essence of the delusion in v. 35 has appeared in many guises since then, but Christ remains as reigning supreme over all. Christianity is a living religion because its founder is still alive and continues to give of his own life to others (John 1:4).

Christianity is a life-changing religion (24-25). Demetrius was concerned about the effect Christianity was having upon Ephesian society, especially financially. When radical change comes to a community as a result of growing Christian influence, it is always for good. Moral transformation takes place as inconsistencies are exposed in various areas of life. Christianity interferes with any sinful accumulation of wealth as honesty is promoted. It explodes false illusions as it destroys self-trust and self-seeking. It disturbs cherished ease because, in serving a higher cause, the Christian is usually at odds with his peers and life becomes less comfortable as a result.

Christianity is a law-abiding religion (37). False religions betray themselves by using the weapons of the world, such as violence, threats and intimidation, which true Christianity never will deploy (2 Cor. 10:3-4). Although Christianity may provoke opposition when self-interest is exposed, it poses no threat to public order. It has no need. Its kingdom is not of this world (John 18:36). God is spirit and so Christianity is a spiritual religion, and its involvement in the physical realm, while real and significant, is not predominant (Eph. 6:12). Christianity is set on preparing us for the world to come (2 Cor. 5:1-5).

Acts 20:1-16   Church life in the days of the apostles

God's people – gathered. This passage records various occasions when believers were together in different circumstances (1,2,4,7,16). Frequent fellowship should be a noted characteristic of believers. We are united by stronger ties than the bonds of family, race or culture. If Christ dwells in each of us, the more we are together, the more of Christ we should experience as we see something of him in each other and share something of him with each other. We should want to be in each other's company for ministry, companionship and assistance.

God's Word – declared. Paul took every opportunity to declare God's Word (1,2,7). Fellowship has its benefits but it also has its limits. In itself it does not save people (1 Cor. 1:21). God has spoken to man and has called men to pass on his Word to others to establish and strengthen their faith. Nothing should be allowed to usurp the primacy of the declaration of God's Word in the life of the church or the individual Christian. It can easily become downgraded when it is re-packaged into another format.

God's day – hallowed (7). These disciples evidently met regularly and not on the Jewish Sabbath. It seems to have become a voluntary celebration of the resurrection. The fact that it was still a working day probably explains the timing of the meeting. Synagogue attendance may still have continued with Jewish Christians, but Gentile believers had more liberty to meet. We have a day set aside to meet with God, along with specified times and places to facilitate it and yet we let other things put us off.

God's Son – remembered (7). The centrality of the breaking of bread on these occasions shows that the purpose of these gatherings was primarily God-ward rather than man-ward. They obediently met in a joyful celebration of their salvation, remembering the death of their Saviour and no doubt being enriched by their contemplation of the grace of God in Christ. Our sense of worship will increase the less we think of ourselves.

God's power – received (12). The power of God was seen as Eutychus was restored to life. He was strengthened by God physically but the church was strengthened spiritually as the work of God was seen. Seeing the work of God in the life of others is always beneficial to believers, especially when the dead are brought to life.

God's work – continued (3,11). Nothing could stop Paul from continuing what God had called him to do (2 Cor. 11:24-28). He was relentless, despite threats and worse. What an example to us to persevere amidst difficulty and not grow weary in well doing (Heb. 12:1-2; 1 Peter 1:13-19)! Have you put your hand to the plough and looked back? We must learn to say, 'I can do all things through Christ who strengthens me.'

Acts 20:17-24   Paul: an example of Christian service

Paul was on his way to Jerusalem (16), and was waiting for a connection. He was only 30 miles away from Ephesus, and not wanting to miss his connection he asked the elders to come to him, rather than go to them. Luke was present to record the only address to Christians in the Acts of the Apostles, highlighting:

A demonstration of faithfulness (18). Paul had stayed in Ephesus for at least two years (19:10), so the young church there had known him well. Perhaps the victim of a smear campaign again, Paul reminded them that he had lived a transparent life among them. If tempted, they had no grounds to doubt the authenticity of his life and message. His appeal was based on their own observation of his consistency. Neither he nor they had anything to be ashamed of.

A dedication to Christ (19). The reason for the transparency of his life was that he served the Lord – not men. He was not arrogant but humble. He was not dictatorial, taking advantage of his position, but caring, demonstrating a tender concern for, and strong association with, those in need. He was not diverted or discouraged by opposition, but maintained a high degree of loving service.

A determination to help (20). Paul had wanted to be as helpful to the church as possible, so he did not keep back difficult truth they needed to know about. Whether in public or private, he spared no thought for himself, but was focused, energetic, thorough and confident.

A declaration of truth (21). He made the truth known to all without discrimination, for all had an equal need. He upheld the centrality and simplicity of the gospel by proclaiming repentance and faith. Every sinner has offended God and they must turn away from their sin to him with genuine contrition. As they do that, they will see that he has provided a Saviour for them in the person of his own Son and they must put their trust solely in him.

A compulsion of the Spirit (22). As he had been compelled by God to preach the gospel to them before, so now he was constrained by the Spirit to go to Jerusalem. He was subject to a higher authority. He had committed his future into hands of God and left the outcome with him. His conscience would not allow him to act in any other way and he was prepared to face the consequences.

A communication of God's will (23). He had been moved on by a word from God (21:10-11). His own spirit was bound to the Spirit of God. It may have appeared that he was acting against reason (21:12-14), but he had the assurance from God himself that he was doing the right thing.

A completion of the task (24). Paul was willing to be used by God in any situation. He was not being careless with his life but careful. He would harness his energies to remove any doubts about the gospel, and continue to convince others of its truth. The gospel was too important for him to pamper himself.

Acts 20:25-38   Fundamental features of a Christian church

The second part of Paul's address concerned the church.

The church is purchased (28).

(a) *It was formed through a divine transaction.* The church was brought into being by God, belongs to him and exists for him. By his own action, he has acquired a people for himself.

(b) *It is defined by the blood of Christ.* The action God took was to provide his Son, Jesus Christ, as an atoning sacrifice for the sin of those people. Won at such a great cost, the church is clearly of great value to him.

(c) *Leadership has been provided.* If the church was brought into being in such a way, God would not then leave it unattended. He has appointed overseers for it through his Holy Spirit. They are to act in accordance with the nature of the church. As sheep, the church needs shepherding.

The church is persecuted (29-31).

(a) *It is vulnerable to attack from outside.* Satan is intent upon its destruction. The church in Ephesus received more apostolic communications that are preserved in the Bible than any other congregation. This event is thought to have taken place about AD 56 and Paul's epistle to the whole church arrived about five years later. Then came two letters in fairly quick succession to the leader of the church, Timothy, after a further three years or so, and finally one arrived from the apostle John, about thirty years later (Rev. 2:1-7).

(b) *It gives rise to distortions of the truth from within itself.* Some of the leaders would stray from the truth and take others with them. One of the temptations of leadership is to try to extend one's influence, and if it meant introducing new revelation to do so, then some would even do that.

(c) *It needs guarding – and they were the ones to do it.* In order to guard others, the shepherd must keep watch over himself first. They needed to remember that the church belonged to the Father, that the Son and died for it and that the Spirit had appointed them to lead it. They were to be aware that a powerful enemy would attack a vulnerable people and they were to conduct themselves with constant vigilance, as Paul had done.

The church is preserved (32-35).

(a) *It is under God's protection.* Although attacked, it would not be endangered. Only its own disobedience would destroy it. God would preserve a testimony to himself and remove what was not of him. If men were faithful to God and his Word, they could leave the future of the church in the hands of God.

(b) *It is protected by the Word of God.* The means God uses is his own Word. He will not only work beyond them for their good, he will work within them too. His Word will save, sanctify and secure them.

(c) *It is preserved by selfless sacrifice.* Paul had no thought for himself in his service to the church. Like Jesus, he gave himself for the good of all.

Acts 21:1-17   Some key Christian characteristics

Joyful fellowship. Fellowship is more than friendship. It is not just a gathering of people with a common interest. It is the product of a common experience which is deeper than any ties of blood or race. People are bound together because of God's dealing with them individually (1 John 1:3,6-7). Fellowship is not created but is expressed because of a relationship that already existed. It is expressed in various ways:

Affection: 'torn ourselves away' (1). There is an awareness that other believers are precious to you and you are affected when something happens to them (20:37).

Longing: 'having sought out' (4; 'finding', NIV). You want to meet and spend time with other believers in preference to other people.

Concern (4,11). Disciples at Tyre and Caesarea were anxious about Paul's safety. We should not be afraid to warn others when we consider they might be taking a wrong course of action.

Harmony (5-6). Even though their advice was rejected, all the disciples in Tyre still commended Paul on his journey. We should do all we can to preserve unity even when there is disagreement over an issue.

Ministry (5,9-10). In Tyre the believers shared in the ministry of prayer with Paul, and in Caesarea Paul and his companions benefited from the ministries of believers also. All believers have the ability and obligation to help each other.

Hospitality (4,7-8). One aspect of ministry evident in all three places is hospitality. A home open to other believers is a tangible demonstration of our oneness in Christ.

Companionship (16). Other believers joined the party to complete the journey (see also 20:4). They took the opportunity of providing practical support in the labours of others – perhaps to guide or guard. There are many opportunities for similar supportive roles to assist Christian workers today.

Spiritual sensitivity (4,12). Through the direct testimony of the Holy Spirit, believers in Tyre and Caesarea warned Paul that he would suffer if he went to Jerusalem. Paul already knew it (20:22-23). The Spirit was not forbidding him, simply telling him what to expect. The believers took the warning a stage further and urged him not to go, but Paul knew he must do. When the Spirit speaks on a issue, he says the same thing to all parties involved. We must be careful not to misinterpret him.

Costly commitment (13). By continuing on his appointed way, Paul showed that he had an even greater commitment to Christ than to the church or his own well-being. He would defy others and deny himself in order to pursue the course he knew the Lord wanted him to take. In order to keep ourselves close to Christ, we may sometimes have to take decisions which seem strange to others.

Acts 21:17-36   A slave to all, to gain many

A good report (17-20). Always ready to welcome other believers, the Jerusalem church gave a warm reception to Paul and his companions. The leadership was given a detailed account of God's work through Paul and rejoiced at what they heard. We should take every opportunity to hear about, and rejoice in, the work of God elsewhere.

A polite request (20-26). Many Jewish believers continued to uphold the law after their conversion and had been wrongly informed that Paul spoke against the law. Because Paul had been welcomed by the leadership, he was asked to demonstrate his willingness to uphold certain ceremonial aspects of the law in order to avert a split. His thinking on this issue is shown in 1 Cor. 9:19-23 and he agreed, out of respect for:

Weaker brethren. He was willing to adjust his lifestyle to accommodate those who had not come to the same understanding as him. He was showing how his oneness with them as a fellow believer was more important than the issue itself.

Church leadership. He agreed to their request, being willing to adjust his behaviour while he was with them, since they knew what was best for their own church.

The gospel. He remained immovable on that and he was acting without compromise and without sin. No moral obligation was being imposed on others for it was a secondary issue.

Observance was voluntary and personal, a matter of conscience. His action was only a temporary concession which would bring the blessings of greater love and obedience. He would 'gain' others in fellowship, assurance and maturity and maintain the unity of the Spirit in the bond of peace.

The law. By showing that he was the master of the law, not a slave to it, Paul put the law in its proper place. He used his liberty from it to show his subjection to it, thereby demonstrating that obedience was voluntary – after obeying Christ first (Gal. 5:13-18).

Christ. Jesus had done the same thing. By his incarnation he did not surrender any of his rights, but chose to withhold his exercise of them (Phil. 2:3-8).

A serious riot (27-36). While fulfilling this request, Paul was recognised by unbelieving Jewish visitors to Jerusalem who started trouble which endangered his life. An innocent action was misunderstood with serious consequences. An action intended to help the church enraged the world. Consideration for others can lead to unexpected problems. But troubles are part of the providence of God and these were predicted (20:22-24), and began events which take us to the end of the book. They opened up a new ministry for Paul – to the authorities and to Rome. Sometimes help comes from an unexpected, worldly source to preserve a godly ministry. It may not have been sought, but it was needed. The church may be powerless, but God is not.

Acts 21:37 – 22:21   Paul's testimony

This is one of three accounts of Paul's conversion (see also 9:1-19; 26:9-23). The original charge against him was given in v.28, which was that he taught and acted against the God of Israel. Paul refutes that and demonstrates the opposite by:

His condition (22:1-5).

(a) *He was approved by man.* His religious pedigree was very impressive. In education and observance, he identified himself with everything his Jewish hearers would hold dear. He equalled and excelled them in his Jewishness and should have qualified for their acclaim, not their condemnation. But...

(b) *He was disapproved by God.* He had sincerely believed he was serving God by what he did, but the opposite was the case. He discovered that what he had done arose out of ignorance and unbelief (1 Tim.1:13). What pleased God was not his persecuting zeal but the revelation of Christ in his life which came later (Gal.1:15-16). He, above all, had reason for confidence before God, but his conversion to Christ showed that it had been of no account to God (Phil.3:4-7).

Many today are still under the illusion that they have much which will commend them to God. Such pride can only be broken down by a revelation of Christ.

His conversion (6-16).

God entered Paul's life dramatically, and from that moment on the Damascus road he was:

(a) *Blinded to man.* His physical blindness was real but it was also symbolic. Up to then, all he had seen was men. Now he was blind to the world of men, because at the same time he was ...

(b) *Sighted towards God.* All he could see was 'the glory of the Light' (11). He could see nothing but God. As his life unfolded, it showed that his sight remained firmly fixed on the glory of God.

Believers can still pay too much attention to the world of men and lose sight of the light of the world. We need to gaze more frequently on the 'Fairest of ten thousand' in wonder, love and praise.

His commission (17-21).

Having been given an inkling of what lay in the future for him, it seems that Paul's mind had begun to race and naturally expected that his life had prepared him for a work among his own people (19-20). But it was not so, and Paul had to learn the important lesson that what was:

(a) *Undesirable to man* – in an unexpected and perhaps initially unwelcome change of direction in life, was in fact ...

(b) *Desirable to God* – because he has plans which are greater and better than ours.

We may think we know the mind of God for our sphere of service, but we must learn to wait upon him for clear guidance and perhaps prepare ourselves for the unexpected.

Acts 22:22 – 23:11   An example of Christian fortitude

In facing various difficulties, Paul presents a positive example to us.

Paul before the secular world (22-29).

(a) *He accepted that he was at the mercy of an unjust world.* Paul was an innocent victim, badly treated. He was in the hands of someone who acted first and asked questions afterwards. The world has its own agenda – which does not include God or his people.

(b) *He adopted a peaceful and polite method of protest.* It is proper for a Christian to stand up for justice and avoid unnecessary suffering. Sometimes there is no need for martyrdom when a protest is not directly related to Christian testimony and the antagonism is not an expression of anti-Christian feeling.

Paul before the religious world (22:30 – 23:10).

(a) *Honesty.* Paul makes three statements which have this characteristic: He had always acted according to what he believed God wanted form him (1). He had been unselfish but misinformed. We do not know the reason why the high priest could not be identified (5), but Paul's apology reinforces his commitment to abide by the Word of God. Although the resurrection was a point of contention (6), his comment was a true statement of his position and would have opened up the way for testimony to Christ.

(b) *Piety.* Paul stood up for the things of God twice, rather than for himself. His response (3) expressed righteous indignation at such an affront to justice in the offensive treatment given to a fellow Jew. Jesus protested in a similar situation (John 18:23). Luke 12:11-12 could suggest that Paul's comment was prophetic, given the fact that it came true ten years later. His comment in v.6 would have been supported by evidence if he had had the opportunity to speak further. He was not guilty of any personal offence but aggravated an unresolved doctrinal dispute.

(c) *Humility.* He admitted his mistake in v.5 and made no attempt to present himself in a favourable light in v.6.

Paul before the Saviour of the world (11).

(a) *Companionship.* Paul was alone but the Lord stood with him. He came uninvited. He not only sees our need, but cares enough to respond personally. Exceptional events prompted an exceptional appearance.

(b) *Courage.* Jesus said more than 'cheer up'. His words meant, 'Draw from me the courage you need for this situation.' Paul needed to hear that because the prophecy of 21:10-11 had come true. Had Paul made a mistake by his insistence on going to Jerusalem? There was no rebuke.

(c) *Commendation.* Jesus assured Paul that his testimony in Jerusalem was accepted. It was not a mistake. Paul had taken the opportunities given.

(d) *Commission.* Paul was to look forward, not back. His work in Jerusalem was over but it was time for him to move on to a new and greater phase.

Acts 23:12-35 The plot against Paul

This passage presents a contrast between the greatness of sin and the greatness of God.

The greatness of sin (12-15). It is:

Restrictive: sin binds and imprisons people so that they cannot escape it.

Compulsive: springing up spontaneously to provoke immediate action.

Extreme: not content with half measures but aims for the extremity of death.

Blind: unable to see it is working against God, blinkered.

Contagious: not restricted to an individual, easily spread, involving the innocent.

Bold: makes presumptuous demands with no respect for authority.

Proud: boastful of its intentions and confident of success.

Premeditated: not always accidental but calculating and purposeful.

Deceitful: encourages others to sin to further its own cause.

Harmful: unconcerned about its detrimental influence on others.

Foolish: ultimately self-destructive and doomed to failure.

This terrible catalogue evident in the conspiracy against Paul is not far removed from our experience. The nature of sin can be grossly underestimated, even by believers. It is a real and powerful force which needs radical treatment. Its power has been broken at the cross, but are we still letting it have dominion over us? Although the battle within us rages still, it is won and that is how we must live.

The greatness of God (16-35). God is not mentioned in this passage but his hand is clearly on these events. Two features are evident:

Preparation: Before the threat was even conceived, the Lord had already prepared Paul to face the future, whatever may have been involved. Paul was not in any real danger because God was already at work, strengthening his servant for the new phase of ministry ahead of him. Although his next destination had been revealed to him, Paul did not know the details of how he would get there. It is the same for believers. The Lord has assured them where they are going, but has chosen not to reveal what the journey will involve. The enmity of others may seem fearsome, but the outcome of their action is ordained by a greater power and part of a higher purpose. He expects us to trust him.

Providence: Having made a promise to Paul, the Lord kept his word and provided help for him. This time, it was not in the form of an angel or an earthquake but his nephew. God's ordering of events sometimes takes us by surprise because they seem so ordinary. Preparation is part of providence as purpose is indistinguishable from performance. What God says, he will do — never fear, only trust and obey.

Acts 24:1-21 Paul's defence before Felix [1]

In the course of his defence before Felix, Paul highlights three basic elements of genuine faith as illustrated in his own life.

I worship God (14). Paul worshipped a God he knew (John 4:22). He was not worshipping in ignorance. God had made himself known in two ways:

In history. He is the God of 'my fathers'. He has been identified by his actions in history as the God who cares for his people. Throughout succeeding generations his actions have been consistent with, and not contradictory to, his character.

In Scripture. He has caused authentic records of his activities in history to be set down. He has also revealed his requirements to mankind – a code of conduct he expects them to adhere to, while leaving them under no illusions about the consequences of failure. In this way man discovers that not only can he know God, but he is also answerable to him. This sense of accountability to God is one of the hallmarks of true religion: a humble dependence upon him both for this life but especially for eternity.

I have hope in God (15). This accountability ought to lead us, as it led Paul, to trust God wholly and unreservedly for our eternal well-being. Paul spoke of resurrection, as others did. But there was a certainty about it for Paul because its reality was grounded in the unchanging nature of God, the demonstrable faithfulness of his dealings with his people and the undoubted trustworthiness of his promises. Others had no such assurance. Because they knew nothing of God personally, their 'hope' of resurrection was little more than wishful thinking. Life after death is guaranteed, but only as a gift of the same God who gives life before death. Is our hope of eternal life based on our aspirations or God's declarations?

I live for God (16). Like the Old Testament saints, we do not yet enter into what has been promised (Heb. 11:39-40). Although we have a glorious prospect in view, we do not live now in such a way as to persuade or placate God or earn a place in his presence. Anyone who is sure of his God and his heavenly home knows he has a debt which can never be repaid. Our life is both an expression of gratitude and a desire to honour the God who has given us everything. Pleasing God does not come automatically. The Scriptures are in our hands to guide us, and the Spirit is in our heart to enable us, but it is hard work. If our faith is real, we will never be satisfied with our Christian life. We will always be aware that we are not as holy as we ought to be, and while we long to be more pleasing to him now we have a greater longing to be with him – which is far better.

Acts 24:22-27   Paul's defence before Felix [2]

Do you know anyone who is like Felix? He was:

Knowledgeable (22). Felix knew much about Christianity – its beliefs and practices. He had information about the person of Jesus Christ and was interested in what he heard. Perhaps we have a 'contact' like this, maybe a churchgoer.

Kind (23). Felix treated Christians well. They harmed no one and he had no cause to harm them. He may not have gone along with all they said, but he would not stand in their way if they wanted to do what they believed was right. Your friend may be favourably disposed to upright Christian people.

Keen (24). Felix listened to preachers and spoke to them about spiritual issues. He welcomed opportunities to hear more and thought what he heard was important enough to invite other people to hear it too. This is the kind of person you hardly need to invite to a meeting because they would be there anyway, but you are unsure of what is going on in their heart.

Convicted (25). Felix was affected by what he heard and it made him feel uncomfortable. His conscience was pricked, but what he heard was rather too close to the mark for him, and instead of submitting to the truth he backed off. He would not take the next step and become committed because he realised some of the personal implications of what he had been told.

There are two suggestions why he would go no further.

He loved life too much (26). It seems he thought there was something to be gained by being open to Christianity. If he could use Christianity to his own advantage, he would, but as soon as it demanded anything from him, he wanted nothing more to do with it. He would still be civil, and talk and listen, but he was no longer willing to be convinced. There was just too much at stake and he was not prepared to make that sacrifice. He had not seen that what he would gain by trusting Christ far outweighed anything he might lose.

He pleased men too much (27). Whatever Felix knew about God, he still had more regard for men. He was more concerned to be in favour with man than with God. He wanted to try and make this life as easy as possible for himself, but in doing so forfeited the blessings of the next life. Despite speaking about the judgement to come, he had no sense of his accountability to God.

If you are in touch with someone who seems to be near the kingdom, keep praying for them and witnessing to them. If you have lost touch with such a person, keep praying for them and trust that God will use someone else to witness to them.

Acts 25   Paul before Festus

Paul was subjected to scrutiny by the authorities. It was not a trial but a hearing. The charges against him were:

(i) Heresy – teaching against the truth of the law – even though he upheld it. He considered it fulfilled in Christ.

(ii) Sacrilege – against Jewish religious practices, even though he had not abused the sanctity of the temple. He considered it to be a type of Christ.

(iii) Treason – he was no threat to the Roman authorities. Others had caused the riot, not him. Let us learn from Paul how to acquit ourselves before the world when we are unjustly accused.

With a clear conscience (10). Satan is both the accuser of the brethren and the father of lies. Sometimes the world is very eager to pick up the least fault and magnify it out of all proportion.

A declaration of innocence. Paul had wronged neither God nor man and invited any fair test to be used to prove it. We need to live with a clear conscience, so that if we are accused we can cite evidence to the contrary (1 Peter 3:16).

A confession of wrongdoing. The world may be correct in its accusations. If so, we must make an honest confession, but if not we must stand against falsehood because self-defence can be a proper defence of righteousness.

With a clear conviction (11).

A willing submission to divinely constituted authorities. Paul was within his rights to use the machinery of the law to the uttermost.

It was not a matter of submitting spiritual issues to secular judgement. It was the only way to get a fair hearing. It was not a matter of retaliation (Matt. 5:39), but preservation. In taking the initiative away from his accusers he was trusting in the protection of God, not denying it.

A willing submission to a divinely revealed plan. He had expected to bear witness in Rome (23:11), and saw the harmony of human responsibility – protesting his innocence – with divine sovereignty. Speaking with conviction does not simply come from knowing that one is right, but particularly that one is right with God. To speak with conviction means that one must first have a conscience void of offence, but also a submissive spirit which gladly accepts the revealed will of God whatever the cost. A Christian will not be able to stand boldly against the world if he is uncertain of himself, but even less if he is uncertain of his God.

With a clear testimony (19). Festus was convinced that Paul was innocent (25) and that the charges against him were of a religious nature. He also knew that the central features of Paul's claims related to the death and resurrection of Christ. Of all that you have said or done in relation to your faith, what are the key elements that people would select as being central to it – the fact that you go to church and do not smoke or swear? Festus knew about the living Christ from Paul. Although the world may not accept him, they should at least hear our testimony to him as the only explanation for the life that we live before them. Christ should be the distinguishing feature of the Christian.

Acts 26:1-23   Paul's vision of Christ

This is the third account of Paul's conversion recorded in Acts and it is useful to put them together. Here we consider what the Lord revealed of himself to Paul.

His glory (13). Paul knew the light was divine because of its source and nature. It came from heaven – not the sky, and was brighter than the brightest earthly light. Thus he was confronted by the fact that heaven had opened before him and that some of its glory had been directed to him. His natural response was to fall to the ground in awe. He learned that Jesus, whom he had despised, is the central figure of heaven's glory. He had been resurrected and ascended, just as his disciples had claimed. Paul's misconceptions about Jesus were dashed in a moment. It was he who was the heretic, not the disciples of Jesus. We too have beheld his glory, but by faith, not sight.

His knowledge (14). Jesus did more than identify himself as the object of Paul's venom. He showed himself to be alive and familiar with Paul's activities. Only deity could overcome death and possess knowledge that defied space and time. Paul was singled out of that group as being personally known by Jesus. All we are and have been is known to the Lord. He also knows what we will become. An encounter with him reveals the worst aspects of ourselves, but it also reveals that he has accepted us as he found us, without sifting through our past sin.

His authority (16). Jesus gave Paul a command, a commission and a promise. Initially Paul was told to stand up, then he was called upon to testify, and finally he was promised protection and success. Jesus has authority over the purposes and revelation of God as well as the physical and spiritual life of men. Paul discovered that all authority in heaven and earth had been given to Jesus. From that moment he was working for the person he had been working against. Are we more constrained by the words of men than we are by the commands, commission and promises of Christ?

His grace (18). Instead of being punished for his persecution of the followers of Christ, Paul was pardoned and called to serve him. Paul's experience was such a clear example of God's grace that it naturally became a prominent theme in his ministry. He was living proof of God's grace, as he often testified (1 Tim. 1:15-16). We may not have lived lives in active opposition to Christ before we came to know him for ourselves, but the fact remains that we did not deserve the grace he showed to us. We may not have much opportunity to draw attention publicly to the grace of God within us, but we must not allow ourselves to lose the wonder of it in our hearts.

Acts 26:24-32   Almost persuaded

Agrippa had been brought up in Rome and was the brother of Drusilla (24:24) and Bernice (25:13). He had been given the kingdom of his father, Judea, after his father's death (12:23). Agrippa's father had killed James (12:1-2), his great-uncle had killed John the Baptist (Matt. 14:3) and his great-grandfather had killed the babies in Bethlehem (Matt. 2:16). We may think that such a man has little in common with us today, but we find traits in him that are evident still.

He accepted the Word of God (27). Agrippa had adopted Jewish ways when he became king and so was familiar with the Jewish Scriptures. He had become something of an expert, someone who seemed to care about his people and took an interest in their way of life. There are many caring, serious minded people today who would say their lives are guided by a Christian sense of values found in the Bible. Far from discounting it, they endeavour to live by it.

He rejected the Word of God (28). But also like many today, Agrippa was content as long as he could remain master of the Scriptures. As soon as they began to master him, he would turn his back on them. Although God the Holy Spirit can take his own word and apply it to the heart, the hearts of some will resist his influence. That is a dangerous position to be in and Paul did not want Agrippa to do that.

Instead he wanted Agrippa to be like himself (29), and become:

Regenerated by the Word of God. Paul had known the Scriptures before his conversion, but the Word had become flesh. Christ had spoken to him personally and his life had been transformed. He had been mastered by the Messiah and had willingly surrendered himself to his authority. He had a new life and the life he lived in the flesh he lived by faith in the Son of God who loved him and gave himself for him.

Motivated by the Word of God. Paul's life was constantly governed by what God said. His new life had started that way (19) and continued in that way. He kept himself under the influence of the Word of God, turning neither to the right nor the left. Is it our sincere desire to see our lives conformed to the image of his Son? If so, are we making enough effort to ensure that it is found to be in keeping with his Word?

Sanctified by the Word of God. By the power of the Holy Spirit, the Word of God does its work in the heart and life of the believer. It is living and powerful (Ps. 33:6a; Luke 4:35-36; John 15:3; 17:17), so that habits and attitudes are changed, sins are cleansed away and a purifying process takes place. Often painful but ultimately glorious, it can change a Saul into a Paul, and even changing an Agrippa into a Paul is not beyond the power of God.

Acts 27   Paul is shipwrecked

This long narrative records how Paul took the opportunity of these events to speak of God. This presents us with a challenge of how ready we are to speak for God in times of adversity. Paul said:

I belong to God (23). God was the rightful owner of Paul in at least two ways. First of all, God had made him and so he was his creature. Then God had redeemed him and so he became his servant, indebted to him for being rescued from the clutches of sin. Yet Paul knew that, above all, he belonged to God as a child belongs to his father. There was an unbreakable relationship between them which meant that God protected, guided, instructed and sustained Paul out of love, not obligation. As a result, Paul was able to call on God for help – not only for himself, but for others also. Because Paul belonged to God, 276 people were safe. How much are we exercising the privilege of belonging to God on behalf of others in need at home or at work or in our neighbourhood?

I serve God (23). God had called and equipped Paul to serve him in a certain way. His life had direction and purpose. He did not live for himself, indulgently lapping up God's blessings. He worked – not for them, but for the God who gave them. His life was ordered by God and he knew it was not going to end yet (23:11). God has not called us to be idle or fruitless. We may have a different role from that of an apostle, but we are as much servants of God – who calls and equips us to work in whatever sphere he has placed us. There may be obstacles around us and fears within us, but God does not call us to do the impossible.

I believe in God (25). A key part of the relationship between Paul and God was communication. God spoke and Paul trusted what he said for two reasons. First of all, God is trustworthy by nature. He could not be God if he was proved to be unreliable. Also, Paul's own experience had proved God to be trustworthy. Paul knew that on previous occasions, what God said, came to pass (for example 20:23; 21:11). Do we trust God unreservedly? Do we need more evidence before we do so?

I give thanks to God (35). Paul's belief in God was an inspiration to those around him because he translated his trust into action. He thanked God and ate food to strengthen him for the life ahead – which he knew would not be lost. In this way he publicly acknowledged the provision and care God gave him in the midst of their common adversity. Thanksgiving can become a formality if we are not careful. This is more than just saying grace at a meal. Is our thanksgiving mixed with faith? Is our thanksgiving open to public scrutiny? Is it a spontaneous, constant and permanent expression of our relationship with God?

Acts 28:1-15   Paul on Malta

Our Christian faith brings us into fellowship with both God and man and this passage illustrates features of both relationships.

Fellowship with God means preservation (3-5). The snake bite should have been fatal but God preserved Paul because:

(a) It was God's purpose that Paul should go to Rome (23:11).

(b) God's power was demonstrated in his survival, which along with the subsequent healings, authenticated the preached word.

Paul did not always escape harm (2 Cor. 11:24-27), but his life was preserved until his work was done. The same truth applies to every believer, even those who have a much lower public profile than Paul. Jesus tells us we are to pray for our physical and spiritual preservation (Matt. 6:11-13), but we must trust him to provide it.

Fellowship with God means presentation (6-10). It seems Paul could hardly go anywhere without taking the blessing of God with him. It is very difficult to imagine that during his three months on Malta he kept silent about the things of God. Although no preaching is recorded, he would at least have explained why and how people were healed. Are we the kind of Christian who can introduce God into various situations we encounter? How can we be preserved by God without giving testimony to the fact? We may not have a supernatural gift, but something

of our fellowship with God ought to overflow into our daily life.

Fellowship with man means gratitude (11-15). The very appearance of Christian brethren prompted thanksgiving in Paul. He had heard of them already (Rom. 1:8), and his thanksgiving would be likely to include:

(i) the work of God in their lives;

(ii) their genuine expression of love in travelling so far to meet him (40 miles);

(iii) his own safety.

The fellowship of believers is one of the most precious consequences of our salvation and should be a daily cause for thanksgiving. As we meet with other believers, we should rejoice that God has saved them as well as us and that he has brought us into touch with each other for our mutual support. We should also repent of any wrong attitudes we have towards other believers – neglect or criticism perhaps. We should correct those attitudes and behave lovingly to all (1 John 1:7).

Fellowship with man means encouragement (11-15). Paul had an ordeal to face and the fellowship of other believers was a source of strength to him. Even Paul was not self-sufficient. He needed the support of others. It is not a sign of weakness to rely on others, but rather a recognition of God's design of the church. Can you bring encouragement to someone today? Ask the Lord to show you who is in need of your help at this time (Heb. 10:24).

Acts 28:16-31   The centrality of Christ

We cannot trace with any certainty what happened to Paul after the last page of the recorded history of the early church. Two factors are evident. Firstly, the consistent pattern of rejection by the Jews (for example 17:5) resulted in the decisive concentration upon ministry among the Gentiles. Secondly, the constant preoccupation in the preceding narrative – the fearless proclamation of Christ – continued unabated. Let us note three factors in relation to this.

Christ is central to the Scriptures (23). Paul was addressing people who were familiar with the Law and the Prophets, but were unfamiliar with the fact that they pointed to Jesus as the Christ. Peter (ch. 2), Stephen (ch. 7), Philip (ch. 8) and Apollos (ch. 18) all did the same thing. They spoke of how the course of Jewish history had been preparing for the coming of Jesus of Nazareth. They showed that although his name was never mentioned explicitly in the earlier scriptures, he perfectly fulfilled the true Messianic expectation. Many readers of the Bible have not discovered that Christ is its central theme. It is not primarily a book of history, morality or philosophy. It is first and foremost the revelation of Jesus Christ.

Christ is central to salvation (27). To reject this centrality of Christ is more than just rejecting a particular interpretation of the Bible. It becomes a rejection of the salvation that is found only in him, for there is only one name given under heaven among men by which we must be saved. If Paul's hearers admitted he was right, at the same time they were admitting they were wrong – and they could not do that. They had created their own way by which they believed they could get to heaven and would not be persuaded otherwise. There are plenty of people like that around us today, but ultimately God's just condemnation of their rebellion will glorify him.

Christ is central to service (31). Verses 30 and 31 describe how Paul spent much of his time when he first lived in Rome. He had come with that intention (Rom. 1:15). He did not want to go sightseeing, set up a tent making business or find a good lawyer. Anything else was secondary. He knew what God called him to do and he was not disobedient. But he did more than preach Christ. He lived Christ – for him and in him. Can we say the same thing? Have people around us got the impression that our lives are church-centred rather than Christ-centred? For Paul, preaching was the obedient expression of his Christ-centredness. What is ours? This book, so full of Christ, ends with a man who was full of Christ giving a message that was full of Christ. We would do well to imitate him (1 Cor. 11:1).

Readings in

Hebrews

by Clifford Pond

WINDOW
ON THE
WORD

Authorship. The author of this book is uncertain. The internal evidence is that he was a Jewish believer who was very familiar with Old Testament and had suffered for his faith (10:34). He also had an extensive knowledge of the problems faced by the early church as this letter was not addressed to a single congregation but to the church in general. The traditional view is that Paul was the author, but many of the features of Paul's writings are absent, such as the absence of a greeting and the lack of use of Christ Jesus. Other possibilities are Apollos, Silas or Barnabas.

Date, recipients, purpose. The letter must have been written before the destruction of the temple in AD 70, for sacrifices were still being offered (10:2,11; 13:10-11). Timothy was still alive (13:23) and Clement referred to its existence in AD 95. The writer received his knowledge of the gospel from eyewitness (2:3). There are forty Old Testament quotations in the book and numerous references to Old Testament laws and types which have become obsolete through the New Covenant. Written to demonstrate the superiority of Christ over everything that came before him (1:2; 2:9; 3:1; 4:14; 12:1-2), it therefore showed how Christianity fulfilled Judaism (8:7-13;10:11-18; 12:18-24). The writer's intention was to encourage Jewish believers not to revert back to their Jewish faith because of the trials they were facing (6:1; 10:36-39). The Old Testament was not being dismissed, but built upon.

Outline. In 8:1a, the writer points to a summary of the previous chapters, suggesting he had outlined what we have in Christ.

He is greater than prophets (1:1-3), angels (1:4 – 2:18), Moses (3:1 – 4:2), Joshua (4:3-14), Aaron, the Levitical priesthood and Melchizedek (4:14 – 7:28).

From 8:1 – 10:18, he explains how Christ is the mediator of the New Covenant, which replaces the Old Covenant, because he has offered up a better sacrifice than all those offered before.

From 10:19 to 13:25, there are various exhortations based on the truth that we have such a high priest. They begin with appeals to draw near to God in worship and to persevere in faith, the latter illustrated by many Old Testament examples and completed by encouragements to practical holiness and godly Christian living.

Hebrews 1:1-3; Matthew 17:1-8   Listen to him

It is very unlikely that Hebrews was written by the apostle Paul. Alternatives have been suggested such as Apollos, Silas, Luke and Barnabas, but in the absence of a signature it is best to admit that we just do not know.

The readers were most probably Jews who professed to be Christian believers, who had suffered for their faith and perhaps were still being persecuted by hard-line Jews and Roman authorities (10:32-36). It seems that, because of their trials, they were tempted to turn away from Christ and revert to their Old Testament roots. Throughout the book, the writer extols the greatness of Christ and his superiority to all others. He shows his readers that Christ is the fulfilment of all they will find in the Old Testament, and he warns them of the dire consequences of renouncing him (3:12).

The sense of the opening passage (1:1 to 2:4) can be made out by linking two clauses: 'God has spoken to us by his Son' (1:1-2); 'we must pay more careful attention, therefore, to what we have heard' (2:1). The writer is ready and willing to acknowledge that God spoke through the Old Testament Scriptures (2 Peter 1:16-21), but he shows the folly of going back to them from Christ who is God's Son and God's last word. Not only so, but as time goes on he will show that they would find Christ in the very Scriptures to which they wanted to return (Matt. 5:17-18).

The message here is the same as that to the disciples on the Mount. As Moses and Elijah faded from view, they were told: 'This is my Son, you must listen to him.' In vv. 2-3 of today's passage, we have a sight of the Lord's glory as God's eternal Son. He is the very out-shining of God's splendour, the maker and sustainer of all things, and, following his atoning work on the cross, he has inherited universal authority (Matt. 28:18; John 17:2). He is worthy that every knee should bow to him in love, trust and submission.

Over to you:

1. The writer gives us an example of the message being more important than the messenger. Are you willing for your name to be forgotten?

2. When we neglect the truth about the Lord and his glory, we are open to the danger of drifting altogether from the faith.

3. In our multi-faith society, the best thing we can do is point to the unique greatness of Christ.

4. Why not go back to each element in this description of the Lord of glory and worship him?

Hebrews 1:4-14   The Son – superior to angels

Why this sudden reference to angels? It is because the readers were inclined to revert to their Old Testament roots in Judaism, in which there was an almost superstitious reverence for angels. This was partly because of the involvement of angels in the giving of the law at Sinai (2:2; Acts 7:38,53). Furthermore, some Essenes, who were influential among the Jews, taught that Christ himself was no more than one of a number of angelic mediators between man and God. So the writer takes time to demonstrate, from the very Old Testament Scriptures to which the readers wanted to return, that Jesus Christ, God's Son, is infinitely superior to angels both in who he is and in what he accomplished.

Note: Differences between the New Testament text and our Old Testament arise because our Old Testament is translated from Hebrew, but the writer here is quoting from a Greek translation known to us as the Septuagint (LXX).

The Old Testament quotations show the superiority of Christ over angels in a number of ways. No angel is ever called God's Son. The angels themselves are called upon to worship and serve the Son, whereas the Son occupies a position of universal and everlasting power and authority. In fact, the Son is equal with God.

Not only do the angels wait on the Son, but their very mission is to serve the interests of the Lord's people who are destined to share his glory (14). Every power arraigned against him, physical or spiritual, secular or religious, political or ecclesiastical, will be entirely subdued and banished. No angel has ever had anything like such authority.

Over to you:

1. Our generation is fascinated with the unseen spirit world. We need to keep our eyes on Jesus so as not to be distracted (Col. 1:15-18).

2. It is possible to think too much of angels, but also to think too little of them. They are examples to us of humble service and devotion to God.

3. It is possible that we owe more to the ministry of angels and their protective care than we realise.

4. Why not confound the next Jehovah's Witness at your door with 1:8? – the Son is God!

Hebrews 2:1-4; Matthew 7:24-29   'Careful attention' needed

We now see why the writer was so keen to show the Son to be superior to angels. The account of the giving of the law in Exodus 20 does not mention angels, but from Deuteronomy 33:2; Psalm 68:17 and Acts 7:38,53, we learn that they were involved. The argument is that if breaking the law, which angels helped to give, merited God's judgement, much more would neglect of the word given by no less a person than God's own Son.

The word, given by the Son, is now identified as 'great salvation'. Christ came, not simply to replace one code of conduct by another, but to replace a way of law by a way of grace (salvation) and all the law could not do (Rom. 8:1-4).

We need to give full weight to the implication of these verses. The consequences for those who neglect, or let slip, the word of Christ, are the same for those who are 'disobedient' to the law given at Sinai, namely God's judgement. This is the same teaching as we find in Matthew 13:20-21 and 1 John 2:19. It is true that they may be backsliders and in God's mercy return to him in due time. But we dare not make this assumption, and this is the warning the writer was spelling out to his readers here and in later passages (6:4-6; 10:26-31).

The powerful works Jesus performed were signs that he was who he claimed to be. They were also wonders, giving rise to astonishment among those who saw them, and miracles, demonstrations of things beyond human power or wisdom.

Over to you:

1. Careful attention involves both the reading of the word and putting it into practice (Matt. 7:24).

2. To say that we love the Word of God and yet neglect it or fail to obey it may reflect seriously on our spiritual state (Matt. 7:26-27).

3. Far from neglecting the reading and study of the Scriptures, we should apply ourselves to them regularly and systematically.

4. If you are tempted to give some attention to religious books, such as the Koran and others, remember that none of them has anything like the authentication that God has given to the Bible (4).

Hebrews 2:5-16   A suffering Saviour

At least three themes are interwoven here, leading to the application: 'Because he suffered … he is able to help' (18).

Christ – not an angel but a man. The argument from Psalm 8 is that man's original authority (Gen. 1:27) was lost through sin (Gen. 3), but Christ took man's place and regained it (6-9). The angels never had this authority, nor do they have it now (5). Since the angels have not sinned, they do not need to be saved; but man has sinned, and so Christ took a human nature, like Abraham's and his children's, to rescue such (16) and make them holy – acceptable to God (11-13).

As a man Christ suffered. In himself Christ was perfect, but without suffering for our sins he could not be a complete Saviour (10). He tasted death (9) means more than a little sip. He was made flesh (John 1:14). His pain was not diminished because he was God; rather, his revulsion at sin would have intensified the agony he endured (14). By his death, Jesus robbed Satan of any power to bring again under God's wrath those for whom Christ died (14-15).

He suffered to bring many to glory. The suffering readers of Hebrews must not miss the fact that the sufferings of Christ were his road to glory (9), taking many sons with him. The world to come (5) is God's kingdom in time and eternity. Without the suffering there would have been no glory for Christ or for us.

Over to you:

1. The only explanation of the state of the world that fits all the evidence is that man has lost the authority he once had, and now can control neither the world nor himself (Rom. 8:20-22).

2. Some evangelicals believe that Satan has power over whole areas and must be defeated by prayer and marches before they can be evangelised. But Satan is defeated already (14-15; John 12:31; Col. 2:15). Our business is to preach the good news.

3. No cross – no crown – neither for Christ nor for us.

4. The whole transaction of Christ's coming and suffering for us was by the grace of God (9); it was on the basis of God's mercy apart from human effort or merit.

Hebrews 2:17-18; 2 Corinthians 1:3-11   Able to help

These two verses form an application of vv.5-16. To people suffering for their faith, the message now is that Jesus Christ who died to save them is, for that reason, totally able to help them. In doing this he is filling out the two main elements in the work of the Old Testament high priest: atonement (17), and help and encouragement (18).

The word for atonement (17) is translated 'propitiation' in the AV here and in Romans 3:25 and 1 John 2:2; 4:10. The NIV marginal note has: 'that he might turn aside God's wrath'. We must never lose sight of the fact that our sins incur God's wrath and that Christ's death alone can appease it. This is not at all the same thing as offerings made to gods in pagan religions. Their gods make cruelly impossible demands on them, even to the extent of child sacrifices, whereas God in love and mercy, who is the offended one, has himself provided the propitiation in the suffering of his only Son.

In addition to all the benefits flowing from the cross which we have seen (2:10-11,14-16), we are able to draw strength and comfort from Christ's sufferings themselves. The word translated 'help' is rendered 'ropes' in Acts 27:17. This is instructive. The ship was in a violent storm and in danger of breaking up, so ropes were passed under it to hold it together and save it from foundering. Believers who are suffering hardship in one form or another may feel they are falling apart. They need to know that their master understands, and is able to comfort and to fortify, like strands in a rope that will keep them secure.

Over to you:

1. There is a modern aversion to the idea of God's wrath. But it is clearly taught in Scripture (1 Thess. 1:10). If we deny it, we rob ourselves of a personal understanding of God's love.

2. Human help for those who suffer is limited. Either we can sympathise but not help, or we can help but we do not understand. Our Lord has no such limitation.

3. Just as the sufferings of Jesus are put to use in helping his people, so we must understand that one reason why we suffer is that we can help others in their plight (2 Cor. 1:3-7).

4. Our Lord is well able to minister to those in need, without human aid, but he often uses people like us, and we must always be ready at his disposal.

Hebrews 3:1-6   The Son – greater than Moses

Apart from Abraham, no one was more highly esteemed among the Jews than Moses. If the readers of Hebrews were going to be dissuaded from returning to the Old Testament religion, they would need to be convinced that Jesus Christ is superior even to the great lawgiver.

The writer works this out in terms of position in God's house. This is not a building, but a household, the people of God (Num. 12:7), which would ultimately mean the church, that after Pentecost would include Gentiles as well as Jews (Eph. 2:14-19).

There was no doubt that Moses was faithful to God in his service in God's household. In fact, the writer is quoting from Numbers 12:6-8, where God is showing the special privilege Moses had above others, in that he spoke to Moses not by dreams and visions, but directly, person to person. Yet the writer is saying Jesus Christ is greater even than Moses. The difference between him and Jesus Christ, was the difference between a steward in a household and the firstborn son (1:2; Col. 1:18) in his position of privilege, authority and inheritance. This illustration is not perfect, because Moses, the leader, was also himself one of God's people. He was part of the house that Christ is building (Matt. 16:18) and subject to the Lord.

Once again, the test of being a true child of God, belonging to his household, is 'if we hold on ...' and persevere in the faith. This is a constant theme in Hebrews, and we might say, by the time we reach its end, that this has been the predominant theme of the book.

Over to you:

1.   Do you think it is possible for us to give more respect to human teachers than we do to Christ himself? Is it really a good thing to be called a Wesleyan or a Calvinist?

2.   Church elders must always remember that, though they are leaders, they are church members, the same as the people they lead under the same Lord. They are both shepherds and sheep!

3.   Independent churches are committed to the principle that Christ is the head in local church. Is this just a lovely idea, or is it a reality in your church?

Hebrews 3:7-11   Spiritual rest

The whole passage from 3:7 to 4:13 is complete in itself, so today we will take an overview of it, leaving detailed notes for the next two days.

The argument of the passage is that since, as we saw yesterday, Christ is superior to Moses, then disobedience to Christ must carry even more serious consequences than those suffered by the people in the desert. It is essentially the same kind of argument we met earlier in 2:1-4. What is the 'rest' frequently mentioned here? Having been rescued from slavery in Egypt, the people of Israel should have been ready to occupy the promised land of rest, but most of them failed to do so because they were hardened in unbelief and disobedience to Moses (Num. 13 and 14).

Both the psalmist and the writer of Hebrews see more in the 'rest' of the promised land than merely the possession of a strip of land. It is a spiritual rest that finds its fulfilment in Jesus Christ and his deliverance from the guilt and power of sin, into fellowship with the living God (Matt. 11:28-30). This we enjoy now in anticipation of the perfect rest that awaits us in glory (Rev. 14:13).

The words of Psalm 95:7-11 were penned by the psalmist, but here they are said to be the words of the Holy Spirit. This is one of the many confirmations we have that the writers of the Old Testament set down what they were taught by the Holy Spirit (2 Tim. 3:16; 2 Peter 1:21). The implication here is that the same Holy Spirit is speaking through the writer of this book.

Over to you:

1. The older hymns often see the crossing of the Jordan into Canaan as a picture of death and entry into the promised land of heaven ('When I tread the verge of Jordan'). There is no doubt that this is our ultimate goal, but do you think it is better to see the promised land as a picture of the Christian life now, with its rest in Christ, but also its fight to possess and nurture the blessings God has for us in this life?

2. Is it true for you that what the Bible says, God says, not only about salvation but also about how you handle your church life and your family life?

Hebrews 3:12-19   Don't harden your hearts

Just as the people in the desert hardened their hearts in unbelief, and similarly so did the people in the psalmist's day, so the readers of Hebrews were in danger of the same by turning away from Christ. This passage up to 4:13 is an extended appeal to them to think again, or else they too would suffer God's wrath. Our writer borrows the urgent appeal made by the psalmist to press home his message by repeating his 'today', which implies that there may not be a tomorrow! We notice three exhortations:

1. Don't turn away (12). The readers should examine their hearts because defection from Christ arises from an inner sinful disposition.

2. Encourage one another (13). Christian fellowship is an essential part of keeping us faithful to Christ. This includes encouragement, strengthening and warning (Col. 3:16; Heb. 10:24-25).

3. Hold on firmly (14-15). We share with Christ all the blessings that implies, only if we persevere in the faith and go on as we began.

All this calls for self-examination, provoked here by pointed questions. Three points are being pressed home:

1. Just as the people in the desert rebelled despite the amazing goodness of God to them (16), so we can easily forget all that Christ has done for us.

2. Just as the Lord punished the people in the desert for their unbelief (17), so defection by us is very offensive to God and merits his wrath.

3. Just as the blessing of the promised land was forfeited by unbelief (18-19), so we cannot think we will receive gospel blessings if our hearts are hardened in unbelief.

Over to you:

1. It is always dangerous to put off necessary reformation and correction in our relationship with the Lord. Tomorrow will not do!

2. We too readily blame circumstances, persecution, etc., for decline in our spirituality when all the time the problem is sin's deceitfulness.

3. Is there real fellowship in your church in which you actively strengthen and encourage one another in these testing days?

4. Do you think the communion service has been given us to be constant reminder of God's love, mercy and grace, and so to help us hold fast to him?

Hebrews 4:1-13   Out and in

The writer now explains more explicitly what he has in mind. The 'rest' promised to the people of Israel, and that was still available in the psalmists' day, pointed on to the 'rest' promised in the gospel of Jesus Christ (Matt. 11:28-30). Just as the promise held out to the Israelites was both rescue from slavery and entry into Canaan (Exod. 6:6-8), so the gospel is about both rescue from the guilt and power of sin and, at the same time, entry into the 'rest' of peace and assurance in Jesus Christ. The people of Moses' day failed to grasp the whole message by faith; this must not happen to us. It is God's rest into which believers enter, the rest he enjoyed after six days of creative work. Each of the six days had an end (Gen. 1:5,8,13,19,23,31), but the seventh day of rest had no end (Gen. 2:1-3). God rested for ever from creation work, not because he was tired, but in order to contemplate the perfection of all he had made, and to delight in it. Reconciliation to God through faith in Christ means that we share in his satisfaction with the finished work of Jesus Christ through his life, death and resurrection. We rest in Christ, not only one day each week, but every moment of every day. Although Joshua did lead the people into the promised land, he could not lead them or us into gospel rest: only Jesus Christ can do that. There is a better rest than Canaan, heralded by one greater than Moses, and provided by one greater than Joshua.

The exhortation is to strive to enter this rest (11; Luke 13:24). Many people have a great struggle to rid themselves of every vestige of self-trust and simply rest in Christ.

The writer's words were the Word of God (12-13), subjecting the readers to serious self-examination. This can be very painful because none of our thoughts, motives or intentions are hidden from the Lord.

Over to you:

1. The hymn writer Philip Doddridge had a great spiritual struggle, until he could say:

> Now rest, my long divided heart,
> In Jesus Christ, who loves you, rest
> and never from your Lord depart,
> enriched by him, by him possessed!

2. Is your Sabbath rest enjoyed only one day a week, or is it your constant experience?

3. Since the Word of God is like a sword, we must expect it to be painful and penetrating, mustn't we?

Hebrews 4:14-16; Matthew 8:23-27   Throne of grace

The writer begins with 'Therefore', but what follows does not flow logically from what has just been said. There are two possible connections between this new section and what has gone before. Perhaps this is simply picking up on previous references to the priesthood (2:17-18; 3:1). Or, maybe, this follows from the heart searching of the previous verses, with appropriate comfort and strengthening that only Christ can give.

The original readers may have been taunted by their Jewish persecutors, that, as Christians, they lacked a visible, wonderfully attired high priest (Exod. 28). The answer was that, though he is invisible, Christ has surpassing greatness. Whereas the Old Testament high priest went but once a year into the Holy of Holies, this was a picture of Christ, who in reality entered heaven itself and stayed there (Lev. 16:15-17; Acts 1:1-11; Heb. 7:25). Not only was Jesus greater than Aaron in what he did but also in who he was, the Son of God.

Our Lord did not necessarily suffer the exact problems we do (e.g. cancer, childbirth), but he was familiar with the same kind of physical pain and emotional stress that are involved in our experiences. The double negative 'we do not ... who is unable' strongly emphasises the positive nature of his sympathy. He feels with us (Acts 9:4).

The throne of grace is the throne of God where Christ sits at his right hand (1:3; Col. 3:1). For those who come to him trusting in Christ, it is not one of judgement, but of pardon and strength and enabling grace – not sympathy with no ability to help, nor ability to help but no sympathy. Our approach to the throne should be without hesitation, doubt or fear, and yet with a due sense of awe and reverence. No time is unacceptable, improper or inconvenient, so why not come to him now?

Over to you:

1. What need do we have of any kind of human priest when Christ the Son of God is our great high priest?

2. When you are tempted to give up, 'set your hearts on things above, where Christ is seated at the right hand of God' (Col. 3:1).

3. Why Matthew 8:23-27? Because Jesus is still the same as he was then – believe it!

4. Do you think a Christian should ever say, 'No one knows how I feel'?

Hebrews 5:1-10   Our Great High Priest

To people who were tempted to defect from Christ and return to their Old Testament roots, the writer here underlines the suitability of our Lord to be our high priest and how perfectly he fulfils all that Aaron and his descendants foreshadowed. We can notice five ways in which Aaron was suited to the office and how Jesus Christ more than matched them.

1. He was a man (1a); not an angel, but a man, because only so could he represent humankind. Our Lord's humanity was clearly seen in the Garden of Gethsemane (7; Luke 22:39-44). He was not afraid of death as such, but his identification with our sin, its guilt and punishment, was totally abhorrent to him. The sinfulness of Aaron was not reflected in Christ, but his perfect humanness is (4:15).

2. He was the representative of the people before God (1b). This was the function of the priest, and this is what Jesus Christ was (6).

3. He provided salvation by offering gifts and sacrifices to God on behalf of the people (1c). Our Lord provided eternal salvation (8-9) by offering himself in obedience to God. This was a new experience for him, and without it he would not have been a complete ('perfect') saviour.

4. He understood the needs of the people (2-3). Being human, he shared their experiences and their failures and so was able to sympathise with them and help them.

This has already been shown to apply to Jesus Christ (4:14-16).

5. He was appointed by God (4; Exod. 28:1). No one outside Aaron's family was allowed to take this office (2 Chr. 26:16-21). Christ was appointed by God (6,10), but in at least two ways his priesthood excelled Aaron's. Christ's, like Melchizedek's, is a royal priesthood (Gen. 14:18; look again at 4:16), and it is 'for ever'.

Note: Sometimes coming to faith in Christ is spoken of in terms of obedience (9) to him or to the gospel (Rom. 1:5; 2 Thess. 1:8; 2 John 4). Faith must always show itself in obedience. Obedience without faith is futile human effort. Faith without obedience is false profession (James 2:16).

Over to you:

1. Should not our Lord's voluntary submission to the Father have a large place in our love for him?

2. Our Lord's sufferings are portrayed in Scripture, not to draw out pity for him, but shame for ourselves (Luke 23:27-33).

3. What lessons may we learn from Christ in Gethsemane as to how we ourselves can face the crises in our lives?

4. Have you understood that the gospel is not only an offer, it is a command to be obeyed (Rom. 6:16)?

Hebrews 5:11 – 6:3   Serious immaturity

One reason why the original readers of this book were tempted to defect from Christ was that they may have lapsed into immaturity because they had not advanced in their spiritual understanding. In these verses, we can trace four signs of 'spiritual babyhood'.

1. Low understanding (11). It is not that the deeper truths are obscure, or especially difficult to understand, but because we are too often spiritually lethargic.

2. Forgetfulness (12). Not only are small children forgetful, but older people often have problems in remembering. The readers had evidently been professing Christians for some time, but they had forgotten much of what they had once known (Matt. 13:4,19).

3. Poor appetite (13). Just as infants tend to reject good food, preferring what is not so good for them, so a sign of spiritual immaturity is a dislike of the solid food of biblical teaching, while wanting to stay with the milk of the simple gospel.

4. Lack of exercise (5:14 – 6:3). Lack of physical exercise in a child is disastrous, and so is failure to exercise our spiritual minds. Spiritual maturity comes through training or exercising ourselves in righteousness (Phil. 1:9-10), discerning truth from error, good from evil and right from wrong.

Note: The foundation described here is basic Old Testament teaching. It is foolish to stay with this when the glorious New Testament fulfilment in Christ can be clearly seen.

Over to you:

1. If you have been a Christian for less than ten years, are you growing in spiritual understanding? If you have been a Christian for more than ten years, can you now explain the Christian faith to a seeker? If not, why not? Reflect on Ephesians 4:11-12.

2. Are you one of those professing Christians who prefers 'blessed thoughts' to expository preaching?

3. Do you with great eagerness examine the Scriptures every day to see if what the preacher says is true (see Acts 17:11)?

4. Those who remain immature in the faith most easily succumb to the latest unbiblical heresies and fashions, or lose interest in spiritual things altogether when life becomes difficult.

DAY 84 ✓

Hebrews 6:4-8   A serious warning

These verses have been a cause of great distress among Christian believers because, at first sight, they seem to teach that it is possible for someone who is born again to fall away from Christ and be eternally lost. Further consideration will lead us to see that those described here, despite appearances, are not true children of God. Two reasons for this are:

1. That to see them as true believers is to make Scripture contradict itself. The consistent teaching of passages that raise no questions is that those who are born again, by grace persevere in the Christian life and are secure in Christ (John 3:16; 10:28-30; Rom. 8:35-39; 1 Peter 1:3-5).

2. That we have quite a number of examples in Scripture of those who seemed to bear the marks of spiritual life, such as we have here in vv. 4-6, but who later were seen never to have been true believers (Balaam – Num. 22–24; Rev. 2:14; Saul – 1 Samuel 9–31; Simon Magus – Acts 8:9-24; professing Christians – Matthew 7:21-23).

Such people may have:

'been enlightened' – possibly enough to have been baptised;

'tasted ...' – possibly even been used in gospel work;

'shared ...' – like Judas Iscariot;

'tasted the good Word ...' – knowing the Bible thoroughly;

'... and the powers ...' – seeing God at work;

and yet know nothing of inward regeneration. They do not fall away from salvation because they were never saved.

The writer helps us with a parabolic illustration (7-8) of the teaching in vv. 4-6. The parable is of the two plots of soil, both receiving seed and plenty of rain, yet one yields only weeds while the other produces a good crop. The conclusion is that if a professing believer does not go on with the Lord, bearing spiritual fruit (John 15:5-6) then, despite the profession, he or she is not a true believer but is under God's wrath. As in our Lord's parable (Matt. 13:1-9,18-23), everything depends on the condition of the soil – the human heart.

Over to you:

1. If you are a true believer, this teaching will not drive you to despair but to diligent self-examination.

2. Self-examination (2 Cor. 13:5) means making sure that our spiritual confidence is in Christ alone and not at all in ourselves, and that we seek to live a life that pleases him.

3. If we are not growing in grace (2 Peter 3:18; 1:5-11), then very likely we are slipping back and may be in danger of falling away.

Hebrews 6:9-12   The need for diligence

The warning of vv. 4-8 has been very challenging, and it may be that some of the readers whose faith was real and genuine had been driven to question whether they were true believers. But, as we see throughout this book, the writer blends warning with exhortation (9-12) and encouragement (13-20).

The purpose of vv. 4-8 had not been to drive true believers to despair, but to encourage them to self-examination (2 Cor. 13:5) and to perseverance in their faith, not turning back, but going on to maturity (2 Peter 1:10).

'Dear friends.' Here speaks the hopeful pastor who understands that only God knows who is a backslider and who is apostate.

'Better things.' Things such as genuine repentance, a living faith in our Lord Jesus Christ and perseverance in godliness and gospel witness (John 15:8; 2 Peter 1:5-11).

'Work ... helped.' In the circumstances, this may have needed considerable courage and would be evidence of a true faith.

'Each of you.' Individual believers were not to hide behind the activity of others. Each must prove the genuineness of his own faith.

'Diligence to the very end.' The final proof of spiritual life is not what we have been, but what we go on being to the end of our days.

'Inherit.' There is no such thing as universal salvation; this is only for those who persevere in 'faith and patience'. None of us will be saved unless our lives are consistent with our profession of faith.

Over to you:

1. Do you take seriously the warning of Scripture?

2. If preachers do not sometimes give themselves to consecutive exposition, they will more than likely neglect the really heart-searching passages. Pray for your preachers.

3. Are you diligent in daily reading in all the Scriptures?

4. Do you still have the same zeal for Christ and his kingdom as you did when you were baptised?

Hebrews 6:13-20   Encouragement and certainty

Having faced his readers with the dire consequences of turning away from Christ and exhorted them to persevere in following him, the writer now gives them encouragement to do so because of the certainty of the security that true believers have in Jesus Christ. This all depends on the trustworthiness of God's promises, which is first illustrated in the experience of Abraham (13-15) and then is shown to be focused in our Lord Jesus Christ (16-20).

The fact of God making an oath is prominent in these verses. God does not need to do this: his bare word is sufficient because he is totally to be trusted. But for our sakes, God makes an oath, which means that he swears by himself because there is nothing or no one greater than he. By this, God is saying: 'If what I promise does not happen, then I will cease to be God'; it is as certain and secure as that.

God's oath to Abraham (Gen. 22:16-18) has been abundantly fulfilled in his numberless progeny, both natural and spiritual (Gal. 3:26-29). This illustrated the trustworthiness of the oath of Ps. 110:4 that Christ would be a priest for ever, and would be the absolute security of those who trusted him. Just as the anchor of a ship is buried unseen in the depths, so Christ, our great high priest for ever, has entered, unseen to us, into the presence of God.

Christ is both our representative before God through whom we come to him, and our forerunner who is the guarantor of our ultimate entry into God's presence (John 14:3).

Over to you:

1. Did you know that God wants you to be certain of your salvation, and that his warnings are not designed to leave you in doubt, but to lead you to assurance?

2. Whatever storms of life we may encounter, we should keep our minds firmly fixed on Jesus (Isa. 26:3).

3. Did you realise that when God said, 'I will remember their sins no more', he really meant it? It is not presumptuous to be sure of that.

4. Remember, what is unseen is eternal (2 Cor. 4:18).

Hebrews 7:1-10   Melchizedek

The teaching of chapter 7 is based on the three verses in Genesis 14:18-20. There are two elements in this brief story to which our writer draws attention.

1. The absence of any reference to either the birth or the death of Melchizedek, thus foreshadowing our Lord's timeless priesthood.

2. That Abraham gave Melchizedek a tenth of the spoils he had gained from his armed conflict. This showed the superiority of Melchizedek to Abraham and his successors, foreshadowing our Lord's priesthood to be greater than Aaron's.

The argument of vv. 4-10 is in a form that is unusual to us, and seems rather complicated. It is, however, based on the principle of representation that is familiar to us. For example, at the end of the Olympic games, we might have said that we gained so many gold medals. We had nothing to do with it, but our athletes represented us. Or we may say, 'We won the battle of Waterloo', when we were not even alive at the time. But we were 'in' our victorious army. In today's passage, two main themes are being worked out.

1. That Melchizedek was greater than Abraham because he blessed Abraham and Abraham gave him tithes. This is because the priest represents God and so has a higher status than those who bring tithes to him.

2. That Melchizedek was greater than Aaron, because as a descendant of Abraham, Aaron was 'in' Abraham when he was blessed by Melchizedek and gave him tithes.

The point of the argument is that Christ's priesthood is in the order of Melchizedek, and is therefore superior to Aaron's. Therefore, to return to the Aaronic or Levitical system is not only contrary to New Testament teaching, it is contrary also to the Old Testament itself when rightly understood.

Over to you:

1. Had you realised that what the Bible does not say is just as important as what it actually says?

2. In the day of grace, should our standard of giving to the Lord measure up to the Old Testament standard?

3. Do you rejoice in the principle of representation as it is applied to our relationship to Jesus Christ in Romans 5:12-21; 6:3-4?

4. Should the fact that our actions cast a shadow of light or darkness on our successors concern us?

Hebrews 7:11-19   Near to God

In the New Testament, 'perfection' almost always means completeness, or perfectly achieving the intended purpose. The purpose of a priesthood is to enable people to be related to God, and the last words of today's passage spells it out: through Christ, we actually and really draw near to God!

The writer suggests that if his readers had read their Old Testament with spiritual eyes, they would have asked themselves why, after many years of the Aaronic system, God spoke of another priesthood (Ps. 110:4). If the Aaronic system was adequate, why was another necessary? The answer would be that it could only be a picture or visual aid of the reality that was to come. Obviously, God who established the old was perfectly at liberty to introduce the new, which would achieve what the old could never do.

Just as Melchizedek was both a priest and a king, so was our Lord. This is why, though he was to be a priest, he came from the royal line of Judah rather than the priestly line of Aaron.

One step further: the new priesthood is not based on law at all. It is of an entirely different order. Our salvation does not rest on any legal system but on the eternal Son of God.

Over to you:

1. We need to take care not to conclude from the strong language here that the Old Testament law is entirely redundant. It is obsolete as a way of salvation, but its moral requirements are still valid.

2. Are you aware of our need to be reverent in our approach to God, and yet of our liberty to do so as his children?

3. Are you living in the bondage of law, or the liberty of grace? Are you a slave or do you enjoy the freedom of a love relationship with the Lord?

Hebrews 7:20-24   A better covenant

The Levitical priesthood was established by God but without an oath, leaving the way open for change. The oath of Psalm 110:4 made certain that the priesthood of Christ was unchanging and for ever.

The whole subject of this part of Scripture has to do with God's dealings with sinful people and his provision of a way for them to be reconciled to him and to draw near to him. This scheme is called a covenant. This does not mean, as in human relationships, an agreement between two equals. Rather it is something imposed by God on those he makes his own. He promises them many undertakings such as salvation, provision for all their needs and ultimate glory. At the same time, God sets his requirements of his people before them, which they must obey on pain of chastisement.

Here it is called a better covenant, in contrast to the one made with the people through Moses (Exod. 19:5). This is the New Covenant of Jeremiah 31:31-34. Christ is the guarantor (Luke 22:20), because he keeps the terms of the covenant for us, which we cannot do! Our part in this covenant depends entirely on the perfection of his life and the suffering of his sacrifice for our sins.

Over to you:

1. When you sing, 'Nothing in my hand I bring, simply to your cross I cling', is your hand absolutely empty, or are you still trusting even a little bit on your respectability or your Christian service?

2. Are you quite assured that simple trust in Christ is your salvation because this is guaranteed by God's oath? This means that if Christ failed you, then God would not be God; your salvation is as sure as that!

3. God's requirement of us is that we become like his Son. This must be our aim, not in order to be saved, but because we love the Lord and want to show our love and gratitude in the way that pleases him best. Not only so, this was one reason why he saved us (Rom. 8:29).

Hebrews 7:25-28   The only Mediator

These verses are the writer's pastoral application of all he has been saying. The priesthood of Jesus Christ is complete and permanent, and so the salvation of those who trust him is also complete and permanent. Christ, and none other than Christ, meets our need.

The Levitical priesthood fell short in many ways. The sinfulness of the priests themselves and their mortality contrasted sharply with the perfection and eternal nature of our Lord. Furthermore, the Old Testament sacrifices had to be repeated over and over again, but the offering of himself by Jesus Christ was once for all.

When the priesthood of Christ is called 'perfect', it means that it totally and completely achieves its purpose. It leaves nothing, absolutely nothing, to be added to it or subtracted from it. Christ is now exalted in the heavens in the presence of the Father, there for ever to represent us and intercede for us.

We rightly speak of the finished work of Christ for our salvation based on his one sacrifice for sins for ever. But we must not lose sight of his continuing work of presenting the virtue and value of that finished work continually before the throne of God (Col. 3:1-3).

Over to you:

1. Do you have a 'therefore' in your mind when you read the Bible? We must always apply to ourselves what we read.

2. You celebrate the birth, life, death and resurrection of our Lord. Do you give as much thought and thanksgiving for his ascension into glory?

3. Are you rejoicing that Christ saves you completely, to the uttermost and for ever, and are you seeking to live the kind of life for which he saved you (Eph. 1:4)?

Hebrews 8:1-5   Christ sitting – not standing

It is not easy to work out the line of reasoning here from one verse or group of verses to another. But we can see quite clearly a gradual unfolding of the supremacy of Christ over the Levitical priesthood. Parallels and contrasts with the Old Testament ritual are interwoven. Seed thoughts are sown at one stage and then later they are developed and applied. For example, the ascension of Christ was mentioned at the very beginning, and the idea of covenant, offering and intercession have been intertwined. From now onward, all these themes will be worked out in detail. The foundation has been laid for them to be applied to Christ and his high priestly work on our behalf.

1. Our Lord is interceding for his people in the very presence of God on the basis of what he accomplished on the cross. His sitting indicates a completed task in contrast to the 'standing' of the Levitical priests (10:11).

2. Our Lord's priesthood could not be on earth because he was not from the tribe of Levi, but from Judah. Furthermore, there were already plenty of qualified priests for the earthly ministry. This was not our Lord's sphere of ministry.

3. The importance of the tabernacle and all the priestly service that was done there, was not in itself, but in the eternal reality it represented. This is why the copy needed to be correct, so that it would faithfully illustrate Christ and his saving work that was to come.

Over to you:

1. Since what the world knows about God is largely what they see in us, ought we not to be very careful that our lives faithfully represent him?

2. Do you see your pastor as the one who goes to God for you and speaks to you from God? Or do you have direct communication with the Lord?

3. If you are a pastor, is your aim the same as Paul's in 1 Corinthians 2:5?

Hebrews 8:6-13   The New Covenant

Much of the argument of chapter 7 was centred upon Psalm 110:4. From here up to 10:17, the reasoning will be dominated by Jeremiah 31:31-34. The implication is that the people of God should have been prepared to welcome the new regime brought in by Jesus Christ if they had understood their own Scriptures.

The 'wrong' of the Levitical priesthood was not in itself, since it was instituted by God, but in the failure of the people to adhere to its terms.

The New Covenant is given to the houses of Israel and Judah. From Paul we learn that this now embraces all who are in Jesus Christ, both Jews and Gentiles (Gal. 3:26-29). In the New Covenant, the Lord will give these blessings to his people because of what Christ has done (Luke 22:20):

1. He will give them an inward love of his law.

2. In a new relationship, he will protect and provide for them.

3. They will be assured of his love and security in him.

4. Their sins and shortcomings will be forgiven and forgotten.

The old regime would disappear with the destruction of Jerusalem in AD 70. It had no further usefulness.

Over to you:

1. Satan is expert at reminding us of our past sins. We put them to flight by refusing to remember what God says he will not.

2. Is your Christian life a matter of meetings and observances, or is it an inward matter of joy, peace and overflowing hope (Rom. 14:17; 15:13)?

3. Does this ring a bell? – People reared in sound traditions approved by the Lord, fail to notice from the Scriptures that those traditions will need to be abandoned for a better way. They refuse to countenance change, even if it is clearly required by Scripture. They lose the Lord's blessing.

Hebrews 9:1-10   The invitation

In these verses we have a reminder of the structure for Old Testament worship (1-5) and then the use that was made of it (6-10). This is described in Lev. 16 and was to be an illustration preparing the way for the provision of the New Covenant, of which the writer will give a detailed explanation (9:11 – 10:18).

1. There are two emphases in the description of the structure. One is on the richness of it all, making the fulfilment in Christ yet more glorious. The other is the Most Holy Place, stressing that in all this, the whole purpose was not a mere system of ritual, but a means of entry into God's presence.

2. We have already seen the contrast between the mortality of the Levitical priests and the undying nature of Christ's priesthood (ch. 7). Now there are three more weaknesses in the Old Testament ritual to be observed:

(a) The high priest had to repeat his entry into the Most Holy Place annually, whereas Christ is sitting for ever in God's presence.

(b) The high priest had first to offer sacrifices to atone for his own sins, whereas Christ was sinless and therefore his one sacrifice was a perfect provision for others.

(c) The high priest's offerings did not offer a lasting peace of conscience, but this is what our Lord gives (14).

Over to you:

1. Is entry into God's presence a reality to you? It is all too easy to go through outward forms and to miss the wonder of what prayer really is.

2. Is your devotional life so orderly that it is in danger of becoming a mere ritual? Or is it so disorderly that it lacks depth and direction?

Hebrews 9:11-15   Consciences cleansed

All that has gone before has prepared the way for the most instructive and heart-warming presentation of the gospel (9:11 – 10:18). It should be placed alongside Romans 3:19-26 as salvation viewed from another perspective. Here we turn from symbolism to reality, from the passing glory of the Old Covenant to the eternal glory of the New.

1. At his ascension (Acts 1:11) our Lord entered heaven itself, there to remain (Col. 3:1) until his return (28).

2. The blood of Christ was more valuable than all the animal sacrifices put together (1 Peter 1:18-19; Acts 20:28). It was not necessary for his death to be repeated; it was once for all time.

Our Lord did not take literal blood into heaven (1 Cor. 15:50), but the shedding of his blood was the basis of his acceptance with the Father and of his intercession for us.

3. Christ's sacrifice obtained eternal redemption for us, not the passing ceremonial cleansing of the Old Testament ritual.

4. It was also an internal redemption, providing lasting peace of conscience (the answer to v. 9), and no fear of condemnation at the judgement (Rom. 8:1).

5. While this is disputed by some scholars, the natural meaning of v. 14 is that all three persons of the Trinity were active in providing our salvation.

6. In the terms of the covenant, God provides all that is needed for our salvation. In return, he requires us to live for him (Rom. 12:1-2).

7. We enter into salvation by being called (Rom. 1:6-7; 1 Cor. 1:24). This is the Spirit's work within us, powerfully overcoming every obstacle and leading us to Christ.

8. By nature we are all under the Old Covenant which was a slavery because it meant a futile effort to keep the law and escape judgement. Just as the Israelites were delivered from slavery in Egypt, making bricks without straw, by the blood of the New Covenant, we have been released from the bondage of sin and death.

Over to you:

1. Is your conscience clear? If it is, you will no longer fear the judgement. Your conscience will make you feel your Father's displeasure but not his banishment.

2. Are you a Trinitarian believer, giving praise to Father, Son and Holy Spirit for your salvation?

Hebrews 9:16-22   Precious blood

The writer is so concerned that his readers should not fail to understand what he is saying about the blood of Christ, that he turns to an illustration from everyday life. He picks up the thought of inheritance from v. 15 and points out that we cannot claim an inheritance provided for in a will until the testator dies. Our inheritance is inscribed in the New Covenant (8:10-12) and we are able to claim this because of the death of Christ for us (Matt. 26:27-28).

The ratifying of the New Covenant by the blood of Christ was foreshadowed in the Old Testament ritual:

Verses 18-20 – this is recorded in Exodus 24:4-8.

Verses 21-22 – this must be a reference to Exodus 40:9 and Leviticus 8:10. The fact that blood was used is additional information given us by the writer here.

The statement at the end of v. 22 is at the very heart of the gospel. It is not enough simply to point to Jesus Christ; it falls short of the full gospel simply to point to his life, or his teaching, or even to his death. What matters is the meaning and purpose of his death, and the focus on the shedding of his blood.

Over to you:

1. When preaching the gospel, it may be right to do no more than to point to Christ as the object of our faith. It may be inappropriate to go into the detail of substitutionary atonement every time. But when bringing people to personal faith, they must understand this dependence on the precious blood of Christ.

2. Be sure that the teaching here expands your understanding of the Lord's Supper and enriches your spiritual participation in it as a means of grace.

3. Why not sing:

Not all the blood of beasts
on Jewish altars slain
could ever give the conscience peace
or wash away its stain:

But Christ, the heavenly Lamb,
takes all our sins away –
a sacrifice of nobler name
and richer blood than they.

Hebrews 9:23-28   The three appearances

The teaching of these verses is gathered around three appearances of Jesus Christ, in heaven as our high priest (23-25), on earth (26-28a), at his return (28b). Each of them is once for all, not to be repeated.

1. Our Lord's appearance in heaven to intercede for his people is for ever (7:25), in contrast to the Old Testament high priest who had to repeat his appearances in the Most Holy Place. There are two problems in v. 23 for which we can only suggest explanations:

(a) Clearly heaven itself did not need to be purified (Hab. 1:13). Perhaps the meaning is that when sinful people approach God in the name of Jesus Christ, they are covered by the virtue and value of his blood.

(b) The plural 'better sacrifices' is puzzling. Perhaps the plural indicates the superior worth of Christ's sacrifice over all the others put together.

2. Our Lord's coming is described as an appearance which distinguishes it from all others for whom birth is the beginning of life. He came at the end of the ages (compare with 1 Cor. 10:11); his death was the complete and final fulfilment of all that the Old Testament ritual foreshadowed. Death is not the end, nor does it lead to reincarnation; it brings us face to face with our maker.

3. There will come a moment when Christ will appear on earth for the second time (Acts 1:11; Rev. 1:7). This will not be to add to our salvation, but to complete the work by freeing us from the presence of sin in ourselves (1 John 3:1-3), and in the world (Rom. 8:22-25; 2 Peter 3:12-13). Waiting for him does not mean doing nothing (2 Thess. 3:10), but serving him (Matt. 24:42-46; 25:14-30) and preparing ourselves for his presence (1 John 3:1-3; 2 Peter 3:11-14).

Over to you:

1. Are you rejoicing in a threefold perfect salvation – the death of Christ cancelling the penalty of your sin, the intercession of Christ and the ministry of the Holy Spirit giving victory over the power of sin, and the return of Christ to deliver you from the presence of sin for ever?

2. Are you preparing yourself for the moment when you stand before the Lord who gave himself for you?

Hebrews 10:1-18   The Father's will

From 7:1 it has been our privilege to see the glory of Christ displayed in the perfection and completeness of his work to provide for us acceptance with God and peace of conscience. This has been presented to us by means of parallels and contrasts with Old Testament ritual, making that ritual now redundant, like the uselessness of a visual aid compared with the reality it represents.

There is much here that repeats what we have already seen. The writer is showing his readers the tremendous importance of the once for all, finished nature of Christ's work for sinful people. They must not lose sight of him. For full measure, he introduces confirmation in a new quotation from Psalm 40:6-8 from which we can deduce:

(a) That the plan of salvation was made in eternity before the world began (Rom. 8:29-30; Eph. 1:4).

(b) That our Lord agreed to his part in the plan before he came (1 Tim. 1:15).

(c) That he did not come to persuade the Father to receive sinners, because the plan originated with the Father and with agreement between both the Father and Son.

(d) That the plan foresaw the inadequacy of the Old Testament ritual by providing the final answer in advance.

There are two covenants. The covenant of grace, which is between unequals, provides blessings and imposes his requirements on those he has chosen. The covenant of redemption was between equals. In eternity, before time, the Father, the Son and the Holy Spirit determined the plan of redemption. The Father chose his people, the Son would suffer the price of their pardon, and the Spirit would apply new life to their hearts.

Over to you:

There are too many professing Christians resting the assurance of their salvation on such unreliable props as their parents' faith, a decision they once made, their church membership, or the kind of life they live.

In 3:1, the writer said: 'Fix your thoughts on Jesus', and since then we have seen many good reasons for us to do so. Can you say that your hope is built on nothing less than:

1. The finished work of Jesus Christ?

2. The promise that in Christ your sins will no more be remembered?

3. The fact that you are loved with an 'everlasting love' (Jer. 31:3)?

Hebrews 10:19-25   Therefore ...

This book is strewn with 'therefore's' (2:1; 3:1; 4:1,14; 6:1), but the one here in v.19 is probably the most significant. It looks back to all that has gone before about the glory of Christ and all he has done for sinful people and says: 'In the light of these things, let us notice with care what it should mean to us in practice.' This application goes on, in various ways, to the end of the book.

In today's verses, we look first to our relationship with God (19-23) and then with our fellow church members (24-25).

1. 'Let us draw near...' (22; 4:14-16). We can do so with confidence because Christ has opened the way. Just as the veil of the temple was torn apart, never to be repaired (Mark 15:38), so access to God's presence was opened, never to be closed again (John 14:6; Heb.7:25).

'Sincere heart' – undivided, trusting only in Christ.

'Full assurance' – certain of acceptance through Christ.

'Hearts sprinkled' – our guilt has been removed (9:14).

'Bodies washed' – having openly confessed Christ in believer's baptism.

'Hold unswervingly' – remaining true to Christ and his promises (4:14; 6:18-20).

2. 'Let us consider ... one another...' (24). There is an essential link between being rightly related to God and our relationship with his people.

'Consider...' – members are to be deeply and continuously concerned for one another. A church is a living body (1 Cor.12:12-27; Phil.2:3-5).

'Spur one another on...' – towards a loving and caring community.

'Not give up meeting...' – there is interaction between spiritual coldness and carelessness, and slackness in attendance at regular church fellowship. One feeds the other.

'Encourage one another' – church membership must be more than merely sitting together and singing from the same book. We are to get alongside our brothers and sisters to strengthen their resolve to persevere, and even tenderly and lovingly to warn them (3:13; Rom.15:14; Eph.4:16).

'The day approaching' – the day of our Lord's return, when we must give an account of what kind of church members we have been.

Over to you:

1. Are you great on doctrine, or on Christian experience? Both are vital, and the latter should follow the former.

2. Have you realised that without any movement of any kind, just where you are and how you are, you can enter the very presence of the eternal God, unrestricted by time, circumstances or ritual?

3. What kind of church member are you?

4. Are you growing in maturity enough to be able to give spiritual help to others?

Hebrews 10:26-31   No other way

The book of Hebrews is in the Bible to make us examine our spiritual state, and today's portion, along with 2:1-3, 3:12-15 and 6:4-6, specifically point to the terrible danger that we can appear to be true believers and yet fall away from Christ. This is an exposition of Matthew 13:20-21.

According to these verses, it is possible to receive the knowledge of the truth, but then to take up a deliberate and determined stance of rejection and opposition to it. In Num. 15:27-31, a distinction is made between deliberate and unintentional sins. The problem in our verses is not with sins that are contrary to our predominant desire to please God, but with a determined attitude of defiance against God, regardless of the consequences. Such a stance puts a person outside the provision of Christ's sacrifice, and since there is no other way of salvation, beyond all hope under God's judgement.

To turn away from Christ is more serious in God's sight than breaking the law of Moses for three reasons:

1. Such a person has trampled the Son of God underfoot. To turn away from Christ is to reject the one who is God's eternal Son and to side with those who crucified him (6:6; Matt. 21:33-41).

2. It is to treat as an unholy thing the blood of the covenant. The blood of Christ is no longer treated as precious (1 Peter 1:19), whereas it is of the greatest significance in God's plan of salvation (Matt. 26:28).

3. It is to insult the Spirit of grace. It was the Holy Spirit who led them into the truth of the gospel. In rejecting the gospel, they are spurning the Holy Spirit who brought them thus far.

To depart from the gospel is to dishonour both God the Son and God the Holy Spirit. No wonder the Father is offended! He is not to be trifled with. He is the living God and cannot be sidelined. He is not open to discussion or evaluation (Matt. 10:28).

Over to you:

1. Do you think that we should point out such passages of Scripture as this to those submitting themselves for baptism?

2. A head knowledge of Christian truth is very important, but if it does not move our hearts to love the Lord and motivate our wills to serve him, it can be very dangerous.

3. Self-examination should not lead us to depression but to thankfulness for God's work of grace in our lives.

Hebrews 10:32-39   You did run well...

All through this book we are being warned about how far into a Christian profession people can go before turning their backs on it all. Here we see that such people may even go through much hardship, suffer insults, persecution and material loss. In the past they had not only stood firm themselves, but had also encouraged others to do so.

Paul faced the same problem in Galatians 3:1-4, where the people were tempted to add Old Testament law to their faith in Christ. For Paul this was an insult to Christ and just as bad as forsaking him altogether, which the readers of Hebrews were tempted to do. The challenge here is the folly of turning away from Christ, especially in the light of their past experience and the logical sense of persevering with him.

The promised reward is the inheritance we have in Christ (6:15; 9:15; Rom. 8:17; 1 Peter 1:3-6); it is eternal life (John 17:3) and is none other than union with God himself (Gen. 15:1). All this will be revealed in its fullness at the coming of our Lord Jesus Christ (1 Thess. 4:13-18).

In the meantime we may pass through perplexing times as did the people in Habakkuk's day. The message for them was the same as for the readers of Hebrews, and it is the same for us today – 'my righteous one will live by faith'. (See also Rom. 1:17; Gal. 3:11).

Over to you:

1. Is your church diligent in warning new converts of the hazards of the Christian life, and the awesome consequences of defecting from Christ for whatever reason?

2. Should we pray much for those all over the world, who are persecuted for their faith in Christ, that they may have courage to endure it, and not yield to the temptation to turn from Christ?

3. We are saved by faith in our Lord Jesus Christ (John 3:16; Eph. 2:8). Are you equally convinced that, having been saved by faith, we go on to live by faith in and through every experience?

Hebrews 11:1-7   Faith defined

The original readers were in danger of wilting in the face of persecution and they were reminded that they must live by faith. But what does that mean? First the writer defines faith (1-3) and then he shows how people in Old Testament days applied their faith in most extraordinary ways.

Faith is a faculty of the spiritual life we have in our Lord Jesus Christ. This means that believers are sure about spiritual realities, to which unbelievers are completely blind. This faith is not vague hopefulness, but God-given certainty about things impossible to prove. For example, none of us was present when the world began (Job 38:4), and so we cannot prove anything about what happened. Faith bridges the gap with certainty that the origin of creation is God himself. Before he spoke, there was nothing apart from him (Ps. 33:6-9). God gave existence to everything (Ps. 90:2).

We see, then, that faith is directed to God himself, his wisdom, power, authority, goodness and purposes, and trusts him completely.

The first example is Abel's humble reliance on the mercy of God (Gen. 4:3-4). There may be some truth in the idea that Abel's offering was accepted because it involved blood shedding (Heb. 9:22), whereas Cain's did not. More likely, the emphasis is on their spiritual state. God looked in favour on Abel and his offering because it represented a heart of trust in God and his mercy, which Cain's did not.

Enoch walked with God (Gen. 5:21-24) in an age of increasing godlessness (Gen. 6:1-8). Against this trend, he tried at all times to please God. He went directly to heaven, by-passing the experience of death as did Elijah (2 Kings 2:11), and as will those who are alive when the Lord returns (1 Thess. 4:16-17).

Noah's faith (Gen. 5:28 – 9:29) was believing and obeying God even though there was no evidence in his land-locked home that there could or would be a flood.

Not until the New Testament is the glorious truth about the imputed righteousness of Christ spelled out (Rom. 3:21-22; 4:4-5). Noah and all the Old Testament believers were heirs of that blessing.

Over to you:

1. Is your worship a mere ritual, or is it humble gratitude to God for his saving mercy?

2. To what extent is your life influenced by the standards of the world rather than by the pattern given us in Christ?

3. Is your faith vague optimism that everything will work out comfortably, or is it firmly grounded in the character and word of God?

Hebrews 11:8-19   Abraham

Abraham (Gen. 11:27 – 25:11) was the one the Jews revered as their father (John 8:31-41), and Paul used him as the great illustration of justification by faith only (Rom. 4; Gal. 3:6-9, 29). The author of Hebrews picks out three ways in which God tested his faith with increasing intensity.

1. The test of total commitment (Gen. 11:31 – 12:9). The call was to leave a large civilised but pagan society (Josh. 24:2) to live in tents in a place he knew nothing about. The Lord gave Canaan to Abraham and his posterity as their inheritance, but his faith looked beyond that to the eternal city (Rev. 22:1-5).

2. The test of the humanly impossible (Gen. 12:2; 18:11-15; 21:1-3). Abraham was about 100 years old and Sarah about 90 years old when God said they would have a son. He believed that God could do the humanly impossible.

3. The test of what he did not understand (Gen. 22:1-19). Two questions would arise in his mind. First, how can God who hates human sacrifice tell him to sacrifice his son? How could God, who promised a great nation through Abraham's son, now command him

to kill him? Abraham's faith went so far as believing that God could raise Isaac from death.

None of the Old Testament believers were perfect, but they were God's people and they trusted him. He owned them as his and he was their God (Exod. 3:6; 4:5).

Over to you:

1. Have you left the world's side and its idols to entrust your life completely to God's love, wisdom and power? This is at least part of the meaning of believer's baptism – have you obeyed the Lord's call to total commitment?

2. Do you believe that God can do in your life what you cannot do for yourself? There is no way we can live the Christian life with our own resources, but we can with his enabling. We cannot serve the Lord in such a way as to bring him glory by our own strength, but he can work in and through us.

3. Left to ourselves, we will crumble with defeat and disillusionment when we are faced with situations we cannot make sense of. It is only by God-given faith that we can trust him in the darkest hours and be 'more than conquerors'.

Hebrews 11:20-31   Men and women of faith

The examples multiply and the variety of experiences of faith seems endless.

Isaac (20; Gen. 27:27-33). By faith he recognised the hand of God even in and through improper human scheming.

Jacob (21; Gen. 48:20). Despite being now under Egyptian rule, his whole attitude was one of trust in the future prosperity of his people.

Joseph (22; Gen. 50:24-26). No doubt he could have had a great Egyptian funeral, but God's purpose for his people meant more to him than any pagan honour (Josh. 24:32).

Moses' parents (23; Exod. 2:1-2; 6:20). The extraordinary appearance of baby Moses (Acts 7:20) made them realise that God had a special purpose for him, so they defied the authorities.

Moses (24-28) forsook a princely status and wealth, and the vile idolatry of the Egyptian court, for a life of hardship with his people. His eyes were not on passing glamour, but eternal glory. God's people were his people. At the age of 80 years he might well have settled down to a quiet life, but God intervened and he committed himself to God's plan, persuading the people to display lamb's blood on their house to escape death (Exod. 12).

The Israelites (29). With the Egyptian chariots at their heels, the only way of escape was a path through the Red Sea (Exod. 14:16-28). They acted on the bare promise of God.

Jericho and Rahab (30-31). The story of Jericho (Josh. 6) is about doing God's work in God's way, even if it seems contrary to human reason. Rahab was a woman in a pagan society, an idolater and a prostitute, and yet she came to faith.

Over to you:

1. Will you leave your children a legacy of optimistic faith in the living God?

2. Would you agree with the godly man who said that his highest privilege on earth was to be a member of his local church?

3. Have you realised that no experience of life is wasted for the Lord's purpose in your future here and in the life to come?

Hebrews 11:32-40   Others

Not all that the four judges (32) did is to be commended, but the writer, led by the Spirit, tells us that their great motivation was faith in God.

Both David (1 Sam. 16:1 – 1 Kings 2:10) and Samuel (1 Sam. 1:1 – 25:1) were able by faith to lead the nation towards godliness in the face of great difficulties.

The prophets were constantly opposed and sometimes physically assaulted (1 Kings 19:1-2; Jer. 38:1-13).

Up to v. 35a is a summary of the trials endured by many Old Testament believers because of their faith. Some of this, here and in the following verses, may refer to the terrible sufferings of Jews in the period before the Lord's coming.

The word 'others' (35b), marks out a difference between those in the previous verses who were sustained in their sufferings, and those (35b-38) who had no relief and whose lives were taken from them. They were faithful to death (Rev. 12:11).

Verses 39-40 are a kind of summary of chapter 11. The examples of faith demonstrated faith as trusting in the wisdom, love and power of God, and in his faithfulness to his promises. The focus of their faith was not in temporal blessings but in eternal safety, security and satisfaction. All this would be fulfilled in Jesus Christ and be shared by all who trust him in every age.

Over to you:

1. In our desire to comfort people, we may give them the false impression that if they trust God they will have relief from their trouble. But it may not be so and they may be required to hold fast without relief, and perhaps even to death. The ultimate blessing of the gospel is the presence of God in glory.

2. Do we need to beware of being critical of new Christians when, in their zeal, they seem to do improper or unwise things? God accepts what is done with sincere faith even if it is misguided. But they must learn, as they grow in grace, to be more biblical.

Hebrews 12:1-4   Fix your eyes on Jesus

'Fix your eyes on Jesus' could very well be seen as summarising the message of the whole book. The purpose of chapter 11 was to draw attention to the object of those people's faith which was a glorious spiritual and eternal inheritance. Some of those people may have dimly understood that this blessing would focus on a coming one, who was our Lord Jesus Christ.

The cloud of witnesses are not angels, nor are we to think of those who have gone before as peering down at us from heaven. Those heroes of faith witness to us of the strength and courage that come from faith focused on Christ. For each of the examples in chapter 11, the way of faith was marked out for them by the Lord. For us, the life of faith will mean different challenges as God works out his purpose for each of us. Whatever that may be, we are to persevere in it and go on patiently to the end with no thought of giving up.

The Lord is our supreme example, but he is more than that. He begins his work of grace in us and guarantees to bring it to completion (Phil. 1:6). He is with us at every stage from start to finish. It was this completion and perfection of his work that was such a large element in the joy that was set before him.

In suffering for Christ, we are following in his footsteps, but ours has not resulted in death as it did with Christ and many others of his disciples. So long as we look to Christ and the eternal glory, we will be enabled to maintain our struggle against sin and all that opposes him, no matter what the cost. If we dwell on our difficulties and sufferings and take our eyes off the Lord, we will lose heart as did Peter (Matt. 14:22-33).

Over to you:

1. If you think of your salvation only as something arising from your decision, do not be surprised if assurance is something that eludes you. But if you understand that your decision was made possible by the Lord beginning his work of grace in you and that he promises to bring it to completion in glory (Rom. 8:29-30) then your assurance will rest in him and not in yourself (Rom. 8:38-39).

2. Is your Christian life at a standstill? In describing it as a race, the Scripture tells us that it is progressive and should always be advancing in spiritual strength, understanding, usefulness and, above all, Christlikeness (2 Peter 3:17-18).

3. No doubt you admire our spiritual forefathers, but do you also share their faith and their zeal for God?

Hebrews 12:5-17   God's loving Fatherhood

The writer has a pastoral heart. As we have seen, he is faithful in his warnings, but at the same time he is keen that his readers will prove to be true believers and children of God. It may well be that they have resented their suffering and were asking, 'Why must we be persecuted like this?' The answer is that God was neither careless about their problems, nor punishing them as though they were unbelievers, but was dealing with them as a loving Father, which must necessarily include painful discipline and correction. They should already have known this from their Old Testament – Proverbs 3:11-12.

So they should not be surprised at their painful experiences, because they were proof of God's love for them as their Father. Therefore they should patiently endure their suffering, knowing that God loved them too much to leave them without correction.

At their best, our human fathers use discipline to develop our character, correct us and prepare us for life in this world. God's purpose is to prepare us for life in eternity. This means that all he does for us and to us aims at holiness (12:14; Rom. 8:28-30). By its very nature, discipline is unpleasant and often very painful. If we remember God's purpose and the glory that awaits us (Rom. 8:18), we will more willingly submit to his discipline, throwing off feelings of resentment and self-pity and applying ourselves with vigour to the spiritual race. If we do this, others will not stumble because of our bad example; rather, those who were beginning to waver will be strengthened and encouraged.

Verse 14 completes the illustration which began at v. 1. They must make every effort to run the race. As they do so, they must try to be at peace with all the others in the race. A healthy response to discipline is not only an individual matter but also involves our concern for each other. Striving for holiness will mean watchfulness over our fellow church members (see again 3:13; 10:24-25). It is possible for a church member to prove not to be a true believer ('miss the grace of God'). Such a person will be a grievous influence ('bitter root') causing others to stumble. The bitter root can take many forms of which two are mentioned: sexual immorality and carnality, thinking and living with more concern for the natural and fleshly than for the spiritual – of which Esau was a clear example.

Over to you:

1. Parental love is not best expressed by allowing children to work out their own standards, but by positive correction and clear guidance.

2. What are the ways in which God exercises discipline over us? How can we recognise them? Does the experience of Job help, or Paul (2 Cor. 12:1-10)?

3. How can we exercise our responsibility to our fellow believers without having a critical spirit?

4. Some people speak of losing their faith when trouble hits them, while others stop attending church services. You may not go that far, but are you bitter or resentful?

Hebrews 12:18-24   A radiant church (Eph. 5:27)

These verses provide us with a glorious climax to the whole argument of the book. People who were tempted to return to their Old Testament roots are shown the tremendous contrast between that tradition and the amazing privileges and prospects that belong to believers in Jesus Christ. The contrast is described in terms to two mountains, Sinai and Zion, each representing spiritual principles, the one law and the other faith.

The law given at Sinai was not designed to show people the kind of life they were able to live, but rather to expose human sin and helplessness (Rom. 3:19-20; Gal. 3:19-25). This is why the giving of the law was accompanied by terrifying signs (Exod. 19:10-25; Deut. 4:11-12; 5:1-26), and even the man of God, Moses, trembled, because if this is all we have, we are under the wrath of God. If the readers decided to defect from Jesus Christ, they would be putting themselves back under the Sinai regime, with no means of escape from the awesome consequences. Not only so, let them consider the tremendous privileges and blessings upon which they would be turning their backs.

Mount Zion was the city of David (2 Sam. 5:7), and it was the place where God chose to dwell among his people (Pss. 9:11; 74:2). It was a place of beauty, strength and security (Ps. 48). In all these ways it became a suitable picture of the New Testament church in which Christ reigns (Ps. 2:6; Isa. 28:16) and from which the Word of God is sounded out (Isa. 2:3).

In Revelation 21:1-2, the church is seen to be the 'Holy City' and the 'New Jerusalem'. It is the spiritual and heavenly realm into which all believers are brought by grace.

While angels are not part of the church since they had no need of redemption, they are in constant attendance on believers (1:14) and share with them in extolling the glory of God and the wonders of his grace (Rev. 5:11-12).

'Firstborn' in Scripture does not primarily refer to order of birth, but to the position of privilege held in families by the older brother. All believers are 'heirs of God and co-heirs with Christ' (Rom. 8:17). Their names are written in heaven (Luke 10:20; Rev. 20:15) and nothing can remove them.

In Christ we have access into the very presence of the living God (Eph. 2:18) without fear of rejection. There also are the spirits of righteous men made perfect. This is the great company of the redeemed already in glory (Rev. 7:9-17) awaiting the day of resurrection. The church on earth and in heaven is one.

Finally and gloriously, we come to Christ who by one sacrifice made redundant all others, and by whose blood alone access into God's presence is guaranteed (Eph. 2:13).

Over to you:

1. Are you afraid for the future of the church of Jesus Christ? Dwell long on Matt. 16:18.

2. Are you trying to reach heaven by obedience to God's laws? Don't you see that this brings you under God's wrath (John 14:6)?

3. Are you tempted to 'give up'? This is probably because you have never realised what a wonderful thing it is to be a Christian.

Hebrews 12:25-29   The final appeal

The writer of this book is a faithful pastor. We would have almost certainly ended on the positive note of the previous section. But here, the writer does not end his message without a final warning of the dire consequences of defection from Christ.

In v. 25 we are right back to the beginning (1:1 – 2:4). Since Christ is who he is, then there is only one thing to do, and that is to listen to him (Matt. 17:5). The argument surfaces again in 10:28-29, and it now has greater force since the glory of Christ and his total sufficiency have been amply demonstrated.

The seriousness of holding on to Christ is further demonstrated by reference to the great final sifting and cleansing that will take place when Christ returns. When the law was given at Sinai, there was a tremendous upheaval (Exod. 19:18), but that was nothing compared with what will happen at Christ's Second Coming. Then the whole universe will be involved (Matt. 24:29; 2 Peter 3:10-13).

The quotation from Hag. 2:6 spoke of events about to take place then, but, with the inspiration of the Holy Spirit, the writer here tells us that they foreshadowed events at the end of time. Only those things that are spiritual and eternal will remain.

Here is the response to persecutions and every attempt to discredit and destroy the church of Christ. Even if at times the enemy appears to be succeeding, he will ultimately fail. Christ's kingdom is indestructible: it stands for ever.

So instead of trembling for fear, we should be thankful that the wisdom, love and power of God in Jesus Christ will be vindicated. We should be full of awe and praise, and give ourselves in worship and service to him. Doubt must be banished from our minds!

The last word in this final appeal is a reminder that while the eternal God is longsuffering and full of grace, he is nevertheless not to be trifled with. All our dealings with him must be real and honest.

Over to you:

1. Our passage today concludes the message of the book. As such it presents a challenge to all preachers in respect to the way they end their sermons. Some just taper off. Others merely summarise what they have been saying. Others finish with a promise to continue next time. With the example here before us, we will be sure to leave our hearers with a clear application either of comfort or warning, or of instruction to be obeyed.

2. The media ensure that our minds are bombarded with a bewildering confusion of voices. There is only one voice that carries final authority, that of the Son of God. Are you listening to him?

3. The evangelical world seems to be divided between those whose worship is joyful but flippant, and those whose worship is reverent but formal. How can we be both full of awe and full of exuberance?

Hebrews 13:1-8   Love and trust

The main argument of the book is complete. Now the writer has in mind the effects that stress and persecution can have on believers individually and in their church relationships. It is all too easy in times of trouble to forget the requirements of love and of trust in the Lord.

Remember to love one another. In vv. 1-4 various aspects of love are mentioned. It is significant that when our Lord was about to leave the disciples, knowing they would pass through hard times, he tells them not to forget to love one another (John 13:33-35). We can so easily resort to self-preservation and self-interest, and forget the needs of our fellow believers.

Loving hospitality is an important part of both Christian fellowship and witness (Rom. 12:13; 1 Tim. 3:2; Gen. 18). This can be a blessing not only to those needing it but also to those giving it.

Our concern for those who suffer for their faith should not be merely formal, but with real feeling and, where possible, it should be practical (Matt. 25:31-46, 1 Cor. 12:26). Loose morals are a common result of hard times. Sex is a gift of God, but must be enjoyed within the constraints of God's law (Exod. 20:14; 1 Thess. 4:4-8). In the twenty-first century, this is increasingly an essential element of Christian witness.

Remember to trust the Lord. Trust resulting in contentment is also a very important part of Christian witness at all times, but especially in difficult times. Thomas Watson says that contentment is a blend of faith, believing God does all for the best, love, thinking no ill of God, and patience, submitting cheerfully to what God orders wisely. There is always the temptation to look after 'Number One', even if this is at the expense of other believers. There was a situation like this in Neh. 5.

The love of money is always spiritually harmful (1 Tim. 6:6-10,17-19). It is covetousness, breaking the tenth commandment (Exod. 20:17). The positive side of this is contentment (Phil. 4:11-12) arising from confidence in the faithfulness of God to his promises (Deut. 31:6; Josh. 1:5). God says: 'Never, never will I leave you; never, never, never will I forsake you!'

The readers are reminded that they have not only the example of those in Old Testament days but also of those by whom they were taught, whose inspiration had been the unchanging Christ.

Over to you:

1. No matter what our situation might be, we must be sure to maintain our love for our brothers and sisters in Christ, and our trust in the character and promises of God.

2. Have you considered what a powerful witness there is in a contented life in this acquisitive generation?

3. Have you considered opening your home for fellowship with God's people, encouragement to young people or 'coffee' with your neighbours?

Hebrews 13:9-17 Remain true to Christ

Under pressure of trials or persecution, there is temptation to avoid the reproach of Christ, and to be disloyal to church leaders.

Christ is our satisfying good (9-10). On the Day of Atonement, the priests were not allowed to eat any part of the sin offering (Lev. 16:27), but we can at any time feed spiritually on the sacrifice of Christ (John 6:53-59). This eclipses all discussion about the rights or wrongs of certain foods.

Shared disgrace (11-14). Just as the body of the sacrifice was taken outside the camp under God's curse, so Jesus was made a curse for us outside the camp (2 Cor. 5:21; Gal. 3:13). By this, those who trust in him are made holy, their sins being blotted out. Therefore, we must be willing to share his rejection and reproach.

Spiritual sacrifices (15-16). All believers now are priests (1 Peter 2:4-5, 9-10), to offer to God not animal sacrifices with a view to pardon, but spiritual sacrifices because pardon has already been received (Rom. 12:1-2).

Submission to leaders (17). The word 'authority' (NIV) has been added by the translators. The text should read 'obey your leaders and be submissive'. Christ alone has authority in the church through his word. Elders have authority only as they are true to Scripture. The obedience required is not blind or unquestioning, but an attitude of submission based on love and respect, as in marriage (Eph. 5:22).

Elders are to earn the love and respect of the people and to minister with diligence (Acts 20:28; Matt. 20:25-28). Ultimately they are responsible to God.

Over to you:

1. Ask the Lord for grace and courage so that you will not be ashamed of him in any situation (Luke 9:26).

2. Are you exercising your privilege as a priest to God, or are you leaving everything to your minister?

3. Do you idolise your past minister while making life difficult for your present one?

Hebrews 13:18-25   The fellowship of prayer

Christianity can be described as a fellowship of prayer. Every relationship among believers should be marked by every kind of prayer, thanksgiving and intercession. Leaders with their members; member with member; the life of the body is prayer.

The readers asked to pray for the writer (18-19). This is a good example for all leaders. It is all too easy for them to give the impression that they do not need help in their life and in their work. All leaders are exposed to false accusations and unfair criticisms. What they need is not self-defence but ability to live lives that are above reproach (1 Tim. 3:2).

His prayer for his readers (20-21). They were in a troubled and distressing situation, so he first of all commends God to them as the one who can give them peace. This he is able to give them because of both the sacrifice of Christ for them and his rising from death. Not one or other of those, but both validated the eternal covenant into which they have entered through faith in Christ. Unlike the Old Testament priests who were imperfect and mortal, Christ is the ever living good and great shepherd of his people (Ezek. 34:1-16; John 10:1-28).

On the basis of the all-sufficiency of Christ, the writer is able to pray for them with confidence. To equip means both to repair and to prepare. Those who serve the Lord need to be kept in constant good repair, and to be given all things they require for the work to which they are called (John 15:16; Eph. 2:10; Phil. 2:13).

The great aim of our life and our work is to please the Lord. We need to be the best that we can be. In this we are totally dependent on him, and therefore the glory is his and not ours.

His final prayer for them is, 'Grace be with you all.' This is more than merely saying good-bye. It is saying, your needs are very great, but the grace of God, his wisdom, love and power, is more than sufficient for your need (2 Cor. 12:9). Amen!!

Over to you:

1. Can your church leaders be sure of your well informed prayers for them?

2. Do you give yourself time in the midst of your busy life to turn to the Lord for the spiritual repair of your love for him and for his people, and your zeal for his truth and the gospel?

3. Now that we have completed this series of notes on the book of Hebrews, is there something new that you have learned about Christ and the gospel? Do you need to face a new challenge to advance your spiritual life?

Readings in

James

by Ron Hollands

WINDOW
ON THE
WORD

Author. James, the son of Alphaeus, was an apostle and is mentioned separately from James, the son of Zebedee (Matt. 10:3). James, the half-brother of Jesus, is also mentioned separately (Mark 6:3; Gal. 1:19). He is generally acknowledged as the leader of the church in Jerusalem (Acts 15:13). He had been present in the upper room (Acts 1:14) and was the one to whom Jesus appeared privately (1 Cor. 15:7). He is one who is thought to be the author of this epistle.

James probably wrote from Jerusalem to Hellenistic Jewish Christians outside the city. It is possible he was writing to those who had been scattered by persecution (Acts 8:2), to instruct them in practical and ethical behaviour. He died about AD 62.

Content. James writes with authority in a similar way to the pronouncement of Acts 15. He does not address sins more commonly found among Gentiles, such as idolatry and immorality. He does not address the Judaisers against whom Paul fought. There is no reference to Acts 15 and so it is likely to be the earliest epistle. The word 'church' only appears in 5:14. The gathering place for believers is called a synagogue (2:2). The epistle takes orthodox Christian teaching for granted and has little doctrinal content. The conduct James advocates is based on that teaching and he is showing how the superstructure of Christianity rests on a foundation that already exists. Paul writes of justification by faith without works. With no contradiction, James writes about how genuine faith is demonstrated by works.

There is a prophetic wisdom about this epistle. It is a passionate plea for obedience. Within 108 verses, James gives 50 commands. In both style and language, there is moral astuteness linked with practical application. There are echoes of the teaching of Jesus (cf. Matt. 7:16 and James 3:12; Matt. 6:34 and James 4:13; Matt. 7:28 and James 1:22,25).

James 1:1 Meet the author ✓

Christianity is not for Sundays only and the letter we begin today takes us out into the working week. Workers' rights are touched upon in one place, along with things like money, gossip and relationships. When we go to church, we deal with class discrimination. More 'religious' themes are not ignored, such as prayer and trusting God for everything. Let us begin, though, by meeting the writer of the letter that bears his name.

1. James makes little of himself: 'a servant'. Suppose I tell you that I am directly related to the organiser of the biggest ever wildlife preservation project in history to date? We can get a certain 'buzz' from being related to or known by famous people. In my case, though, I would have little to brag about as Noah is your relative too.

James, though, introduces himself not as 'James, half-brother and former playmate of Jesus of Nazareth' but simply as James, his servant (literally 'slave'). He would have joined with Apollos and Paul to affirm they were 'only servants, through whom you came to believe' (1 Cor. 3:5). Knowing he had been transformed from unbelief (John 7:5) by a personal meeting with his risen Lord (1 Cor. 15:7) to become the major leader of the Jerusalem church (Acts 15:13-21; 21:18), James preferred the spotlight to be elsewhere and so:

2. James makes a lot of his Saviour: 'the Lord Jesus Christ'. When translating the Old Testament into Greek, 'Lord' was used for 'Yahweh'. Also, like Paul in the opening greetings of his letters, James quietly asserts Jesus' deity by placing him alongside God the Father.

As *Jesus* ('the Lord saves'), God the Son assumed a human nature with a name highlighting his mission to sinners (Matt. 1:21).

Christ (literally 'the Anointed One') is a title rather than a name. In the Old Testament, prophets, priests and kings were anointed and the Lord Jesus combines in one, all three.

As *Prophet* he brings God's Word near to us (Heb. 1:1-3a).

As *Priest* he brings us near to God (Heb. 1:3b; 4:14-16).

As *King* he exercises his wise and loving rule over those who, like James, willingly submit to his 'crown rights'.

3. James manifests a love for all the saints: 'scattered among the nations'. While 'the twelve tribes' may refer to Christian Jews living outside the Holy Land (including some still 'scattered' after earlier persecutions: Acts 8:4; 11:19), it could figuratively denote the entire Christian community: the 'Israel of God' (Gal. 6:16). How wide are your sympathies?

To ponder: 'Him exalting, self-abasing, this is victory' (John 3:27-30; 2 Cor. 4:5).

James 1:2-4 Tested for good

'The Christian life is a bed of roses – thorns and all.' James knew that his readers (present and future) would 'face trials of many kinds' (2) and to help us cope with them, he challenges us with:

1. A reality to face. It is a case of 'whenever' and not 'if ever'. The Lord Jesus warned that 'in this world you will have trouble' (John 16:33) and the apostles taught their new converts that 'we must go through many hardships to enter the kingdom of God' (Acts 14:22). So 'do not be surprised … as though some strange thing were happening to you' (1 Peter 4:12).

2. A reaction to cultivate. Trials are a common human experience, but 'pure joy' is an uncommon reaction to them and one needing cultivation. Not that we, in some masochistic way, are to rejoice in the trial itself. Neither is this a call to 'put on a happy face' before others and try to live in denial. When going through a rough patch, we can be tempted to think life does not make sense. Yet James, like Paul, mentions a family secret: 'because you know' (3; compare Rom. 8:28 – 'we know'). In respect of our trials as Christians, there is:

3. A reason to grasp. God's infinite wisdom, not 'bad luck', is somehow at work in our trials, even though we may not fully grasp in this life why 'the dark threads are as needful in the skilful Weaver's hand as the threads of gold and silver in the pattern he has planned'. Where, however, we cannot trace God's hand, we can, in the light of Calvary, go on trusting God's heart.

James does, though, give us some insight into what God may be accomplishing through the 'trials of many kinds' when he assures us that there is:

4. A result to await. The word 'testing' that James uses speaks of a refining process, intended to burn away 'impurities' like self-confidence and develop qualities like 'perseverance'. This is an ability not simply to bear things with passive resignation but courageously and with a vibrant confidence in God's good purpose. It is the quality displayed superlatively in those martyrs who face death, like Hugh Latimer, with a: 'Be of good cheer.'

God's ultimate goal in our trials, though, is that we 'may be mature' (4): to be what we were made to be and 'become mature, attaining to the whole measure of the fullness of Christ' (Eph. 4:13).

To ponder: The ancient silver refiner was said to skim the impurities until he could see his face in the molten metal. The application to our 'testing' is obvious (Rom. 8:28-29).

James 1:5-8   True wisdom [1]

All we learned from the previous verses might sound fine, but what if you still feel your lack of ability to make sense of your current trials, let alone how best to steer through them? What you will need is 'wisdom'. That is the God-given skill to discern and apply God's Word in real life situations or the ability to be spiritually 'streetwise'. James will explore further what it is to be wise in 3:13-18, but now let us note:

1. The source of true wisdom is the giving God (5b). As an incentive to ask of him, remember that God gives *generously.* 'Count your blessings, name them one by one' if you doubt it, not forgetting that you do not deserve the least of them. If you still doubt, then view Calvary in the light of Paul's 'from the greater to the lesser' argument in Rom. 8:32. If God has already spared no cost for you in not sparing his Son, his greatest gift, how much more can you trust him to provide the less costly 'all things' like wisdom to see you through. As already implied and as an added incentive, remember too that God gives *graciously* ('to all') – even giving temporal blessings to those who are ungrateful and ungodly in return (Matt. 5:45). As a final incentive, note that God gives *gladly* ('without finding fault'). He does not greet his children with: 'Oh, not you again', as an exasperated human parent might.

2. The securing of true wisdom is through prayer offered in faith (5a,6a). With such incentives that our giving God inspires, we have every reason to ask in faith. James reminds us that faith is the essential component in prayer (6). We must not minimise the fact that, as Thomas Watson says, if 'prayer is the key of heaven, faith is the hand that turns it' (Heb. 11:6). This leads James on to underline the fact that:

3. The stumbling block to true wisdom is doubt (6-8). The 'doubting' James censures is surely not that of the sincere but struggling Christian who prays, 'I do believe, help me overcome my unbelief!' (Mark 9:24). The word literally means 'judging between two' and may rather indicate those who are vacillating in their total commitment to the Lord, like God's people in Elijah's day, wavering 'between two opinions' (1 Kings 18:21) – indeed two gods. The Chinese speak of a person with 'a foot in two boats'. The outcome for such a divided heart is a generally unstable life (8), like a storm tossed sea (6b) and no God-given wisdom (7).

To pray: '…give me an undivided heart' (Ps. 86:11).

James 1:9-11; 2:5   True status

People like the idea of having some kind of status. When you were younger, did you dream of being a famous footballer, ballerina, chief executive, politician – or even to marry into the royal family? It did not really matter what it was so long as you had status – even to be famous for fifteen minutes. James turns such thinking on its head by asserting that:

1. The lowly should take pride in being lofty (9; 2:5). Now not everyone 'in humble circumstances' can take pride in having a high position (9) and not everyone who is 'poor in the eyes of the world' is 'rich in faith' (2:5). But if you are also among the 'poor in spirit' you can take pride, not in yourself, but in what God has given you in Christ: a 'high position'. You have real status, for yours is the kingdom of heaven (Matt. 5:3). The Lord Jesus will give you the right to sit with him on his throne (Rev. 3:21) – even to judge angels (1 Cor. 6:3). So, too:

2. The lofty should take pride in being lowly (10-11). Not all Christians lack status in this world. When Jesus called the rich young ruler to give away all his wealth and follow him, this was not a call to all rich people to go and do likewise. Yet James wants Christians to be alert to the fact that whatever wealth and status they may have in this world, it is at best only fleeting and fading and that our glorying should be in something other than what God in his goodness has given us in terms of position or possessions in this life. Naked we came into this world and naked we shall leave it (Job 1:21; 1 Tim. 6:7). When one of the millionaire Rockefellers died, his accountant was asked how much he had left. To this he replied, 'Everything'. All this world offers 'will pass away like a wild flower' (10). 'Solid joys and lasting treasure none but Zion's children know' and that is no mean exchange. As the missionary martyr Jim Elliot put it: 'He is no fool who gives what he cannot keep to gain what he cannot lose.'

Yet we Christians must beware of letting the world's status-seeking mentality squeeze us into its mould. What sadder epitaph for a professed Christian could there be than: 'Demas, because he loved this world, has deserted me ...' (2 Tim. 4:10)?

To ponder:

I would not change my blest estate
For all the world calls good or great;
And while my faith can keep her hold,
I envy not the sinner's gold.

(Isaac Watts)

James 1:12-15   Tempted by evil

James uses the same Greek word for both trial and temptation, depending upon the context and our response. Indeed, 'all trials have in them an element of temptation and all temptations have in them an element of trial'. Temptation is a certainty (13a: 'When tempted...') for us all (14: 'each one of us is tempted...'), so when tempted to evil, you must:

1. Admit the reality (14-15) of that within you which responds to external stimuli to do wrong. The word translated 'enticed' was commonly used to refer to fishing bait. The 'bait' of temptation may not be evil in itself and its very attractiveness can be God-given. The tree of knowledge had a God-given beauty which was like the rest of God's handiwork, 'very good'. But the snake twisted it into a 'bait' to lure Eve into taking a good thing that was 'off limits'. Still today, despite God's later prohibition: 'You shall not covet' (Exod. 20:17), Satan uses our desires and what is desirable to lead us into that which, if left unchecked, can lead to spiritual death (15).

2. Accept your responsibility (12-13). Blame shifting has been ours from the beginning. Yet temptation to evil never comes from God (13). He tests to bring out the good but it is Satan who tempts to bring out the bad. Beware again of blame shifting: 'each one is tempted ... by *his own* desire ... (14). Although in v. 12 James appears to be using the word 'trial' in the broadest sense, the call to persevere surely encompasses temptation to evil. Someone has said that temptation is not sin but a call to battle. Yours is the responsibility to take up arms and James indirectly points to that which will:

3. Assist your resistance (12b,15). One method of resisting is to 'nip sin in the bud', as the analogy of conception and birth (15) would imply. As to *motivation*, it is noteworthy that James describes those who persevere as 'those who love him' (12b). Jesus said: 'If you love me you will obey what I command' (John 14:15). So keep your heart richly supplied with incentives to love Christ more and thus resist sin more readily.

4. Anticipate your reward (12), knowing that 'God does not crown your merits as your merits, but as his own gifts' (Augustine). You will have 'stood the test' by grace alone.

To ponder: Never be complacent about temptation (1 Cor. 10:12). 'The best of saints may be tempted to the worst of sins' (Matthew Henry).

James 1:16-18   The true God

We have seen that people may blame God instead of themselves for being tempted (13). This self-deception casts aspersions upon God's goodness and James may have it in mind when warning his readers not to be deceived (16), before proceeding to affirm that God is the source only of good (17). A wrong view of God may explain many spiritual problems. For example (bearing in mind James' focus on God's giving in v.17), 'every problem in prayer is traceable to a misconception of God'. So, reflect upon the fact that:

1. God is good (17a: 'every good and perfect gift is from above'). Jesus taught that our Father only gives 'good gifts' to his children (Matt. 7:11), while Satan's earliest deception of humanity was to question God's goodness, insinuating that God was selfishly holding something back (Gen. 3:4-5). Bethlehem and Calvary refute Satan's lie and prove that God has not withheld the very best from those who deserve only the very worst (Rom. 8:32).

However, to say that God is good to us is not to say that he will simply indulge us. As fallen creatures, the good we need is often remedial and our Father loves us too much to shrink from bringing into our lives what will secure his goal that we 'be conformed to the likeness of his Son' (Rom. 8:28-29) – including 'trials of many kinds' (2).

2. God is unchanging (17b: 'from the Father ... who does not change'). Although the heavenly bodies move in courses set by 'the Father of the heavenly lights', he who ordains their variation and change is himself subject to none. There is nothing 'shifty' about him, for example one day generous and the next day mean or never certain to deliver on his promises. He is therefore dependable, so that, even in a time of great distress, it is still possible to affirm: 'great is your faithfulness' (Lam. 3:23).

3. God is sovereign (18: 'He chose to give us birth'). James concludes his vindication of God's character by highlighting for his readers a gift that outshines 'every good and perfect gift' that pertains only to this life. Their spiritual birth, he stresses, is the result of God's free choice. Nothing less than this supernatural remedy could reclaim those subject to 'death' (15; Eph. 2:4). Yet the Holy Spirit normally works through 'the word of truth' (18; Eph. 6:17; 1 Peter 1:23), calling for an intelligent, though God-enabled, response of repentance and faith. James assures these early converts that they are a guarantee, as 'firstfruits', of a great final harvest (Rev. 7:9-10).

To ponder: 'Here is your God!' (Isa. 40:9).

James 1:18-25; 2:8   True learners

The Lord Jesus Christ indicated what it means to be a true disciple when he said: 'If you hold to my teaching ('continue in my word': AV), you are *really* my disciples' (John 8:31). James concurs. True disciples are always learning.

1. What they learn (18,21,25; 2:8). The Spirit-empowered Word had already given them new life (18) and, says James, it can *go on* saving them (21). To describe it as law (25; 2:8) which says 'Do and live' (Deut. 4:1; 30:16) might seem forbidding to those who are saved by grace, which, through new birth (18) says: 'Live and do'. But the gospel says 'do' and not just 'live' (22). The Law drives us to Christ to get right with God and then Christ sends us back to the law to show us how to *live* right before God, by his enabling grace.

For James to join together law, which may spell restriction for some ('Thou shalt *not...*'), and freedom, might seem a contradiction (25). Yet God's 'perfect law' is that of your Maker, who knows how best you work. Moreover, true freedom functions within wise bounds, for example, a fish is not more free on land, nor is a motorist driving on the wrong side of the road. Alternatively, by 'law that gives freedom' James may simply mean the gospel (John 8:32; Rom. 8:2).

In summary, the law is about love (2:8); not just towards your neighbour but also towards God (Matt. 22:35-40).

2. How they learn (19-21) is with what Calvin calls 'a mind disposed to learn' (21b: 'humbly accept'). This will require them to disentangle themselves from their past non-Christian behaviour that hinders the 'implanted' Word (21: does James have in mind Jesus' parable of the soils?), to listen without quibbling (19) and to look 'intently' (25). The word pictures a person bending over something to see it better, like Mary, who 'bent over to look into the tomb' (John 20:11).

3. Why they learn (22-25) God's Word is that they may live God's Word (22): God's law of love (2:8: Eph. 5:1-2). Who would go to a mirror and ignore what they see (23-24), especially if something needed attention? Not to make the necessary adjustments would make having a mirror pointless. Yet God's law, being 'perfect', shows us ourselves as we are. Having seen ourselves, we might prefer to forget what we have seen. Yet 'the word of truth' also shows us our Saviour and what he can do by his grace to improve the ugliness we discover.

To ponder: 'The only thing that counts is faith expressing itself through love' (Gal. 5:6).

James 2:26-27; John 17:13-19   True religion

Continuing his theme of 'living what we learn' (22), James distinguishes between religion that 'is worthless' (26) and religion that is 'pure and faultless' (27), setting before us three signs of what we might call authentic spirituality. 'True religion's more than notion', not only experientially as 'something that must be known and felt', but also evidentially as something that must be seen and heard, as in:

1. Controlled speech (26). James will expand upon this topic in 3:1-12, but the emphasis here is on keeping 'a tight rein'. As the Lord Jesus said that it is 'out of the overflow of the *heart* that the mouth speaks'(Matt. 12:34), it surely follows that only a change of heart (the new birth James speaks of in v.18) and a subsequent Spirit-controlled life will effectively lead to controlled speech. 'No man can tame the tongue' (3:8) but God can. Controlling the tongue you already have may be a surer sign of the Spirit-filled life than speaking in other tongues.

James links the next two signs together under the heading 'religion that God our Father accepts' (27) to make an important point by moving us in two opposite directions at once. Firstly, into the world in:

2. Caring service (27a): 'to look after orphans and widows'. At the time they were the two most vulnerable groups of people, with no man to support them. Today,

Christians are to champion the vulnerable, for example, the unborn and anyone who 'slips through the net'.

James then moves us away from the world: 'to keep oneself from being polluted by the world' through:

3. Continuous sanctification (27b). Christian communities are 'scattered *among* the nations' (1:1) and thus *in* the world. To be effective, however, they must be 'salt' (Matt. 5:13) not 'of the world' but 'set apart' from it. Yet at the same time, they must be salt that is scattered where it counts, that is, in the world'. They must not be *aloof* from the world by just staying in the salt cellar in a sort of 'holy huddle', but shaken out in caring service in order to be a preservative, as salt was in Jesus' day. However, if we must not be aloof from the world, neither must we become *assimilated* into the world. If we become so, the salt 'loses its saltiness' and 'is no longer good for anything' (Matt. 5:13), having, by assimilating impurities, lost its effectiveness. Thus, caring service must go hand in hand with continuous sanctification. We need God's help to hold in tension not being 'of the world' and yet being 'in the world'; to be, at the same time pure salt and scattered salt.

To ponder: You can be too earthly minded to be any heavenly use (John 17:18-19).

James 2:1-13   Favouritism

'All one in Christ' can sometimes seem more like: 'All animals are equal, but some animals are more equal than others' (*Animal Farm:* George Orwell). It is so easy for worldly thinking to govern the kind of welcome we give people into the Christian community. When it comes to favouritism, James is very clear and uncompromising.

1. Favouritism can be short-sighted (1-5). We may judge by outward appearance but people are not always what they seem. The 'poor in the eyes of the world' may be 'rich in faith' (5). Beware of superficial judgements like: 'They're just oldies' or 'Not more of those young people from the estate.' Stop for a moment and ponder Isa. 53:2-3. 'Nazareth! Can any good come from there?' (John 1:46). So too the finely attired rich may, in God's sight, be, spiritually speaking, in 'filthy rags' (Isa. 64:6) and a potential bane rather than a blessing, thus proving that:

2. Favouritism can be stupid (6-7), that is, when we flatter and fawn over those who will in the end, for all their seeming potential, bring us nothing but trouble. Calvin observes that it seems odd to honour one's executioners and in the meantime to injure one's friends. History illustrates the folly of courting the favour of those who prove to be a disaster. We need to beware of assessing people for church office in purely worldly terms. A 'whiz kid' with figures will not automatically make a good church treasurer, even though some mathematical ability is desirable.

3. Favouritism is certainly sinful (8-13). It *contradicts the law of God* (10-11). To break one commandment is to break all because it is the law of love and favouritism is clearly unloving. What also gives God's law its indivisible character is that it *reflects the character of God* (11: 'He who said ... also said'). It should be unsurprising that the God of truth is against false witness and God who is faithful is against adultery. Favouritism clearly contradicts the character of him who 'does not show favouritism' (Acts 10:34). Finally, favouritism *contradicts the gospel of God,* which is all about mercy triumphing over judgement (12). How can those who by profession are 'believers in our glorious Lord Jesus Christ' (1), who 'welcomes sinners and eats with them' (Luke 15:2), exhibit such an inconsistency by their practice?

To ponder: 'Accept one another ... just as Christ accepted you ...' (Rom. 15:7).

James 2:14-26   True saving faith

Faith alone truly saves but true saving faith is never alone. That statement summarises not only today's Bible reading but is the central concern of this letter. James, far from denying 'faith alone', considers saving faith so vital that he is at pains to distinguish it from its counterfeit. Our eternal destiny in heaven or hell turns upon knowing the difference (14). When James writes: 'You see that a person is justified by what he does and not by faith alone' (24), he does not mean that we are saved on account of works as well as faith. Rather he means that works are the evidence of true faith, just as a hallmark identifies genuine silver. Martin Luther was so troubled by an apparent conflict with the apostle Paul that he dismissed James as 'an epistle of straw'. Yet James' message can be summarised from a phrase in Galatians: 'The only thing that counts is faith expressing itself through love' (5:6). Despite his reservations, in the preface to his *Romans*, Luther effectively concurs with James' real message when he states: 'Faith is a divine work in us ... It never asks whether good works are to be done; it has done them before there is time to ask the question and it is doing them always.'

James makes his case by using four illustrations, two of which describe false faith and two describe that which is true.

1. **False faith (15-19)** can be seen in its treatment of others. Its 'compassion' towards others in need (15) is cheap, being shown in word only and not in deed (16). If true faith expresses itself in love, then true love expresses itself in deeds (1 John 3:18). On the last day, such a lack of real compassion will expose those with false faith (Matt. 25:41-46).

For his second illustration, with a gentle touch of irony, James asserts that such 'faith' cannot boast (19) as it is no better than that of demons. It may even be inferior as their faith at least causes them to 'shudder' before God (19).

2. **True faith (20-26).** In marked contrast, true faith expresses itself in costly love to God and costly compassion towards others. Abraham showed that he was truly 'God's friend' and that true faith will obey God first of all, at any cost, by being prepared to sacrifice his dearest (21-24; Matt. 10:37). Rahab's faith was not content merely with cosy words but rather, at great personal risk, with costly deeds of love. This is the test of true faith that will mark all like her on the last day (Matt. 25:34-40).

To ponder: 'Faith ever seeks to walk in light and ever works by love' (source unknown).

James 3:1-12   Taming the tongue

James has already asserted that authentic spirituality will be seen in a bridled tongue (1:26) and he now shows its necessity, while admitting that this is humanly impossible to accomplish (7-8). He knows that what with man is impossible is not so with God (Mark 10:27). Those who have experienced new birth (1:18) can know the sanctifying influence of the Spirit-implanted Word (1:21) and today's reading is part of James' contribution to that Word that sanctifies (John 17:17) and leads towards maturity (2: 'a perfect man'; 1:4). The tongue 'has the power of life and death' (Prov. 18:21), as can be seen in:

1. How influential it can be (1-5). The bit in a horse's mouth or the rudder in a ship can control direction out of all proportion to their size (3-4). So too is the tongue in its potential influence for good or ill, especially in the case of those who are in a commanding position (1-2). Let those who aspire to teach God's Word remember they must give an account (1), and for some this could be fearful (Luke 11:52). But the influence of the tongue for good or ill is not confined to what we hear from professional teachers. James also highlights:

2. How incendiary it can be (5b-6). Just as a negligent smoker's discarded cigarette can set ablaze an entire forest, so unguarded or malicious words can destroy reputations and relationships grown over many years. During the Second World War the fear of enemy spies prompted the UK government to issue the poster: 'Careless talk costs lives.' This is a slogan we should always remember. Someone has said, 'The jawbone of an ass was a killer in Samson's day. It still is.'

Yet what an incendiary power for good the Spirit-controlled, heaven-inflamed tongue can be! One book about the rapid early spread of Christianity is called *The Spreading Flame*.

3. How inconsistent it can be (9-12). The evangelist John Blanchard recalls how a friend once told him that one of the most challenging sermons he had ever heard was called 'Ten minutes after the benediction.' It spoke of those who 'moved in moments from the Gloria to gossip, from creed to criticism, from praising God to wounding men'. Think back upon your recent conversations over refreshments after the Sunday service.

To ponder: 'What's down in the well comes up in the bucket' (origin unknown). 'Out of the overflow of the heart the mouth speaks' (Matt. 12:34).

To pray: 'Set a guard over my mouth, O Lord; keep watch over the door of my lips' (Ps. 141:3).

James 3:13-18   True wisdom [2]

Further to 1:5-8, James now expands upon true wisdom that 'comes from heaven' (15; 1:5 – 'from God, who gives …'). In contrast to the selfish, strife generating and satanically inspired 'wisdom' of the world (14-16), true God-given, heaven-sent wisdom produces a sevenfold harvest. In answer to the question, 'Who is wise?'(13), James' answers in v. 17 provide us with a God-given self-diagnostic tool.

1. **Do you seek to be holy ('pure')?** The word 'suggests the notion of shrinking from contamination, of a delicate sensibility to pollution of any kind (1 John 3:3). Do not, though, confuse this with being fussily over-scrupulous!

2. **Do you seek harmony ('peace-loving', 18: 'peacemakers'),** not by quietly 'minding your own business', nor even by patching up quarrels, but by having the foresight to prevent their arising? Such are truly 'blessed' (Matt. 5:9). By mentioning purity first, though, James cannot mean peace at any moral price. Yet 'if it is possible … live at peace with everyone' (Rom. 12:18).

3. **Do you seek to be humane ('considerate')?** Are you always ready, without ignoring faults, to make allowances for and be magnanimous towards others and know when it is actually wrong to apply the strict letter of the law? Would you not want so to be treated (Matt. 7:12)?

4. **Do you seek to be humble ('submissive', NIV; 'willing to yield', NKJV;** 'open to reason', ESV)? This does not mean being ready to yield to any and every opinion (Eph. 4:14) but to be open-minded enough to listen to reason and to God, causing 'yet more truth and light to break forth from his holy Word'.

5. **Do you seek to be helpful ('full of mercy and good fruit')?** James has already warned against a religion of cosy words, without caring and costly deeds (2:15-16), and here he emphasises that true mercy is not just feelings but actions ('good fruit'). If you were on trial for being a Christian, would there be enough evidence to convict you?

6. **Do you seek to be honourable ('impartial')?** The word literally means 'undivided'. It is the opposite of the waverer described in 1:6-8: a person who lacks fixed principles and can be susceptible to partiality. Are you, instead, a person of settled integrity, not swayed by the current 'correctness', yet also remaining open to reason (submissiveness)?

7. **Do you seek to be honest ('sincere': literally 'without hypocrisy')?** One of John Bunyan's characters is Mr Talkative, who is 'a saint abroad and a devil at home'. Do you, in contrast, 'walk the talk'? Jesus had scathing words for religious hypocrites (Matt. 23:27-28).

To ponder: What kind of harvest are you producing (18)?

James 4:1-3   Family strife

Christians are called to spiritual warfare, but not within their own ranks. How sad that anyone should have felt the need to write a book entitled: *How to spot a church split before it happens (and to do something about it)*. James tackles strife among Christians by noting:

1. Its seriousness (2: 'You kill'). They were probably not literally murdering one another, but James may be using strong language to emphasise its seriousness. Perhaps he also recalls some words of the Lord Jesus (Matt. 5:21-26).

All strife is bad, but when it is among Christians it is particularly so, because it denies the blood-bought *ties* that bind together those James frequently describes as 'brothers'. How our heavenly Father must be grieved by his children's squabbling. Moreover, it spoils the *testimony* we are called to bear, by obscuring the essential mark by which, the Lord Jesus says, the world will identify us as his disciples (John 13:34-35).

2. Its source (1: 'your desires ... within you'). Church strife can create a public scandal, but arise from a very private source. As so often, the heart of the problem is the problem of the heart. There is a legitimate place for the inevitable difference of opinion, based upon conscientious conviction, that flows from the fact that 'now we see but a poor reflection' (1 Cor. 13:12). Yet it should be possible to disagree without being disagreeable: with 'fights and quarrels' (1). Often, though, 'wrong motives' (3), like 'envy and selfish ambition' (3:16), may lie at the root of strife. James highlights covetousness (2): the selfish hankering to get what feeds one's own 'pleasures' (3). When each is out only for themselves, it will inevitably lead to strife.

3. Its solution (3: 'ask ...'). Identifying the source of strife ('within you') points to its solution. It is to get our hearts genuinely into the presence of God. By blocking our wrongly motivated self-willed requests ('you do not receive'), God may be driving us to subject our wills to his (7). We still have open the avenue to ask properly: 'You do not have because you do not ask God' (2b). Therefore 'our desires ought to be bridled and the way of bridling them is to subject them to the will of God ... what we in moderation wish, we ought to seek from God himself; which if it be done, we shall be preserved from wicked contentions, from fraud and violence, and from doing any injury to others' (Calvin).

To pray: 'Grant unto thy people that they may love the thing which thou commandest, and desire that which thou dost promise' (Book of Common Prayer).

James 4:4-10   Combating worldliness

Until now, James has referred to his readers as 'brothers' (see 1:2,16,19; 2:1,5,14; 3:1,10,12. Now he calls them 'adulterous people'. Those familiar with the Old Testament would pick up James' allusion to its frequently naming God's people's unfaithfulness to him as spiritual adultery (Jer. 3:20). James begins with:

1. A searching enquiry (4-5). Friendship in the Bible often denotes the serious commitment of being in covenant with someone, as was Abraham's (2:23), who was in covenant with God. The world we must not befriend is 'the spirit that animates fallen mankind, the spirit of self-seeking and self-indulgence without regard for God' (J I Packer).

Verse 5 is difficult and is variously translated. If taken in the context of James' addressing 'adulteresses', it could read: 'God jealously longs for the spirit that he made to live in us' (NIV footnote). As the jealous Lover of our souls (Exod. 20:4-6) he will tolerate no rivals and will do whatever it takes to 'woo' us back to himself (Ezek. 14:4-5; Hosea 2:6-7,14-16). James wants action and so he follows with:

2. A serious exhortation (7-10). Ten commands follow, each in a tense denoting the need for decisive 'once for all' action. 'Submit … to God' (7a) means voluntarily to enlist under God's command; not being press-ganged. 'Resist the devil' (7b) should remind us that once we enlist under God, we should expect an enemy attack and, to resist him successfully, we will need to 'come near to God' (8a). Yet, if God seems distant, who has moved? As God is holy, though, coming near to him will necessitate repenting (8b: 'wash … purify') of wrong outward actions ('your hands') and wrong inward attitudes ('your hearts'). If we think that 'grieve … mourn … wail … change…' (9) seem extravagant expressions when it comes to repentance, this might say more about our superficial view of sin than any alleged exaggeration by James. Finally, coming before God will cut you down to size: 'Humble yourselves before God…' (10). Yet the way down is also the way up ('he will lift you up').

None of this will be possible without:

3. A supernatural enabling (6). Until now we have overlooked what is possibly the key verse and which highlights the Christian's 'invisible means of support'. God's grace even enables the humble disposition to receive what is required. The jealous Lover is also the gracious Lover. What is more, when the burdens grow greater, 'he gives us more grace'.

To pray: 'Lord, grant what you command and command what you will' (Augustine of Hippo).

James 4:11-12; Matthew 7:1-5   Kangaroo courts

James' condemnation of an 'unbrotherly' (11) judgemental spirit reflects the teaching of Jesus. We are, though, our 'brother's keeper' and in neither teaching was the intention to forbid, for example, brotherly 'care-fronting' (Matt. 18:15-20) or judging teachers to be false, as the Lord exhorts us to do in the very chapter in which he says, 'Do not judge' (Matt. 7:1,15-20). What James has in view is when Christians, in judging others, usurp the place of God, the 'only one Lawgiver and Judge' (12), with their own 'kangaroo courts'.

1. When this may occur. We may *focus on the person rather than on their actions*, going beyond addressing what is humanly verifiable and presuming to judge the heart, which only God can do (1 Sam. 16:7; Jer. 17:10). James may have this in view with the expressions 'slander one another' and 'against his brother' (11) that focus on the whole person.

We can also usurp God's place as Judge when we *go beyond what Scripture warrants* in judging others' actions. We can, in effect, 'judge the law' (11) by trying to 'improve' upon its assumed lack of clarity. The Pharisees did this with the law of Moses, by trying to 'fence' it with their many burdensome traditions. Christians can fall into this trap, even out of good intentions. Paul addressed a bone of contention in the Roman church about a matter not dogmatised in Scripture. He did so, not by calling for a denial of personal conviction (Rom. 14:5), but for a mutual respect of one another's consciences, while also warning against 'playing God' by judging one another (Rom. 14:3-4).

James exposes the underlying critical spirit that violates, by 'speaking against' it (11), the royal law of 'Love your neighbour as yourself' (2:8): that love that 'is ever ready to believe the best of every person, and will credit no evil of any but on the most positive evidence' (Adam Clarke on 1 Cor. 13:7: '[love] always trusts').

2. Why this may occur. The Greek personal pronoun 'you', placed first for emphasis in the last phrase of v. 12, implies: 'You there! Who are you to judge ...?' and calls for self-examination on the critic's part. Could a readiness to demote another be fuelled by a desire to promote oneself? We should first judge our own sin in order better to deal with what we suppose is another's (the import of Jesus' instruction in Matt. 7:5). Also, we must do so 'gently', while watching 'yourself, or you may be tempted' (Gal. 6:1).

To ponder: 'Never put your finger on someone's faults unless it is part of a helping hand' (source unknown).

James 4:13-17; Luke 12:13-21   Facing the future

'We should all be concerned about the future, because we will have to spend the rest of our lives there.' However, there is a right and a wrong way to face it.

1. How not to face it (16: 'you boast and brag'). Plan for the future if you wish, says James (13), but do not presume even upon tomorrow (14). To counter this cocksure attitude, James asserts three sobering truths:

(a) *Your ignorance* (14a: 'you do not ... know'). God has opened for you an account in the Bank of Time and given you a deposit. He knows how much you have 'spent', but this 'bank' issues no statements and allows no overdrafts. Your 'deposit' will certainly be used up. 'There is nothing more certain than death; nothing more uncertain than the time of dying. I will therefore be prepared at all times for that which may happen at any time' (Warwick). The Lord Jesus may of course come again first, but you are also ignorant of that appointed date. The only time you have to repent and believe is now (2 Cor. 6:2).

(b) *Your transience* (14b: 'You are a mist ...'). Time passes more quickly than you think. 'Swift to its close ebbs out life's little day' – like a vanishing mist or like the steam from a kettle. Do not therefore act as though this life were for ever. Remember the rich fool (Luke 12:19-20).

(c) *Your dependence* (15: 'If it is the Lord's will, we will live ...'). You are literally living on borrowed time and he who lent it ordained all your days 'before one of them came to be' (Ps. 139:16).

Although less explicit than about how not to face the future, James does hint implicitly at:

2. How to face it.

(a) *God is the sovereign of time* (15a: '... you ought to say "If it is the Lord's will" '). Even though we need not always openly articulate it, we should always plan with that qualifying thought.

(b) *You are a steward of time (17)*. Remember that lost time is never found. Frances Ridley Havergal showed great perception when, in her famous 'Consecration Hymn', she began with: 'Take my moments and my days.' If the Lord has your time, he has everything. Notice that James focuses on the good we might fail to do with our time (17). While sins of omission are easily overlooked, the Lord Jesus highlights them when speaking of the 'goats' (Matt. 25:41-46). No wonder the dying James Ussher prayed, 'Lord, forgive most of all my sins of omission.'

To ponder: 'You ... say, "Today or tomorrow ..." ' (13). 'But God said, "This very night ..." ' (Luke 12:20).

James 5:1-7a   Future reckoning

Why does James bother to address unbelievers who are not going to read his letter? That the unbelieving rich are in view seems clear from the fact that he calls them 'you rich people' (1) and not 'brothers' (a term to which he returns in v. 7). What is more, all he can promise them is condemnation. So to what purpose is this prophetic-like outburst? James seems to have two in view:

1. To console his readers. The tell-tale 'then' (7) implies that James' first readers have been living with the consequences of the oppression and injustice afflicted by these 'rich people' (he also alludes to them in 2:6-7). In such conditions, God's people can become discouraged (Ps. 73:13), even envious (Ps. 73:3-4) and, above all, question God's justice (Mal. 2:17).

James, however, obliquely assures them that a day of reckoning is at hand, by rhetorically addressing their oppressors (1). What the 'rich people' will face will be formidable: the verb 'wail' conjures up the agonising sound it describes. The word actually has the sense more of a shriek, 'howl' (KJV, ESV).

They are charged in vv. 3b-6 with greedily hoarding up wealth to live in self-indulgent luxury. Far from showing generosity to the poor, they have unjustly cheated workers of their wages and condemned innocent people who were doing them no harm. Yet all that they have gained will turn to loss, and worse. It will testify against them and be like fuel to ignite their destruction (3). We detect in James not the dispassionate listing of charges by a court clerk but words of moral outrage that have caused some to dub him the 'Christian Amos'.

Later on in the chapter, James affirms that this day of condemnation for the ungodly will be a day of consolation for God's people (7-8,11). In view of this, he calls them not to fret or worse but to persevere. You can almost hear him saying with Paul, 'Do not take revenge, my friends, but leave room for God's wrath' (Rom. 12:19).

Yet, too, James' rhetorical condemnation of the riches may, at least implicitly, be:

2. To challenge his readers. The end of the ungodly should challenge rich Christians 'not to be arrogant nor to put their hope in wealth ... to be rich in good deeds, and to be generous and willing to share ...' (1 Tim. 6:17-19). It should also challenge all oppressed Christians not to envy their rich oppressors.

To ponder: 'I envied the arrogant when I saw the prosperity of the wicked ... till I entered the sanctuary of God; then I understood their final end' (Ps. 73:3,16-17).

James 5:7-11   A grace for the stressed

Christians, like others, are subject to trials and stresses and often precisely because they are Christians. Here James highlights the grace we will need for stressful situations.

1. The pressures we may face. Previously we have seen that James' first readers may have been especially conscious of pressure from the oppressive rich (1-7a). Historically, such oppression has often led 'the workmen' to cry out' (4) and unite in revolution. Instead, James issues a call to patience (7a,8a). However, he knows that stressful external circumstances can lead us to be less than loving towards our fellow believers and exacerbate any existing tensions within the Christian fellowship (9). He therefore reflects upon:

2. The patience we will need. The verb translated 'patient' literally means 'long tempered' and is part of the composite 'fruit of the Spirit' (Gal. 5:22). Chrysostom described it as 'the spirit which could take revenge if it liked but refuses to do so'. It is the grace that is ready to forgive those who wrong us and is ready to bear with others who annoy us, even 'in the face of suffering' (10). It makes a good companion to 'perseverance' (11). We met this word in 1:4, where we thought of it as an ability not simply to bear things with passive resignation but courageously and with a vibrant confidence in God's good purpose. In terms of 'passive resignation', we have not heard 'of the patience of Job', who wrestled hard with God's dealings with him. But we do know of his 'perseverance' (11). Despite everything, he courageously stood firm (8).

3. The perspective we should have. Hope, it has been said, is the mother of patience (Rom. 8:25) and James reminds us of the 'blessed hope' (Titus 2:13): 'the Lord's coming' (7), which is 'near' (8). Indeed, 'the Judge is standing at the door' (9b). If there were no prospect of the divinely promised 'autumn and spring rains' (7; Deut. 11:14; Jer. 5:24), the farmer's patient sowing, watering, weeding and waiting would be pointless. Yet how much more certain is 'the Lord's coming'. To keep this in view, and what lies beyond it, should put our pressures in perspective (Rom. 8:18). 'What the Lord finally brought about' for Job (11) was but a faint this-worldly prefiguring of what lies in prospect for Christians currently under pressure. Yet note too that the prospect of Christ's coming ought also to make us look to our behaviour (9; 1 John 3:3).

To ponder: Revelation 7:9-17.

James 5:12; Matthew 5:33-37; 23:16-22   False and flippant speech

We have already seen how James recalls the Lord Jesus' own teaching and here is perhaps the most explicit example. Neither teaching forbids lawful oaths which, sadly, are necessary in a world of sinners. In a court of law, you may be a stranger and your integrity unproven. What is censured, though, is:

1. Insincerity. People had a way of wriggling out of commitments by a trick of the tongue, for example by arguing that to swear by anything other than God when making a solemn promise or assertion made it less binding (Matt. 23:18 – 'it means nothing'). However, both James' and Jesus' point is that your word, whether what you promise to do or what you assert to be true, should always be as good as if you were under oath. All our life, including our commitments, whether or not God's name is mentioned when we make them, is constantly open to God. This is Jesus' point in Matt. 23:19-22. We will give an account to him one day for 'every careless word' (Matt. 12:36).

When making promises, therefore, 'make them cautiously and keep them conscientiously' – as far as you can. When making assertions of truth, make sure they are 'the truth, the whole truth and nothing but the truth'. A half-truth represented as a whole truth is an untruth. And 'nothing but the truth' would include a fact combined with a mere opinion

stated as though the composite were a fact, for example, 'She didn't stay at church today. She's deliberately avoiding me.' Remember that a text taken out of context is a 'con' (a deception) and provides a pretext for whatever you choose it to mean.

This teaching also implicitly rebukes what underlies such evasive insincerity, especially when solemnly avowed, that is:

2. Irreverence. Such misuse of God's name in vows may have been the immediate application of the third commandment, but underlying the command not to 'misuse the name of the Lord your God' (Exod. 20:7) is required 'the holy and reverent use of God's name, titles, attributes, ordinances, word and works' (*Westminster Shorter Catechism* Question 54). It is essentially a call for an attitude of heart towards God that the Bible calls 'the fear of the Lord'. By this is not meant that cringing fear that causes the demons to shudder (2:19) but to have such a reverence for God our Father that readily and lovingly obeys his will, submits to his discipline and worships him in awe, with speech that does not betray it.

To ponder and to pray: 'O how I fear Thee, living God, with deepest, tenderest fears' (F W Faber).

James 5:13-18   Counsel from 'camel knees'

An ancient tradition has it that James was nicknamed 'Camel Knees', because his devotion to prayer caused calluses to develop on his knees. If so, his prayer counsel deserves our attention as it is divinely inspired. He deals with:

1. Personal prayer (13). Communion with God is not to be reserved only for the bad times but also for the glad times. Furthermore, as James seems to imply, 'those blessings are sweetest that are won with prayers and worn with thanks' (Thomas Goodwin).

2. Pastoral prayer (14-16a). Note firstly, the *condition*. The word translated 'sick' in v.14 implies 'weakness' and the different word in v.15 means literally, 'the weary, worn out one', being used only elsewhere in Heb.12:3 and Rev.2:3. It implies more than just a physical condition, if indeed it actually is, and it seems to be associated with sin (15b-16). Sickness usually has no direct link with particular sin (John 9:3; 11:4). An extreme spiritual 'weariness' would fit well contextually with the call to persevere in spite of stresses without and within (7). Secondly, it is the 'sick' person who issues the *call* (14), with no suggestion of doing so instead of employing medical remedies. The Lord Jesus said that the sick need a doctor (Matt.9:12). Paul appreciated his 'dear friend Luke, the doctor' (Col.4:14) and recommended wine for Timothy's digestive problems, a common remedy of the day (1 Tim.5:23). Whether the anointing is symbolic, as a 'visual aid' to focus faith, or medicinal is disputed and there is no reference to laying on hands. The *consequences* do not imply that all physical healing is open to sufficient faith, assuming the condition here described has a physical component. James would be contradicting himself were he to mean that (4:15) and the wider teaching of the New Testament on prayer in general and healing would also preclude this (1 John 5:14; 2 Tim.4:20).

3. Prevailing prayer (16b-18). Elijah exemplifies the powerful and effective 'prayer warrior' (16b). We should note, however, that his prayer *assumed certain prerequisites*. He was 'a righteous man'. Being clothed in Christ's righteousness and adopted as God's children, 'we may approach God with freedom and confidence' (Eph.3:12). At the same time, our prayers may be hindered by cherished sin (4:3; Ps.66:18). Note too that Elijah's request (17: 'that it would not rain') was implicitly *grounded in God's promises*. In this case it was a 'negative' one (see Deut.11:13-17). Remember that 'the possibilities of prayer run parallel with the promises of God' (E M Bounds).

To pray: 'Lord, teach us to pray' (Luke 11:1).

James 5:19-20; Galatians 6:1-2   Pastoral care

1. Who should care. James states 'someone' and not 'the elders', as in v.14. Although some are especially gifted for pastoral oversight (Eph.4:11-12), most spiritual gifts are endowments to 'specialise' in an area where all are to be involved. Thus, all are, in measure, to pastor one another (Rom.15:14).

2. Why we should care. Trace James' frequent description of Christians as 'brothers': 1:2,16,19; 2:1,5,14; 3:1,10,12; 4:11; 5:7,9,10,12. The familial *'ties that bind us'* provide a compelling reason to care. You are your 'brother's keeper': 'the brother for whom Christ died' (1 Cor.8:11). The *temptations that beset us* also call out for mutual caring. Any of us may 'wander'. The picture is not of a sudden headlong rush into sin but an 'almost gentle straying', like a boat drifting away. 'Indeed the safest road to hell is the gradual one – the gentle slope, soft underfoot, without sudden turnings, without milestones, without signposts' (C S Lewis: *The Screwtape Letters*). Finally *the tragedy that might otherwise befall us* should motivate us to 'care-front' (20): future ruin will be averted ('save him from death') and, instead, a much more wholesome experience for the one rescued and those around him or her ('and cover a multitude of sins').

3. How we should care. One old church covenant quaintly reads: 'We do promise to watch over each other's conversations and not to suffer sin upon one another, so far as God shall discover it to us, or any of us; and to stir up one another to love and good works; to warn, rebuke and admonish one another with meekness, according to the rules left to us of Christ in that behalf.' This was certainly not meant to be a charter for busybodies (2 Thess.3:11; 1 Peter 4:15: 'a meddler'). It does perhaps, though, challenge our tendency towards excessive independence and an individualism that fails to recognise our responsibility towards one another. Studying the 'one another' passages in the New Testament could be a fruitful exercise. Yet we will best care when we engage in constructive rather than destructive correction (Eph.4:29). That means to restore one another we will each need to be *fit* to do so: to have that spirit of gentleness that Paul expects of those who seek to 'restore' (Gal.6:1). This is a word used for setting a broken limb or for mending nets (Matt.4:21). That is why a judgemental spirit is no good for the delicate task of metaphorically removing 'the speck from your brother's eye' (Matt.7:1-5).

As Thou hast sought, so let me seek
Thy erring children lost and lone.

(F R Havergal)

Readings in

1 Peter

by Ray Beeley

WINDOW
ON THE
WORD

THE FIRST LETTER OF PETER

The letter was written by the apostle Peter, perhaps using Silas as his scribe (5:12). It is likely that he was in Rome when he wrote, with the reference to Babylon being spiritual rather than literal. He writes to Christians generally, not to a specific congregation or region, thus indicating how far the gospel had spread by this time. As an apostle to the Jews (Gal. 2:7), this would apply to Jewish believers, but he also writes to Gentiles (1:14,18; 2:9-10; 3:6; 4:3-4). He wrote to help them stand firm in the faith as they faced persecution (1:6; 2:12; 3:14-17; 4:12-16). He exhorts them to maintain an exemplary character before a godless world. It is thought that Peter arrived in Rome about AD 60 and was martyred there is about AD 68. There was a growing anti-Christian mood in Rome, leading to open and orchestrated hostility in AD 64. The letter was probably written then.

Style and vocabulary. Peter's style is good literary Greek, suggesting the help of Silas. He writes to exhort, not to give detailed exposition of doctrine, although his exhortations are clearly doctrinally based. More than sixty words in the original Greek are not found elsewhere in the New Testament. Although he covers various themes, a recurring thread is suffering and glory (1:11; 3:18-22; 4:13-14; 5:1,4,10,11). He wrote to inspire the Christians with hope (1:3,7,13,21). Persecution is to be expected and salvation will be glorious. Following Christ in the pilgrimage of faith presents a stark contrast to living in the world.

1 Peter 1:1-2 Rejoice!

It is suggested that the main theme of this letter was to encourage beleaguered Christians. Many were slaves subject to cruel masters, and Christians suffered quite often even before the fierce persecutions under Nero (AD 54-68). The mention of Babylon in 5:13 is most probably symbolic of Rome.

Some have argued that the letter was written for Jewish Christians, but there is no reason to exclude others!

The vital choice (1-2; Ephesians 1:4-6; Romans 8:29). The initiative here is God's not men's.

1. Sojourners. The places mentioned included the nationalities mentioned at Pentecost (Acts 2:8-9), including Jews of the Dispersion and Gentile God-fearers. They were 'strangers scattered' (KJV) – small groups from various towns of people reckoned a little odd by their neighbours – because they were not idolaters and had a completely different approach to life.

The expression is also spiritually significant because they knew that they were by nature 'strangers, alienated from God' (Eph. 2:12-13) but were now citizens of a heavenly kingdom.

The 'scattering' may indicate persecution, as had happened to Aquila and Priscilla (Acts 18:2-3) and to Paul at Thessalonica (Acts 17:1-9) and Ephesus (Acts 19:23-41).

In the prayer of David in 1 Chronicles 29:15, 'strangers' (AV) suggests the idea of people who are completely dependent upon the goodness of another.

'Strangers' is rendered by 'pilgrims' in the NKJV – to convey the idea of 'those residing on earth but belonging to heaven' (Phil. 3:20).

2. Secure. God had set his favour upon them. In v. 2 there is an inescapable Trinitarian thought: God the Father had set his love upon them apart from any work on their part (John 15:16). They were sanctified by the work of the Spirit in their hearts. The price of their sin had been paid by the death of Jesus – 'the blood of Jesus Christ'. Nothing could change that (Rom. 8:35-39).

3. Set apart. God had a clear purpose in their choice. These 'nobodies' were to be 'somebodies' in eternity! In Christ they were a 'new creation' (2 Cor. 5:17), forsaking their attitude of rebellion as children of Adam. They were chosen 'to obedience' – the work of God within them would produce this effect in their lives now on earth. God's choosing did not undermine human responsibility but directed it into right channels.

Verse 2 is completed by a blessing that speaks of the abundance of God's love reaching out to the hopeless. They now enjoyed peace with God, and the gracious help of the Holy Spirit.

For our direction: Christians should remember to which kingdom they belong (2 Cor. 5:17). They have been bought at great price (1 Cor. 6:20). That is a comfort when men set us at nought, and a challenge when we are tempted to make ourselves too comfortable in the world (Matt. 6:33).

The confession of Psalm 115:1 should be ours. All the glory for our salvation belongs to God.

1 Peter 1:3-5   His great mercy

The very thought of the great grace of God's salvation in Christ should fill our hearts with gratitude and excite praise.

Gratitude. Let us think of it as 'a duty' (Rom. 12:1-2) – our spontaneous response to his great love for us (1 John 4:19). Such love should inspire obedience (2). At the very least, it is good manners to say 'Thank you' for favours received!

In v. 2 we are reminded of God's great initiative of love. Nicodemus (if he came to faith) and Zacchaeus, Peter, Paul and the repentant thief stand on common ground – 1 Timothy 1:15. Backgrounds and sins were very different, but all were sinners 'without hope' apart from Christ.

There is a wonderful demonstration here of the Trinity and the work of pure love (1 Cor. 13:4-5). The Son was equally God with the Father but came in obedience. The Holy Spirit was also equally God but condescended to be sent by the Father and the Son. Together they work to give salvation.

Gift. God deals with us who deserve nothing but wrath, by way of generous giving. 'Mercy' is the key. Men cannot 'birth themselves' – another must give life.

He gives 'new birth' to sinners who have forfeited the right to life.

He gives 'hope' to those who have no hope.

He gives 'resurrection power' to those dead in trespasses and sins.

He promises a 'sure inheritance' to undeserving rebels.

That is what 'grace' means (Eph. 2:12-13).

Guarantee. All believers are shielded by God's power (5) – the power revealed in the resurrection (3). Our prayer should be for understanding of that (Eph. 1:17-20; Rom. 8:31-39). His purpose is that 'we should be conformed to the image of his Son' (Rom. 8:29). This is the salvation we are to 'work out' (Phil. 2:12-13; 1 Peter 1:13).

Some scholars have remarked that Peter is being very Pauline here, but it is better to note that the Spirit was the teacher of both – no wonder they agreed!

Great faith is based on what God has done in Christ. *Great hope* is based on what he has promised. *Great love* is demonstrated in his love for us. *Great perseverance* depends on what he is doing in us now. All this follows from the new birth.

When you feel forsaken, or tempted to give up, consider the greatness of the plan, the person who has commanded it, and the one who has worked it out. Remember the death of Jesus on the cross for you, and his resurrection from the dead. The believer is *in him*! Plead with him to fulfil his promise and get you there! Faith in his sacrifice ensures forgiveness. His resurrection guarantees eternal life.

Question: Is your faith so personal and your love so real that you have a joy in it that is inexpressible (8)?

Answer: God desires this for you, so persevere in asking him for it until he grants the request (Matt. 7:7-11). Then, be thankful!

1 Peter 1:6-9 The result of trials

These verses begin the application of the 'great and precious promises' received by faith (2 Peter1:4).

Persuasion. 'In this you greatly rejoice.' 'This' refers to what we have in Christ (3-5). Because it is sure, depending as it does on the infallible Word of God, we can rejoice in it because we are assured of it! It points us to a future that cannot be spoiled in any way (4-5) and is reserved for us by God's power (2 Tim. 1:12).

Jesus passed through death into endless resurrection life, and when united with him by faith this is your sure destiny.

Pain. Suffering is an inevitable part of our present experience. Jesus warned the disciples that there was a cross to be taken up (Matt.10:38; Mark 8:34-38). The cross of Jesus was unique in that he alone could pay the price for the sins of others before God, but his followers were called to share the pain of rejection by the world which being identified with him would bring. Peter speaks of 'suffering grief in all kinds of trials' and later adds more (1 Peter 2:19-21).

Purpose. The common human reaction is the complaint, 'Why is this happening to me? I don't deserve it.' Peter puts forward a different view: Here is the demonstration of the reality of faith. Your firm convictions produce this trouble and God's grace will enable you to persevere. They are evidence that you belong to him. Peter is not encouraging these believers (or us) to seek martyrdom, but explaining the inevitable consequence of consistent Christian living. As gold is purified by fire, so will your faith be! God is using your trials for your good and for his glory.

Proof. Your endurance is the proof of the genuineness of faith. But more, it is the expression of your love for the Saviour. These believers had never seen the Saviour, but they loved him because they had received the gospel and had the witness of the Spirit in their hearts.

Prospect. They had embraced the promise of God that the Lord Jesus would be revealed, and even now they were receiving 'the salvation of their souls'. The body might be disfigured by physical suffering and would surely die, but they would be presented perfect before God with exceeding joy (Jude 24). Their salvation was a present reality and a future hope.

This is the 'ultimate tense' of salvation – we *are* saved; we *are being* saved; we *shall be* saved. There is this unbreakable chain (Rom. 8:29-30).

'The soul is the spirit in union with the body; the spirit is the soul out of that relationship' (Jay Adams). The salvation of your soul means the final redemption of the body!

Realistically you will experience sadness.

Hopefully you embrace God's great plan.

Joyfully you look past present sadness to the fullness of the glorious inheritance of which your present salvation is the firstfruit.

1 Peter 1:10-16,23-25; 2 Peter 1:16-21   The living word

Having set out the gospel in clear and challenging terms, Peter draws special attention to 'the Word of God', first proclaimed by the prophets. This concentration on 'the Word' and the Old Testament prophets is important because there is a modern tendency even among Christians to ignore or neglect it. In this passage Peter makes it vital to the Christian life – it is through the Scriptures that we come to know the truth and experience its power.

The wonder of the Word (10-12). This is the Word of God himself! See Psalms 19:7-10; 119:49-50; Isaiah 55:10-11. Peter speaks of two 'sources'

(a) *The prophets.* Much of its significance was hidden from them but they realised its importance and faithfully recorded what they received. They had received it through the Holy Spirit. This was not the product of their own thinking – it was supernaturally conveyed to them by God. It was revealed to them that the fullness of this truth was for a future generation, and so they recorded it faithfully.

(b) *The apostles.* The message was completed (in Peter's day) by apostolic preaching applied by the inward work of the Holy Spirit. The same Spirit was at work in the prophets and the apostles. The message spoke of 'the Christ' (one sent and equipped by God) and his sufferings and the glories to follow.

The whole idea of 'Messiah suffering' was alien to most Jewish thinking and 'foolish' to the majority of people (1 Cor. 1:21-24). Yet this was what had been recorded and was now preached. The Old Testament had been clear about both aspects in the life of the Deliverer.

His sufferings were foretold in Genesis 3:15 (the bruised heel of the seed of the woman); Psalm 22; Isaiah 53; Zechariah 12:10.

The glories to come were spoken of in many prophecies in Isaiah (including the latter part of chapter 53), and in many psalms including Psalm 110; and in Daniel 7:13-14.

All had been realised in the facts concerning Jesus (1:2-3). Even the angels did not fully understand.

The modern church is losing sight of this truth, making many decisions without any reference to God's Word, or filtering the truth through so-called human wisdom (1 Cor. 1:20-21).

Questions:

1. Do you believe the Word of God, or what people are saying about it?

2. Are you depending upon the opinions of men, or is the Holy Spirit your teacher?

Act upon the truth: Receive the Scripture as God's Word. Follow the example of the prophets by diligent searching under the authority of the Word and the Spirit. Learn, as they did, that there are limits to human wisdom. Understand that it is not for us alone: we are to share it! Seek and submit to the Holy Spirit. Embrace the Lord Jesus as the fulfilment of the promises. Live accordingly – an obedient, pure and holy life. Expect the 'glories' – Jesus will return victorious!

1 Peter 1:13-16   The outworking of the gospel

This gospel was intended to produce results (13) – there were consequences of believing.

1. Hope. There was hope in an 'ignorant' (14) and 'aimless' (18) world. Hopelessness seems to be a trait of the modern world. Men have ceased to ask, 'Why are we here?' and many have become immersed in the pursuit of pleasure. The more unfortunate have given up on life altogether! For many, the marks of modern life are hopelessness and turning to drugs.

2. Discipline. The readers were called to discipline – 'gird up the loins' means 'prepare like a soldier for action'. This, again, is something alien to much modern life, of which self-indulgence has become a part. Often this has also become part of the life of the church. Prayer and the careful study of the Word of God have been neglected in the quest for what is termed exciting worship.

3. Obedience. They were to be 'obedient children' – fully aware of their new relationship with God, they were to obey and please him. Liberty and fun have become the order of the day, and obedience to the Word of God has been branded as legalism.

4. Holiness. Israel had been called to holiness (15; Lev. 11:44-45) and the Christians were now in the new and intimate relationship of being separated to God with the moral consequence of purity. In the Old Covenant, Israel was intended to be a separate people, marked by circumcision and obedience to the law. Their decline was marked by the desire to become like the nations.

In the New Covenant, believers are no longer in bondage to the law (Rom. 8:15) but we are ruled by the Spirit, who has imparted new desires which are pleasing to God (Rom. 8:3-10). We have become members of a new kingdom in which Jesus is King, and we seek to live as those who are redeemed by him (Col. 1:12-14), pleasing to him in every way (Col. 1:10). The Christian has 'set his heart' on something different from the life of the world (Col. 3:1-4). That involves a transformed life style (Col. 3:5-14) requiring that natural inclinations are 'put to death'. There is no place for compromise in these matters. The Holy Spirit is within us to enable us to do this work.

Once again Peter and Paul at one!

Holiness has become a dirty word suggesting hypocrisy and remoteness from the realities of life. Peter rejects all that, as he addresses his appeal to slaves (2:16-18), husbands and wives (3:1-7) and applies the truth to all Christians (3:8). Life is lived with a different object in view (4:2).

Holiness is not demonstrated by a formal mode of dress, or a written code of behaviour, but by an inward desire to seek and please God, as is patterned by the Lord Jesus.

Our hope will be fulfilled when the Lord Jesus returns in glory (1:7-9).

Basic truths at which men stumble today are the physical resurrection of Jesus and his visible return to earth in glory.

1 Peter 1:17-21   Ransomed from futile ways

In verse 13 Peter has started to draw out the consequences of faith in the Lord Jesus Christ. 'Holiness' (15) is the sum of it, but here he is drawing out various aspects of it.

1. Realising responsibilities (17). Christians will call upon God as Father (as in the Lord's Prayer) for they alone have this privilege of an intimate relationship with God. This will have its consequences because their Father is the Judge. He is the Judge of all men, but this has special significance for the Christian, because the Father is looking at him to find something to praise (1 Cor. 4:5). We should be showing some evidences of being sons. Sin in the Christian is serious but is covered by the blood of Jesus: God is now looking for evidences of the work of his Spirit in the new heart. It is a matter of wonder that he will reward such works (Matt. 10:41-42).

The 'fear' of the Christian is of loving reverence for such a holy and almighty Father, continually repentant, confidently dependent and eternally grateful.

2. Recognising what you are (17). The Christian is a temporary inhabitant in this world. He does not really belong to it, having a better hope. 'Stay' (NKJV) means living as a temporary resident ('as strangers', NIV). By God's grace we now belong to a different kingdom (Col. 1:12-14). As Peter has already said, we have a different destiny (1:3-4).

3. Remembering the price paid (18-19). The 'precious blood of Christ' was of infinite value because of the pre-eminence of the person who gave himself as a sacrifice, and also because of the preciousness of what it obtained.

The idea of 'the lamb' relates back to the Old Testament where the sacrifice was to be without blemish. The probable reference is to the Passover lamb (Exod. 12:3-13) which not only delivered Israel from death but pointed them to pilgrimage and a different destiny. Even gold is corruptible by comparison.

4. Reflecting on the wonder of it (20-21). To emphasise the precious nature of Christ, Peter takes a moment to reflect on it.

(a) The plan was conceived before creation, bringing home the supernatural nature of it, and that it owed nothing to our deserving.

(b) It was manifest – actually demonstrated in history. 'The last times' indicates the finality of what was done. God has no other purpose to supersede this.

(c) 'You' – this salvation had specified people in mind (1:2) and they have received it.

(d) The plan is consummated in the person of Christ who has brought them to faith and hope in God. God raised Jesus from the dead and exalted him (Phil. 2:11).

The attention of the believer is focused on the Lord Jesus Christ.

Realise the privilege and responsibilities of saying 'Christ died for me'.

Reflect on such wonderful love. Mercy has made it possible (1:3-4).

Respond with 'reverent fear'.

'If Jesus Christ be God and died for me, then no sacrifice can be too great for me to make for him' (C T Studd).

1 Peter 1:21-25   Purified souls

Here are revealed fundamentals of true faith to 'you who believe'.

1. Resting on facts. God had promised after Adam and Eve's fall into temptation by the devil that 'the seed of woman would bruise the serpent's head' (Gen. 3:15), which promise was fulfilled in the person and ministry of Jesus. 'Jesus Christ – raised from the dead and glorified (21).

That is a very brief summary of the person and work of the one upon whom faith depends.

(a) *He came from heaven.* There was an incarnation by which God came into the world as a man.

(b) *He died.* Reference has been made to 'the blood' (2,19). The significance of that is revealed as an acceptable sacrifice (a lamb without blemish).

(c) *He rose again (3,21).*

(d) *He is glorified* – in the resurrection, the ascension and in a future coming (7).

2. Revealed in the Word – the truth, the enduring Word of God. Peter had already spoken of that (10-12). True faith is inseparable from the Scriptures (of Old and New Testament) and issues in obedience. The Spirit operates through the Word enabling us to obey. From the beginning God had dealt with man through his Word. Man's part was to trust and obey.

3. Received by new birth. Jesus had told Nicodemus that he needed to 'be born again'. Christians have been born again. They need that personal inward sanctifying work of the Spirit (2). This had been promised through the Old Testament prophecies of the New Covenant (Jer. 31:31-34; Ezek. 36:24-27). This is not an option but a necessity!

4. Restoring purity. By nature we are stained by sin. The Word of the gospel pointing to the cross and the inward work of the Spirit restores that which was lost by the sin of Adam and Eve, as David anticipated in Psalm 51:1-12.

Augustus Toplady wrote of the 'double cure of sin – cleansing from its guilt and power'. That is what the gospel brings to us.

5. Resulting in love of the brethren. There is a bond between Christians as members of one family of God. This is the inevitable result of being born again by the Spirit of God into the same family, but is something to be cultivated as believers 'obey the truth'. New birth has imparted something that was not there before, but it is to be nurtured by the Word of God, which is our spiritual food (2:2-3). Faith in and obedience to the Word of God are part of the essential responsibility of being members of God's family. One consequence is that we are bonded into the one family of which God is the Father.

Revelation and regeneration are fundamental to biblical faith – God must work in us before we can live for him.

We receive God's gift and work it out by faith (Phil. 2:12-13). The Word of God is his instrument, and faith in the promises leads to their accomplishment (22).

Christian love is intensely practical: it follows the example of the Lord Jesus (2:21). See the practical outworking in 4:8,10; 5:5b.

1 Peter 1:25 – 2:3   Grow up into salvation

The thought of 1:25 is carried over into the first verses of chapter 2. The Eternal Word is the word that makes us grow.

1. Affirmation of truth. Before Peter begins to exhort his readers (2:1), he reminds them of the gospel (1:25) which had been preached to them (1:3-5), its Old Testament connections (1:10-11), its eternal authority (1:24-25) and the historical facts concerning Jesus (1:21). Christians are not building on 'sinking sand'!

2. Assurance offered. Peter's use of 'therefore' at 2:1 makes clear that action is to be taken on the basis of this gospel and that the result is assured. Because of the nature of this gospel of the grace and power of God this is a reasonable course to take (echoing the thought of Romans 12:1). The sprinkled blood (1:2) is a reminder of the effectual cover of the blood of the Passover lamb.

3. Attitudes rejected. Paul frequently adopted a 'put off, put on' theme (Eph. 4:22-24; Col. 3:5-10; and the same pattern is followed in Gal. 5:16-25). New birth will issue in a new way of life which will be in opposition to our former natural inclinations. 'Deceit, hypocrisy, envy and slander' are all fruits of self-centred living resulting from the corruption of the human heart as a result of turning away from God. 'I'll do it my way' has become the call sign of the age and is the pathway to destruction.

Jesus is the perfect example of the better way (2:21-23). We can follow him only because

of his atoning blood and the power of his risen life.

4. Appetite cultivated. As believers we have received a new nature which is to be built up. This can be done through seeking strength and direction from the Word of God. It is accomplished, not by casual interest, but by earnest application – 'craving' is the word used. Psalm 119 describes this – see vv. 147-148 and vv. 30-37 as examples.

5. Aim in view. The NIV speaks of 'growing up in salvation'. Once again we find Peter and Paul at one (Phil. 3:7-14), as we should expect in Christ's apostles. Simply, this means dependence upon Christ and increasing Christlikeness. To the believer he is 'the way, the truth and the life' (John 14:6).

There is an intensity of response here, lacking in many Christians and churches today. The self-centred approach of the godless world has become the pattern for many professing Christians, accompanied by the desire for a comfortable time. Faithful believing is looked upon as narrow minded fanaticism. Is it really remarkable that the church in the United Kingdom is making little impact as Christians are more interested in enjoying themselves rather than enjoying Christ?

Does being a Christian really affect your way of life? If you were put on trial for being a Christian, would there be evidence enough to convict you?

Is the Christian faith your steering wheel or a spare wheel kept for emergency?

1 Peter 2:4-10   A spiritual house raised on a living stone

Salvation (1:5,10) had been one of the great topics of the Old Testament – realised first for the Jews in the deliverance from Egypt, and repeated throughout their history by deliverance from various enemies. There was also promise of a future salvation of which the others were but a pale shadow (Isa.45:21-23; 49:6).

In this epistle of Peter salvation becomes personal in the Lord Jesus Christ.

1. Salvation revealed in the Word of God. This had become very evident in 1:10 and now it is demonstrated by quotations from the Old Testament (6,7,8,10).

The first three liken the Saviour to a 'stone', a 'living stone', just as the Lord was referred to as 'the Rock' in the Old Testament (Deut.32:3-4; Ps.62:2). The fourth is taken from the prophecy of Hosea, speaking of the restoration of an alienated Israel. See Isa.28:16.

2. Salvation realised in a person. In vv.4-7 this person is 'precious', because of who he is (1:3-5) as well as because of the gift of salvation he brings. For these early Christians the reference to 'a living stone' would probably stir thoughts of the stone removed from the tomb!

Many thoughts are stirred by the quotations concerning the stone: it was 'precious'; the building would be incomplete and insecure without it; it was successful in that it became 'head of the corner' and caused enemies to stumble; it was unique as 'a living stone' giving life to those who built their lives upon it.

All this was foretold centuries before it happened and those who prophesied it were mystified by it (1:10-12). Remember that the Jews generally could not conceive of a suffering Messiah and Peter had been appalled by the idea of it (Matt.16:22).

3. Salvation rejected by the rulers. His person and the salvation he brought were rejected by the rulers. In spite of the evidence of the miracles and the wonderful teaching he brought, the rulers of the Jews rejected him and harried him to death, preferring their traditions and human effort to the free gift he brought for those who would believe.

The Scriptures had consistently emphasised that this way was doomed to failure (Isa.8:20; Hab.2:3-5).

4. Salvation for a people. The people of God are of an entirely different order.

(a) They come to Christ as 'the living stone'. Men reject them as they have rejected him, but they are chosen of God and precious to him. There is a careful balance between the choice of God and the faith of men in v.4. Both are a necessary part of a unified whole but 1:2 has indicated that man is very much the junior partner.

(b) In him, they are being built into a 'spiritual house' and a 'holy priesthood'. They are the reality of which the Old Testament tabernacle and temple and the priesthood were a pale reflection (Heb.9 and 10). They were able to offer acceptable sacrifices, which the Jew could never aspire to in the old dispensation outside the ritual. Their faith in Jesus Christ made all the difference.

(c) They are to live to his praise.

Is he precious to you? Do you live to glorify him?

1 Peter 2:11-12   Conduct yourselves honourably

In a couple of verses, Peter summarises what it means to be the people of God and a royal priesthood in very practical down-to-earth terms.

1. A relationship to recognise (11a). Peter uses just one word to address these believers – 'beloved' – speaking of their relationship to God in Christ, as expressed in 2:9, and then of their relationship to one another.

John 17, 1 John 3:16-24, Galatians 4:8-19 and 1 Corinthians 4:17-21 explain this: the last two show us how to cope when believers go astray: we should not be quick to write them off!

2. A reaction to express (11b). There is a telling modern comment on this: 'In our fallen world whether Rome in Peter's day or New York or London in ours – the corruption of bodily desires for food, drink and sex sweeps over us like a flooding sewer. The apostle calls the Christian to be "out of it", out of the compulsive urgings of hammering sexual music, the seduction of pandering commercials, the sadism of pornographic films and paperbacks. In fleshly temptation the devil promises life but his assault is against life.' The writer, Edmund Clowney, might have added the more innocent-sounding quest for amusement and self-fulfilment among the dangers of this present age.

The main problem is inward – the fallen nature and the remnants of indwelling sin in the believer create a desire for such things (Gal. 5:17-21; Rom. 7:14-24).

What Peter deals with in a few words is a very large problem. Love cannot pretend that it is not there.

3. A responsibility to accept (12). The apostle's answer is not to withdraw from the world, but to live positively in it.

There is the recognition that we live in a 'pagan' world in which the majority are in bondage to false desires and world-views. Peter's answer is not so much in the world of argument as in positive living (12a).

The believer may be misunderstood because unbelievers do not understand his motives, but they are to be impressed by the good things he does. That was the teaching and example of Jesus (Matt. 5:13-16; Acts 10:38).

The power of evil is to be recognised and overcome in the power of the risen Christ (Rom. 12:21).

'Having your conduct honourable' (12) means living lives of positive integrity and goodness. Paul reflects the same truth (Phil. 4:8).

The unbelievers' 'glorifying God on the day of visitation' is a problem to interpreters. Some suggest that 'visitation' can be used in a good sense of bringing mercy and that for some, seeing the good works of believers, will lead to their conversion, by which they will glorify God. Others argue that 'visitation' generally speaks of judgement and that, on that day, those who reject the witness will be compelled to acknowledge the faithful witness of God's true servants. On either interpretation, God is ultimately glorified by the faithful living of his people.

We must take seriously the dangers posed by life in this age (1 John 5:19) and the duty of the Christian to live positively for the glory of God.

1 Peter 2:13-19   Submission to authority

It is made very clear, that even with an unsympathetic government, the Christian is not a troublesome revolutionary, though his allegiance to the rule of God may on occasion create tension, as Peter's experience showed (Acts 5:29).

(a) *As citizens.* The Christian is to be a good and obedient citizen, keeping the law where this does not conflict with the law of God. The state authorities are to be regarded as 'ordained of God' – their purpose is to do good and punish evil. This authority is seen as part of the providential governance of God.

(b) *As slaves.* The Christian slave is to be faithful even to the harsh master, although he suffers unjustly. Christians were not directed to revolt against the institution of slavery, but it is significant that Christian influence eventually led to the downfall of the institution. It should be observed that the overthrow of the institution in Peter's day would have led to widespread social collapse and that many masters were reasonably just in their treatment of their slaves.

'Submission' and 'respect' are key ideas in our relationship with both (compare Romans 13:1-7).

Verses 15-16 give clear practical reasons for this pattern of behaviour:

(a) There were always those who made false accusations – like some who used the Christian celebration of the Lord's Supper to accuse Christians of cannibalism.

(b) Because they refused to worship Caesar as a divine being there were those who were perverting the truth of Christian freedom into lawlessness. Christians are free from bondage to law and sin but they do not use their freedom as a cover for sin (Galatians 5:13).

The application of apostolic teaching to modern life is complex.

1. Peter was able to assume Christian unity. 1 John 4:15-18 lays down a good general principle. It is easy to be critical of believers who do not see things just as we do. What instruction do we have in the New Testament which deals with relationships among believers? Matthew 18:15-17; 20:25-28; 1 Corinthians 15:3-4; 1 John 4:7-11; 2 John 10.

2. Non-conformity to the world may be aggressively expressed and give unnecessary offence. God is a God of order. Government is God-given. The teaching of Jesus in the Sermon on the Mount is most helpful – Matthew 5:1-16. See also Romans 12:14-19,21; 13:1-10; Philippians 2:14-16; Titus 3:1; Hebrews 12:1; 1 Peter 2:12; 1 John 2:15-17. True wisdom in outlined in James 3:13-18.

Christians are not revolutionaries but should so far as possible seek to be good citizens. Through the ages, the question has been raised about the Christian's attitude to an unjust government. Some have pointed to the later pattern of submission for slaves (20), and of Jesus (23), but others claim that there is a right to resist oppression. The possibility is then that civil war may be even more painful than unrighteous government.

3. 1 Timothy 6:3-16 is a good code for practical living in the world.

4. Living to the glory of God must be our supreme ambition.

5. We conform to society's law when this does not contradict the revealed law of God.

1 Peter 2:20-25   The Master's example

This is a vital passage that quotes the example of Jesus and indicates its far-reaching importance. Regarding his example, he restored the ear of one of the soldiers sent to arrest him (John 18:10-11; Luke 22:49-51). Consider the spiritual significance of this passage:

Suffering (20-23). The example for the Christian is that of the Lord Jesus himself who raised no noisy protest at his unjust suffering but committed the case to God. We live in an ungodly world where sin reigns for the moment, and the Christian must expect to be involved in its suffering, but God has a much better inheritance for the Christian (1:4-5). Psalm 73 is a good example of how the believer has an answer to the problem, which is also faced in the prophecy of Habakkuk.

As sons of Adam, we should expect to be involved in the consequences of Adam's sin (1 Cor. 15:22). We now 'groan as in the pains of childbirth' but 'we wait eagerly for the redemption of our bodies' (Rom. 8:22-23).

The death of Christ according to the Bible is much more than an example, but example it is.

Saviour (24). The real purpose of Jesus' sufferings is as 'sin-bearer'. The whole passage is strongly influenced by Isaiah 53, and it is from there that we must draw our doctrine of the meaning of Christ's death. He took upon himself the curse that was our due. The New Testament makes clear that Jesus was 'without sin' (2 Cor. 5:21).

The reference to the tree reflects Paul's use of the words in Galatians 3:13, taking up the idea that 'to be hanged on a tree' was to be accursed (Deut. 21:23). Faith in his death would produce the change of life from the dominion of sin to a life of righteousness. Jesus himself used the example of the brazen serpent (John 3:14-16) to show that faith in his death would produce the change.

Shepherd (25). The one who died is viewed as risen and watching over the believer. The shepherd essentially guides, protects and provides for his flock. Jesus had spoken of himself as 'the Good Shepherd' (John 10:11) and that his death was essential to his work. Jacob first spoke of God as shepherd (Gen. 48:15).

The application of the example of Christ's sufferings is not without difficulty – does it demand pacifism?

It is pointed out that the New Testament nowhere demands that converted soldiers leave the army. It is accepted that the government rightly 'bears the sword' to bring punishment of the wrongdoer, which is commonly taken to justify national resistance to powers of evil. A distinction is made between personal reaction and civic responsibility. What is very clear is that there is no place for personal vindictiveness (Rom. 12:17-21).

Our daily life continually reminds us of the devastating reality of sin. The perfect example of the Lord continually convinces us of how far short we come of the glory of God, but the sacrifice of the Lord Jesus declares that the penalty has been paid, and his shepherd care assures us of his unfailing compassion.

1 Peter 3:1-7   Submission in the home

Peter continues to apply his teaching on submission after the pattern of the Lord Jesus. 'Likewise' refers back to the general principle in 2:13.

1. The circumstances in which Peter spoke. More space is devoted to the instruction of the wife because Peter was speaking to a church that would be predominantly Gentile and where the Jews involved would be legalistic rather than spiritual in their approach. The wife's position would call for more adjustment.

This was important because Christianity brought a new perspective on marriage, particularly in the Roman context where women generally followed the religion of their husbands. This would create special difficulty where the newly converted wife had an unconverted husband. There were two particular problems:

(a) The wife's profession of faith would look like an act of rebellion.

(b) The wife's zeal to see her husband converted might lead to 'nagging' and resentment.

Christian submission meant putting biblical teaching ahead of personal inclinations. The 'headship' of the husband was to be accepted respectfully.

2. The calling of the wife (1-6). Peter is dealing particularly where wives had unbelieving husbands (1). He is not saying that husbands could be converted without hearing the word of the gospel, but is pointing out that the witness of a godly life was a priority.

'Chaste conduct accompanied by fear' (2) – most translations suggest that this refers to purity and respect in relation to their

husbands, alleviating any suspicion, but some suggest that the fear is towards God.

The real attraction should not be that of outward adornment but of 'a gentle and quiet spirit' (3).

The example of 'former times' (5-6) is important although those women did not always observe it perfectly. Sarah could be wilful, but generally she was in submission to Abraham, particularly in surrendering Isaac to the Lord, although she is not mentioned in Genesis 22. She was submissive not slavish.

3. The character of the husband (7). The 'submission' of the husband is no less real but different in nature. He is the leader but he and his wife together are the heirs of life – they are a partnership (Gen. 2:23-24). Disunity will hinder their prayer life. The horizontal relationship will affect the vertical. His behaviour should always be considerate. The woman is usually less physically powerful, and particularly in child-bearing, would require protection. The wife's 'weakness' does not imply inferiority.

Practical godliness often opens the door for spiritual witness.

Peter is not saying that women should be unconcerned about outward appearance but that it is not the major priority.

The emphasis on a harmonious spiritual relationship in marriage must condition modern thinking. Unity in Christ is more important than individual rights or material wealth.

There must be a restored emphasis on 'being heirs together' and mutually encouraging prayer life: both husband and wife should be seeking to encourage one another spiritually.

1 Peter 3:8-12   The humble mind

Peter continues to apply his teaching on submission after the pattern of the Lord Jesus.

In v.4 Peter had spoken of the 'incorruptible beauty' of the Christian wife: here he is speaking more broadly of the beauty to be seen in a fellowship of Christians. In a way he is still dealing with 'submission' – the submission of Christians to one another and to the authority of the Word of God.

1. The tender sympathy of the Christian believer (8-9a). Jesus prayed that unity should mark his church (John 17). Peter here exhorts believers 'to be of one mind'. To attain that, it would be necessary for all Christians to show compassion and love towards one another, remembering that all by nature are fallen men. This should be a particular feature of relationships between Christians (Eph. 4:32 – 5:2). Compassion and humility are essential elements of Christian behaviour perfectly expressed in the life of Jesus (Matt. 9:36; 11:29).

Verse 9 seems to spread the net more widely to include others outside the Christian fellowship. Revenge should play no role in Christian behaviour (Rom. 12:17-21).

Christians should be distinguished by forgiving restraint.

These are features of the one who has been truly 'born again' by the Word (1:23). We become 'sons' (Phil. 2:15) by trusting in the Son (2:24; 3:18).

2. The patient search of the Christian believer (9b-12). An authoritative guide for Christian behaviour is found in Psalm 34.

What we say is a vital aspect of the Book of Proverbs and demonstrates our true character.

Gentle truthful speech, caring behaviour, and seeking peace, are marks of godliness. These virtues were perfectly expressed in the life of Jesus, and are evidence of the new birth and being a child of God.

3. The final source of authority for the Christian believer (10-12). The Old Testament which was the source for the truths of revelation is also the court of appeal for godly behaviour. Its value is expressed for life here and now. Living by God's Word will confer life and good days, and will result in answered prayer, because this is the proper lifestyle for the child of God.

The final word (12) has an immediate and a future aspect. The eye of the Lord includes protection as well as approval. Peter's view of 'calling' (9), is to 'a living hope' (1:3), and a future inheritance.

The unity prayed for by Jesus in John 17 is achieved by practical obedience to vv. 10-12. There is no place for self-will or self-esteem in the Christian life.

In this so-called enlightened modern world, the Scriptures of Old and New Testament remain the standard for Christian behaviour. How easily the church has strayed from the path of Christian unity by trying to establish it by wrong methods! It is not to be found by watering down apostolic truth but by nurturing Christian sympathy with humility and patience. There has been a marked failure to express the compassion of Christ. Most of us judge more readily than we forgive.

1 Peter 3:13-17 Facing reality

1. A realistic assessment (13-14a). Peter has quoted from Psalm 34, showing the blessings of a sincere walk before God. In normal circumstances one might expect a quiet life in the community, but Peter does see the possibility of suffering. The impact of sin on individuals and the community is drastic (1 John 5:19). Jesus faced rejection even though he went about 'doing good' (John 3:19; 5:40). He taught that persecution was likely to happen (Matt. 5:11-12). Paul spoke of blessing through suffering (2 Cor. 1:4-5; 4:7-12).

2. A blessed assurance (14-16). 'Even if you do suffer, you are blessed' – that is God's promise. 'Do not fear' is a quotation from Isaiah 8:13-14 where God made a promise to Judah in the face of the alliance of the northern kingdom of Israel against Judah during the reign of the evil King Ahaz. The promise was made to a generally unbelieving people and expressed the unfailing divine compassion. Believers have nothing to fear when they rest on such promises.

On their side, the only requirement is to 'sanctify Jesus as Lord' which means honouring him and his word, obeying his commands and trusting his promises, which is not unreasonable in the light of his resurrection. In the face of Satan, the power of evil and death itself, he has triumphed. Peter has already spoken of the Christian hope (1:3).

3. The perfect answer (15b-18). Persecution is not a disaster but should be seen as an opportunity for witness. This was the answer of Peter who at one time had failed so badly. It required more than human strength.

(a) It is expected that if we are truly 'sanctifying Christ in the heart' we shall be ready to give an answer because our fear of men has been laid to rest. It is recorded of one Romanian believer in the Ceausescu regime that when threatened with a beating by the Chief of Police, his answer was 'You cannot lay upon me one stroke more than my Master permits.' The official dismissed him with a warning!

(b) The answer is based on reason from the fact of the resurrection. The Christian faith based on miraculous acts of God transcends human reason but is not contrary to it.

(c) Christians are to answer with 'meekness and fear'. The NIV suggests 'gentleness and respect'. 'Meekness' is a quality of Jesus (Matt. 11:29), meaning not pushy or self-assertive, and should mark disciples (Matt. 5:5). The 'fear' may refer to God and proper respect for authorities ordained by him.

(d) Bold words cannot honour God unless supported by a consistently godly life. The clear conscience is one enlightened by the Holy Spirit and seeking to honour God. God's approval is what really matters. The example of Jesus should be the believer's pattern.

(e) Christ's experience demonstrates the triumph of hope in the face of suffering (Heb. 12:2).

Heed Paul's warning in Acts 14:22 – 'We must through many tribulations enter the kingdom of God.'

In this present fallen world we may well be called to bear the pains of childbirth. Jesus called disciples to 'take up their cross' (Matt. 10:38).

1 Peter 3:18   Christ's suffering

This verse shows the link between earthly life and the spiritual realm. The earthly life is inevitably doomed because of sin, but because of Jesus there is something better (1:3-4). If we accept the interpretation of the following verses that Christ preached through Noah, it is clear that the message of salvation through faith in grace alone was always God's message to fallen man. How he accomplishes it is progressively revealed in Scripture.

The purpose of it. The expression 'for sin' may well be understood as 'a sin offering' pointing to his death as the fulfilment of the Old Testament 'sin offering'. The animal was offered as a 'sin-bearer' taking upon it the penalty due for sin to bring reconciliation to God for the believer who offered the sacrifice. Jesus was the reality to which the Old Testament sacrifices pointed. They had to be offered continually: his sacrifice was 'once for all' (Heb. 10:10-14); they were spotless, but only animals: he was a sinless man, God become man, to offer the one perfect sacrifice (Heb. 9:13-14).

Substitution and propitiation (to turn aside wrath) are New Testament truths (2 Cor. 5:21; Gal. 3:13; 1 John 2:2; 4:10).

Faith in the Lord Jesus results in peace with God (Rom. 5:1).

The people redeemed. They were 'unrighteous'. Once these were 'in darkness' and 'no people' (2:10). By nature, they were sinners, lost and alienated from God – 'dead in trespasses and sins without hope' (Eph. 2:1,14), but by grace they are reconciled and born again!

The proof of their hope. Their Redeemer, God incarnate, was 'put to death in the body' – a real man, he suffered the divine judgement on sinful men. He was raised in the spiritual realm – the resurrection was evidence of the 'incorruptible inheritance' (1:3-4). There is debate about the phrase 'in' or 'by the Spirit': does this refer to the Holy Spirit, to his spirit or 'in the spiritual realm'? In the context the last alternative is most probable.

The power involved. There is a power involved here which transcends sin and death. Christ by his suffering and death brought these sinners to God. The sovereign God revealed as Father, Son and Holy Spirit (1:2) accomplished his purpose of grace by his sovereign power through the sacrificial death of his Son.

The promise realised. There is a great promise realised in the phrase 'bring us to God'. After Adam and Eve had sinned God had made a promise that the seed of woman would bruise the serpent's head (Gen. 3:15). Although Adam and Eve were driven from the garden and became subject to death, God did not abandon them. Through the death and resurrection of Jesus, the reconciliation was achieved (2 Cor. 5:19-21).

Eternal life is something to enjoy now by faith through the perfect sacrifice of the Lord Jesus. How wonderful is the planning, patience, power and love of our glorious infinite God! We should be happy to obey his will (4:1-2).

At the beginning of the letter Peter speaks of 'joy inexpressible and full of glory'. Is that your response?

1 Peter 3:18-22   Triumphant through suffering

Luther commented that this was 'a more obscure passage perhaps than any other in the New Testament', and so we must handle it carefully, seeking to deal with it in context.

Peter has been calling for positive Christian living in terms of submission, and so the following passage is best understood as an encouragement to a positive view of Christian suffering in terms of identification with Christ and opportunity to witness.

1.   The sufferings of Christ (18). Following the statement of v.17 about suffering for righteousness sake, Peter again quotes Christ's example (as in 2:21), but there is more here. 'Made alive by the Spirit' has been variously understood. Since there were no capital letters in the Greek it may be read as a reference to Christ's human spirit raised from the dead – 'made alive in the sphere of the spirit' – but it is equally possible to see the work of the Holy Spirit in the resurrection, as in Romans 1:3-4. The NKJV makes both references (18-19) apply to the Holy Spirit.

2.   The steadfastness of Noah (19-20). The best understanding, helped by the reference to the Spirit of Christ in 1:11, seems to be that Christ, by the Spirit, preached through Noah. Noah's patience was God's work in him. 'The spirits in prison' refers to the unbelievers of Noah's day in bondage to sin. His steadfast patience and faith as he built the ark and waited patiently in it for the end of the Flood was God's work in him. 2 Peter 2:5 speaks of him as 'a preacher of righteousness': as he built he declared the reason for his faith (15). He must have endured much mockery as he built the ark. No one listened, and only his family with him in the ark were saved (eight persons). Here is an example to follow!

3.   The salvation of God (21-22). The Flood has its antitype in baptism. It is a symbol – not about the removal of dirt from the body, but about identification with Christ in his death and resurrection. 'The answer of a good conscience' would best be understood as 'the appeal to God for a pure conscience': as Noah by faith trusted the ark as God's provision for his security, so the Christian trusts Christ to bear him through the judgement. Or, it may suggest a pledge to keep a pure conscience in future – an obedient walk (Col.2:6).

Understood in this way the passage is an encouragement to the Christian in the face of suffering – having the example of Jesus himself, and Noah, in steadfast endurance of suffering, and the assurance of Christ's triumph in the resurrection. We are identified with him who removed the burden of sin by suffering for it (18), and rose triumphantly to give evidence of his victory.

The Christian has strong reason to persevere in the face of adversity, and encouragement to persevere in the face of evidence that only a few seem to be saved.

At times the Christian church has prospered, but there have also been times when it has seemed in danger of extinction.

Remember that the Christian church started from small beginnings and the New Testament shows how it faced many adversities. But it will always triumph in Christ.

1 Peter 4:1-6   What do you want out of life? [1]

The argument relates back to 3:16-18 and 2:24. Because of the sufferings of Christ, sufferings inevitably accompany the Christian life (Matt. 5:11). Jesus had spoken of the necessity of taking up the cross (Matt. 16:24). Baptism (3:21) symbolised identification with Christ.

1. The choice to be made (1-4). He expects Christians to prepare themselves for suffering. 'Arm' is a strong word. Paul spoke of the need to put on the Christian armour (1 Thess. 5:8; Eph. 6:10-18; Rom. 13:12). The Christian life requires resolution!

Having the 'same thought' means having the same approach as Jesus himself, being convinced that it is better to suffer for doing right than for doing wrong.

Having 'ceased from sin' means not being without sin, but having resolved to make a clean break with it, as is explained in v. 2. The believer's object in life is no longer to satisfy selfish human desires but to do the will of God.

The decision to obey God and follow the Lord Jesus means rejecting sin even when that may involve physical suffering. The believer does not seek martyrdom, but consistent Christian living may involve it.

The past unregenerate life with its main object of self-indulgence is rejected (3).

The man of the world will think the Christian attitude strange and will speak evil of it (4).

2. The condemnation to be faced (5-6). There will be an inevitable day of accounting for both the living and the dead (5). Believers are included but covered by the blood of Jesus. For the Christian there will be a time of reward (Matt. 5:12; 10:40-42).

For this reason the gospel was preached to Christians who have died (6). The world might pass a contrary judgement upon them, but they may have full assurance in Christ. (This addresses the same fear as that expressed in 1 Thessalonians 4:13-18.)

3. The comfort to be found (6). The experience of past believers is a present guide. At present men pass judgement upon believers. They may be falsely accused, persecuted by all, and condemned by governments, but as they persevere in their obedience to God they can be confident that they will be vindicated by him in the final judgement.

Peter does not offer any immediate alleviation of their lot, but encourages them to persevere in their commitment to God confident of their vindication in the final judgement. This verdict fits with the situation in 1:5-6 – there may be many trials now, but there is a glorious inheritance ahead.

This truth is a comfort to those who have loved ones who have died, and an exhortation to those still alive to live in the strength the Spirit gives.

The wisdom of human spirituality is authenticated by Scripture. Make the Bible your final authority: depend on what God says in his Word, not what man thinks.

1 Peter 4:7-11　What do you want out of life? [2]

1. The coming of Christ (7). The stage is set for the final act. The return of Christ and the last judgement are always seen as imminent. This will be the final event in the history of the world as we know it and is referred to very frequently in the New Testament on the authority of Jesus himself (Matt. 24:27-31; Mark 13:26-27; Luke 21:25-28).

2. The consequence for the believer (7b). Faith in Christ changes everything. Peter has already reminded these Christians, who are 'strangers scattered' in the eyes of the world, that they are 'a royal priesthood and a holy nation'. Most Jews had lost sight of that truth (Deut. 14:2; 23:14; 26:16-19). Paul spoke of the Christian as 'a new creation' (2 Cor. 5:17). Having Jesus as Lord changes everything!

Therefore the believer is to live according to God's will, as Jesus did (John 5:30; 8:28-29; Matt. 3:17; 17:5).

'Serious and watchful' means having a proper slant on all things – personal ambitions, pleasures and happenings in the world understood in the perspective of God's salvation and eternity – so that prayer may be effective.

The real point of living is the privilege of personal access to God in prayer as to a Father (Matt. 6:9). Prayer is a most effective weapon in the Christian's armoury.

3. The commitment required (8-11). The importance of 'love for one another' is again mentioned (8; 1:22).

Proverbs 10:12 is quoted. This is not about atonement before God, but points out that Christians should not give or easily take offence. Such love preserves unity by forgiveness.

'Hospitality' (9) includes the idea of helpfulness in every way.

In the use of spiritual gifts (10) the object is not selfish but to serve one another. The gifts are 'manifold' – of various kinds to meet every sort of need.

The speaking (11) is not confined to preaching, but the reference to the 'oracles of God' probably refers to the Scriptures and that all our speaking should be in accordance with them. The desire of the believer should be to glorify God through Jesus Christ.

To think about:

The life of the Christian is to be loving, earnest and committed. Live as God would have you live. Jesus' life on earth was the perfect pattern.

We should think through the biblical implications of Christian suffering. Do we really want to be made holy and to glorify Christ?

Do not lose sight of the day of accounting. The Christian life involves a clean break with the past, devotion to Christ who has shed his blood for us, and reverential fear of God who is the Judge of all.

Does love mark our attitude in our Christian service, in the fellowship of the church, and especially when we have differences as Christians, in readiness to forgive?

How precious is your prayer life? Is it pleasing to God?

1 Peter 4:12-19   Suffering as a Christian

Peter here completes his extensive covering of the subject of Christian suffering.

1. Realise the need for testing (12-13). Peter speaks of a 'fiery ordeal', probably with a particularly fierce persecution in view, but he knows well enough from the teaching of Jesus that 'taking up the cross' is an integral part of the Christian life and means more than giving intellectual assent to the fact of Jesus' death or wearing a symbol of it. Peter's personal experience and that of the early church in the Book of Acts bear witness to the reality of suffering for Christ. The letter suggests that those who received it were already having a hard time.

To be a Christian will inevitably bring conflict with the forces of evil, both human and spiritual, and misunderstanding by those who claim to be neutral.

This is an inevitable test of genuineness. The Christian is often referred to in Scripture as a soldier, and for soldiers conflict is inevitable. Jesus has left an example. Believers should rejoice to be identified with Christ in this way. Suffering is an anticipation of the glory to come. Christian baptism symbolised death and resurrection, suffering and glory to follow. The Christian 'hope' involves this (1:6). Peter has a sense of the reality of suffering now, and a lively anticipation of the coming glory.

Suffering does not in itself bring gladness, but there is joy in demonstrating how greatly one loves him and in the assurance of the glory to come.

2. Rejoice in God's sufficiency (14-16). The Spirit who sustained Jesus rests upon believers to enable them to endure the persecution and witness a good confession that glorifies the Saviour. Peter himself had experienced this (Acts 4:29) and there was the example of Stephen in Acts 6:15.

The glory of Christ is more than a future hope: it is a present possession by the Spirit's help even in the midst of adversity.

This will happen only where there is a way of life pleasing to God (15).

Do not be ashamed of suffering for Christ – but be sure that it is for him!

3. Recognise the fact of judgement (17-19). Peter here is reflecting Ezekiel 9, where judgement began at the sanctuary, and Malachi 3:1-3.

If things seem so bad for believers that hardly any will escape, think of what will happen to those who know nothing of God's forgiveness!

In view of this coming judgement, those who suffer according to God's will, not because of their wrongdoing, should entrust their lives to their faithful Creator and continue to do what is good in the sight of God.

It is wrong to suggest that being a Christian means having an easy time in this life. See the teaching of Jesus in Matthew 10:34-39.

Polycarp at the stake prayed to be received by the Lord as a rich and acceptable sacrifice. That is what the Spirit will do in devoted hearts. How deep is our commitment?

Our suffering for Christ becomes a pledge to us of the reality of our belonging to Christ, producing joy and strengthening hope.

1 Peter 5:1-4   Duties of elders

1. The suitability of the teacher. Having encouraged the people of God to live God-glorifying lives, Peter gives directions to the leaders, because in the past the leaders had done much to lead the people astray (see Ezekiel 34). Peter writes as a fellow elder, not glorifying his rank as an apostle, but as a witness of the sufferings of Christ. He has made clear that the sufferings of Jesus as Redeemer were at the heart of his ministry as 'the Anointed' (Messiah). At the same time, he is assured that he will be 'a partaker of the glory that will follow'. He had been admirably trained as a fellow elder, having learned from experience. Prior to the transfiguration, he had been corrected and humbled (Matt. 16:21-27); later he had denied his Lord (Mark 14:72); and after the resurrection his heart and motives were searched (John 21:15-18). He had learned humility the hard way, and from his experience he was fitted to prescribe the pattern of elders' behaviour. He called them to be willing, enthusiastic and humble, as examples to the flock, rejecting any thought of material or personal gain. Both Jesus and Paul also gave solemn warnings against covetousness (Luke 12:15; 1 Tim. 6:6-10).

2. The superiority of the Saviour. Jesus is called 'the Chief Shepherd' (4), impressing Peter's readers with the example of humility but at the same time exalting the Saviour as the one who had accomplished all that so many past leaders of Israel had failed to do.

3. The service to be offered. 'Eldership' was an office the church had derived from the Jewish system. It was for responsible mature men (compare the teaching of Paul in 1 Timothy 3:1-7 and Titus 1:5-9). This position of authority was also a position of humble service, in the appointment of God, and not to be coveted for selfish ends.

4. The satisfaction of the reward. At the same time there is the assurance of a rich reward – 'a crown of glory'. This is assured, not by our efforts or achievements but by grace, but at the same time it is spoken of as a reward, indicating that faithfulness and diligence in the Lord's service do not go unnoticed (Matt. 10:40-42; 19:27-28; 25:34-39).

For consideration:

The experience of Peter confirms the Christian proverb: 'No cross, no crown.'

Because those called as elders were also sinners by nature, their training must involve pain. There are no short cuts to conforming to the pattern of Christ.

God will humble before he exalts. A basic quality for Christian leadership is humility.

We see the care of God in training his men, using even their failures. Such a God inspires our confidence.

The perfect pattern is not Peter, but Jesus himself. We do not follow men but Christ. If we imitate men it is because they have first learned to imitate Christ (1 Thess. 1:5-6).

Never lose sight of 'the glory that will follow', because the path down here on earth will be tough. But the final reward will be abundant.

1 Peter 5:5-14   How the flock is kept

Peter concludes his letter with instructions and assurance for the Christians who he has compared to a building (2:4), a priesthood (2:5), as pilgrims (2:11) and as a flock (2), as already implied in 2:25.

Directions to the flock (5-9). Elders (5) probably refers to the older men rather than the official 'elders'. The mention of 'submission' to them probably indicates their responsibilities as fathers or heads of families. Younger people are addressed since they were probably inclined to be self-assertive, but all are encouraged to be humble and submissive, as in chapters 2 and 3, on the authority of Proverbs 3:34.

Above all, there should be humility towards God (6-7), expressed in trusting his rule, reflecting Psalms 37:5, 55:22 and Philippians 4:6-7. God's care transcends our anxieties. The prospect of future exaltation is balanced with the assurance of his present care.

The exhortation to level-headedness and watchfulness (8) in the light of the subtlety of Satan's attacks (compare 4:7), is typical of the New Testament letters (1 Thess. 5:5-8; Eph. 6:11) as he is often seen working through false teachers (2 Cor. 11:14-15). The imagery of the lion is borrowed from the psalmist's frequent comparison of his adversaries to ravaging lions.

The believer is called to steadfast resistance (9), knowing that Christians everywhere are subject to such attacks.

Deliverance to expect (10). The God who had delivered Israel from Egypt and kept them on the wilderness way is well able to keep his people now. He is the abiding source of grace who will strengthen, settle and make them complete. Though they may have to face suffering in the present, he will bring them safely to his eternal glory. The great themes of the letter are repeated – grace, suffering and glory.

The final greeting (12-14) names Silvanus as co-operating in the writing of the letter and exhorts them to 'stand in grace'. From beginning to end the gospel is about grace that brings the peace of God.

The kiss was a common form of greeting in the Near East. Men kissed men and women kissed women.

Peter's special relationship with Mark is shown. It is believed that Mark wrote his Gospel on the basis of Peter's eyewitness testimony.

Something to think about:

There is a word in v. 5 to remind the older men that all have a responsibility both by word and example to give guidance on the Christian way. In this age where youth is so important, we need to be reminded of the importance of respect of age and the value of maturity and experience.

What particular lessons are to be learned from the various figures for the church?

Embrace God's grace in Christ; accept the inevitability of suffering; cultivate love and humility; resist every assault of evil; live in expectation of glory and rejoice in God's grace in Christ.

Readings in

2 Peter

by Ray Beeley

WINDOW
ON THE
WORD

THE SECOND LETTER OF PETER

This short letter was one of the latest to be included in the canon but was accepted as canonical by influential Early Fathers of the fourth century and recognised by the late fourth-century Councils of Hippo and Carthage. It claims to come from the hand of the apostle Peter, but this has been challenged on the grounds of its difference in style from 1 Peter and its close resemblance in chapter 2 to the Epistle of Jude. The first objection may be accounted for by Peter's employment of a different scribe, and the second by the fact that the two men had similar concerns. It is not clear which letter was written first. It has been suggested that both men used a common source. False teaching, especially involving sexual immorality, seems to have been a common problem in the early church, as is seen in 1 Corinthians and the early chapters of Revelation. Both the doctrine and the moral requirements of the letter accord with apostolic teaching and it may be received with confidence.

It is helpful, if we can, to determine the object the author had in view when first he wrote the letter. Sometimes it is clearly stated in the letter (as in Jude 3), but, more often, we have to try to determine it from the contents of the letter. For this reason it is helpful to read the complete letter, perhaps three or four times, and to note down some of the 'strategic statements' and any sequence of thought that we can find. In 2 Peter it is not difficult to discern a pattern as follows:–

Chapter 1 – the Christian's anchor. We are called and chosen (10) – God has revealed himself in Jesus Christ and this brings joy and peace. We have been given all that we need for a life of godliness. Most important to this is the Word of God. Our response is faith and diligence.

Chapter 2 – the Christian's adversary. In 1 Peter 5:8, the devil himself is the great adversary, but here it is false teachers within the church perverting the truth. They even deny the Lord who bought them (1). Not having come to faith in Christ alone for salvation they are presenting 'another gospel' (compare 2 Corinthians 11:4). They are covetous and deceitful (3), bold and arrogant (10), depraved (12, 19). Such people will be judged – 'paid back' (13). In particular, they are denying the doctrine of the Day of Judgement, the Second Coming of the Lord Jesus (3:3-4).

Chapter 3 – the Christian's assurance. There is an anticipation of this in 2:9. The hope of v. 2 is based on the words of the prophets, the Lord himself and the apostles. 'The Day of the Lord will come' (10). The Old Testament prophets had anticipated that this would be a day of judgement for the ungodly and a day of salvation for the righteous (compare 2 Thessalonians 1:7-10). The response of the believer is diligence (14) and growth (18).

The letter exalts the grace of God in salvation and encourages believers to be diligent in working it out. This is against a background of the mockery of unbelievers and the assurance of the righteous judgement of God on immoral professors. The most serious adversary is the enemy within!

2 Peter 1:1-2   Greetings

The greeting of the first two verses is important enough to merit a section all to itself.

Verse 1. Peter states his authority for writing – he is the servant and special messenger of Jesus Christ. Although we do not have apostles in the formal sense today, it is still true that all believers should be his servants (John 13:16) and apostles, in the more general sense of messengers sent by him into the world with the gospel (Matt. 28:16-20; Mark 16:20). It is important that we have this sense of a personal commission and responsibility.

The reference to 'our God and Saviour Jesus Christ' is significant. It is distinguished from 'of God and of Jesus our Lord' in v. 2. The latter distinguishes the two persons of the Trinity, but the most natural reading of the first indicates that Jesus is God. This seems to have been the conviction of the apostles from earliest times after the resurrection (consider Thomas' statement in John 20:28). The Trinity is an important tenet of the Christian faith and states that Jesus was God and a perfect man, appointed by God as the Christ, the one anointed by God to be Saviour and Lord of the people of God.

Peter addresses the Christians as those who have come to faith 'through the righteousness of our God and Saviour Jesus Christ'.

(a) The expression affirms the perfect life of the Lord Jesus Christ, his righteousness which, through faith, is put to our account before God.

(b) It also indicates the justifying righteousness of God, which comes to us through faith in the Lord Jesus (Rom. 3:21-22) and accepts us in him. There is no difference between Peter and Paul on this matter.

The 'faith' here, is personal trust in Jesus Christ, and is received as a gift of God (Eph. 2:8-9). In other contexts, as in Jude 3, it refers to the 'body of truth', as in Acts 6:7 and 1 Timothy 4:1.

It is significant that Peter does not 'pull rank' but indicates that their faith is as good as his. In him and in them there has been that saving work of the Holy Spirit bringing them to faith.

The word 'precious' indicates a key thought in Peter's thinking – precious blood (1 Peter 1:19), precious faith (here), precious promises (4) and the Lord himself (1 Peter 2:4,7), bearing witness to the uniqueness of gospel salvation. By trusting the Word we come to Christ, and by acknowledging his death on our behalf as a ransom sacrifice – 'by his blood' – we come to God (Exod. 12:13).

Verse 2. Believers have come into a personal 'knowledge' of God through the Lord Jesus Christ. Once they were ignorant and blind but now they have a personal relationship with God. Their knowledge is far from complete and it is expected that it will grow (3:18), but they have been reconciled and know God as their Father.

This brings 'grace' and 'peace'. They have come into the sphere of God's favour whereas once they were aliens (1 Peter 2:9-10). There is no human merit in this: it is all by the unmerited good pleasure of God. Once they were enemies, but now they are reconciled and know the peace of God (Rom. 5:1).

2 Peter 1:2-11 Called and chosen

Verse 2. Believers have come into a personal knowledge of God through the Lord Jesus Christ. They have come into the sphere of God's favour although once they were aliens (1 Peter 2:9-10). Kistemaker comments that 'knowledge' refers not only to facts but also to an experience of fellowship.

Verse 3. The power of God has brought this about. On the one hand, this excludes all human effort, while on the other, it guarantees its success. Believers are brought into the sphere of life and godliness, re-created in the image of God from which they had fallen away: they are restored to enjoy eternal life, what Henry Scougal described as 'the life of God in the soul of man'.

Verse 4. God's instrument in this gracious work is the exceedingly great and precious promises, the Word of God, that we may escape the corruption that is in the world as a consequence of turning away from God to self-fulfilment, that is, sin! Peter makes much of the importance of the Word of God in the Christian life.

Verses 5-8. Men turn to Christ, by the call of God, and enter into a process of development to demonstrate a godly character, which requires their cooperation and diligence. It is generally agreed that the word 'add' is drawn from the Greek theatre and is used of the patron who provided for the needs of the chorus, in generous cooperation with the poet and the state in putting on the plays. For us it means the diligent application to working out what God has worked in us (Phil. 2:12).

Virtue – 'excellence' – the word suggests 'the proper fulfilment of anything' – God will make us what he intends us to be.

Knowledge – knowledge of God leads to practical wisdom that is pleasing to him.

Self-control means aiming to please God rather than to fulfil self in every sphere of life.

Perseverance – which is not turned aside by adversity or opposition.

Godliness – the practical result of what God has done in us in v. 3, the renewal of the divine image.

Brotherly love – our relationship to our Christian brethren – the kinship of like natures.

Love – Like our God, who has 'so loved the world' (John 3:16), we are to give ourselves to a hostile humanity.

Verses 9-10. As these marks of a true believer begin to demonstrate themselves in us, they will increase our assurance. The word 'diligence' is used again, stressing our zeal and perseverance.

Verse 11. The object of it all is entrance into the 'everlasting kingdom of our Lord Jesus Christ' – the objective of the Christian lies beyond this present life. For the unbeliever there will be eternal judgement (ch. 2); for the believer, eternal life.

Let us focus the mind on:

Gift (3) – our new life is the gift of God.

Growth (5-9) – there is to be the development of our personal character in cooperation with the grace of God.

Goal (11) – the eternal kingdom.

The centre of it all is the Lord Jesus Christ. Have we received the gift? Are we diligent to grow in our faith? Are we focused upon the goal?

2 Peter 1:12-21   The Word of God

Verses 12-15. Peter knows that he will soon die, but he is imparting a truth to them that will abide forever. His object is to emphasise the abiding truth of the Word of God.

What he has told them regarding the gospel will bear repeating. We are reminded of the *confidence* we should have in the gospel and our *concern* for its proclamation. It is vital that it should be made the foundation of the believer's life.

Verses 16-18. Peter uses the transfiguration as the infallible evidence of the glory of Jesus' person as 'the Son of God', and the essential fact of his sufferings. It was a real historical event.

It confirmed Peter's confession that Jesus was the Son of God. From that time Jesus began to teach the disciples about his sufferings and death, always including in this the fact of the resurrection. For whenever the Lord Jesus spoke of his death, he always added that he would rise from the dead. Here is the 'essence of the gospel'.

Verses 19-22. Even more important than the apostolic experience is 'the more sure prophetic word'. Commentators have differed about how to understand v. 19. Does it mean that the apostolic experience confirms the prophetic word, or does it mean that the prophetic word is even more reliable than any apostolic experience? Both preach the same gospel but the Word is foundational. The subsequent verses indicate that Peter's prime emphasis is on the Word rather than his experience. Calvin comments that 'since the Jews were in no doubt that everything the prophets taught came from God, it is no wonder that Peter says that their word is more sure'.

This Word is a 'light shining in a dark place', echoing the thought of Psalm 119:105. It reveals the moral darkness of the world in which we live, and the sure guidance of God's revelation. As we read we should pray that the Word will do its work in us. The idea of light coming into a dark place is also used prophetically of the difference Jesus' coming into the world makes (Isa. 9:2). The Word of God is the light that points us to him who is the light of the world (John 8:12).

'The morning star rises in your hearts' has been read in the following ways:

(a) The phrase 'in your hearts' has been taken with 'knowing first' in v. 20.

(b) There is a growing anticipation of the Day of the Lord.

Verses 20-22. Peter emphasises the essential nature of biblical prophecy as the Word of God. No prophecy of Scripture originated in the prophet's own mind.

There are three important things to note in this passage:

(i) The apostolic testimony was based on facts: the gospel is about the facts of the coming of the Son of God in the flesh, his death on the cross for the redemption of sinners, and his physical resurrection from the dead.

(ii) The ultimate authority for the early church was the prophetic word (the Old Testament);

(iii) Their expectation was of the Lord's return in glory.

If the Word of God is truly 'a lamp to our feet and a guide to our path' it will point us to the person of the Lord Jesus Christ and a glad expectation of his return.

2 Peter 2:1-9   False teachers judged [1]

There are three main topics in this passage:

1. The *recognition* of the false teachers – they are exposed.

2. The *reality* of the divine judgement – rebels against the Lord will be called to account.

3. The *rescue* of the godly – there may be delay but it is sure.

Verses 1-3. As there were false prophets in the Old Testament, so there will be in the church. We are warned against them and we must be definite in rejecting them. The devil's main attack is upon the Christian – unbelievers are his already! He will use false teachers to pervert the truth (John 8:44). The apostles were more concerned with this as a danger than with persecution. Peter characterises these teachers as deceitful and destructive. They will claim to have been 'bought by the Lord', using the language of sound theology, to accomplish their deceit. But their judgement is sure. We need to be watchful and prayerful, rejecting the teaching, but seeking to correct and rescue the teacher.

Verses 4-8. Peter uses three examples of the divine judgement:

(a) There is virtually nothing said of *angels that sinned* (4) in the Old Testament, though some claim that Genesis 6:1-4 is a reference to it. More is said in the Apocrypha, but Revelation 12:7-9 is a clear reference to it. Peter and John, enlightened by the Holy Spirit, did not need the Apocrypha!

In vv. 5-8 the two human examples are both cited with reference to 'the godly who escaped' (9).

(b) The Bible does not tell us elsewhere that *Noah* was a preacher of righteousness, but it is plain that his lifestyle had a ministry. Obedience was a feature of his faith (Heb. 11:7). He doubtless answered curious enquirers about what he was doing.

(c) *Lot* in Genesis 18–19 is a pathetic figure escaping 'by the skin of his teeth'. Peter speaks of him as a righteous man who was tormented by the sins of Sodom. Both estimates of him are true! There are some important things to learn from him:

(i) A covetous spirit may draw the believer back into the world, demonstrating the impact of the remains of indwelling sin in the believer.

(ii) Lot was unhappy with the world in which he lived, but he was stained by it (see Genesis 19:7-9) – his compromise affected his moral standards and judgements.

(iii) He was righteous in that God rescued him from the judgement upon Sodom – he was a sinner justified by grace alone.

(iv) Considering the narrative in Genesis, we must appreciate the importance of the intercession of Abraham in this process – we too should be diligent in interceding for sinners.

Noah is an example of what a believer should be in a sinful world, and Lot an example of the lifestyle we should avoid.

Verse 9. The Lord knows how to deliver his people. Look up 1 Corinthians 10:13, and make a note of some Old Testament illustrations of it. Thank God that he rescued such a one as Lot. Be sure of grace, but do not presume upon it. This verse, in the context of what Genesis teaches us about Lot, exalts the patience of God.

2 Peter 2:10-22   False teachers judged [2]

Such is the importance of the subject, that there is a further passage on the subject of false teachers.

Verse 10. There will be sure judgement on those 'who walk according to the flesh' – they have never been born of the Spirit of God as demonstrated by repentance and faith.

Commentators have difficulty in determining the meaning of 'dignitaries' or 'glories'. It may mean angels. Some think it refers to demons. Yet others think it refers to the glorious attributes of God or Christ. The verse plainly indicates that the false teachers have no true concept of the exalted nature of spiritual things or of the seriousness of the spiritual warfare.

Verse 12. By their actions they betray their unregenerate nature, which will be judged.

Verse 13. They actually partake in the love-feasts of the church, behaving in a corrupt, deceitful and immoral way, leading unstable souls astray. It is expected that the Lord's people will behave in accordance with his holy character (Col. 3:3-10), but this speaks of unstable people in the churches who have not been regenerated.

Verse 15. The false teachers are likened to Balaam who was brought in to curse Israel (Num. 22 – 24) and eventually suggested immoral measures to lead them astray (Num. 31:16).

The expression (14) 'having eyes full of adultery' implies sexual immorality. Adultery may be understood spiritually (Hosea 2:4-5), but physical immorality is an expression of rebellion against the divine will (the seventh commandment). The heart of the problem is the problem of the heart – we have a sinful nature resistant to the truth of God.

Verse 17. Peter employs two figures of speech to show that the false teaching brings no lasting satisfaction, is unstable and uncertain and doomed to eternal darkness.

Verse 18. The false teachers, by the boasting of their empty conceits, lure back into error some who have started to escape from the pollution of the world. Pride is a mark of the sinful nature. Peter deals realistically with the fact that there are some who start out on the Christian path who remain vulnerable. He gives a solution to this danger in 1:5-7. The true believer gives diligence to fulfilling the purpose of the gracious calling of God.

Verse 19. The false teachers promise liberty but actually bring bondage to corrupt unregenerate nature.

Verses 20-22. Peter is not suggesting that Christians can fall away, but is pointing out that these false teachers, who once appeared to walk in the way of righteousness, have actually turned away from 'the holy commandment'. The New Testament makes clear that a true believer will not behave in this way. He may, on occasion, have a terrible struggle with temptation, but will cry to Christ for deliverance (Rom. 7:21-25).

Those who turn back to the pollution of the world merit the severity of the judgement they will incur. They show by their lives that they are strangers to the basic gospel call to repent, having failed to understand the moral imperatives of the holiness of God and the corruption of the human heart. While having some knowledge of the forms of Christianity, they are strangers to the Holy Spirit's work of regeneration in the human heart.

2 Peter 3   The return of Jesus Christ

The letter concludes with a new focus on the Second Coming as the final fulfilment of the promises of God and the occasion of the final judgement of the false prophets.

Verses 1-2. Peter is writing to believers to stimulate them to wholesome thinking based on the Old Testament prophets and the apostolic writings, which are ranked as of equal importance and of the same absolute authority.

Verses 3-4. He warns that there will be scoffers in the last days at the promise of the Lord's return.

Verses 5-6. These false prophets wilfully forget the power of the Word of God, which had been the agent in the creation of the world and in the judgement of the Flood. It is infinitely powerful and reliable.

Verse 7. This Word would again be fulfilled in the judgement of ungodly men. The former judgement was by water, the final judgement will be by fire. We must learn to live in expectancy that the Word of God will be fulfilled in the face of human contradiction.

Verses 8-9. The delay of the Coming must be understood in the light of God's different time-scale, and his patience in giving men time to repent. The use of 'us' here limits the 'any' to believers.

Verse 10. The 'day' will come suddenly and in awesome power.

Verses 11-13. The reaction of the believer to this should be holy and godly living.

Verse 12. There is a sense in which we may 'hasten the Coming' by persistent prayer, like that of Abraham for Lot, and godly lives as an effective witness to unbelievers.

Verse 13. We embrace the promise, looking forward to new heavens and earth.

Verses 14-15. Peter makes a renewed call to diligent and blameless living, glad of the delay in the Coming as giving an opportunity for salvation. This surely implies not only godly living, but evangelistic zeal.

Verses 15-16. The reference to Paul's teaching is important, as ranking his teaching with 'the other Scriptures' and reminding us that in his teaching there were things that were hard to understand and could be misconstrued. This is reflected in Romans 3:7-8 and the contention created by the Galatian controversy.

Verses 17-18. The letter concludes with a renewed warning lest the readers be led astray, and a positive exhortation to grow in the grace and knowledge of the Lord Jesus. Grace, godliness and growth are fundamental to the Christian life.

The whole chapter directs us to three important lessons:

(i) The Word of God is true – you can base your life upon it.

(ii) The work of God is faithful – the promises and warnings of his Word will be fulfilled, with a consummation at the Second Coming.

(iii) The will of God is merciful – he exercises it patiently for the salvation of all his people. Like Noah, we should trust and obey the Word of God, and wait patiently for its fulfilment. Repentance (3:9) is an important key – as we turn from human speculations to patient trust in the fulfilment of the promises of God.

Readings in

1 John

by Keith Weber

WINDOW
ON THE
WORD

THE FIRST LETTER OF JOHN

The writer. The epistle is anonymous. It is written in the first person singular to a specific group of people who knew the author well and whom he knew well – see, for example, 2:1,12-14,19,26. The reason for its anonymity is probably that the author was so well known to his readers that he had no need to identify himself.

The epistle's association with the apostle John goes back to a very early tradition emanating from Polycarp, the famous martyr, a contemporary and disciple of John. Also, the style and thought are similar to John's Gospel (compare v.1 with John 1:1, and 5:13 with John 20:31). Some have suggested that 1 John is a letter accompanying the Gospel to explain its purpose (see 1:1-4; 5:13).

The readers. The churches with which John was most closely associated were in Asia Minor (modern Turkey), the group to whom he addressed the Apocalypse (see Revelation 1:4,11), and particularly the church in Ephesus. Hence the epistle makes substantial reference to the heresy of Cerinthus, who was based in Ephesus.

The date. This letter was written considerably later than Paul's letters for, in referring to the enemies of the gospel, John does not distinguish between Jews and Greeks but simply speaks of 'the world'. This indicates it was written after AD 70 when Jerusalem was destroyed and the Jewish persecution of Christians ceased. But since there is no reference to Roman opposition, it was before AD 96, the possible date of Revelation. A date in the '80s is therefore indicated.

The purpose. This was to counter troubles from heretics (2:18-22; 4:1-6) and nominal Christians who professed much (1:6,8,10; 2:4,6,9) but still committed sin (3:4), hated the brethren (3:15) and did not believe the teaching about Christ (5:10). Possibly the heretics were the nominal Christians.

The heretics comprised some in the Greek world who were trying to combine the gospel with Greek and oriental ideas. This became known as Gnosticism because it claimed special 'knowledge' of God. They, of all Christians, were 'in the light'. We can see from 1:6 and 2:4,9 that John is proposing tests for this claim. The three tests are righteousness, love and belief. He goes through these three times. The first series is in chapters 1 and 2. These tests are valuable to us: *(i)* to apply to people or movements that make claims to special experience (4:1); *(ii)* to apply to ourselves to see if we are truly Christian. If we 'pass', it will give us assurance (5:13). If not, we know what to ask God for.

1 John 1:1-4   The apostle commences his evidence

Introduction. John's style of writing is strikingly unusual. The relative simplicity of his language belies the complexity of both the structure and the substance of the letter. It is difficult to break it down into separate sections because it contains several overlapping and recursive themes. Even a cursory reading will reveal that the letter abounds in sharp contrasts and comparisons, which for the most part are encapsulated in terse statements – short, sharp and punchy, the combined effect of which is intended to demolish all opposition to the truth. The intention is that, by the end, when he simply says, 'Little children, keep yourselves from idols,' we should know exactly what he is talking about.

So what was John's purpose in writing, and why write in this way? The elderly apostle had lived long enough to see various heresies beginning to afflict the church. Though the particular brands of false teaching then in circulation may receive mention as we proceed, it is important to recognise that his method of combating these was to remind his readers of the fundamentals, not in this case by closely reasoned arguments so much as by means of the clear testimony of reliable witnesses.

The weight of the testimony (1-2). Note the fourfold witness given in this verse – 'heard', 'seen', 'looked upon', 'handled'; observe also the 'we': this is not the doubtful testimony of *one* person who *might* have seen something, but the incontrovertible evidence of a number of witnesses over a period of time, who declare that 'Jesus is the Christ' (compare 2:22), and that 'he has come in the flesh' (4:2-3). There is no denying it,

however hard some may try. It has always been the aim of false teaching to detract from the person of Christ, to deny his deity, or his humanity, or both. If Christ is not 'the image of the invisible God' (Col. 1:15) then we are even now in the darkness of ignorance of God.

The purpose of the testimony (3-4). It is to draw in the hearers, and is summed up in the two words, 'fellowship' and 'joy'. The former has two aspects: fellowship with other believers and, together, fellowship with God. Clearly from what John has to write later these two are indivisible. The latter, joy, is the product of such fellowship. Most of what appears in this letter is concerned with what is essential to true fellowship, and this is absolutely consistent with the apostle's stated intention.

But what is fellowship? This is something the apostle takes up in the following verses. In Acts 2:42-47 we have several indications of what it is: it is expressed in unity of mind and heart both in what is believed and in what is practised; it is seen where believers love to be with one another, gladly to share together in their knowledge and experience of the Lord and gladly to support each other in their needs according to the utmost of their ability. This relationship among the many within the church is a manifestation of that of each one with the Lord. Corporately there is a return of praise to God the boundless giver. Joy, though the word is not mentioned there, pervades that passage.

How does our experience answer to this description? If it answers well, then we shall delight in what John writes. If it is deficient, then he writes that it might not be.

1 John 1:5-10   The basis of fellowship

Light and darkness (5). That 'God is light' should be the basis of the apostle's message may seem strange and remote, until we understand his meaning and recognise that he is concerned with the behaviour of professing Christians. In the Scriptures light is associated more with enlightenment than luminosity, with illumination of the mind more than the surroundings, with revelation, truth, fellowship, righteousness; whereas darkness is associated with the absence of these things or with their opposites. The following scriptures make the point: Psalm 36:9; Matthew 4:16; Luke 2:32; John 3:19-21; 8:12; Romans 2:19; Ephesians 5:8-14; Colossians 1:13; 1 Peter 2:9.

Saying and doing (6-7). When we come to the realm of religious experience people are often gullible. 'All right,' says James in effect, 'you *say* you have faith? *Prove* it!' (see James 2:18). While here John says as much to those who claim to be in fellowship with God. It is not unreasonable to expect that our own claims to spirituality or that of others should be subjected to the scrutiny of certain criteria.

What, then, are the criteria presented against which this claim to fellowship with God is to be measured? Firstly, it is walking, or living, in the light, already defined; secondly, it is practising the truth (6); thirdly, it is living in fellowship with other believers (7); fourthly, it is in acknowledging ourselves to be sinners (8); fifthly, it accords a central place to the saving work of the Lord Jesus Christ who shed his blood for our sins (9).

Concealing and confessing (8-10). The believer who is living in fellowship with the Lord would rather not have sin, but is only too well aware of how things really stand. On the other hand, the deceiver who makes claim to live in fellowship with the Lord would claim also to be without sin. Such a one, being in the dark, sees neither the true nature of sin nor the significance of the price that was paid for sin at Calvary. What is a rich promise to one, full of consolation, is irrelevant to the other. The humble confessions of the believer are starkly contrasted with the vaunted claims of the deceiver. To conceal our sin is a mark of pride and self-sufficiency; to confess it is an evidence of contrition and dependence upon the sufficiency of Christ to deal with the problem. To conceal is to retain the burden; to confess is to be relieved of it. To conceal is to remain bound; to confess is to enter into glorious freedom.

Our fellowship with one another depends upon our confessing our sins to the Lord and being forgiven. If we are not in fellowship with the Lord we cannot be in fellowship with one another. If we are dirty we might be reluctant to come to the light for fear that our moral filth will be exposed. But we must come so that we may be cleansed. There is no fear of light if it shows up how clean we are, and in Christ we are clean. The Christian, living in fellowship with the Lord, enjoys the enormously liberating experience of not needing through shame to conceal his life from other believers. For what has been dealt with in Christ cannot be raked up again to torment us.

1 John 2:1-4 A tonic for the contrite; a bitter pill for the presumptuous

An affectionate encouragement (1-2). The problem of sin is the greatest problem the Christian has to face throughout life. Until his dying day it remains so. Yet there is progress and there is victory. John is well aware of the tension here, even as Paul was when he wrote Romans 7. We should not commit sin, but we do; we have a desire not to do so, but we still do. We are given the means not to do so; but we do not always avail ourselves of those means. So John here by his teaching provides incentives not to sin. But where his readers fail, he does not fetch the stick to them. Rather, with the tender and loving appeal addressed to 'my little children', he directs our attention to the one upon whom we can still call. Satan would accuse us that, if we have fallen in the light of all the privileges we have, we have no grounds on which to come to the Lord. Not so, says John. That is the very circumstance in which we (note that 'we' – as if to say, 'You are not alone in your problem') – 'we have an advocate with the Father, Jesus Christ the righteous'. Because he is both righteous and the propitiation for our sins, we can call upon him, and call upon him in precisely such circumstances; for his person and work thus described are the very grounds upon which fellowship with God is restored and preserved. His work has satisfied the law's just demands. His advocacy with the Father demonstrates beyond shadow of doubt that there is no longer any case against us.

There is nothing miserly, grudging or restrictive about what Jesus Christ accomplished at Calvary – the efficacy of his death prevails throughout the world where people call upon him in truth. What John is teaching here is not what is called universalism; he is rather giving rich encouragement for troubled Christians to look at the glorious nature and extent of Christ's finished work on the cross and take heart that they may yet call upon him and find in him all sufficiency to answer to their need.

Keeping or rejecting (3-4). John has just been writing about fellowship with God and walking in the light, and especially the light of the dark side of Calvary. He now introduces and links two new things: knowing God and keeping his commandments (3). We have come into the knowledge of God through the forgiveness of our sins – how do we know that? Not through any experience we may have had in the past, says John, nor on account of any feelings we may have now. Such things are not reliably subject to scrutiny: our assessment of them is not fixed. What matters is how we stand in relation to what God requires of us, his commandments. The acid test lies in our obedience: do we have a heart for obedience to his commandments? That is not to say we may not fail from time to time – he has just acknowledged as much. 'Oh, let me not wander from your commandments! Your word I have hidden in my heart, that I might not sin against you', says the psalmist (Ps. 119:10-11), who also consistently declares his interest in, and love for, the commandments of the Lord. *Keeping* his commandments is more than Pharisaical observance: it is treasuring, guarding, meditating upon them as words of supreme worth and delight. Should that not be the case with any reader, there is a serious question as to whether you have ever known him. Forget your feelings: face the facts.

1 John 2:4-11   Getting the facts into focus

Saying and doing (4-5). We have the same kind of contrast as in 1:6-7, but the writer has moved from the first person plural to the third person singular. Having dealt with the risk of our deceiving ourselves, he is now concerned with the threat imposed by others who might deceive us. Our own fellowship with God is paramount; but how should we respond to others who also claim to know God? Should we welcome them with open arms and without question? No! As with ourselves, there are objective tests to be applied. John does not mince his words: if any such person does not give obedience to the revealed will of God the place of first importance in his life, he is a *liar*. By contrast, however, we can be sure that anyone who does keep God's Word has experienced his grace.

The inward and the outward (5-6). John now has something further to write of our relationship with the Lord. Having described it in terms of fellowship with him and walking in the light, and then of knowing him and obeying him from the heart, he now adds the concept of our being *in* him (5). We now come to the way in which we should be conducting our lives if we say we are abiding in him, that is, if we have a settled, ongoing, intimate relationship with the Lord. If you are in a train, you will go where the train takes you. If you are 'in' Christ, you will go where he takes you. But, more than that, you will conduct yourself as he did. He described himself as the light of the world (John 8:12), as always doing those things which pleased his Father, and as keeping his Father's word (John 8:29,55); he was described by others as the one who went about 'doing good' (Acts 10:38). Dare we say we are abiding in him without going about our lives with Christlike behaviour?

The old and the new (7-8). In what a perplexing way John writes! First there is the puzzle of whether the commandment is old or new, and then there is the question of what it actually is! It is good that we should have our attention fixed in this manner. Firstly, John has nothing new to write – no stunning new revelation, nothing to add to what has been said already. The foundation has been laid, and the revelation given is sufficient. He was not adding in his letter anything the readers did not already know. No new philosophy was being introduced to be followed. He was simply testifying to home truths. So why do so? For the simple reason that the old truths come to us with new power as we receive further enlightenment. The old is new every time we encounter it! This is the wonderful thing about the Christian life. We do not follow worn out teachings or get tired of the limitations of the Bible as we might of any other book. That is because the Bible does not have limitations as other books have, for it is the living and active Word of God (Heb. 4:12).

Love and hatred (9-11). 'A new commandment I give to you, that you love one another' (John 13:34). In and of itself, love for the brethren was not new at all (see, for example, Lev. 19:18); what made it new was the rest of the sentence: '... as I have loved you, that you also love one another'. As we grow in the knowledge of the love of Christ, so his commandment acquires increased depth of meaning, as should also our response to it in our relationship with our fellow believers. If we are honest, there are those of our brothers and sisters in Christ with whom we find it difficult to get on, and for a variety of reasons. The one who said, 'Love your enemies' (Matt. 5:44) also said, 'Love your brother' – even the one of whom you expected better! That is where the real test lies!

1 John 2:12-14   Christian experience

What John writes (12-13), and what he has written (14) amount to much the same thing. There is no need to move away from the great cardinal truths of the faith. The whole of the Christian life rests on these foundations: the forgiveness of sins, reconciliation with the Father, and the consequent progress in grace.

The three categories of persons he addresses, 'little children', 'fathers', and 'young men', refer to what they are in their Christian, rather than their natural, lives. John's letter is directed to help all Christians, whatever the extent or limitation of their Christian experience.

The 'little children' (12), just begun in the Christian life, though perhaps knowing little else at this stage, rejoice in the knowledge of sins forgiven. To them it is everything to know that they have peace with God through the removal of the fetters which bound them. And so it should be, that whatever they have to look forward to and grow up into in their Christian lives, nothing can begin to compare with what it means to be forgiven. What is wonderful is that our sins are forgiven 'for his name's sake': that is, on account of his name. In that name is invested all that he came into the world to do (Matt. 1:21), and all that he actually accomplished through his death, burial, resurrection and ascension. It is perhaps the greatest tribute we can pay him to acknowledge that our sins are forgiven 'for his name's sake': our regeneration is attributable to what he is and what he has done, not to what we are or what we have done. Let us live in the good of it.

The 'fathers' (13) have been Christians for many years, are rich in knowledge and experience. Their encouragement from the pen of the apostle is based on their knowledge of God. They have grown in the knowledge of his person and his works; they have found him to be a faithful, covenant-keeping God; they have experienced his compassionate care and timely provision for their every need. They have found him in every way to be a sufficient God (though that description is really too mean to use for one whose grace has abounded towards them – Eph. 1:8).

The 'young men' (13) are those in the midst of their Christian warfare, proving the armour of God given them. In the name of Christ they are treading the tempter down and knowing what it is to gain the victory through the strength which God supplies.

Then John seems to repeat himself – at least, he goes through the cycle again of little children, fathers and young men. Only this time he addresses the 'little children' using a different word, perhaps for those who have begun to understand something more of the family into which they have been brought. They have known the Father, they understand that they have been adopted into the family of God's elect, of which God is the Father and Jesus Christ the elder brother (see Hebrews 2:11). For the fathers and the young men there has been a tense switch, already noted; and concerning the latter group he amplifies a little by referring to their strength and the Word of God abiding in them. Indeed, it is the Word of God which is their strength and glory (Luke 4:4; 1 Peter 1:23).

In all this John is really underlining that all Christians have all that they need in Christ. Their whole lives are undergirded by the truths spoken of. To move away from these, to seek new experiences or so-called knowledge, would be a disaster.

1 John 2:15-17   The divergent courses of love and lust

Two loves. We have to appreciate that interpretation of Scripture must relate to context. John, in his Gospel (3:16), declares, 'For God so loved the world…', while here he warns Christians not to do so. The language is the same, but the meaning so different. The comparison, however, will serve a purpose. God's love for the world is that which motivated him to do something to change it from its state of corruption, and on that basis he sent his Son into the world that through him the world might be saved (John 3:16-17). When a Christian is tempted to love the world, the story is very different, for it is allurement away from God, as if the pleasures and enjoyments of this life were of greater worth than fellowship with God. It would seem that is what happened to Demas (2 Tim. 4:10). Should we be in any doubt as to what John means by 'the world', he explains himself in v.16. It is concerned with 'lust' and 'pride' rather than the legitimate enjoyment of all that pertains to the created order as God intended it to be. Self-gratification and covetousness, personal prestige and power are the kind of things John has in mind here, which includes *anything* which interferes with fellowship with God and the love for him which expresses itself in wholehearted submission and service. Sadly, these things invade our churches sometimes, and we know their fruits. See Philippians 2:5.

Two origins. Love, which fixes upon an object, whether it be God and his children, or the world, has also a source, or an origin. What is it which drives your affections? Is it 'of the Father', or 'of the world' (16)? It must be one or the other. There are times when we need to ask ourselves just what it is which motivates us to do the things that we do.

Bear in mind what John has been saying concerning what is of paramount importance and significance: the forgiveness of sins, knowledge of and fellowship with God, and victory in service; and now contrast that with the lust of the flesh, the lust of the eyes, and the pride of life. The former is spiritual, the latter worldly. The former starts with the grace of God in the heart and ends with the glory of God in the life. The latter starts with the attractions of what is in the world around us and ends with the indulgence of self in this life. They are like oil and water which do not mix; they are separate closed systems. One has reference to what pleases God, the other purely to what pleases self. The lust of the flesh refers to all that feeds our self-indulgence – and what that is will to a certain extent vary from person to person; the lust of the eyes feeds the lust of the flesh, representing the principle of covetousness. The pride of life concerns the establishment of *self* in the world. In these three phrases John comprehends all that is 'in the world'. Someone may object with an appeal to much that is good in the world, and yet we must always ask ourselves what the origin and the end of these things are, for if not 'of the Father' then they are 'of the world' and are not serving the interests of the kingdom of heaven.

Two ends. In v.17 'passing away' is contrasted with 'abiding for ever'. We are reminded of what Paul said about a man's works being tested by fire (1 Cor. 3:13-15). What matters is not our estimation of the worth of something, but God's. That applies to 'good works' as to anything else. How much of man's work, even much supposedly good work, will pass away and be accounted as worthless in God's reckoning! Remember the ending of the parable of the sheep and the goats in Matthew 25:31-45, and also note the irony of the contrast in Matthew 7:21-23.

1 John 2:18-23   Antichrist and antichrists

It may surprise us after so many centuries to see John's reference to 'the last hour'. The last hour before what? He does not say, but we may safely infer that the return of Christ is in view. Since the early days of the New Testament church there have been people who have stood in opposition to Christ. More sinister than pagans who oppose the gospel message through the ignorance of unbelief, these 'antichrists' have their origin in the church, or at least in its visible manifestation, for 'they went out from us' (19). Taking their knowledge of Christianity with them, they turn it against the Lord.

Judas Iscariot betrayed his master by abusing his privilege in the intimate circle of the Twelve. 'The antichrist', of whom all who have gone before him are but precursors, will be the embodiment of evil: heading up the opposition to the Lord he will assume to *himself* the authority which he has usurped. From what John writes, it is likely that he too will have his origin from within the organisation of the church. Of him, however, the true child of God need have no fear, for the Lord himself will consume him with the breath of his mouth and destroy him with the brightness of his coming (2 Thess. 2:8).

Such defectors from the faith can cause deep alarm to Christians. The alarm springs from what they *appeared* to be. Had they not once appeared to be believers no one would have been surprised at their later opposition. It is always highly disturbing to hear those who vigorously declaim against the Lord Jesus Christ by declaring that they once were Christians but have now been enlightened and thrown it all off; the more so if they are people who were high in our regard and were accepted as true believers. John sets his readers' minds at rest on this point. He acknowledges the deception (19), firstly that they had been within the church, and secondly, that it is *by their departing* that their true colours are revealed. We see only the outward man, but God looks upon the heart and knows what goes on there. Satan is a deceiver, and he uses instruments of deception.

'If *they* went, what about me? Perhaps *I* will not last the course?' No. For all the initial outward similarity between these antichrists and true believers, there is a world of difference in reality. The true child of God has received the Holy Spirit (20), an 'anointing' which sets him or her apart to God: it is the mark of God as opposed to the mark of the beast (Rev. 13:16-17). Under the Old Testament dispensation the anointing oil was used in setting people apart for specific service – see, for example, Exodus 30:30; 1 Samuel 16:12-13; 1 Kings 19:16. In David's case, of course, the actual entry into office took place only much later, after many hazards and extremities. The anointing a true believer has received from God marks him or her out as God's special possession, as a person separated, sanctified, to God. Whatever the hazards or extremities in the way, nothing can thwart what God has purposed to do. This anointing with the Holy Spirit has brought us into true knowledge – the knowledge of God through the forgiveness of our sins and reconciliation with the Father, in which Christ Jesus is central.

Contrast this with the antichrists, who by their defection demonstrate that they never had this anointing, who acknowledged Jesus Christ only so long as it suited them, and when they had done with him they discarded him and trampled upon his name, his work and his people. See Hebrews 10:26-29.

1 John 2:22-28   Remember your roots

Those who apostatise such as John describes are always called antichrists, because it is always Christ who is the subject of attack (22-23). It is not that they necessarily deny God: their invective is aimed at Christ. (They certainly deny the Father, for he is the God and Father of the Lord Jesus Christ.) Why? Because 'no one has seen God at any time. The only begotten Son ... he has declared him' (John 1:18). Christ is the image of the invisible God (Col. 1:15), he is God manifest in the flesh (1 Tim. 3:16). Were it not for him, God would still be unknown, and we would still be in the dark. It is because of who Christ is, combined with his accomplishment at Calvary, that he is always the subject of attack. Never in the history of the world has any man been treated with more contempt, been more vigorously and bitterly opposed, more deliberately subjected to character assassination by means of every method available, than the only Man whom angels worship (Heb. 1:6) and who alone is worthy of the highest praise, our Lord and Saviour Jesus Christ – the one before whom every knee shall bow!

John is really writing by way of reminder at this point (21). We need our minds stirred up by way of remembrance (2 Peter 3:1, speaking of scoffers and smooth talkers – and note the word 'lusts' there also). We need to be reminded, lest we substitute carnal for spiritual wisdom.

From the beginning (24). See how preoccupied the apostle seems to be with this phrase. He has used it of God the Son (1:1; 2:13-14) as well as of the message of the gospel (2:7, here, and later at 3:11). God does not change, neither does his word. It is we who change, and it is we who forget. John is repeatedly directing our minds back to where it all began, not only in our experience but also in the eternal purposes of God. What we heard was good news sufficient to secure eternal life for us (25). Nothing need be added: all has been done. It was not a mere introductory message requiring subsequent additions or modifications as the initiates grew in their knowledge of the system; it was not something to be discarded once the converts had attained to a measure of maturity. No, it was a whole, a complete, a full gospel which was heard, believed and received, and it is good to all eternity.

Abiding (24,27,28). This is another word the apostle uses repeatedly (2:6-10, here, and 3:6,15,17,24; 4:12,13,16 – though the NIV and the AV translate the same word variously). The gospel of the forgiveness of sins is as valid for the believer today as when he or she first believed it, and we are daily to live in the good of it. It was the basis of our acceptance of the Lord Jesus Christ into our lives, and it is also the basis of our ongoing relationship with him as we abide in him.

In marriage a man and a woman covenant together, each publicly making vows concerning the other. Their whole life as man and wife is built upon – is a filling out of – the vows they made at the beginning, and woe betide them if they neglect them. Now whereas a woman may in the course of time find grounds to be disappointed in her husband, the same cannot apply to the relationship between the child of God and the Lord Jesus Christ. The Christian life is built upon what happened at the beginning, and comprises a developing relationship with One whose perfections become more apparent with time. Unlike the marriage covenant, which applies only 'until death do us part', the promise the Lord has given us is of eternal life. It is an everlasting covenant (Heb. 13:20).

1 John 2:24-29   Don't get sidetracked

John is particularly concerned about those who attempt to deceive Christians (26) to rob them of what they have in Christ. Paul was concerned about much the same thing when he wrote to the Colossians of their not being 'moved away from the hope of the gospel which you heard' (1:23), and when he urged them, 'As you have therefore received Christ Jesus the Lord, so walk in him...' (2:6). The gospel of Christ, and the covenant relationship sealed with his blood, are sufficient to guarantee the believer's eternal security and happiness.

When John wrote of the knowledge given to believers on account of their having received an 'anointing' (20), and when he writes here (27) that, for the same reason, they do not need that anyone should teach them, we must be clear that he is writing in the context of the subversive teachings of deceivers, and by no means suggesting that his readers have already attained to a complete understanding and need be taught nothing further concerning the faith. The point being made is that there is no 'secret knowledge' to which they have yet to attain, nor is there any insufficiency in the gospel which they received or in the Lord Jesus Christ. They have no need to move away from that message, nor from him: the word of life is to abide in them, and they are to abide in him (24). To do otherwise, to be taken in by the plausible words of the devil's spokesmen (for that is what they are), is bound to end in bitter disappointment and shame (28). It is precisely the same tactic that Satan used

in the garden with Eve, and people are still being taken in by it. When God came to Adam and Eve in the garden, they were covered with shame and hid themselves. How will it be otherwise with us when the Lord Jesus Christ comes again if we have allowed ourselves to be enticed away from the only gospel to embrace the doctrines of demons (1 Tim. 4:1)?

The New Testament writers are uniformly strong on this point. Jude writes of the necessity to 'contend earnestly for the faith which was once for all delivered to the saints' (Jude 3), while Peter declares that God's 'divine power has given to us all things that pertain to life and godliness, through the knowledge of him who called us by his own glory and virtue' (2 Peter 1:3). Both these writers, having pointed out the sufficiency of the message which has been proclaimed, proceed to expose the subtle ways in which false teachers shift the centre of attention (2 Peter 2:1; Jude 4).

Returning to John, having reminded his readers of a truth, he again rounds it off with the inescapable logic of a very practical application in v. 29. Cut through the veil of words in which people envelop themselves, strip away their outward display, and ask the question, 'Are they practising righteousness?' The standard of righteousness is the Lord Jesus himself, who is the Righteous One, and if anyone's manner of life bears resemblance to, and acknowledges, his, then it is an indicator that he or she is born of him.

1 John 3:1-3   What we are and what we shall be

If we would know ourselves, our status and our prospects, we must look away from ourselves and meditate on the love of God towards us, a love which has devised a way for him to call us his children and for us to address him as 'Father'. This is by the Spirit of adoption sent into our hearts (Rom. 8:15; Gal. 4:6). Comprehending his love, which is infinite in all its dimensions (Eph. 3:18-19) is not the work of a moment! It should be something of which the Christian is always aware, always beholding. At one time one aspect will present itself, at another time a different one, but always the same love. 'O love, thou bottomless abyss!' Our busy world makes unreasonable demands upon us. We would be the better for a regular 'beholding' of the love of God, its 'manner' and its bestowal upon us.

We could wish we understood more of 'what we shall be' (2), but our knowledge of what 'we are' should allay any fears on that score. If we are God's children then we are safe in his care and the happy recipients of all his promises. He has not revealed what we shall be, but he has revealed that we shall be like our Lord Jesus Christ at his appearing. It is what we are which gives us security for what we shall be. What we shall be is rooted in the manner of love the Father has bestowed upon us in bringing us into his family.

If we are not looking forward to what we shall be it is because we have not sufficiently taken stock of what we are. Oh sad, sad Christian who, having lost sight of such love, shivers in the only warmth this world can afford! What comfort is there outside the love of God, and what lack of it is there within it?

A Christian will often feel lonely in the world. The sense of not belonging there is fully justified, for the Christian does not belong there. 'The world does not know us' really indicates there to be a fundamental cleavage between 'the world' and 'the Christian'. Though points of contact may remain, the organic unity has been severed. Those who 'did not know him', that is, who were ignorant of the real Jesus, the Son of God, will be just as ignorant about those whom he is not ashamed to call brethren (Heb. 2:11), those who are 'called children of God'. Such a state of affairs is to be expected. We are strangers and pilgrims here, looking for a better country, that is, a heavenly one (Heb. 11:13,16). Our joy is in what has been revealed, our hope in what has been promised.

Yet again, the apostle translates into hard evidence the testimony he has been giving. Here it is the response to the hope of which he has been writing (3). What God has set us apart for and is preparing us for is evident in the way we look forward to it and prepare ourselves for it. There is the Godward aspect of the work, and there is the man-ward aspect of it. If God is at work within us, then we will work accordingly (see Philippians 2:12-13). If the Holy Spirit indwells us, then it is to be expected that the outworking of this will be in holy living. It cannot be otherwise. A person who says he is rejoicing in being a child of God and looking forward to glory, who at the same time is living in this world on intimate terms with it, is not to be believed. If you are not purifying yourself, then it is clear you do not have this hope – you are hopeless. If you do have this hope, then you will be seeking to be what you will be at his appearing.

1 John 3:4-10   What we do is what we are

That is John's thesis here, and very blunt about it he is too. Some Christians have used this passage, among others, to teach Christian perfectionism; others, sensitive to their own failings, have found it deeply disturbing. Exactly what is John saying? Certainly we are right to listen to him with the utmost seriousness without watering down what the Holy Spirit has caused him to write.

As sinners we have a natural bias, accepting sin as an inevitable part of life, to treat it rather lightly, even to the extent of glossing over it at times as of little consequence, or perhaps, worse, of not identifying it at all. If we do so we are imposing our own standards on our behaviour. John reminds us that there is a standard which has been set by God: his law. Acting in a manner which ignores, flouts, contradicts or deviates from his law is to be lawless: it is sin (4). Most of us seem to understand well enough that a person who flouts the laws of the land is a menace to society and ought to be locked up. Many of us are a little less vociferous about the deserved consequences for flouting the law of God!

John has already recognised (1:7 – 2:1) that the Christian is not free from sin: it is a problem which remains with him throughout life. But that is not what he is dealing with here. A lively child will stumble from time to time and suffer cuts and bruises, but get up and get going again. A child diseased in the legs will never be up and about and active. John is here not beaming in on what happens occasionally, but on the way of life; not on events, but on activity. It is all a question of

'doing' sin (4), or 'doing' righteousness (7). What are you 'doing' in your life? What you 'do' is what you are! A minister of the gospel who is one thing in the pulpit and another outside it is to be given no credibility, for he is not 'doing' his job, however professional his conduct may appear to be in one department! A 'Sunday Christian' is not a Christian at all. Whatever public image you project, if your private conduct does not match up to it then you are not 'doing' what you would like people to think you are.

However hard we try to be otherwise, we always revert to type. This is as true in the spiritual realm as in any other. John does not want anyone to be deceived on this score (7). He is writing here about how the governing principle of our life manifests itself, whether we are children of the devil (8) or children of God (9). A bad tree cannot bring forth good fruit. 'A good man out of the good treasure of his heart brings forth good things' (Matt. 12:35).

Jesus said of the Pharisees that they 'did' the works of their father, the devil (John 8:41). They were not doers of righteousness, for all their outward show. They taught the law, but they did not do it (Matt. 23:3). It is not hearers of the word who are justified, but doers of it (Rom. 2:13).

What John has stated positively in v. 7 he states negatively in v. 10. No middle ground is therefore allowed to exist. You are either one thing or the other; there is no sitting on the fence. The question remains: what are you 'doing'?

1 John 3:10-11   What Christ has done makes us what we are

Removal and destruction. There are two things said of the Lord Jesus Christ in the earlier verses in relation to what he came into the world to do: to take away our sins (5), and to destroy the works of the devil (8). Both were accomplished in a single stroke at Calvary. Refer to 2 Corinthians 5:21 and 1 Peter 2:24. To take away our sins involved his bearing them. He actually took them upon himself, suffering the full weight of punishment that they deserved. In so doing he disarmed principalities and powers, making a public spectacle of them, triumphing over them (Col. 2:15).

The devil has wielded his power only on account of his hold on man who was created in God's image as the crown of his creation. Christ's work on the cross has loosed his hold, has broken his grip. In this one action the power of the devil has fallen apart, his work destroyed, his claim annulled. The cross – a stumbling block to the Jews and foolishness to the Greeks (1 Cor. 1:23) – is the glorious fulfilment of Genesis 3:15. A proper appreciation of these things clears away any doubts about the meaning of this passage. How can anyone 'abide' in him in whom there is no sin and yet remain in sin? It is not possible. Or how can anyone who has the life of God – his 'seed' – in him (9) live the life of the ungodly? It behoves all of us who read these verses to weigh them carefully, lest in any there should be an evil heart of unbelief (Heb. 3:12).

It is an amazing fact that children of wrath should become children of God (Eph. 2:3; 5:1). Adoption into the family of God's elect (Eph. 1:5) is more than transposition: it is also transformation, for which only the concept of rebirth (9) is adequate to explain it.

Verse 10 serves as a link between the previous emphasis on righteousness and the introduction of teaching on love. It is interesting to observe that before he has anything much to write on the subject of love (although he has mentioned it in 2:9-11) he should focus on our positional relationship with God, in terms of what we are and where we stand through the forgiveness of sins, being brought into a new relationship with the living God, obeying his commands, standing apart from our former way of life, acknowledging Jesus Christ for who he is, and living in such a way as demonstrates that we believe his word of promise. It is only after all this that he refers to loving our brethren. Why? It would almost seem to contradict what we hear through many popular religious media, where love is placed at the head of all things – at least, it used to be, and the reason for its recent demise is found here. The reason is quite clear: love has foundations on which it must be built; it has a root from which to derive its nourishment so that it can grow and flourish. So it is that, as he develops what he has to say about love, John relates back to what he has written before, about righteousness (12), rebirth (14), truth (18), obedience (22), faith (23). On what is your love for your brother founded?

Expected, but not automatic (11). This is the message about love. We have already noted that it needs a framework in which to operate. So, for example, love does not suppress the truth or put righteousness to one side in order to gain its end. Self-interest may do that, but not love. Love has to be worked at, it has to be cultivated and developed. It is not based on feelings, though they may grow as time goes on.

1 John 3:12-18   The responsibility of love

Intractable jealousy (12-15). Bearing in mind that John is writing about love, we might think it strange that he take such an extreme example as Cain to demonstrate what it is not. Yet his choice is particularly apt, for Cain of all people ought to have had at heart his brother's welfare. His reply, 'Am I my brother's keeper?' (Gen. 4:9) is not only an attempt to conceal his guilt but also shows a callous disregard for a fundamental responsibility. What about people who say such things as, 'What he does is none of my business'?

There are two aspects to Cain's problem which are characteristic to some extent of all unbelievers. Firstly, his sinfulness was exposed by the righteousness of his brother's life (12). A believer's righteous conduct is often a thorn in the side of the unbeliever. Secondly, his offering was rejected whereas Abel's was accepted (Gen. 4:4-5). There was clear evidence of the favour of God towards the believer, arousing jealousy in the one rejected. Cain chose to remove the offence not by doing something about his conscience but by doing something about what was provoking it – he killed his brother. We need to pray that Christians maintain a clear testimony by righteous living (12) and by loving the brethren (14). It is inevitable that such lives will arouse hatred (13) because of the sharp condemnatory contrast to the world around us. Also, whatever people say, they often see that Christians have what they do not have, enjoying the blessing of God upon them. Paul could write of provoking his fellow Jews to jealousy (Rom. 11:14), but in order that some of them might be saved. He had a high price to pay for such a noble concern!

Cain 'was of the wicked one' and had self-interest at heart. We may not be aware of the power of self interest until someone else is preferred before us, and then it can come to the fore in various forms of resentment. Love, on the other hand, seeks the good of others irrespective of any benefit to ourselves … and indeed of any worthiness in them – witness the love of Christ towards us (16).

When we read that Jesus laid down his life for us, we should not think only in terms of his death. What he did in going to the cross was the culmination of his life of service (see Phil. 2:7-8). It was all of a piece. So when we read of our laying down our lives for the brethren, we should see it in its panoramic perspective. Without doubt we will not be prepared to die for our brethren if we do not set their interests above our own now. It is a very serious question to ask: do we esteem others better than ourselves (Phil. 2:3)? Are we concerned for their welfare to the extent that our own takes second place – even our very lives? 'Yes,' we may say, 'we are.' Well then, says the apostle, here is a practical test whereby we may measure the sincerity of our words: How is it if we see a brother or sister in Christ in some situation of real practical need, and we have the means of helping him or her (17)? Of course, perhaps we don't get close enough to our brethren to be in the position of understanding their needs. Shame on us if that is the case! But then, if we do see them, we may argue that had they managed their affairs better they would not be in the situation in which they now find themselves, and so we find an excuse to shut our hearts against them! Did God's love take that attitude towards us?

Today's reading has content enough to warrant our searching our hearts and thinking hard about our behaviour towards our brethren. Let us carry v. 18 with us today and through life.

1 John 3:18-22   A rich promise

We start where we left off yesterday – and so we must. We find that our lives fall short of our profession, and certainly of our desires, as Christians. One of our problems is that we do not know our own hearts. But God knows them. What we read of here is not our satisfying ourselves concerning the sincerity of our hearts (in which we may be self-deceived) so much as our opening ourselves to the searcher of hearts (see Jeremiah 17:9-10), for it is what we are 'before him' (19) which matters. Though we may know of nothing against us on this score, our persuasion must be in the light of his Word, for it is only in that light that we may have any true confidence.

So John permits of the two possibilities of vv. 20-21, both of which have a single end and give an opening to great comfort to the true believer. We find a striking illustration of the apostle's teaching in the following case: When Peter declared to the Lord, 'I will lay down my life for your sake' (John 13:37), though he fully meant what he said he did not fully know his own heart. The discovery was a bitter blow (Luke 22:62), and would perhaps have finished him had it not been for what took place later on the shore of the Sea of Tiberias (John 21:15-19). It is here we see that Jesus' replying question, 'Will you lay down your life for my sake?' (John 13:38) had a double edge, for here the Lord dealt with the heart which condemned the man, replacing it with a better-founded confidence, one which would result in Peter's doing what he had declared he was prepared to do. Peter was persuaded of the genuineness of his love for the Lord and was to concentrate on giving

his life in service for the Lord's people, by following him.

So if, though we have the desire to lay down our lives for our brethren, our hearts condemn us, we have the wonderful encouragement here that God is able to do something about the problem. Our omniscient, all-wise God knows how to deal with our hearts! This leads in to a most remarkable statement. Hitherto John had referred to Jesus receiving from his Father whatever he asked because of his keeping his commandments and doing those things which were pleasing in his sight (John 8:29; 11:22; 15:10). He now declares that this is the same portion for all those who have confidence before God. The self-same privileges are accorded to believers now which were accorded to the Son himself in his days upon the earth.

This is a promise we need to take seriously. It is set very firmly in the context of loving the brethren. If we love the brethren – if indeed we are prepared to love them in accordance with what John sets before us here – we immediately find ourselves in need of resources which we are unable in and of ourselves to meet. This is why the promise is given. It is what is meant by 'asking in his name' (John 14:13-14); it is what is involved in doing the works that Jesus did and greater (John 14:12). For it is the continuation 'of all that Jesus *began* both to do and to teach ...' (Acts 1:1) – a continuation of the building founded upon the apostles and prophets, Jesus Christ himself being the chief corner-stone (Eph. 2:18-22). It is a work in which all are involved who are true disciples of the Lord Jesus Christ.

1 John 3:23-24   Don't be hoodwinked!

The company love keeps. Love always operates in the realm of believing on the name of Jesus Christ (23), of living in fellowship with him (abiding 'in him, and he in him', 24), and of being obedient to his commands (23-24). It never operates outside these things, a point John is at pains to stress; and the more one reads what he has to say, the more one realises that there is an indissoluble unity among love, fellowship and obedience: none has priority over any other, there is no tension among them – love is not more important than obedience, nor is fellowship with God to be placed above love towards the brethren. They stand or fall together. If you are not loving as described here, then you are not 'abiding in him', nor are you 'keeping his commandments'. If you are doing one, then you are doing the other. So before we convince ourselves that we love our brethren as we ought, let us ask a parallel question, for to answer one is to answer the other: Do we keep his commandments? By 'keep' we understand (as we have said above – on 2:3) the kind of 'keeping' so graphically described by the psalmist in Psalm 119 – see for example vv. 11,14,20,24, 35,59,60,97 – it is so difficult to make selection because the whole psalm breathes the psalmist's delight in and dependence upon the Word of God. Let us make it our earnest prayer that we go on to maturity in our Christian lives.

The company love shuns. John has more to write on the subject of love (4:7 onwards), but now he seems to interrupt his flow with a caution to his readers to exercise discernment. He is quite clear about the necessity of this (4:1).

It has been said that love is blind – an observation which has a measure of truth in it. But though it may rightly be blind to the blemishes and imperfections of its objects, it must not be where truth and error are concerned, so as to compromise in these areas. Love which 'rejoices in the truth' (1 Cor. 13:6) is not of a kind to turn a blind eye to what is false.

Satan, being a master of deception, has no scruples about misleading people, and even in the matter of love false prophets can give a good impression (they are 'seem to be' prophets). We are not to be taken in by or to follow after those, however exemplary their conduct may appear to be, who deny the essential deity and humanity of our Lord Jesus Christ. It is not their track record over how many 'converts' they have, or what extensive 'good deeds' they are doing by which we are to assess them, but rather their position with regard to the essentials of the gospel.

False prophets are always, directly or indirectly, pointing out supposed shortcomings in the gospel and in gospel believing people. Their aim is to undermine our confidence, which they do by shifting the centre of attention from fundamentals to peripherals. They would have our attention directed to where they want it – which is away from where it ought to be. We must be neither bullied nor intimidated into giving way before their influence. The Christian has the Spirit of God (3:24; 4:2) and true 'knowledge', and therefore the right to discriminate and stand apart from error. Are you doing so?

1 John 4:1-6   'By this we know...'

There is a great encouragement given to God's people in these verses. It is the double 'abiding' – we in Christ and Christ in us (3:24; 4:4). Paul could speak about 'Christ in you, the hope of glory' (Col.1:27); see also John 14:23. The Holy Spirit, the Spirit of adoption, bears witness with our spirit that we are children of God (see Romans 8:13-16). In other words, by the Spirit of God we *know* that we have this relationship with the Lord Jesus Christ. It is for this very reason that on the one hand we become uneasy when people say things which compete with what we have come to believe, whereas on the other, positively, our hearts warm to those who, we discover, share our beliefs from the heart. It is not just a matter of their crossing their t's and dotting their i's in the same places as ourselves; it is not a case of their having the same ideas as us about certain subjects: it is the witness of the Spirit of God, and so our fellowship is on a spiritual level. Otherwise we could have no more justification for the position we have taken than they have over theirs.

There is a conflict going on all the time between those who have the Spirit of God and those who are of another 'spirit'. Basically, any 'spirit' that does not confess the Lord Jesus Christ is of the 'antichrist'. He who is in the believer is the Spirit of God himself. He who is in the world is the spirit of antichrist. We who have the Spirit of God know that we have moved from the position of being 'in the world' to being 'in Christ'. The world used to have our ear, but has so no longer. The very fact that we have been set free from the law of sin and death (Rom. 8:2) is testimony to the truth that 'he who is in you is greater than he who is in the world' (4). Let us never lose sight of the fact that the warfare, waged within us and all around us, is a very real conflict between the Spirit of God and the spirit of antichrist. The latter has been dislodged from our lives and rages against us – but to no avail, for victory is ours through our Lord Jesus Christ, though the battle be fierce. The cross bears testimony to that.

John's statement in v. 6 would be sheer arrogance and presumption were it not true. On what grounds can anyone dare to make such claims, to be 'of God' and to know God? The answer is to be found only in the divine initiative. If we are 'of God', it means that God has taken the initiative to make us his; if we know God, it is because he has chosen to reveal himself to us. If we have been given the Spirit of God, if we abide in him and he in us (3:24), then we are quenching the Spirit if we are shy of this truth. The personal relationship we have with the Creator of the universe is a stupendous privilege and one shared by all who love the truth. 'He who knows God hears us' is really an indication of the understanding which exists among true believers. At the purely human level they may be separated by language, culture, age and generation; but the Spirit of God, who is the Spirit of truth, transcends all these natural barriers (which in any case have their origin in the fall of man in his disobedience), creating a bond which the world simply cannot understand.

Those who pride themselves on some secret knowledge or wisdom simply mistake the matter. True knowledge comes from God, and those who have it know it, and are distinguished on account of what he has done in them. Their glory is in that they know him (Jer. 9:24).

1 John 4:7-11   A question of motive

Perhaps in the light of the foregoing we can now return to the subject of love with a heightened awareness of what it involves. In chapter 3 the motivation for our loving our brethren was based upon what our Lord did for us in laying down his life for us (3:16). If he did that for us, then we ought to be self-giving in our behaviour towards our fellow believers. It is in a sense an example to follow, and doing so is a reflection upon what God himself did for us. Now here in chapter 4 the apostle takes us a stage further, beyond what God *did* to what God *is*. He sent his only begotten Son into the world for us because he *is* love.

There are occasions when, though we do the right thing, what actually motivates us leaves something to be desired. So, for example, we might give our time or our money or our abilities in helping our brethren out of nothing more than a sense of duty, or because our consciences so trouble us that we dare not fall short of what is required, or we do it because we know it is the right thing to do and it becomes a sort of automatic response to the situation. John has moved on now from 'doing' for others because of what God has 'done' for us – love in action – to probe into the heart of God, so to speak, to the love which is the motivation of all that God did. God did not send his Son into the world that we might live through him (9) because it was the right thing to do, or because the situation demanded it. He did it because he loved us. Furthermore, he loved us not on account of what we were, or of anything he saw in us; that is, his love was in no way externally motivated or driven. He loved us because he *is* love. God *is* love, and love is *of* God. This is the love to be followed which is twice set before us in these verses (7,11).

It is well worth asking ourselves not only whether we love the brethren, but *why* we love them. Oh that we had more understanding of the love of God!

God only knows the love of God;
O that it now were shed abroad
In this poor stony heart!
For love I sigh, for love I pine,
This only portion, Lord, be mine,
Be mine this better part!

(Charles Wesley)

1 John 4:11-13 Implications of God's love working in us

The opening words of v.12 are reminiscent of those of John 1:18. There the statement that no one has seen God at any time was preparatory to his speaking of the revelation of the Father through the Son. But what is the purpose of John's saying the same thing here? We can perhaps find a link in John 14:9-11, where Jesus declared himself to be the revelation of his Father – 'He who has seen me has seen the Father'. But then he went on to speak of his being in the Father and the Father in him, as evinced by his works. 'Do you not believe that I am in the Father and the Father in me?', he asked Philip. In other words, the overwhelming evidence was before Philip would he but open his eyes to see it.

Now read vv.11-12 here again, but this time omitting the first sentence of v.12 (to the semi-colon in the NIV). Our proper response to a recognition of God's love towards us is to love one another. That is what we *ought* to do. But *if* we do, what does it prove? It proves that God abides in us, and his love has been perfected in us. In other words, more than its being a demonstration of our being objects of the love of God, it is an evidence and outworking of the stupendous fact that God himself has come and made his abode with us (John 14:23). The love which we display towards one another is *of the same kind* as the love which he displayed towards us in Christ. It is *his* love working in us and through us. Which takes us back again to v.11 to reflect more soberly upon what is really meant by 'we also *ought*'. The question is, do we? What is our love towards one another? Is it really of the same kind as the love of God towards us? It ought to be … but is it?

This is not the first time the apostle has referred to God abiding in the believer – see 3:24. But whereas there the evidence was in keeping God's commandments, which is personally orientated, here it is love, which is orientated towards others – it is outgoing.

Right in the middle of the profound argument of vv.11-12 is the statement, 'No one has seen God at any time'. 'No man could do the works this man does if God were not with him,' they said of Jesus (see John 3:2). 'By this all will know that you are my disciples, if you have love for one another,' said Jesus (John 13:35). Taken together, we have the evidence of what is not immediately seen. The love of God towards us, and its outworking in us and through us towards others is the evidence of the unseen God abiding in us. When God so loved the world, what did he do? He sent his only begotten Son into the world, the Son who declared the Father. By his love he revealed himself through his Son. By his love towards us he reveals himself, he makes himself known – and not to us only, but through us to others. Our response to the riches of the grace of God towards us is the most powerful testimony which exists in all the world of the reality of God, and it is the incontrovertible evidence that God himself really abides in us by his Spirit.

Verse 13 is a restatement of 3:24b but in a different context. We are dependent upon the Spirit of God for loving as well as for keeping God's commandments. Obedience and love, which he both requires of us and works in us, are his witness in us, to us, and through us to others.

1 John 4:14-19   Two incompatible things

'Bold shall I stand in that great day, for who aught to my charge shall lay?' To talk about boldness in the day of judgement (17) is easy enough when it is not observed to be close at hand! Perhaps those who have had the experience of looking death in the face will know more about it. There is a difference between boldness and presumption. We may be presumptuous now, but we cannot be then. However, we can be bold both now and then. Presumption is based on a false foundation; boldness on a true. The true foundation is the finished work of the Saviour of the world (14), the Son of God (15).

We must keep in sight all the time that the love of which the apostle is speaking is the love of God – or our response in kind to his love, because it is an outworking of it – his love working in and through us. Boldness is contrasted with fear. Will we be confident, or will we cower? If you are not sure about this, then the answer is to be found only in knowing more fully this love.

Our *testimony* is that he has saved us, leading to our *confession* is that he is God's Son (14-15), in just the same way as the testimony of the man born blind led him inexorably to the conclusion that the one who restored his sight was from God (John 9:25,33). Both knowing and believing are involved (16). We know it because we have experienced it; we believe it because what we have experienced has only one explanation. If we have experienced God's love in saving us from our sins we are led infallibly to certain conclusions about the Son. Thus v.16 is our rational response to our experience of the love of God towards us, giving us life and forgiveness and reconciliation through the Son (9-10).

The love described in v.17 is not just the love of God towards us, which has been perfected in us (12), nor is it just our love towards God because of what he has done for us. The point here is that there is a mutuality about it (summarised in v.19), based on the relationship between the Christian and God, which is one not of fear, but of love. How this contrasts with what we might term 'religion', which involves worship of the unknown, servile submission to its rules and regulations, and the bondage of fear! To know that God 'so loved us' (11), and to be brought into a relationship in which we can respond to and reciprocate that love, necessitates the removal of everything which sets God at a distance from us, or us from him, namely sin. This love brings us right through to the day of judgement, a day which will hold no terror for the believer who is loved with an everlasting love.

The reason given for our boldness is given at the end of v.17: 'because as he is, so are we in this world'. Christ is seated at the Father's right hand, the object of his Father's complacent love, crowned with glory and honour on account of his suffering by which he accomplished all that he came into the world to do, namely to bring many sons to glory (Heb. 2:9-10). For him the work of judgement is past, consigned to history. To fear is to contradict what he has done. If he himself bore our sins in his own body on the tree (1 Peter 2:24) there can be no wrath, no torment, for us. We are 'clothed in his righteousness alone, faultless to stand before the throne'.

1 John 4:19 – 5:3   Love assessed

'I love mankind, it's people I can't stand!' The wit who coined that phrase made a telling point. It is easy to have a nice idea in general terms, but will it stand the test in particular cases? In v. 20 John cuts through the waffle to see if there is any substance behind it. Having written as he has about the love of God for us and the wonder of such an effectual love, it might be our almost natural response, if we have felt the impact of it, to say, 'I love God'. But wait a minute: John's concern all the way through this letter is to give testimony to the truth, and to call upon witnesses to confirm it. The witness he now calls upon is your 'brother'.

How will he, your brother (or she, your sister) assess your love for God? According to your love for him (or her). The stark fact is that if you do not love your 'brother' then you do not love God as you ought. This is not an issue to be sidestepped by an appeal to want of 'lovableness' in your brother. The statement here stands without qualification. Never mind whether your brother is lovable or not. The love of which the apostle speaks is that love of which he was speaking in the previous verses, namely the response of love of a similar kind to that shown by God towards us. God's love for us was not qualified by any virtue or loveliness or deservedness of it on our part.

See how this verse harks back to v.12a: 'No one has seen God at any time'. Anybody who talks of loving God while not demonstrating the same love towards his brother does not know what he is talking about. This love, when it is in evidence, is also proof that God is abiding in us. Its absence is a denial of the same. Love is a communicable attribute: it has to have an object to give it expression. We would never have known that God is love had he not shown it to us in giving himself for us. If the love of God abides in us it must have an object on which to fix itself, a means by which it must express itself. God's love is expressed to all his children; if his love is in us, then it follows that his love *in us* will be expressed in the same way.

Yet again, it appears that John uses a circular argument, for while at 4:20 he appears to be saying, 'By this we know that we love God, when we love our brother,' at 5:2 he says 'By this we know that we love the children of God, when we love God.' However, this kind of circular argument is entirely valid. For love for God and love for the brethren are inseparable, in just the same way as love for God and keeping his commandments are (5:2-3). The link is provided in 5:1 – to love the Father (who begot) is to love his children (those who are begotten of him). The one who loves is also one begotten of God, or born of God. There is, however, a different nuance in 5:2, for our love for the children of God – our brethren – *proceeds* from our love for God. For when we love God, it means that God's love in us mightily motivates us in love towards our brethren, creating in us a yearning for their good, and activating us to the accomplishment of that end.

Is the driving force in your life which is expended towards your brothers and sisters in Christ the love of God? Is it his love which *compels* you (2 Cor. 5:14), that is, it gives you no freedom of movement other than to conform to its dictates?

1 John 5:2-5 Love at work

Love is sometimes set in opposition to law, almost as if they were two conflicting things. If we love God, say some, we need not concern ourselves about the law, for we are not under law, but under grace. The law no longer has any relevance to us. But that is very far from what John is saying here (2-3). Our love for God will give us a sensitivity towards his commandments and a heightened concern to keep them. His commandments are not simply to love God and our neighbour – these *summarise* his commandments. Let us argue from the lesser to the greater: When you love another person, you concern yourself in his or her concerns, seeking to do those things which please him or her. How much more so with God, especially as those things which please him are also intended for our good!

The love of God gives us a different perspective on, and attitude towards, his commandments. They are a burden indeed to those who have little time for their author; but not to those who really love him. 'I have seen the consummation of all perfection', says the psalmist, 'but your commandment is exceedingly broad. Oh, how I love your law! It is my meditation all the day' (Ps.119:96-97). If we still find any of his commandments a burden, then we still have something to learn of his love. The very fact that John mentions this point would seem to acknowledge that God's commandments may be found to be burdensome by some of his readers. Or else it is a device by which he reminds his readers of the amazing transformation which has taken place in their lives, that what was indeed once a burden is now a delight.

Overcoming the world (4-5). Because 'the whole world lies under the sway of the evil one' (5:19) it is quite clear that such love as we have been talking of is greatly opposed. It is simply not accepted in our society; there is no place for it in our world. Our obedience to the commandments of God may cause people to sneer, but the love which is his commandment will make them gnash their teeth and stop their ears unless they are touched by the grace of God. Love gives power to the commandment. 'Be of good cheer, I have overcome the world' (John 16:33). 'Greater is he who is in you than he who is in the world' (1 John 4:4). This is proved not only by the fact that God's people are kept secure while in the midst of this hostile environment, but most especially also by the turning of men and women from darkness to light, from the power of Satan to God (Acts 26:18).

If you are born of God then you have the life of God in your soul; you have been delivered from the thrall of darkness and transposed into the kingdom of God's Son (Col.1:13). That is the first stage in overcoming: it is by faith, and it is his work. Then, from your spiritual infancy you grow in the grace and knowledge of Christ (2 Peter 3:18). This is the second stage in overcoming: it is by faith, and it is his gift (Eph.2:8). But coupled with this defensive, personal aspect of overcoming there is the offensive one with the weapons of our warfare for the pulling down of strongholds (2 Cor.10:3-5): this, too, is by faith, and it is by his empowering. It is all by faith in the Son of God who himself has overcome the world (5). Therefore let us look unto Jesus, the author and finisher of our faith … (Heb.12:2).

1 John 5:6-13   A consistent witness Ꞌ

All the way through his letter John has been concerned to present consistent and corroborative testimony to the truth. Matters of substance are established in the mouths of two or three witnesses (Deut. 19:15). We are concerned with believing that Jesus is the Son of God – as Peter put it, 'You are the Christ, the Son of the living God' (Matt. 16:16). In this passage John appeals to a threefold witness to be received. It is not the fallible witness of men, but the infallible witness of God (9).

But first it is necessary to say that v. 7 in the AV and NKJV is almost universally rejected as not being original but a late addition to the text, being found in only a very few, very late, manuscripts. That is, vv. 7-8 should read simply something like this: 'For there are three that bear witness: the Spirit, the water and the blood; and these three agree as one.' This is not the place to enter into a discussion of the point, except to say that the inspired apostle is arguing that we should receive and accept the threefold witness of the Spirit, the water and the blood (9). When we understand this we see that the argument is not concerned with witness in heaven or on earth, or about the unity of the Godhead in the Trinity, but rather is directed to our acceptance of the person of Jesus Christ for who he is.

The dominant word in these verses is 'witness' or 'testimony'; it is the same word which appears again and again, in verb or noun form, though it may be variously translated as 'witness', or 'testimony', or 'record', or even 'gave' at the end of v. 10 – 'the testimony which God *has testified* concerning his Son'. Called upon to hear this testimony, we at once run into the difficulty of what are represented by the Spirit, the water, and the blood (8). These are the three that bear witness, says John, but back at v. 6 he brings in the Spirit only after declaring the manner in which Jesus Christ came – by water and blood.

We may think we understand the witness of the Spirit, but we ought to suspend our judgement until we have understood what is meant by water and blood. Our second witness in v. 8 is 'the water'. Jesus Christ came by water and blood; not only by water, but by water and blood (6). It therefore appears that the second and third witnesses, water and blood, must be taken *in conjunction*. But what are we to make of the 'water'? In his interview with Nicodemus, Jesus spoke of being born of water and of the Spirit (John 3:5). Various interpretations of that passage, too, have been forwarded. Many have supposed water to be *contrasted* with Spirit there, or with blood here. So that, for example, in the Gospel passage, water is taken by some to represent *natural* birth, and Spirit *new* birth by the Spirit of God. However, there is no difficulty at all if water and Spirit, or water and blood, are taken in harmony, as representing different aspects of the same thing. Here in John's letter the threefold witness of the Spirit, of water and of blood are a witness in harmony ('these three agree as one', 8).

A consideration of these difficulties will serve to remind us that the correct interpretation of any portion of God's Word will be in harmony with the rest, for what we read here applies generally, namely that God's testimony, unlike man's, is absolutely consistent.

1 John 5:6-13   A threefold testimony

Water and blood were uniformly understood in the Old Testament ceremonial law (which prophetically foreshadowed the truths of the New Testament dispensation) of cleansing (purification) (see, for example, Leviticus 8:6; Ezekiel 36:25-27) and atonement (see, for example, Leviticus 17:11). In the case of the priests, the washing with water symbolised cleanness for service. Now Jesus Christ 'came by water'. Our great high priest was altogether clean, without spot or blemish, untainted by sin – 'holy, harmless, undefiled, separate from sinners' (Heb. 7:26). Unlike the Levitical priests, who only *became* ceremonially clean, Jesus Christ *came* that way. 'Which of you convicts me of sin?' he could say to the crowd and in particular to those who would gleefully have seized on the least thing had there been any (John 8:46). The life of Jesus set him apart as the Son of God in the sense that it testified to his being so. But not only so, for he came also by 'blood'. While this may be a counter to some who denied the real humanity of the Lord, that he really was 'flesh and blood', there is more to it than that. Yes, he lived a perfect life in a real human body, but he bore that human body that it might be sacrificially broken on the cross, the altar where his blood was poured out to atone for sin. See John 19:34-35. Yes, he 'came by blood' in order that he might present his own blood in the presence of God to speak for us (see Hebrews 9:11-14). So not only does his life testify that he is the Son of God; his death does the same – see Luke 23:47 and Matthew 27:54.

So, having received the testimony of the water and the blood, how does the Spirit bear witness (6)? Consider the witness of the Spirit after Jesus was baptised (Matt. 3:17), or when he was transfigured (Matt. 17:5), or before his sufferings (John 12:28). This is the testimony God has testified of his Son (9). Yet there is more to the witness of the Spirit than these isolated instances. The witness of the Spirit characterised his whole ministry (Acts 2:22; 10:38), demonstrated in works of power, so that even his severest critics had to concede that God was with him (John 3:2).

We have heard the overwhelming historical testimony of these witnesses, and yet justice is not fully done to the text of v.6 because the witness of the Spirit is also a *present* witness. Not only so, but the water and the blood are also present witnesses, in that to their historical reality there corresponds an effectual reality in those who believe. These are not dull facts about something which happened in the past, but they are of vital importance to us, because they relate to us. Christ's perfect life was *lived for us* who believe, and in his sacrificial death he *died for us* who believe. And his Spirit was *given to us* who believe. For v.10 says, 'He who believes in the Son of God has the witness *in himself*'. Without a perfect life lived in our stead, without a sacrificial death in our place, without an outward and inward testimony to these, we could neither have nor know eternal life in God's Son.

We are first called upon to face the facts presented by God's testimony, and to believe in the Son on the basis of those facts. According to his promise, he gives his Spirit to those who believe in him, so that the Spirit who has testified externally, being the same Spirit of truth, now testifies internally, so that we may *know* we have eternal life.

1 John 5:13-17   Asking for others

This is not the first time John has written on the subject of confidence in prayer and receiving what we ask of him (3:21-22). Formerly it related more to our own need of grace; here it relates more to others' need of grace, for immediately John carries the point through to its application of asking on behalf of others who sin.

We cannot possibly know what God's will is except from what he has revealed of it, and except we have a wholehearted desire to do it. It is only as we are going about our heavenly Father's business that we can even find ourselves in the position where the truths of these verses have any bearing upon us.

What we are told here about asking is indicative of a need which arises in our service for Christ. It is when we are serving the Lord that we are most inclined to feel our own weakness, inadequacy and impotence. We cannot achieve what his own honour and glory demand should be done. His will is the calling out of his own out of the world (John 6:39-40; 10:16), and his work is carried out through the instrumentality of his servants. It should be clearly in our minds that we are serving Christ only as we are going about his will, and that it is his will which is to be done, and which must and *shall* be done. Therein arises our confidence, for all power and authority have been given to him, and he not only hears, but grants our petitions. With some people it makes no difference whether they hear us or not, because they will not or cannot lift a finger to grant us what we ask. Not so with the Lord. For him to hear is for him to answer (15).

The example John brings in connection with such asking (16) has, like so many of his statements, been much misunderstood. It hits upon a significant problem, for God is sovereign in salvation, and how then can we ask in respect of others needing to be saved? Nevertheless, it is no different in essence from any other problem associated with our asking of God, for his sovereignty extends to all things, and so how can we ask in respect of anything? (When John uses the word 'brother' here, as elsewhere in his letter, he is not *necessarily* thinking of brethren in Christ, although much of what he has to say will apply to such.)

When it comes to our praying on behalf of others, it is essential we have right motives. One of these is that 'all unrighteousness is sin' (17), which should move us to pray for its removal. Another is that the glory of Christ is seen in sinners turning to him. The grace of God is manifested in the salvation of those who believe; at the same time the righteous judgement of God is manifested in the condemnation of those who refuse to believe. Samuel was not wrong in praying for Saul (1 Sam. 15:35; 16:1), nor was the apostle Paul wrong in praying for the salvation of his fellow countrymen (Rom. 10:1). We can get into unnecessary tangles over this, as if it is right to pray about this but wrong to pray about that and we don't know how to distinguish between them! John is not classifying sins into venial and mortal sins, nor is he writing with the 'unforgivable sin' in mind. He is talking about men and women entangled in sin to whom the gospel is being presented. Some will hear, and some will harden their hearts. But, whatever their attitude, they are *all bound* under sin, and unless delivered will die in their sins. Our asking is an essential accompaniment of our evangelism, in order that some might be saved.

1 John 5:18-21   Protecting our interests

Verse 18 has echoes of 3:9 and 3:3. John writes of those 'born of God' not sinning. Paul, in Romans 6:2, writes of those who have 'died to sin' not living in it any longer. They are saying the same thing in different ways. There is something utterly incongruous about those continuing in sin who have died to it, or of those who have been born of God behaving in an unrighteous manner (for 'all unrighteousness is sin', 17). Before we start theorising about whether John is writing in an absolute sense or placing things in watertight compartments and whether a Christian who commits sins (as all do) are denials of what he declares here, let us remember that this statement is to be taken in the same way as all other such statements in his letter. John is concerned with grand principles, not with supposed exceptions. Being 'born of God', that is, having the life of God in you by his Spirit, is absolutely incompatible with wrongdoing. We have all had the experience of being told by others, very likely by our parents when we were children, 'You don't do that here,' whether it was talking in a public library or failing to observe the proper etiquette in company. If we knew what was good for us, our reply was not, 'But I just have!' How much more shamefaced should we be when reminded by God's Word that, as Christians, 'we don't do that'! Who is going to stand up and dare to assert that those who are born of God do sin in the sense that it is accepted practice? No: whoever is born of God does *not* sin!

That this is the force of the argument is indicated from the following clause: 'but he who has been born of God keeps himself'. The principle of life within the believer operates powerfully to the end that he should not sin. Such a principle is entirely absent from the unbeliever. It is no use exhorting the non-Christian to strive for the ideals which are consistently set out in the New Testament because they are not met with the desire for conformity to the will of God which characterises the Christian. The non-Christian must be urged to turn to the Lord in repentance and faith because his heart and desires are all wrong. But for the Christian there can never be enough of that encouragement to press on to greater holiness of life because it finds in his heart a corresponding desire to 'keep himself'.

Taking verses 18 and 19 together, we see that there has been a fundamental cleavage between those who are 'born of God' and the rest of the world, which lies under the sway of the evil one, or, literally, is 'in' the evil one. We are either 'in' the evil one or 'in' him who is true (20). For the Christian, as one 'born of God' it is a wonderful truth that the wicked one 'does not touch him'. How eager is the enemy of souls to lay his malevolent hands on us, to enclose us in his secret, sinister embrace! Once we lay there comfortably enough, as does the rest of the world; but, having been released from his clutches and seen the end of his dark designs, it is unspeakable comfort to know that such is our security in Christ that the wicked one does not touch us. 'Hands off!' cries one of infinite power and authority.

How are you keeping?

1 John 5:18-21   'We know … so what?'

We who are of God live in a world which is 'in the wicked one'. In a very real sense the whole world is against us, for it was against him whose life was impaled on a Roman gibbet. The 'mind-set' of all people of whatever culture or background or education; the social and political systems of the world; the norms to which people are expected to conform; the objectives set in life; all are 'anti-Christian', all are the result of the world lying 'in the wicked one'. The whole world system militates against us. When such things are considered it is an amazing truth that we 'who know that we are of God' should survive such hostility. It is a demonstration of the truth that 'he who is in you is greater than he who is in the world' (4:4).

However, there is undoubtedly an implied caution in these verses. It is not simply to be taken for granted that the one born of God keeps himself. There is nothing automatic about it. Keeping oneself requires a mighty and an ongoing effort. When we begin to forget that we are of God, when we start to lose our spiritual bearings, then is the most dangerous time to be in the world, then we are most susceptible to being seduced by its influences.

'We know … we know … we know' is the recurring theme of these verses. Do we? Do you know whose you are? Do you know where you are? Do you know how it has come about? Has the Son of God come and given you an understanding (20)? He came to make his Father known, who is described as 'him who is true'.

All the way through his letter John has presented us with stark contrasts that we might know where we stand, so that by the end we might have a rich assurance of what is true. Of the Lord Jesus Christ, God manifest in the flesh, we can declare, 'This is the true God and eternal life'.

What pathos there is in John's closing word! Idols stand in contrast to the Lord Jesus who alone is worthy of our undivided love, our highest worship, the zeal of our service. With what affectionate concern does he adjure his readers to cleave only to Christ! The Christian has nothing else to live for in this world. Sport, hobbies, entertainments, socialising, food, music, or whatever it may be, are idols in as real a sense as the Mary of Roman Catholicism or the representations of deity in every false religion, but often are not recognised as such. However, if they are not serving the Christian in his or her life for the Lord, idols they are, and idols they will remain. 'But I must have my …' is invariably a denial of the place of pre-eminence of Christ in our lives.

These closing words of the apostle strike at the heart of what is wrong in so many of our churches. You have heard the apostle's gathered evidence. What is your conclusion?

Readings in

2 and 3 John

by Keith Weber

WINDOW
ON THE
WORD

T he 'elect lady', to whom the second later of John was addressed, may well have been a real person with believing children (1:4), but it is possible this might have been a coded message to a church in Asia Minor with which John was familiar. Similarities of style and language suggest that the author was the same as those books in the New Testament which are attributed to the apostle John (cf. v. 5 with John 13:34-35, v. 6 with John 14:23 and vv. 7 and 12 with John 15:11 and 16:24). John was again concerned with anti-Christian teaching which denied the person and work of Christ (7-9). As Christians met in homes, it was important for them not to welcome false teachers, for their heretical teaching would be very damaging. John repeats one of the themes of his first letter but in a more personalised form. He shows once more that abiding in truth is the basis for walking in love. True fellowship with unbelievers is impossible. There are no clear indications about the time and place of writing, but it is likely to have been the same as other letters.

The third letter was written to a believer known to John who regularly offered hospitality to travelling preachers. John gives him both a commendation and a warning. The subject matter is similar to 2 John in that he wants to encourage believers to welcome true preachers of the gospel. Diotrephes was a gossip and guilty of abusing authority in the church by excluding brothers who were being hospitable (9-10). He says that love must prevail within the circle of truth (2-12), as peace must prevail within the circle of friends (13-14). If 2 John promotes exclusivity by denying fellowship to false teachers, 3 John restores the balance by promoting inclusivity among all true believers, whether local residents or visitors.

2 John   Truth and love to be cherished

It has been argued by some that 'the elect lady' was a kind of pseudonym, and that John was actually writing to a church rather than an individual. It is true that he does not name the lady in question in his letter – but neither does he give his own name (which has led some to suppose the writer to be someone other than the apostle John). Let us take it at its face value: a personal letter from the apostle, 'the elder', to a lady who was well known to him, and indeed to many others (1). Who knows but that the letter was occasioned by John's contact with relatives of the lady in question (4,13)? Even supposing it was written to a church, the points he makes remain valid.

A well-known figure (1). There were a number of prominent women in the early New Testament church, most notably, perhaps, Priscilla, who, together with her husband Aquila, were renowned for their service and hospitality, a church meeting in their house – see Acts 18:2,3,18,24-26; Romans 16:3-5; 1 Corinthians 16:19. Phoebe also, from the church in Cenchrea (Rom. 16:1-2), was a labourer whose works went before her. Women such as these were a living testimony to the blessing brought to churches through their following the principle of 1 Timothy 2:9-10. Would that God would give us more of them! See how the 'elect lady' was not only well known but universally loved (1).

A responsibility rewarded (4). John links 'children walking in the truth' with the 'commandment' which had been given. We have no power to convert our children to Christ, but we are charged to bring them up in the 'training and admonition of the Lord' (Eph. 6:4). A mother's influence in the home on her children is incalculable. God has always been pleased to deal with families, and he has always honoured those who honour him. A youngster surrounded by godly influences in a happy home where the Word is taught and the Lord is at work will not easily throw it all away. This woman's children rose up and called her blessed (Prov. 31:28), those who were 'walking in truth'. In these days where there is so little cohesiveness within families, but so often conflict of interests and friction and unprincipled conduct, what a cause of joy it is to see the fruit of a Christian upbringing. One sows, another waters, but God gives the increase. But without sowing and watering there will be no increase!

Much of what John writes here on truth and love and keeping God's commandments has been considered in the notes on his first letter, and so we shall not dwell on them now.

Discernment and discrimination (7-11). If the 'elect lady' was in the position where her house was open to the church then she would have to be especially careful whom she welcomed who might exercise an influence there (10-11). Sadly, not all those professing to be Christians are what they seem to be. The truth has to be guarded against error.

Fellowship (12). There can be much pleasure in receiving a good report of a brother or sister in Christ; even more in receiving correspondence from them or (a privilege they did not have in John's day) speaking with them on the telephone. However, there is nothing like being able to meet face to face those whom one loves in the Lord (12). See Proverbs 27:17, and Philippians 1:23-26. May we make it our ambition so to live in fellowship with the Lord that our fellowship with others fills them with joy.

3 John   Truth and love to be exemplified

This letter was prompted by the return to John of some whom he simply calls 'brethren' (3) – probably itinerant evangelists or missionaries, and possibly those who had been sent out under the apostle's direction – who had given him a report of their reception at the hand of Gaius as well as their rejection at the hand of Diotrephes. Gaius himself may or may not have been an office holder in the church. More than likely he was in the same church as Diotrephes, but if not then he must have been sufficiently acquainted with him for John to be able to write to him in this way. Diotrephes appears to be the leader of the church, and if not the only elder, certainly the one with influence, and acting here in a high-handed way (10). Note that it is not the church with whom John finds fault, but the leader of the church. Nor is he 'having a go' at Diotrephes behind his back, for although this was a letter written to a private person, it appears from what he says that John has been open and public about the problem (9-10). That is so necessary in the church. Where an accusation against an elder is sustained by witnesses and his sin is exposed, he is to be rebuked publicly, as Paul says (1 Tim. 5:19). This man was actually harming the church.

Gaius. To be 'beloved' (1-2) by such a one as John is a rich commendation. What warranted this description of the man? Firstly, his soul prospered (2), which is enlarged upon in the next sentence concerning the truth being in him, and his living accordingly (3). Secondly, he was a man given to hospitality (5-6), using this means to forward the cause of the gospel (8). He had a great heart for all who loved the Lord (5).

Because what Gaius had done was in direct opposition to the wishes of Diotrephes it brought him into a position of conflict.

He has received the brethren, contrary to the instructions of Diotrephes (10). Much heartache is caused when our doing right is disapproved of by others, especially by those who ought to know better, and no doubt Gaius suffered by the censorious spirit of Diotrephes. It is for this reason that John seeks to encourage him by mentioning his faithfulness (5), the testimony of his love brought back by the visitors (6), and the fact that he was doing right, whatever anyone might say, in receiving such men (8). It had not been Gaius' wish to introduce trouble, but he could not compromise on the truth, and so he simply got on with what he was required to do.

Diotrephes. This man was not accused of heresy; it was not his orthodoxy which was in question. The sole charge laid at his door was love of pre-eminence. His actions flowed from that foul source. Christian leader, beware! How came he to that position? Though we are not told, we may hazard a guess that pride concerning the gifts he undoubtedly had, coupled with ambition to see himself 'to the top', from which precarious position he exercised his power and authority to maintain it, were involved. Perhaps he had become dependent upon his office, and acted in so authoritarian a way through a sense of personal insecurity. One has only to think of Saul, the first king of Israel. What he was in the eyes of men was more important than what he was in the eyes of God.

Demetrius. Where he fits into the equation we do not know. Perhaps he was another who had suffered at the hand of Diotrephes. But notice the emphasis John places throughout this letter on 'truth' (3,4,8,12). Truth must be the undergirding principle of our every action in life. It speaks for itself, and from it spring all the other virtues.

Readings in

Jude

by Stan Evers

WINDOW
ON THE
WORD

THE LETTER OF JUDE

This brief letter seems to have been written by the half-brother of Jesus and the brother of James (Matt. 13:55; Mark 6:3). Note how differently Jude referred to them. Jude is a form of Judah or Judas, but he is not the same person referred to in Luke 6:16 or Acts 15:22. He met with the believers after the ascension (Acts 1:14). He wrote to exhort an unidentified community of local believers to contend for the purity of the faith in view of the false teachers who had infiltrated their number. The date is uncertain, but if Peter knew of Jude, it would have to be before AD 68. If not, it could have been as late as AD 80. It is unlikely they used a common source. He warns them of the heretical attacks that were coming from immoral and godless men who taught a distorted view of grace. Any rejection of Christ involved the rejection of Christian morality. Believers were to go on the offensive, without becoming offensive themselves. The use of non- canonical material in vv. 9,14 (the Assumption of Moses and the book of Enoch) caused some to doubt the inspiration of this book at first, but there is nothing contradictory in those references and we can be assured that the whole letter is of God. Paul quoted from secular poets in Acts 17. Note how many of the New Testament letters which are later in time and position deal with the threat of false teaching.

Jude 1   Who was Jude?

The short letter of Jude contains warning (such as v. 4) and comfort (such as vv. 24-25). Believers in the twenty-first century need warning and comfort as much as believers in the first century. Heretical teachers disturb the church today and Christians suffer because of their faithfulness to Christ. It is therefore important that we spend a few days considering this letter to equip us for holy living in this evil world. May I suggest that you read the whole letter each day so that its message fills your mind and grips your soul? How sad that modern Christians often neglect this little book with a big message!

'**Jude, a servant of Jesus Christ**' (1). The term 'servant' reveals three facts about Jude:

(a) *His privilege.* Jude had the honour to serve Jesus Christ, God's own Son, by preaching and by writing this letter. Christ gives weak and sinful people the joy of service, though he could easily work by his own power alone to extend his kingdom.

(b) *His humility.* Jude did not demand a hearing because he was brother to James

and the brother of Jesus Christ. He knew, like John the Baptist, that Christ becomes greater as the preacher becomes less (John 3:30).

(c) *His obedience.* Jude, a servant, obeyed the commands of his master, Jesus Christ. Christians belong to Christ who bought them by shedding his precious blood (1 Cor. 6:20). We are set free from sin's bondage to become servants of Christ (Rom. 6:15-18).

'**Jude ... a brother of James**' (1). The James mentioned by Jude was not the apostle (and brother of John) who was killed by King Herod (Acts 12:1-2). This James was our Lord's brother who became leader of the Jerusalem church and wrote the New Testament letter bearing his name (Acts 12:17; 15:13). Jude was therefore a brother of Jesus Christ and is called 'Judas' in Mark 6:3. In v. 17, Jude makes it clear that he was not one of the twelve apostles.

To think about: 'Look upon duty as an honour and service as a privilege' (Thomas Manton).

Jude 1-2   What is a Christian?

Jude's description of his readers, in the second part of v.1, gives us a biblical definition of a Christian. We take the words as found in the NIV.

Christians are called. There is the *general call* – 'the free offer' – of the gospel to everyone who hears the preaching of God's Word. The sinner may turn a deaf ear to this gracious call.

However, the *special call* – 'the effectual call' – cannot be rejected. The person who hears this call must come to the Lord Jesus Christ for salvation. The effectual call is the voice of God, through his Holy Spirit, compelling sinners to respond to the human voice of the preacher.

Christians are loved by God. The source of God's call may be traced back to his eternal love. 'Those God foreknew he also predestined ... And those he predestined, he also called ...' (Rom. 8:29-30). By the word 'foreknew', Paul means that God loved us before time began. Nothing in those yet unborn could merit his love. Believers were loved not because of foreseen holiness but so that they would 'be conformed to the likeness of his Son' (Rom. 8:29). God the Father displayed his love to his children by the death of his Son (Rom. 8:32). God will never allow anything to separate us from his love which comes to us 'in Christ Jesus our Lord' (Rom. 8:35-39). We are, in the words of Jude, 'kept by Jesus Christ' (1).

The AV/NKJV rendering – 'sanctified' – indicates the outcome of God's call rather than its source. This word means 'set apart for God's use'. We were 'set apart' for God at conversion and become progressively like God as we shape our lives by the teaching of his Word.

Christians are kept. The final section of v.1, 'kept by Jesus Christ', finds an echo in v.24. None of God's children will fail to reach heaven! Commenting on 'by Jesus Christ', Thomas Manton wrote: 'Jesus Christ is the cabinet wherein God's jewels are kept.' The Saviour will not lose any of the jewels bought with his blood.

Christians are called, loved and kept because of God's mercy, peace and love. Therefore Jude prays that his readers will know an increasing measure of these gifts in their lives (2).

To think about: Does the doctrine of the saint's preservation result in spiritual carelessness? No, because 'None are more apt to suspect themselves than they that are most sure in God' (Manton).

Jude 3 Jude the eager writer

The people God had called, loved and whom he keeps safe, live in a world full of heretical teachers. Therefore Jude mixed warning with comfort in his short letter.

What Jude wanted to write (3).

In the first part of v. 3 we read about Jude's:

(a) *Love for believers.* Those who 'are loved by God' (1) are Jude's 'dear friends' (3). His deep concern for his readers made him rethink what they most needed to read even though this meant abandoning his own cherished plans about the book he wanted to write. Are we so preoccupied with our own ideas that we miss the real needs of other Christians?

(b) *Enthusiasm to write.* Jude was 'very eager to write'. We ought to copy his zeal to serve the Lord! But we are to do what he wants rather than what we think he wants. Perhaps we are wasting time and energy on activities and meetings which are unproductive. Maybe God desires us to develop new gifts and to open up new ministries for the benefit of his people.

(c) *The book he never wrote.* What better theme could Jude choose than 'the salvation we share' (3)? However, the dangers facing his readers demanded urgent attention (4).

What Jude felt compelled to write (3).

In the second part of v. 3 we read about:

(a) *Divine compulsion.* Behind Jude's words, 'I felt I had to write', lay divine pressure. Jude wrote God's Word to his readers (then and now), alerting them (and us) to false teachers and their evil doctrines.

(b) *Heartfelt exhortation.* The word 'urge' ('exhort', AV) comes from the Greek word translated as 'Counsellor' ('Helper', NKJV; 'Comforter', AV) in John 16:7. It means 'one called alongside to help'. In his letter Jude gets alongside his readers to help them resist error and to encourage them to remain loyal to the Lord Jesus Christ. Are we urging fellow believers to 'love and good deeds' (Heb. 10:23-25)?

(c) *Revealed faith.* 'The faith that was once for all entrusted to the saints' is now written down in the Bible. We must not add to or amend the Bible (Rev. 22:18-19). We test whatever we hear and shape our lives by God's Word.

We 'contend for the faith' whenever we live a godly life, proclaim the gospel and refute false teaching.

To think about: God speaks once for all in his Word. Are we listening? Are we obeying?

Jude 4-7   A snapshot of heretics

Imagine an explosion at a nuclear power station resulting in dangerous levels of radiation in the air causing contamination for miles around. Jude warns about a contamination that damns the soul. This pollution comes from heretical teaching. But does it matter what people believe? Yes, because wrong doctrine paves the road to an everlasting hell. Bear in mind also that the Bible is God's Word (3) and any departure from it takes us away from God. It would be irresponsible for believers not to warn people about soul-damning dogma spread by false teachers. Jude tells us that heretics are:

1. **Devious.** The words 'secretly slipped in' (4) suggest that these men were members of local churches who had gained acceptance by concealing their error. Heretics 'masquerade as apostles of righteousness' as they copy their true master, Satan, who 'masquerades as an angel of light' (2 Cor. 11:13-15).

2. **Depraved.** In reality these members are 'godless men, who change the grace of God into a licence for immorality' (4). 'Ungodly' means 'destitute of reverence for God' and soon leads to excusing sinful behaviour. Such a person may think: 'God is love and forgives sin so it does not matter how I live';

but this attitude is a contradiction of God's grace which delivers us from sin. This sort of conduct is to 'deny Jesus Christ our only Sovereign and Lord' (4). It is not enough to call Jesus 'Lord', we must serve him as Lord. Jesus said, 'Not everyone who says to me "Lord, Lord", will enter the kingdom of heaven, but only he who does the will of my Father who is in heaven' (Matt. 7:21).

3. **Destructive.** Heretics reap condemnation for themselves and take others to 'condemnation' (4). This was 'written about long ago' (4) in scriptures passages such as Ezekiel 18:20 – 'The soul who sins is the one who will die'– and illustrated in the examples cited in these verses.

The Jews were punished because of their *unbelief* (5), the angels were banished from heaven because of their *pride* (6) and the people of Sodom and Gomorrah faced the fire of God's wrath because of their *immorality* (7). 'Condemnation awaits sinners' is the clear message of these events.

To think about: Note the downward path in these verses. No fear of God leads to excusing sinful living which in turn results in denial of Christ and finally ends in destruction.

Jude 8-11,16 How to identify heretics

In this section Jude tells us more about the false teachers who had 'secretly slipped' into the first-century churches. Such teachers still prey on twenty-first-century churches, so we must pay attention to Jude's signs of false teachers.

Pollution – these dreamers pollute their own bodies (8). Heresy often leads to immorality (see also vv. 4,6). Our bodies are temples of the Holy Spirit and are therefore not to be defiled by sexual sins (1 Cor. 6:15-20).

Rebellion – these dreamers ... reject authority (8). Another mark of the heretic is his rejection of authority, especially that of spiritual leaders and the discipline of the local church. He always wants 'to do his own thing'.

Slander – these dreamers ... slander celestial beings (8; compare 2 Peter 2:10). Perhaps the word 'dreamers' suggests that the heretics claimed special messages from angels which gave them equality with angels and made them superior to other human teachers. But this attitude reveals folly and ignorance – this is the point Jude makes in his puzzling statement in vv. 9-10. They talk about things 'they do not understand' – they have the understanding of dumb animals (10)!

Michael the archangel, the leader of the holy angels, does not dispute with Satan, the leader of the fallen angels. Rather Michael calls on the Lord to rebuke the devil.

Cain ... Balaam ... Korah (11). Some heretics are like wicked Cain who hated his righteous brother Abel (Heb. 11:4; 1 John 3:11-12). Others copy Balaam 'who loved the wages of wickedness' – they aim to make money out of religion as they lead their devotees into depravity (2 Peter 2:15-16; Num. 22–24; Rev. 2:14). A third group behave like Korah, a Levite, who rebelled against the God-appointed leadership of Moses and Aaron (Num. 16).

To think about: Verse 16 aptly sums up the various sorts of false teachers as 'grumblers and fault-finders' who 'boast about themselves and flatter others to their own advantage'.

Jude 12-13   Alarming illustrations

Having told us how heretics behave and given us examples of the variety of false teachers, Jude now gives us six illustrations of the ceaseless activities and dangerous influence of these heretics.

1. The bride (12). The church is often pictured in the Bible as a bride (see for example, Ephesians 5:25-33). Sinful conduct turns 'the beautiful Cinderella into the ugly sister' (Benton) and false teachers are scars ('blemishes') on the face of Christ's bride. These men had no right to sit at the 'love feasts' – a combination of a fellowship meal and a communion service.

2. The shepherd (12). False teachers work for their own good rather than caring for the Lord's sheep. Jude may have in mind Ezekiel's warning about 'shepherds ... who only take care of themselves' (Ezek. 34:2-4). Such shepherds try to lead the sheep away from Christ the good shepherd, but his sheep will never perish. They are safe in the shepherd's hand (John 10:11,28-29).

3. The clouds (12). Heretics promise so much but do not deliver, like clouds in a drought which give no rain. Don't we see evidence of this fact in the unfulfilled promises of the healing evangelists? Christ alone can refresh weary souls.

4. The fruit trees (12). Autumn should be the time when the fruit is ripe for picking. Why 'twice dead'? Heretics are already spiritually dead and will not escape future condemnation (4). 'Blackest darkness' awaits them (13).

Jesus' comments in the Sermon on the Mount and his cursing of the fig tree explain Jude's metaphor (Matt. 7:15-23; Mark 11:12-14,20-21. Read also Gal. 5:22-26). Do we have the leaves of an empty profession but no fruit of a holy life?

5. The sea (13). Just as the storm waves dump flotsam and jetsam on to the land, so false teachers throw rubbish into the church. Trendy teaching opens the door to laxity and worldliness in living and in worship.

6. The stars (13). False teachers who think of themselves as stars shining with spiritual light are destined for everlasting darkness. Christ is the only reliable star for the church (Num. 24:17; Rev. 22:16).

To think about: 'What is the quickest way to ruin the church? It is simply to believe that false teaching does not matter' (Benton).

Jude 14-15   Enoch – the man and his message

In contrast to the wicked conduct of the heretics in vv. 4-13 we read about a godly man named Enoch, 'the seventh from Adam'.

Who was Enoch?

(a) *He was a man who walked with God (Gen. 5:22,24).* He desired God's company so much that he walked with him for over three hundred years. Fellowship with God is the only antidote to the poison of sin and false doctrine. The word 'walked' suggests steady progress and perseverance.

(b) *He was a man who pleased God (Heb. 11:5).* Obedience is the hallmark of the person who walks with God. Obedience is motivated by faith (Heb. 11:6). Obedience to God is our duty and safeguard in days of evil and error.

(c) *He was a man who preached for God (14).* Enoch preached against the wickedness of his generation and predicted the coming of final judgement for all who would not repent of all their sins. Enoch was like an oasis in the desert of wickedness. Service was the outcome of his devotion to God and obedience of God.

(d) *He was a man who went to live with God* (Gen. 5:24; Heb. 11:5). Enoch was taken into God's presence without facing death. He walked from earth to heaven and has been walking with God ever since! Enoch's departure to heaven apart from death declares that there is a future life in heaven for all who trust in Christ. The Saviour died to conquer sin and the grave.

What was the message of Enoch?

Enoch predicted the *Second Coming* of Christ thousands of years before his first coming. In v. 14 Enoch predicts two facts about Christ's coming:

(a) *The Lord's coming is certain* – 'The Lord is coming'. Notice the word 'will' in the following texts: John 14:3; 1 Thessalonians 4:16; 2 Peter 3:10.

(b) *The Lord will come with his angels* – 'The Lord is coming with ... his holy ones'. 'The angels who assisted God to give his law at Sinai will also accompany God in judging the world. How poignant it is that these false teachers who have been slandering celestial beings (8) are going to be judged by celestial beings!' (Benton). Several other passages speak about angels accompanying the Lord at his return including Matthew 13:41; 2 Thessalonians 1:7-8 and various verses in Revelation 16. The AV/NKJV reads: 'The Lord comes ... with his saints', and may refer to believers already in heaven who will come with Christ at his return (1 Thess. 4:14).

To think about: Those who reject Christ as Saviour will face him as the Judge.

Jude 14-15   The final judgement

Enoch predicts a third fact about Christ's coming in v.15: He is coming to judge sinners. The word 'prophesied' (14) means that he is giving us God's own account of that last day.

We read four facts about the final judgement in v.15.

1. The judgement will be public. This fact is implied rather than stated by Jude. The sinner will not be taken into a private room and gently reprimanded for a few minor mistakes. All his secret and open sins will be exposed by Christ the Judge who sees and knows all things.

2. The judgement will be universal. Jude clearly says that the Lord will 'judge everyone' and 'convict all the ungodly' (15). All the names of the ungodly are on his list for the final day of judgement. No sinner can escape the judgement to come, because God has declared that 'man is destined to die once, and after that to face judgement' (Heb. 9:27).

3. The judgement will be based on conduct. Jude uses the word 'ungodly' four times in v.15. We have already defined 'ungodly' as 'destitute of reverence for God' (see notes on vv.4-7). Such behaviour merits, and will receive, God's wrath. Some of the ungodly go deep into their sins, while upbringing or circumstances restrain others.

Some are even religious and respectable but their proud self-righteous lives are still offensive to God. All who are not Christians are in God's estimation 'ungodly'. Though the degree of ungodliness may vary, nevertheless all are guilty in God's sight and will appear at his judgement seat.

4. The judgement will be thorough. Deeds ('all the ungodly acts'), motives ('acts they have done in the ungodly way') and words ('all the harsh words ungodly sinners have spoken') will receive thorough examination by the divine Judge who sees into the depths of every heart. There is no higher court for an appeal or any possibility of a re-trial at a later date. The Judge's word will be fair and final.

Special attention will be paid to the fact that sinners have spoken 'harsh words ... against him' — the Lord Jesus Christ. To deride a Christian is to deride Christ. To use Christ's name in blasphemy is to insult him.

To think about: Jude writes about the judgement of sinners. Paul writes about a judgement day for believers in 1 Corinthians 3:10-14 and 2 Corinthians 5:10. Believers cannot lose their salvation but will be assessed for progress in sanctification and sincerity in service.

Jude 17-19   Remember!

'The apostles of our Lord Jesus Christ' (17) echoed Enoch's predictions about false teachers (14-15). Christ sent the apostles to deliver his message; therefore their teaching (now written in the Bible) is authentic and ought to be remembered by Jude's readers and by ourselves. 'Dear friends' shows Jude's concern to safeguard believers from error (17; see also 3,20).

The last times. It is clear from the opening verses of Hebrews (1:1-2) that 'the last times' (18) span the period between Christ's first coming and his Second Coming. History shows that false teachers have been active since Christ's time on earth, according to his own predictions (see, for example, Mark 13:5-13). Jude and the other apostles (such as Paul in 2 Thessalonians 2 and 2 Timothy 4:1-4 and Peter in 2 Peter 2) tell us to expect false teachers until Christ's return.

Scoffers. Both Peter (2 Peter 3:3) and Jude (18) wrote about 'scoffers' – people who despise biblical morality and laugh at religion. Such people promote homosexuality and argue for lowering the age of consent. Others sneer at those who believe in creation and the miracles of Jesus Christ. Don't become discouraged! Rather see in the words of scoffers a fulfilment of God's Word! One day

God will laugh at those who now laugh at him (Ps. 2:4-6). Perhaps the thought of that day – judgement day – should make us weep and pray for scoffers to 'kiss the Son, lest he be angry' (Ps. 2:12).

People without the Holy Spirit. Scoffers 'do not have the Spirit' (19) and their conduct shows it! They follow 'their own ungodly desires' (18) and 'follow mere natural instincts' (19). It is impossible for sinners not to sin and it is impossible for them to desire what is holy (Rom. 8:5-8). Jesus said that unbelievers are the slaves of sin (John 8:34). But he came 'to proclaim freedom for the prisoners' and 'to release the oppressed' (Luke 4:18). He became a prisoner and died as a transgressor to set the prisoners free!

Scoffers also cause divisions within the church – 'these are the men who divide you' (19). These teachers formed a faction – an elite group – within the church. They apparently thought of themselves as superior to other members. Those who have the Holy Spirit 'make every effort to keep the unity of the Spirit through the bond of peace' (Eph. 4:3).

To think about: Daily togetherness led to daily conversions when the Holy Spirit came on the church! See Acts 2:1-4, 42-47.

Jude 20-21   Building and praying

How can we avoid giving in to error? By paying attention to Jude's teaching in vv. 20-21. We read in these verses about building, praying, loving and looking.

1. Building (20). Heretics are divisive and destructive (19), but we are to build one another up with the bricks of God's Word. 'Faith' is 'the faith that was once for all entrusted to the saints' (3), now preserved for us in the Bible. We grow as we shape our creed and our conduct by the Scriptures.

Why does Jude describe this 'faith' as 'most holy'? We may suggest three reasons. Firstly, the Bible is reliable and true. Secondly, the Bible is derived from God who is holy. Thirdly, the Bible calls us to holiness in contrast to the wickedness of the apostates (4-13,16-19). Jude writes about 'your most holy faith'. Are we using this faith – the Bible – to build ourselves and others up? We build ourselves up as we pray (20) and as we love God and as we love one another (21). Testing times in the life of the individual Christian and in the life of the church are also building and growing times (see Hebrews 12:4-13).

'Contend for the faith' (3) and 'build … in your most holy faith' (20) are inseparable twins. The neglect of either will produce unbalanced churches and weak Christians.

2. Praying (20). Christians 'pray in the Holy Spirit' (20) whereas unbelievers 'do not have the Spirit' (19). God rejects the religious activity of the non-Christian because the Holy Spirit does not prompt his actions. His deeds are performed to earn salvation rather than with a desire to please God. The unbeliever may 'say prayers' but only the Christian knows how to pray. He pleads the merits of Christ and prays in the power of the Holy Spirit; hence God listens to him.

What does Jude mean when he urges us to 'pray in the Holy Spirit'? It is to pray with the power and the assistance of the Holy Spirit. Boldness, fervour, perseverance and faith mark such prayer. Those who 'pray in the Holy Spirit' overcome Satan and their prayers are effective (Eph. 6:18; James 5:16-18).

_____

To think about: Prayer gives us discernment to detect and reject error. Prayer makes us wise builders of one another. Prayer helps us understand our 'most holy faith' – the Bible.

Jude 20-21   Loving and looking

Having looked at building and praying, we think now about loving and looking.

1. Loving (21). God keeps us (1,24), nevertheless we also keep ourselves (21). There is a delightful balance in the Bible between divine sovereignty and human responsibility. Jude's readers were 'to keep themselves within the circle of God's love' (Simon Kistemaker). The father still loved the prodigal son when he went away to a foreign country, but the son had removed himself from the place where he could enjoy the benefits of his father's love to the full. He did not keep himself in the love of his father. We keep in God's love as we keep close to the Lord Jesus Christ. The true child of God, like David, can never stray out of the love of God, however he may through sin lose the comfort of that love and the joy of salvation (Ps. 51:10-13).

We 'keep … in God's love' in three ways:

(a) *By remembering God's unchanging love.* We would do well to read often Scriptures such as Isaiah 49:15-16; Jeremiah 31:3; Romans 8:35-39; 1 John 4:9-10.

(b) *By keeping in love with God.* We should prayerfully face the question which Jesus put three times to Peter: 'Do you truly love me?' (John 21:15-19).

(c) *By loving God's children.* Read 1 Peter 1:22; 3:8-9; 4:7-8.

2. Looking (21). Those who love God are eager to see him and his Son! Two thoughts are wrapped up in the word 'wait': excitement and patience. We should wait for Christ's return with the excitement of a small child impatient for Christmas. We wait with patience because God measures time differently from us (2 Peter 3:8).

In v. 21 Jude gives three reasons for patient waiting:

(a) *Because we will receive mercy.* God's mercy – his pity for us in our sin – saved us in the past, sustains us in the present and will welcome us to heaven in the future.

(b) *Because we will enter into eternal life.* Eternal life is more than never-ending life; it is the adoration of God forever! Boredom will not get a look-in!

(c) *Because we will enjoy fellowship with the triune God.* Father, Son and Holy Spirit – the three Persons of the Trinity – are mentioned in vv. 20-21. We will see the glorious God of the doxology in vv. 24-25.

To think about: The believer and the church which does not have a warm love to the Saviour will soon drift into backsliding and error.

Jude 22-23   Reaching unbelievers

We may say that vv. 20-21 are about the reinforcement of Christians whereas the focus of vv. 22-23 is reaching out to weak believers and to unbelievers.

We see three groups in these verses:

1. Those who doubt (22). Among the doubters are those who have been unsettled by 'certain men' who have 'secretly slipped in' (4). False doctrine or bad teaching causes confusion. Some come to Christ like the leper who said, 'If you are willing, you can make me clean' (Mark 1:40). Others are like the man who said to the Saviour, 'I do believe; help me overcome my unbelief' (Mark 9:24).

We are to 'be merciful to those who doubt' (22). This means showing compassion and patience. Consider Jesus' tenderness to doubting Thomas. Our patience may help doubters towards his confession: 'My Lord and my God' (John 20:28).

2. Those who are in danger (23). Jude's words, 'snatch others from the fire', are rooted in Amos 4:11 ('you were like a burning stick snatched from the fire') and Zechariah 3:2 ('Is not this man a burning stick snatched from the fire?').

The mention of 'fire' points to the peril of the unconverted. We may compare the unbeliever to a man who is asleep in a burning house

and therefore oblivious to the imminent destruction that is about to engulf him and his family. Sinners 'are in the suburbs of hell, the fire is already kindled' (Manton).

We are to 'snatch' sinners from the fire! Sadly, unbelievers often behave like a man in a burning house who complains about his rescuer making so much noise in the street. He grumbles about kill-joy Christians preaching the gospel and laughs at Christians who warn him about an everlasting hell.

The words 'mixed with fear' alert us to danger as we 'snatch others from the fire'. Firemen who go into a burning house put their own lives at risk. To rescue some kinds of sinners we may come near to the fire. We desire to draw sinners out of the fire without falling into it ourselves.

3. Those who are defiled (23). Though all sinners are stained with sin – 'our righteous acts are like filthy rags' (Isa. 64:6) – some sink down into the depths of depravity. Jude's point at the end of v. 22 is this: 'Hate sin, as you would hate stained and soiled clothes.' In practice this means that we don't walk into potentially dangerous situations where we will face temptation.

___

To think about: God's grace can reach all sorts of sinners. Look up 1 Corinthians 6:9-11.

Jude 24-25   To God be the glory!

We may compare Jude's letter to a piece of music which is sometimes deep and sad but the closing finale is exquisite.

Protection (24) – 'To him who is able to keep you from falling'. We are safe because God 'is able' – he is sovereign and therefore nothing can snatch us from his mighty hands (John 10:28-30).

According to John Benton the word 'falling' comes from horse riding. 'God is able to keep you from falling as if you were a horse and he were the rider … He is holding the reins of your life and he is able to guide you and keep you from falling and to put you on the right track and bring you safely home.'

Of course, God's keeping power does not cancel our responsibility. We are 'kept by the power of God through faith' (1 Peter 1:5, AV/ NKJV). Disobedient believers may backslide but they cannot become reprobates. The prodigals will return with broken hearts to the warm embrace of the waiting Father.

Presentation (24) – 'to present you before his glorious presence'. The words 'to present' look back to the Old Testament sacrifices presented by the Jewish worshippers to God. Now we present ourselves to God as imperfect living sacrifices (Rom. 12:1-2). One day God will present us as perfect living sacrifices to himself. Then we will stand before God 'without fault' because Christ the 'lamb without blemish or defect' shed his 'precious blood' for us at Calvary (1 Peter 1:19). The Lord will welcome us into heaven 'with great joy' because his plans in Christ were fulfilled. We too will know 'an inexpressible and glorious joy' in heaven (1 Peter 1:8) because present troubles achieve future joy (2 Cor. 4:17-18).

Praise (25). We direct our adoration 'to the only God our Saviour' – a description rooted in Old Testament passages such Deuteronomy 6:4 and Exodus 15:2. The AV/ NKJV reads 'God our Saviour who alone is wise' and echoes scriptures such as Isaiah 40:13. Such a God is well able to guard and guide believers through this world to the next. We come to God 'through Jesus Christ' – we depend on his merits alone. Our praise recalls the past ('before all ages'), spans the present ('now') and reaches into the future ('for evermore').

To think about: If you desire God's 'glory', then worship him because he is God. If you proclaim his 'majesty, power and authority', then obey him because he is King.

Readings in

Revelation

by Eric Lane

WINDOW
ON THE
WORD

The opening words provide both the title and the theme of the whole book. It would be correct to say that all the books of the Bible reveal Jesus Christ to a greater or lesser extent. Revelation, however, gives us the climax of God's unveiling of the glory of his Son. The Greek term used presents the picture of the drawing back of a veil enabling the viewer to see what had always existed but was previously hidden from view. As the Gospels reveal Christ when he walked on earth, this book reveals him as he is now, enthroned in splendour. He sovereignly moves the whole course of history towards that great day when he will be acknowledged by every tongue as King of kings and Lord of lords.

There is a distinctly heavenly perspective about this book. The background is the time between the first and Second Coming of Christ; but rather than describing particular events in that time, it is the governing principles behind history that the book unveils. All have the revelation of Jesus Christ as their beginning and end.

It is generally accepted that the author of the book is the apostle John who was also responsible for the Gospel and letters in the New Testament which bear his name. The brevity of the reference to him may indicate a personal acquaintance between John and the churches. It is self-effacing with all attention being given to Jesus Christ. This is probably the last of the New Testament books to be written, perhaps about AD 90.

It is likely that the reference to the seven churches are those named in chapters 2 and 3, but we should not limit the application to those. Seven is consistently a symbolic number for a representative, completed perfection. It is possible that each church was made up of a number of congregations, either in the same town or in nearby outlying villages which grew out of and were nurtured by the large town church. He identified himself closely with them and endured what they endured. Patmos was a penal colony. John was in exile there. He had preached Christ and that was the result. This book is a product of persecution.

As we go through this book, we will be reading what the Lord Jesus Christ intended we should read (1:1-3). Jesus put the revelation into terms we would understand. He translated it from the language of heaven into the language of earth, then he gave it to the angel to give to John. The book is unique in the New Testament, being prophetic and visionary. It has many Old Testament allusions and is not intended to be taken literally. The Lord Jesus has provided the visual images we find so puzzling. He has also provided the Spirit of truth to guide us, who speaks not of himself, but shall glorify the Lord (John 16:13-14).

Revelation is presented in terms of God's timing. God wants us to know that 'the time is near' from his point of view. There is an urgency and a need for action as far as God is concerned, but from our standpoint, we cannot see that. Time goes by so slowly for us but these things are written so that we can get a glimpse of the heavenly perspective involved.

Revelation 1:1-8   Introduction: a personal opening

Revelation is not just about the end of the world, but the whole period between the two advents of Christ, which is one of continual conflict. It is basically a letter from John to churches, like other New Testament letters. The overall theme is the conflict of Christ and his church against Satan and the world. The first part (chs 1–11) concerns the battle between the church and the world which persecutes it, and the second part (chs 12–22) that between Christ and Satan. Within this are seven subsections. Seven is a symbolic number in apocalyptic literature representing completeness or perfection, derived from the seven days of the week. Within these subsections are further sevens.

FIRST PART: WAR BETWEEN THE CHURCH AND THE WORLD (chs 1–11).

1:1-3 – a preface. This was probably an editorial preface written when the letters were published later as a book. But they make some important points.

(a) The gospel originated when God purposed to reveal his Son after his return to glory (1).

(b) He does not speak directly to his churches, but to an 'angel' who reveals it to John and through him to the seven churches.

(c) Its form is unique in Scripture, for, although prophets and apostles had visions, they did not write them in the form of letters but spoke directly to people. John, being in prison, could not do this.

(d) When read by individuals or to churches, it will 'bless' them (3). This is urgent because 'the time is short' before the battle between church and world begins.

Verses 4-8 – the letter begins.

Verse 4a is typical of the way New Testament letters begin, with the author, who is John the apostle, the author of a Gospel and three letters. This is followed by the recipients, who are seven churches in Asia (modern Turkey) mainly on the east of the country. These were not planted by Paul, who worked further east (Galatia) but possibly by John himself. In fact there were ten, for Troas, Colosse and Hierapolis also appear in the New Testament.

Verses 4b-5a is a greeting from God the Father, stressing his eternal nature, also from the seven Spirits – the Holy Spirit in all his offices. It is also from Jesus Christ his Son, who lived on earth as his 'witness' (see Isa. 55:4; Rev. 3:14) and rose from the dead – uniquely ('firstborn') then ascended back to glory to exercise dominion over all nations.

Verses 5b-7 are an ascription of praise to Christ, for what he did on earth when he suffered for our sins to bring us into his kingdom as his worshippers ('priests') (5b-6), and for what he will do when he comes back to earth in glory and power, when he will cause all the people of the earth to mourn over their sins, particularly their rejection of him (7).

Verse 8. His qualification for this lies in his eternal nature as 'Alpha and Omega' (beginning and end). On this basis he can pray for God's grace on the churches (4) so that they will enjoy his peace. This was exactly the way Paul opened his letters.

Think about it: The word 'revelation' is 'apocalypse,' telling us the message will come in the form of visions, which radically affects the way we understand the message.

Revelation 1:9-20   John's vision of Christ

Revelation is John's record of the visions he was given by an angel sent to him by God (1:1) of times which were shortly to begin (1:3). These centre on Christ (1:2). It was written to prepare Christians for the battle they faced, so that they would not stumble, as Christ told them (John 16), also Paul (Acts 14:21-22) and Peter (1 Peter 4:12-19). John was writing to comfort Christians in the churches who were beginning to face persecution.

The seven churches represent all churches not only at that time but during the whole of the gospel era up to Christ's return. They are the prototype of what the whole church will experience down the ages.

The 'voice' is that of Christ whom John now saw in a vision confirming the authenticity of the sights and sounds John was to see and hear.

What made John ideal for this ministry (9) – he too was experiencing persecution from Domitian, so he was their 'brother' in this. In fact he was worse off than they, for he was incarcerated on the prison island of Patmos.

What John heard (10-11) – a loud voice ('trumpet') telling him to write down what he heard 'on the Lord's day' (10) and, since he could not tell them in person, to send it to the churches by a messenger, on the circular route described here, which would cover each of the seven churches.

What John saw (12-16) – a vision of the seven-branched lampstand which had stood in the temple before it was destroyed by the Roman army in AD 69. He also saw a figure in

human form ('like a son of man' (13), dressed like a priest (for sympathy, Hebrews 4:15), and wearing a golden sash like a king (for authority). The whiteness of his hair and his blazing eyes indicate a particularly holy person (14), while his bronze feet speak of the immutability of his person, and the sound of his voice signifies the infallibility of his words (15). The stars in his right hand are his authority to judge his people and the sword shows he will fight their battles. Best of all is the glory that shines in his face (16).

What the figure said to John (17-18). John was overwhelmed by the vision (17) but heard 'the voice' reassuring him he had nothing to fear. John had seen him both dead and alive, for he is eternal and will not die again, because he has authority over death – a key not only opens doors but symbolises authority.

What John was to write (19-20) – about the recent vision, which depicted events in the churches then and later (19). Mainly he would see 'angels' like 'stars' shining the truth of Christ to illuminate the dark world around (20).

Think about it: The figure in the vision is the same one whom John had walked with years before, whom he had seen alive from the dead and heard his voice say the words of John 20:27! Now John saw and heard him glorified. Does your faith enable you to see and hear him with the eyes and ears of your heart? This vision prepares minds for bad times ahead. Read Ephesians 1:18 and pray that prayer.

Revelation 2:1-7   Letter to Ephesus

Revelation revolves around cycles of seven: seven churches, seven seals, seven trumpets, seven bowls. It starts on earth with letters to seven churches, then moves to the supernatural sphere in the form of visions, which take us into the realm of angels and demons, of Christ and Satan.

FIRST PART, SECTION 1: LETTERS TO SEVEN CHURCHES OF ASIA (chs 2–3).

It is significant that these letters come at the beginning of Revelation. Putting the letters first shows that these things are happening to people like ourselves. There is real ink on real parchment, read by real people describing real events. There are things going on in the supernatural realm which impinge on Christians in the world today as much as they did on Christians in the past. These are not 'fairy stories'. We are to take them seriously and find out their meaning.

The order of the recipients of the letters probably follows the route to be taken by the messenger delivering the letters. The term 'angel of the church' is probably a symbolic way of describing the churches as 'messengers' of the gospel to the world ('messenger' is the literal meaning of 'angel'). The postman would leave Patmos by sea and dock at Ephesus on the Aegean coast, and from there take a circular route ending at Laodicea.

This letter from Christ describes how the church in Ephesus appeared to its own members compared with how it looked to the all-seeing eye of Christ (1:13).

Ephesus was then a thriving port and Christians were known for their hard work (2), their good deeds and perseverance.

It was a church with a discerning eye for erroneous teaching, especially for those who denied apostolic authority. Paul had set high standards in his letter, so that they would be able to grow in knowledge (Eph. 1:15-19). This had not weakened over the forty years since Paul wrote. They had detected the influence of Nicolas (6), who disagreed with the church's intolerance of certain idol feasts. His adherents were called followers of Balaam (14).

But the all-seeing eye of God and his strong love could detect a lowering of the temperature in Ephesus of the love Paul had stressed in Ephesians 3:17-19. This was depriving their deeds of their power, as he had taught in his letter to the Corinthians (1 Cor. 13).

Here (5a) his message is that their decline in love was not just weakness but sin, the ungodliness which had caused the original fall (Rom. 1:18), and they must repent as they did when they first heard the gospel. This was so serious it would cause their shining light to be extinguished, so that they would become a mere sound and respectable church but lacking any converting power.

Think about it: This is a message for all churches in all ages (7). Do you know of churches like Ephesus? They have good numbers, good pastors, thriving in all departments, with good leaders; they are friendly and have no financial worries.

Could this be your church? Examine yourselves carefully – especially on the issue of love. Is there real love between members? Above all, are all these other good things motivated by fervent love for the Lord?

Revelation 2:8-11   Letter to Smyrna

The letters vary considerably, depending on how well the churches were performing their commission and standing against either persecution (from Jews or the Roman state under the Emperor Domitian) or refusing to compromise with the false teachings which were creeping in, especially Gnosticism.

After delivering the letter to the church in Ephesus, the messenger would have travelled 35 miles north to the next city on his itinerary – Smyrna. This was in some ways a rival to Ephesus. It also had a harbour, and in addition broad streets, well planned, with beautiful buildings. The principal ones were arranged around the top of Mount Pagos and were called 'the crown of Pagos'.

It was on good terms with Rome, especially since a temple had been built in the 30s AD for the worship of the Emperor Tiberius. But emperor worship was not the only religion practised in Smyrna.

The cult of Cybele was popular as she was the chief fertility goddess, important in those times when it was believed that the climate was controlled by gods who required rituals and offerings to be made to them so that the weather conditions would be right for a good harvest. This also explains the references to death and life in vv.10-11. Cybele brought the earth back to life every spring, but Christian believers are delivered from the second death and given the crown of life, which is at least one way by which they are truly rich. This also is probably why the words about Jesus as 'first and last ... the living one who was dead and is alive for evermore' are chosen

from 1:17-18 for his description of Christ in v.8. Each letter begins with one aspect of the earlier vision of Christ. Put together they form a picture of the glory of the risen Christ as the one who dwells in the churches and leads them in the war with the powers of evil.

Verses 9-10. Most of the trouble for Christians came from the Jews, who were particularly powerful in Smyrna. They controlled much of the commerce and business life. They were antagonistic to Christians and used their power to reduce them to poverty. This explains v.9, which accuses them of serving 'Satan', not the Lord, for the Lord's law required Jews to help the poor (Deut.15:3; Ps.82:3; Prov.22:9). The church was not promised that times would get easier; more likely they would get harder (10), but on this occasion the time would be limited – 'ten days' is symbolic of a fixed period. Meanwhile, they were spiritually rich and would end up even richer (10)!

Think of churches you know or know about. There are those (2:9) who are struggling financially, because of low membership or because the members are poor, old or non-earners. They cannot afford a pastor, or can hardly pay the travel expenses of a visiting preacher. But don't confine your search to your country. Think of the 'developing world' where people cannot even afford to feed their families, let alone run a church, or even put up a building. In what ways are they 'rich'? Look up Ephesians 1:7,18; 2:7; 3:8,16; Philippians 4:19; Colossians 2:1-2; James 1:9.

Revelation 2:12-17   Letter to Pergamum

The next of these letters written to ordinary Christians down the ages to prepare them for something extraordinary, was to Pergamum, a town about 55 miles north of Smyrna, on a river, not on the coast. It was built around a large rocky hill overlooking the town below. It was the centre of the paper industry with a library of 200,000 volumes.

Religion. Pergamum was, like Athens (Acts 17:22), very religious. It had not only the usual cults of Zeus, Athena and Dionysus but also a rarer one, that of Aesculapius, the god of healing. There was not only a temple for worship but a 'School of Healing', where some came to be healed and others to learn the art of healing.

The principal cult, however, was of the emperor, whom all had to acknowledge by proclaiming 'Caesar is Lord'. Christians refused and instead proclaimed 'Jesus is Lord'. The huge altar to the emperor could be seen (and still can be) from the town below, gleaming in the sun. This is what v. 13 calls 'Satan's throne'. Christ, who holds the two-edged sword, was aware of this and commended the church because it remained true to his name. At the time of writing the Roman persecution was just beginning and a prominent leader and faithful witness (Antipas, 13) had been put to death. Nevertheless, the church generally remained true to Christ's name.

Heresy. But not all were standing firm. There were those who were following 'the teaching of the 'Nicolaitans', which the letter compares with the teaching of Balaam who prophesied to Israel when they were passing through Moab on their way to the promised land (Num. 25). They had been allowed to fornicate with the Moabite women. If these had been cult prostitutes this would explain how they became involved in idolatry by eating food sacrificed to idols, which was more dishonouring to Christ even than the fornication.

This is not the precise form it took in the early church which was a more general compromise with Gentile practices. The teaching was called 'Gnosticism' (higher knowledge) derived from Plato's teaching, that for those who had spiritual life, what their body did was unimportant. Matter was evil and Christians were delivered from it. They could co-operate with the world in anything and gain influence. They believed that put them in a better position to bring others to Christ.

Some of the early heresies came under God's judgement: Jews ('synagogue of Satan', 9,13), 'Nicolaitans' (6,15) and 'the teaching of Balaam' (14) – probably both Gnostic sects, which mixed the gospel with Greek ideas. In the visions that follow, these and other heresies keep emerging, and some are not destroyed until the final judgement (chs 17–18).

Think! What churches do you know which teach the idea that 'to win the world we must be like the world'? They say we may join in the world's practices and use their methods so that we may win them to Christ. Does it work? We must heed the warning of v. 16 from him who holds the two-edged sword (12). Then we shall know the reward that is hidden from those who follow the ways of the world.

Revelation 2:18-29   Letter to Thyatira

At this point the messenger would turn in a south-easterly direction and travel 40 miles to Thyatira. This city was not dominated by any particular god or religion, but by the trade guilds, of which Thyatira was the centre.

The problems for Christians and churches. These arose from the trade guilds, which had rules of behaviour and customs, but in which worship of the god of the guild had a prominent part in the observance of various days. Membership was compulsory for all who worked in the trade, including Christians, who were obliged to attend the feasts, involving them in idolatry and immorality. To refuse was a serious breach of the rules and could mean a Christian would lose his job. Thyatira was the centre of the cloth trade, and in Philippi Paul had met a lady who had lived in Thyatira and practised dyeing (Acts 16:14). She had become rich, but for Christians to refuse the obligations of the guild was to face poverty. What should they do? A 'prophetess' (20) had come into the church who taught something similar to Nicolas in Ephesus and Pergamum – that it was permissible for Christians to participate in guild feasts. This was justified by the Gnostic view that for Christians who had 'the spirit', what the body did was unimportant. 'Jezebel' was not her real name (names in Revelation are encrypted). More likely it was symbolic – she was doing to early Christians what Jezebel the queen had done to Israel in Elijah's time – led God's servants into sin (20).

The message of Christ to sinning Christians. Into this situation comes the Christ of v.18. He sees the truth. Compromising with sinners is not acceptable to him and he is angry. A happy situation (19) is upset, and he is going to deal with 'Jezebel' and her followers in judgement. After a period of warning (21) he will come in vengeance (22-23). The claim to be a means of winning non-Christians was not sincere but a cover for those who are afraid.

The message of Christ to the faithful (24-28). For those who reject this teaching as Satanic (24) Christ asks one thing: 'Hold on' (25), for he is going to come – now upon 'Jezebel' and her company, and finally upon all such compromisers. If he comes now he will make the Christians who 'hold on' all the stronger (26), giving them authority like his own (27) and even a share in his glory (27). Those who remain faithful receive accolades and rewards (7,11 etc.). All is brought to a triumphant conclusion in the final chapters, 19 to 22.

The message of Christ to all Christians in all times (29). Look out for those who in our day teach compromise to the churches. Christ is searching the hearts of Christians and the teaching in their churches. Are we 'buying' this view in the vain hope it will win unbelievers to Christ? Do not be deceived. It is our difference from the world, not our similarity that convicts them of sin and brings them to faith.

Revelation 3:1-6   Letter to Sardis

A frequent theme of the letters is the 'deeds' of the churches (2:2,5,13,19; 3:1,8). Good as they were, these were not appreciated by the servants of Satan, who stirred up the earth's inhabitants against them (2:8-10,13-15). Sometimes members, and even leaders, of the churches were recruited on Satan's side to corrupt the churches and bring them under God's judgement (3:1-3). Churches suffer grievously at the hands of these (11:1-13; 12:13-17). This persecution is orchestrated by the two great camps used by Satan in his war against the church: evil government represented by 'the beast from the sea' (ch. 13), and corrupt or false religion (represented by 'the beast out of the earth' (13:11-18).

The town and the people (1). Sardis was a town about 30 miles south of Thyatira, the messenger's next port of call. As the letter brings out, the people were comfortable and complacent. They had been unconquered since the Persian and Greek empires. They regarded themselves, and were regarded as, unconquerable, because they were situated on a high fortified hill overlooking a valley so narrow it was easily defended.

They were rich because of the gold in the hills which deposited itself on the riverbanks. The riches of Croesus the King are legendary.

The Christians and the churches. The piercing eyes of Christ saw the truth about their real condition. They had a reputation for being rich in good deeds, but these were the deeds of the spiritually dead.

The call of Christ, who knew the real truth about them was:

'Wake up' (2) – see what Christ sees – that their spiritual life was on the brink of extinction.

Deal with the complacency by 'strengthening what remains', make your deeds complete, let your heart be in them as well as your body.

Bring back to mind what you have forgotten about the need for a loving heart as well as an active life (3). Repent of your lack of love.

Face up to the alternative of judgement, which may happen at any time without warning, 'like a thief in the night', who is in and out of your house before you have woken up.

Take notice of those in the church who are 'more worthy' (4-5), because they are not soiled with the worldly spirit of complacency; follow their example. Covet the things they are being promised – to 'walk with Christ in white' and join his procession on the day of his final triumph, in such a way that you will be acknowledged when the books are opened.

A message for all the churches (6). What he said to Sardis applies not only to all seven churches of Asia, but to churches everywhere at that time, and to churches in all times up to his return.

Think about it: What churches do you know who have a good 'reputation' because they are active and well-organised, well-led and friendly, but their spirituality is superficial and spiritually they are 'dead'? When you go there, you do not feel the awesome presence of the living God, or the glory and beauty of Christ. What such churches need is not more activity but an outpouring of the Spirit's power.

Revelation 3: 7-13   Letter to Philadelphia

The majority of churches (Ephesus, Pergamum, Thyatira and Sardis) received a mixed report, with commendation for those who were standing against various degrees of persecution or refusing to compromise with dangerous heresies. Only two (Smyrna and Philadelphia) receive unqualified commendation, while the remaining one (Laodicea) has nothing good said of it. It is accused of leaving Christ out of its meetings. These reports are highly important, since they were to become typical of churches at that time and in all ages to come. They are warnings to us all, proven by subsequent history.

Philadelphia – a place of opportunity (7-8). Christ is seen as the true and only God who holds the key of David. In Israel a key symbolised authority to enter the temple to make offerings to God (Isa. 22:20-24). Under the New Covenant only Christ, the Head of the church (the new temple) can admit anyone to the kingdom of God, through birth in the Spirit (John 3:5).

Christ can open places and people to hear and respond to the gospel (7; Acts 16:14). Philadelphia was situated where the road from the north-eastern ports to Colosse crossed the road from Smyrna to Antioch. This had made Philadelphia a centre for the spread of the Greek language and culture. In its wake came the message of the gospel, which used the Greek language. This facilitated the evangelisation of Asia Minor. Churches which had 'little strength' (8) could take advantage of the situation.

Philadelphia – a place of opposition (9). The church in Philadelphia was having the same problems as nearby Smyrna – from the Jews. Their defeat by the Romans in AD 70 had greatly weakened the Jewish persecution of the church, but their financial superiority made Christians dependent on them, which the Jews used to pressurise them to reconvert to Judaism. So far Smyrna and Philadelphia had resisted them (9; 2:8-9) but what of the future?

Future security (10). They had successfully resisted until now, but the persecution, far from being over, would get worse: 'an hour of trial' was to come on 'the whole world', perhaps the state persecution under Domitian which was just beginning, or something more widespread, such as a famine, which would affect Jews and Romans as well as Christians, or even one of the Barbarian invasions which would eventually overthrow the entire empire. But whatever it was, Christ's promise to 'keep' them would hold fast.

Eternal security (11-12). The church will survive the final judgement, for these verses refer to 'the new Jerusalem', the eternal kingdom and glory, which follows the judgement, about which there will be much more later in the book (21:2). If they held on until his 'coming', which would be 'soon', they would enjoy three promises:

(a) They would receive 'a crown of life' (11) and be made 'more than conquerors.

(b) They would 'be pillars in the temple', who did not need upholding because they upheld others.

(c) They would 'bear his name, they would belong to Christ forever.

The message for all churches everywhere in all time (13). Whatever the devil hurls at the church to destroy it will fail, for Christ's strength is greater, and his promise to keep us will not fail. See Matthew 24:35.

Revelation 3:14-22   Letter to Laodicea

If the letter to Philadelphia was the most encouraging of the seven, the one to Laodicea was probably the opposite. This was not because of some gross sin in the congregation, nor because of some heresy being embraced, nor persecution breaking out, but because of the wrong attitude of the people.

What the town was like.

Safe. Because of the contours of its location, Laodicea was easily defended, which bred a false sense of security in the people.

Rich (17). It was a centre of the wool and cloth-making trade, also of banking (it bought and sold gold) and was well supplied with fresh water from hot springs about 6 miles away via an aqueduct. By the time it reached Laodicea, however, it had cooled to 'lukewarm' which made it less palatable for drinking and less useful for cloth-making.

What the church was like (14-18). As with places like Ephesus, the character of the Christians derived a good deal from that of the townspeople. This is why Christ is spoken of as 'the faithful and true witness' (14) who knows the truth about the people's 'deeds', that they were not altogether as they appeared. They saw themselves as stable, well-dressed, with secure money and good eye treatment available as and when needed. But they were failing to compare themselves

with the temperature of the water: they were not 'cold', completely lacking in emotion. On the other hand, they were not fanatical, but held their feelings under strict control. They were not extremists and were no threat to the liberal-minded Hellenists.

What Christ thought of the church (17-21). He saw them as being opposite to what they saw in themselves: 'wretched, poor, pitiful, blind and naked'. He was speaking spiritually. Christ could take no more delight in them than we might in a cup of tepid water. He could not stomach them and would reject them. They were estranged from him. He was not in their gatherings (20). They must 'open the door' to him so that his presence would be felt in their gatherings. Then they could share his reign again (21).

The message for the church in all ages (21). Don't seek to be 'acceptable' to the politically correct like the Greeks, who boasted of their 'humanism and liberalism'. Don't be afraid to be called 'extremist'. Be what Christ wants you to be, not what the world will tolerate. Read, ponder and apply James 4:4. What matters most in our churches is that Christ's presence should be felt.

Think about it: Revelation is not haphazard, neither is the church's history; there is a pattern, as in all God's work. He is working his purpose out.

Revelation 4   The vision of God

Christ's church in all the world, in every place and age, is persecuted by the world. In order to calm our fears, this is preceded by a vision of Christ, the church's head, in glory and power. This vision is the background of the subsequent visions.

FIRST PART, SECTION 2: SECOND CYCLE OF SEVENS: THE SEVEN SEALS (chs 4–7).

The second cycle of 'sevens' opens with John's vision of God himself. John sees heaven through an open door (1), through which he hears the voice he had first heard in 1:12, now inviting him to come up and see what must take place. This seems to include all the visions still to come. The open door into heaven symbolises John being shown who is leading the church in its battle with evil powers, namely, he who sits on the throne, called Lord and God (11). John was at once in the Spirit (2), as he had been when he had received the letters from the angel (1:10). What John sees is a throne (2) with a figure on it (3). John does not describe the figure itself but rather its effect – bright and dazzling, like precious stones, signifying God's glory, with an unusual rainbow in the shape of a complete circle rather than a semicircle, and like an emerald in colour. Also surrounding the throne are twenty-four elders wearing twenty-four crowns (4). They represented the Old Covenant church by the twelve tribes, and the New Covenant church by the twelve apostles.

There were more dazzling sights, emanating from the seven Spirits of God, and a crystal sea (5-6). Nearest the throne (6) were four living creatures resembling a lion, an ox, a man and an eagle (7). We do not have the language to describe them because it is supernatural, so they are compared to the strongest earthly beings. These four mighty angels form circles around the figure on the throne, so that all their eyes are on him, ready to do his bidding. These four angelic figures, with their wings and multiple eyes (6b-8a) are those through whom God governs the four corners of the universe. (Ezekiel 1 has the same message.) They also lead all creation in worship (8). What they see is a three-person God who is holy and mighty. The representatives of the church (9) respond: in actions as they fall before him (10) and in words (11) which acknowledge how worthy God is to receive this praise. Not only do those in the circles have their eyes on him but he has his multiple eyes on them.

Think about it:

1. Think about the 'visions' you have read about in the lives of the saints and compare them with the glory here.

2. What will it be like in heaven? The arrangement here of circles around the throne of God means our gaze is directed continually on him alone. We will never lose sight of him nor will he turn his eyes from us. 'They shall see his face' (22:4), as Jesus promised: '... the pure in heart ... shall see God' (Matt. 5:8). What will we do? Worship God: as Creator (4:11) and Redeemer (5:9).

Revelation 5   The book of history

The scene is still as in chapter 4: heaven, at the centre of which is a throne. On it is God himself, the holy and mighty (4:8), who created all things by his will (4:11). He is surrounded by twenty-four other thrones occupied by twenty-four elders, and, nearer the throne, four living creatures (4:6), who lead the rest of the company in an act of worship. The figure on the throne (God) has in his right hand a scroll – papyrus rolled up sealed with seven seals (1), which no one on earth or in heaven has been able to break in order to look inside (2-3). This made John weep profusely (4).

The sealed scroll is symbolic of God's purposes for man and the world, which are known only within the Godhead. The number seven stands for completion or perfection (seven days make one week). Not a single being outside God knows its contents. Why is this? Man does not know what is in the mind of God, because he does not know God (Matt. 11:27). The fall of man into sin (Gen. 3) has deprived him of his knowledge of God (1 Cor. 2:6-16). The Jews did not understand that Jesus was the Son of God. In the Scriptures they had the whole record of God's activity, but it was a closed book to them because they did not know the one from whose mind it had come (2 Cor. 3:14-16). This is our problem today. We not only have the Scriptures, but secular history going back to the earliest times, plus the record of

contemporary events. We do not realise what God is doing in blessing or judgement, which we don't understand because we don't know him. Many Christians, who do know him, are not interested in history because they fail to see it is about God's acts. A man shows what he is like by the things he does, and God is the same, but we fail to see it.

In v. 5 an elder comes to the rescue and tells John of One who has succeeded in breaking the seals, whom he calls the Lion of the tribe of Judah, the one God promised at the Fall (Gen. 3:15), whom the Jews called their Messiah. How has he done it? By becoming a Lamb slain as a sacrifice for the sin of the Fall. This made him 'worthy' (9) to reveal God's purposes down the ages, culminating in the slaughter of the Lamb, by which a world of sinners can become a kingdom of priests, who know God, understand his purposes and sing his praises (11-14).

Think about it! The cross is the key to history! History. Begin here! See how the cross explains the ups and downs of all history, sacred and secular. See how it opens the Bible, how it explains the events of both distant and recent history. Let it teach you more of what God is like and make you a priest, a worship leader. We worship him as the Creator (4:11), then worship him as the Saviour.

Revelation 6   Opening the seals

The history of the world is a sealed book, whose meaning God keeps hidden until he is pleased to reveal it. Christ breaks the seals of the book of history which reveals the persecution endured by the church at the hands of the world through the ages. The judgements here are not the final punishment but warnings that it will come if there is no repentance.

Human theories of history tend to take the circular view: everything goes round and round and leads nowhere. History has no purpose or meaning. But the biblical view is that history is linear. It has a purpose in Christ which Paul calls 'the mystery of his will' (Eph. 1:9) and which is only revealed when he intends it, as he did in Christ's death and resurrection. See 5:1-8.

This happens in stages. Chapter 6 takes us up to the sixth seal. The seventh is opened in chapter 8 and coincides with the first trumpet. The seals take the form of visions: John sees different coloured horses, which depict various forms of judgement inflicted on particular places at certain periods in world history.

The first seal (1-2) shows a white horse whose rider has a bow in his hand and a crown on his head. This represents the righteous rule of Christ, which began when he ascended to the right hand of God, to be finally achieved when he makes all his foes the footstool of his feet (1 Cor. 15:24-25).

The second seal (3-4) reveals a rider on a red horse who is given authority to stir up war between nations, bringing destruction and misery.

The third seal (5-6) shows a rider on a black horse creating severe economic shortage, sometimes due to the wars from the second seal. A poor man's daily wage is sufficient only for a small barley loaf of poor quality, whereas the rich continue to enjoy their luxuries.

The fourth seal (7-8) reveals a pale horse – 'Death,' who spreads death over the world in various forms, resulting from the previous disturbances.

The fifth seal (9-11) concerns the church in particular. While she shares in the afflictions common to man, she also suffers persecution from the enemies of Christ. This is so severe and unrelenting that the afflicted Christians cry out for God to take their part against their enemies. His reply is that they must wait until the number of the faithful is made up and all are delivered together. Compare Hebrews 11:39-40.

The sixth seal (12-17) continues the fifth seal as it describes God's vengeance on the enemies of his Son and his church. But this is only a taste of what they will receive in the judgements of the chapters to come.

Think about it: History is a succession of periods of sufferings for the church and judgements on the world because of its unbelief in God and Christ and its hatred of believers.

Learn to distinguish temporary judgements from the final one. Early Christians thought 2 Thessalonians 1:5-10 meant their persecution was about to be avenged by Christ's return, and gave up their jobs and homes. So Paul had to write 2 Thessalonians 2:1-12 to put them right.

Revelation 7 Opening the sixth seal

The sixth seal has been broken and John sees terrible convulsions breaking out in the material universe (6:13-14), on earth and above the earth, on the continents and the islands. This causes the world's inhabitants to cry out in fear that the final overthrow of all things is about to occur.

God's merciful response (1-3). John next sees four angels placed where they can see all the peoples of the earth. These are just waiting for the word to release their destructive power on the universe. But (2) John sees another angel holding the seal of God (not one of the seven seals of judgement, but a means of distinguishing some from others). He tells the four angels not to release their power until he has marked those who are to be exempt.

Who are the ones marked out (4-8)? The symbolism of the number 144,000 is not difficult to explain, being composed of 12x12x1,000. The first 12 stand for the twelve tribes of Israel, who formed the church of the Old Covenant, whom God brought into covenant with himself at Sinai (Exod. 19). The second 12 represent the twelve apostles, through whom God established his New Covenant in Christ. Those who believed that the Old Covenant contained the promise of a Saviour were just as 'saved' as those who saw, heard and believed Christ was the promised One. The 1,000 symbolises completion – the total number of the saved under both covenants. At present they are suffering persecution (14) but continue to worship (9-15) while they wait for the promise of their final rest to come about (16-17).

The many are one (9-12). The point stressed here is that, however many, they are all really one: one people, one language, one 'dress'. Above all, they sing one song, not the lament of 6:15-17, but 'salvation' (12-17). We are moving on from creation (4:11) to the atonement of Christ (7:14 -17).

Clarification (13-17). So why, John is asked, are present Christians suffering under Domitian? Why are none of them basking in glory? The answer is that for them 'the great tribulation' is not over. Scripture teaches that at every period saints are afflicted. But they will come out of it and share the triumph of those who have already been freed. This vision, like the others, is for all churches in all ages.

Revelation 8   Opening the seventh seal

In this series of sevens, each one tends to lead out of the previous one. The judgements of the sixth seal (6:12-14) become the first trumpet; the seals announce, the trumpets warn. God mercifully delays the final blow while men heed the warning (8:1-2). The prayers of the saints (8:3-5) further hold back the judgement. The trumpets' message is more drastic than the seals (8:6-12).

FIRST PART, SECTION 3: SEVEN TRUMPETS (chs 8–11).

Restoring calm (1-2). The sixth seal led to a climax in 6:12-15, which is the nearest John's visions have reached to the final judgement so far. But the mere expectation of it provokes cries of terror (6:15-17). So God first restores calm before the angels appear to sound their trumpets and bring us to the next cycle of events. God is merciful and has not forgotten his promise to exempt his elect by placing a mark on them (see John 5:24).

The golden censer (3-5). This is God's answer to the cries and prayers produced by the convulsions which accompanied the opening of the fifth seal (5-11; 6:9-11). It sounds as if the final judgement has come – the wrath of the Lamb plunging the whole universe into turmoil. This affects the earth and its inhabitants in a way none of the previous seals have done. Even the most powerful people on earth are made to feel what they never acknowledged before – that this is the last day: the Day of the Lord.

What of the saints' prayers? He takes the censer, fills it with fire and smoke, which causes storms and earthquakes. How this answers the saints' prayers is spelled out by four of the angels who now sound their trumpets:

Four of the angels sound (6-12). They are not warnings of what may happen, but announcements of what will happen.

(a) *The first trumpet (7)* speaks of the earth – the grass and trees.

(b) *The second trumpet (8-9)* refers to the sea – fish and human beings.

(c) *The third trumpet (10-11)* proclaims judgement on inland waters.

(d) *The fourth trumpet (12)* reaches out to extra-terrestrial bodies and becomes increasingly apocalyptic. The 'huge mountain' (8), 'great star' (10) and 'Wormwood' (11) are unidentifiable.

(e) *The eagle (13)* warns us that the final three trumpets are so awful that they are simply called 'woes'.

Think about it: Many Christians are too specific in applying every disaster to the end of the world. Most disasters are simply warnings that there will be a final judgement and they had better repent now. Jesus took this approach in Luke 13:1-5. We must be bold in warning people of judgement to come and not only tell them 'Jesus loves you.' Is our 'trumpet' giving an 'uncertain sound' about judgement and leaving people unprepared for when the final judgement actually comes (1 Cor. 14:8)?

Revelation 9:1-12   The first 'woe'

At the breaking of the seventh seal seven angels appear, sounding their trumpets, which depict the judgement God inflicts on the world for persecuting the saints. The fifth angel announces three woes – more serious warning judgements which increase in intensity as they lead up to the final judgement and the triumph of Christ and his church, which itself is announced by the seventh angel (11:15-19).

The fifth trumpet announces the first woe. This brings us nearer the end of this present universe but not right up to it. It corresponds to the sixth seal in 6:12-15. Much that happens sounds like the final event, but there is more to come under these three 'woes' before we reach the last day. Some of the details are not agreed upon, but it is possible to describe the nature of the period to a certain extent.

An oppressive darkness (1-3). This sounds like the personal descent to earth by Satan in Christ's mysterious words in Luke 10:18. He comes with the power and authority to let all hell loose by opening the shaft leading from hell, causing smoke to arise. The 'smoke' is actually a swarm of locusts, who are given the power of scorpions (3). This graphically describes a period of intense spiritual darkness (2; see Joel 2:1-2), preceding the return of Christ.

A heavy death-wish (4-6). Death is in the air and there is a strong desire to kill, but a restraint is put on this, even on killing vegetable life (4). The servants of Christ, who were marked with a seal, have special protection. So great was the sting of the scorpions and the death-wish they produced that people even wanted to kill themselves, as they did under the sixth seal in 6:15-16. The pain is intense, but while the time is limited (5) it is still considerable, as if something like half of human history is spent seeking an end to life's miseries.

A terrifying appearance (7-11). What did they look like (7)? Not scorpions but monsters. Individually their features were normal, but put together they were frightening. Coming with the force of a cavalry charge, with each rider as a king, having the face of a man but a woman's hair and a lion's teeth (8). They wore mail armour, with wings making a noise like a cavalry charge (9). But worst of all was the sting of the tail (10). They were led by a king from hell whose name is 'Destruction' or 'Destroyer'. Put together, these features form a monster never seen before.

Think about it! We are beginning to learn in these days of terrorism that death and destruction are not the only weapons Satan and his legions use to bring the human race back into his power. This is clever. If he kills us all, he will have none to work or fight for him! But he can terrorise us into serving him. Fear is a powerful weapon. Saul used it against David. The devil can make us terrified by using news items. See Psalm 53:5. The entertainment industry is doing it by its books, films and computer games which strike the imagination.

'Do not be afraid ... for the Lord your God will be with you' (Josh. 1:9).

Revelation 9:13-21   Revolution and civil war

God gives warnings of his judgements to come on the world because of its ungodliness. These increase in intensity as they point to a final decisive judgement. This is revealed in three 'woes' of which this is the second.

Description – what it says. The voice in v.13 speaks from the golden altar, showing it is the word of God himself who may use hellish situations and means when he judges wickedness.

In v.14 the angel is told to release four angels held in bonds on the Euphrates, where the first civil war in the Bible took place (Gen.14). But this later one is much worse. When the angels are released a major civil war breaks out in which a third of the world's population is killed. Vast armies are brought into operation to achieve this (16). Nor is it only their number that is terrifying, but their nature. They are obviously demonic, unlike any horses known to man, for they wear multi-coloured breastplates, they have lions' heads and emit fire, smoke and sulphur which pour from their mouths (17). The death toll is vast (18). Their tails too are lethal – not only shaped like snakes, but carrying a sting which had power to inflict injury (19).

Those left behind continue to trust their own works and practise idolatry (20), witchcraft and general immorality (21).

Interpretation – what it means. Obviously it is about war as a judgement from God. But what kind of war? Everything here points to its being civil war, arising from revolution.

(a) It arises from a dispute from long before. God had been long holding back the angels who stir quarrels into all-out war (14).

(b) The numbers killed in these civil wars are vast (15-16) – a nation fighting its own people loses twice as many as in a foreign war.

(c) A bitter hatred between the protagonists develops which can last for generations (17-19).

(d) Civil wars do not achieve what they set out to do, and fail to bring repentance. Those who do not repent under judgement are given over to the consequences of this failure (Rom. 1:24,26,28). Because it does not have the intended effect, there must be more judgements.

This book is about the war of Christ and his church against the devil and the world he controls (1 John 5:19). This culminates in Christ's victory on his return (17:14). As we approach the halfway point, why not pause to reflect on the overall value of what you are reading? It should help:

(a) To show us what we may expect from a fallen world under the devil who seeks to destroy our spiritual lives (1 Peter 5:8) and the whole church (Matt.16:18).

(b) To show us what response we may expect to our offer of Christ from people who are enemies of God (Rom.5:10).

(c) To show us Christ as our captain who will always be with us (Matt.28:20) and fights for us until the final victory is won (19:1-16).

Think about it: Go over these points until they are firmly fixed in your mind. Then relate every section and chapter to whichever one is appropriate.

Revelation 10   The urgent message – 'No more delay'

Previous judgements should have terrified people and caused them to repent. But it does not have the intended effect. It does not bring 'the rest of mankind to repentance' (9:20-21). There must be more judgements. These involve another 'mighty angel' (10:1).

Although John is told 'there will be no more delay' (10:6), it does not mean time will cease and the end is coming immediately, but that it is the next big event to happen. What does John see and what have we to learn?

More about Christ himself (1-4). He is the 'mighty angel coming down from heaven'. He is 'robed in a cloud' (1:7; Matt. 26:64), for mystery surrounds him. He has a rainbow above his head signifying mercy (cf. Gen. 9:12-17), the little scroll is just one aspect of the big scroll with seven seals (see 5:1-5), showing there is still some history to be fulfilled, in connection with his sovereignty over the whole earth, referred to in the words about his standing with one foot on the sea and the other on the land. This provoked the seven thunders, about which John is not permitted to write, for God is not revealing anything fresh about his plans.

The urgency of the message (5-7). Although the final blow does not fall immediately, those who hear the message have no time to delay their response. Christ has all things under him (5-6) and repeats his warning with a strong oath (6). The sixth angel will sound and 'the mystery' be revealed.

The message must go out to all (8-11). John is told to take the little scroll and eat it, that is, ponder it deeply. He will feel upset to hear of the judgement that will fall on all who do not repent, but he must go on proclaiming it and persuading them to repent, so that they will avoid the judgement and share with him in the blessings of salvation.

Think about it: Revelation does not tell us precisely what will happen and when. But it does tell us that painful and alarming things will happen and that these must be taken seriously. They are judgements on people's unbelief and misbehaviour. We live in days of moral and spiritual decline, along with big disasters which cause poverty. It is no coincidence that such things are happening in days of spiritual decline. People must repent or else ...

The minor judgements, signified by the seals, which constantly fall on the world, are essential to draw attention to ungodliness and the seriousness of the final judgement which is coming. Are we and our preachers seeking to obey this call, or do we think all we need is to tell people 'God loves you'? But this will be meaningless until they face their ungodliness, confess it before Christ and come to him for salvation.

Revelation 11:1-14   The church and the world

We are in the period of the sixth trumpet (announcements) and the second woe (drastic but not final judgement).

The church is separated from the world (1-3). Measuring the temple occurs more than once in the Old Testament, but here it seems to be done to clarify the church's separation from the world. This explains what follows.

The 'two witnesses' are Israel and the church (3-6) – the Old and New Covenant people of God. Israel was called to witness to the true God and proclaim his promises of a Messiah (Isa. 43:10-11). The church is called to declare that these promises are fulfilled in Jesus Christ (Matt. 28:18-20). The world tries to silence it ('trample'), so that the church's preaching and the world's persecution go on at the same time. 42 months = 1,260 days, which symbolises the whole period between the two advents. The church is protected by the Spirit (4), foreseen by Zechariah in his vision of the two olive trees (Zech. 4), for the Spirit has power to inflict severe punishments on the world (5), such as drought and plague (6).

What happens when the 'forty-two months', the age of the gospel, ends (7-10) (Matt. 18:18)? The devil, who has been restrained during this period (20:1-3) will be released, and appear as 'the beast' (7) who will reduce the church to a tiny remnant. The unbelieving world – 'Sodom', Egypt and Jerusalem, where also out Lord was crucified (8) – will gloat over them for the rest of this 'short period', symbolised as the other three-and-a-half years which make up the whole seven days or years which form the full period between the advents (9). They will celebrate this as revenge for all that the world has suffered at the hands of the church during this age (10).

The church finally triumphs (11-12). Just as the church imitated Christ's sufferings, so it will imitate his triumph, for, as Christ was raised and returned to glory, so will the church be. Then those who mocked their defeat will be 'terror-struck' (11) when they see the church taken up to glory (12).

Think about it: How clearly and strongly do you hold the glorious 'Christian hope'? It is essential that you do because, if you live your Christian life faithfully and bear witness to the world, you are bound to be caught up in the sufferings the church has to bear at the hands of the world and its leader, the devil, along with his army of evil spirits. Read what Peter wrote of this in 2 Peter 3:3-9. Some have intense physical suffering, but those who escape this are still 'hated' (John 16:1-4). Notice Peter's 'little while', which corresponds to John's 'short period' (Rev. 20:3).

If we suffer with him we will also reign with him (2 Tim. 2:12).

Revelation 11:15-19   Christ will reign over all

The seventh angel's trumpet blast announces the third woe, to be described in the final eleven chapters. Christ reigns over all and carries out his final judgements. There are universal celebrations (11:15-19). But before this happens, there must be more judgements.

Verse 15 sounds like the end, but it is only the beginning of the end. Christ takes control of 'the kingdoms of the world'. Read Paul's words: 'all things are put under his feet' and that he will 'destroy all authority and power and hand over the kingdom to God the Father' (1 Cor. 15:24-28).

Verses 16-18 are the church's response to this: the 'twenty-four elders' (as in 4:4) represent the church of the Old Covenant (the twelve tribes of Israel), and the church of the New Covenant (the twelve apostles). These submit heartily, 'falling on their faces', and welcome his enthronement (17). This contrasts with the response of the unbelieving world, which is angry because it has lost its battle with Christ and his church. God's wrath is different from human anger: it is righteous (Rom. 1:18), and is poured out on his enemies. None can withstand the power of his wrath.

The final judgement is on:

(a) *all the unrighteous and wicked* who are spiritually dead in their transgressions and sins (Eph. 2:1) and are now condemned to everlasting death under God's eternal wrath (Matt. 25:46);

(b) *God's servants* who willingly accepted his salvation and his reign. They are duly 'rewarded' with the gift of eternal life (Rom. 6:23). This applies to prophets and (other) saints alike (18), because their acceptance of him was sincere – they reverence his name, that is, acknowledge his holiness.

Status in the world does not affect the judgement or reward, which is for small and great alike. The same applies in the supernatural world – those who destroy the earth, that is, the devil and all who serve him will suffer the same judgement.

What shall we make of v. 19? Some say it ends chapter 11, others that it begins chapter 12. It is best seen as a bridge between the two, saying that John will now see with his eyes what he has just heard from the voices from heaven (15). What does he see? God's temple in heaven, originally given to Moses, but destroyed by the Babylonians, along with the ark of the covenant. John will see why God ordained these things. They were like prophecies of the kingdom his Son will set up. He also sees a great storm prophesying what God will destroy, especially the beast (13:11) and 'Babylon' (ch. 18), which will be dealt with in the final 'seven', the 'seven bowls of wrath' poured out (ch. 16).

Think about it: The Old Testament and its institutions are not to be taken literally in the New Covenant, but symbolically of Christ. Blood sacrifices are prophecies of his death.

Revelation 12:1-6   John's vision of the coming of Messiah

The style of Revelation is prophetic ('in the Spirit', 1:10), with visions ('show' and 'saw', 1:1,12). It was a particular form of prophecy – 'apocalyptic' – with vivid illustrations, weird creatures, etc. This formed a kind of code language, used because of the danger of referring directly to the emperor and government. Domitian is called 'the beast' (ch.13), Rome is 'Babylon' (ch.18) or 'prostitute' (ch.17), and the devil is the 'dragon' (20:2).

This chapter opens the second section of the book. The first section was on the war between the church (represented by the seven churches of Asia) and the world. Behind the world are Satan and his followers, and behind the church is Christ, the captain of his believing people. They war against each other.

SECOND PART: THE BATTLE BETWEEN CHRIST AND SATAN.

SECTION 1: THE WOMAN, THE DRAGON AND THE TWO BEASTS (chs 12–14).

John introduces these supernatural beings used in the war against the church.

How Christ became Satan's enemy (1-6). We are taken back to the Old Testament and those who formed the people of God in that age, that is, Israel. In chapter 12 God's people are depicted as a pregnant woman (1). The glory of God's church is pictured by her appearance as a light-bearer (sun and moon). The 'twelve stars' are 'the angels of the churches' (light-bearers to the world 1:20.) Her pregnancy (expectation of one to come) refers to the prophetic nature of the Old Testament, whose theme throughout is the promise of a Messiah. Her pain and crying

(2) describe Israel's longing for the Saviour (Ps. 53:6) and their anguish at the hands of the world. The 'enormous red dragon' of v.3 is identified in v.9 as 'that ancient serpent, the devil and Satan'. The 'seven heads' represent his wisdom, the 'horns' his power, and the 'crowns' his authority. A fallen creature himself, he was able to persuade a third of the angels (meaning a lot, but not a majority!) to join him. He is seen as 'standing before the woman waiting for the arrival of the Messiah, who will be born of a woman, and grow up to reign over the people and destroy the devil and his legions. We understand these prophecies (now fulfilled) better than did the Jews, who saw him as a politico-military figure who would fight against their enemies. Satan aimed to kill the child as soon as it was born and used Herod for this purpose (Matt. 2:1-8). Verse 6 hints at Mary and Joseph's flight to Egypt (Matt. 2:13-15). The symbolic numbers (1,260 days, cf.11:3) represent the whole period of Christ's life and ministry on earth. John sees this in a vision, so that he can understand why he is in prison and warn the churches that they will suffer similarly.

Think about it: Can you take these references to monsters seriously as a suitable explanation of the sufferings of Christians at the hands of the world? Do you find it too fantastic for these sophisticated times? If so, you are playing into the devil's hands. This is just what he wants! John is using this language to conceal his meaning from the authorities who may read his letter. See it as serious Christian doctrine written in the apocalyptic language of visions.

Revelation 12:7-12   War in heaven

The woman's child will defeat the dragon and his followers and lead the New Covenant churches in their battle. They will bear witness to him during his earthly life and heavenly reign (11:15-16). In 12:7-17 these two beings come into conflict: Christ, represented by the archangel Michael (a warrior in Christian literature) and Satan (the dragon).

Satan is defeated (7-9). Verse 7 takes us back to the original fall of man in Genesis 3. Satan tricked Eve into disobeying God, and the result was perpetual war between her 'seed' (mankind) and the followers of Satan ('his angels' or evil spirits). They were given leave to lead the whole world astray. The descendants of Adam and Eve turned from God to idols (Rom. 1:24-25). God maintained a witness to himself through the nation of Israel. They too would defect to idol gods, but God promised a Saviour, one who would come from Israel but who would be stronger than Satan because he is the Son of God. He would deprive Satan of his power to deceive (see Revelation 20:3). 'Losing their place in heaven' and being 'hurled to the earth' (9) is an apocalyptic way of saying they have lost the power and glory they had before and can no longer keep man in ignorance of God and his promise if God wills to enlighten them. There are examples in the Gospels of his defeat at the hands of Christ: in Luke 4:1-13 Satan fails to get Christ to bow to his will; in Luke 10:17-18 the disciples' ability to cast out demons is a sign of Satan's defeat, and John 12:31 points to the cross as the total defeat of Satan.

Christ is victorious (10-12). This was Christ's first victory, duly celebrated by his angels in heaven and shared by those on earth through their testimony to faith in the power of his sacrifice (11). Then he turns his fury against the child and the followers of Jesus. But whatever Satan tries, God resists. But Satan is not giving up – the war continues (13-17). These verses celebrate the accomplishment of Christ's victory over Satan when Christ set up his kingdom of power and salvation (10). Those he saves by his power and through his blood are incorporated into his kingdom (11) and are kept from being deceived by Satan. As a result, they are instrumental in delivering others from Satan's lies by the word of their testimony as they preach or witness to others with the word which has saved them. This will never take place without a cost: they will have to give up their lives to Christ, which in some cases will mean laying down their lives for him. Satan knows his time is limited, which only intensifies his fury (12). This does not quench the volume of the song of praise from those who dwell in heaven, who continue to rejoice as Jesus said in his parable of the lost sheep (Luke 15:7).

Think about it: Do not despair if few are confessing faith in Christ, and do not be surprised if they turn on you or those you know. Christ made this clear, before he suffered, that this would be so (John 15:18-25). 'The blood of the martyrs is the seed of the church' (Tertullian).

Revelation 12:13-17   The history of persecution

Chapter 12 begins the second main section of the book and moves from the conflict between the church and the world to that between Christ and Satan ('the dragon'). This chapter summarises the history of the conflict in the form of an allegory in which each detail stands for an aspect of the war between Christ and his church on one side, and Satan and his evil spirits on the other. The 'woman' (1) represents the Old Covenant church (Israel), out of whom comes the Messiah, the 'child' to whom she gives birth (2). Satan is waiting for him to be born in order to devour him, as Herod sought to do with the baby Jesus (Matt. 2). But the child is protected and will grow up to become ruler of the nations (5). The church, too, is protected by God in order to continue down the ages (6). During this time the two forces fought each other in the supernatural realm (7) and this conflict spread to the earth (8), where Satan with lies and false accusations (10) leads the whole world astray (9). But this fails to destroy the church, which is victorious through the cross, and the Christians' testimony to it (10-12). Thus, although Satan has warred against it from the beginning (13), the church has always found safety under God's protection, as an eagle protects its young (14). But both the New Testament and subsequent history describe how the church was persecuted first by Jews, then by Romans and other nations. Although many Christians died, the church was not destroyed, for God always provided a way of escape; she was like someone alone in a vast desert, out of reach of the enemy (14).

In v.15 Satan finds another method: he raises up heresies which flood the churches. In the second and subsequent centuries, they were riddled with false teaching, particularly about the nature and person of Christ. Verse 16 suggests this had more acceptance with the world (earth) than the church. The church held councils (Nicea, Chalcedon, etc.) which defined the doctrine of the Trinity and the person of Christ and enabled her to continue to be faithful to the Scriptures in these matters and others. Frustrated with his failure to destroy the faith of true Christians with false teaching, Satan turned to nominal Christianity – his most successful tactic in weakening the church, especially over the past two hundred years. People are not attracted to weak, lifeless churches.

Think about it: 13:1 belongs to this chapter: Satan looks satisfied, he has no problem with nominal Christians, but we should challenge them more.

Revelation 13:1-10   The first beast – state persecution

The devil ('dragon') uses two agents in his war against Christ and the church. These he likens to beasts because of their ferocity. The first of these is the beast out of the sea. He represents state persecution of the church. Daniel had a similar vision, but, whereas he was aware of four different beasts, John sees only one with the characteristics of the four: lion, bear, leopard and a monster (Dan. 7:1-7). Just as Daniel's beast was 'like a man' (Dan. 7:4), so the beast John saw had superhuman intelligence ('seven heads') and great authority ('ten crowns'), signifying that in his battle against the church, Satan does not give way to mindless passion, but uses great skill and is given authority (2).

He receives authority from the dragon, which people recognise and regard him as unique in the universe (4). This makes him so proud he feels free to utter blasphemies against the true God. This lasts for the remainder of the present age, symbolised as 'forty-two months' (5). He wields this power over all people (7). The only exceptions are God's elect, whom he chose before the creation of the world (8). It is vital that everyone hears this and takes it seriously (9), because those who are guilty will be sent to a place prepared for them to receive punishment (10). This will encourage the saints to exercise patience, endurance and faithfulness.

What do we in our times see here? We see how the devil uses the totalitarian states of our day to destroy the people of God and even bring down their head, Christ himself! What Assyria and Babylon sought to do to the Jews before Christ came, Satan now seeks to do against Christians. The Jews themselves started this, but they lost their power in AD 70, after which the Roman Empire was the supreme power for centuries. But in the fifth century the Roman Empire collapsed and the Church of Rome became a virtual totalitarian state. Then came the Reformation of the sixteenth century when many nations in Europe became Protestant.

Anti-Christian governments have opposed Christians from the Roman Empire onwards. This will continue throughout the period of Christ's earthly reign as he builds his church through the preaching of the gospel, symbolised in the 'forty-two months'. This can even use those who claim to be Christians but are not saved in terms of v. 8. Christians should not physically fight this (a mistake they made centuries ago) but continue their ministry with faith and patience knowing that those who harm God's people will themselves receive the punishment they deserve (10).

Today Christians have learned that the use of force has no place in Christianity. However, other religions think it does, and nations which embrace these religions persecute Christians with force.

Think about it: First, we must face up to what is happening. We must do what the early churches failed to do (2:4-7): heed the warnings and repent of the backsliding. But we must not give up hope! These hostile states will fall, as the Roman Empire did. Christ is still building his church and it will outlast the kingdoms of this world and of hell itself (Matt. 16:18).

Revelation 13:11-18   The second beast – false religion

John is in the process of seeing a vision of a pregnant woman threatened by an enormous red dragon. She escapes into the desert where she is with her God, which provokes a cosmic war between the angels of God and the army of Satan. This war is fought out on the battlefield of churches on earth (12:1-7). As the vision continues John is shown something of how the devil conducts his campaign against the church by employing two 'beasts'. These are not pets, or domestic or even working animals, but fierce and dangerous ones (12:7b-9).

'The beast out of the sea' who used physical force to try to dethrone Christ and destroy his followers has largely failed, for both are still here, and always will be. True Christians have learned to endure without retaliation. But the 'red dragon' has another agent – 'the beast out of the earth'.

The other beast uses false religion against the church. This one does not use violence, but apes the Christians by being 'lamb-like' (11). He bleats rather than roars, but this is deceptive, for it carries the power of the first beast (12) but uses it differently: instead of attacking Christ and his followers, he tries to show the glories of the first beast, thus persuading them to worship him. It appears friendly, offers comfort and even performs 'miracles'. It claims to have been fatally wounded and then come back to life. He even uses living men (15) who come up with progressive ideas about the creation of the universe, which have persuaded many Christians and drawn them away from God. They affect a nation's economy, so that only those who accept their religion or world-view can trade (16-17). Its true nature is revealed in the number '666' – man's number, one short of 7, the perfect number, belonging only to God. We know this today as humanism, which in various forms is sweeping the board among thinking people.

This beast is very active in some parts of the world where peoples are turning to Christ from their false religion. In the UK we see this in the loss of some privileges and general respect. We have no right to expect the special favours we have traditionally received from the state; rather, if present trends continue, intolerance may turn to actual persecution. We must expect this and not become bitter. In other countries it is a regular occurrence where churches refuse to renounce Christ. We should pray, not for it to cease but for believers to stand firm and not to renounce Christ (1 Peter 4:12; John 16:1-4).

Think! How discerning we must be about teachings which appear helpful and true, especially those that are just humanism in disguise.

Revelation 14:1-5   John's vision of the church in glory

We are still in the period of the seven seals – final warnings before the last judgement (9:13). Under the sixth seal three angels appear, blowing trumpets – announcements that the warnings of 7:1ff are about to be fulfilled. This is the heart of the battle between Christ himself and the devil ('dragon'), along with his agents, the woman and the two beasts.

But first John sees Christ as 'the Lamb standing on Mount Zion' (1) with his whole church of the Old and New Covenants, symbolised by the 144,000 who do not have the mark of the beast and who will not fall at the last judgement but will be in heaven (symbolised by Mount Zion, the new Jerusalem). They are safe, hearing rushing waters (2) and a new song (3).

The living creatures and the elders are the angels, showing John that he was having a vision of heaven, similar to that in chapter 4 which was given to him ahead of the battles he was to see between chapter 4 and chapter 14. This was to keep him from being depressed or frightened by the visions. God has not forgotten his promises! But these promises have conditions attached. It is not enough to have a mark to show they are his elect. Their behaviour must correspond, with sexual purity (4) and faithfulness to Christ. This will prove they have been purchased and belong to God (4; 1:5b-6). Their promises to him are not lies (5).

***

Think about it: What assurance and hope this would have given Christians under the harsh rule of the Emperor Domitian! Since the destruction of Jerusalem in AD 70 and the dispersion of the Jews, Christians had enjoyed twenty years of freedom. Now (in the 90s) they faced the full force of the Roman Empire. The earthquakes and plagues God will send would involve all on the earth, the evil and the good. But the Christians will not be on the earth! They will be in heaven enjoying the blessings of these verses and of chapter 4! They will be with Christ as 'the Lamb', meek and gentle, not as a sheep who may be a disguised ravening wolf! He is the 'Lamb who by his death takes away the sin of the world' (John 1:29).

What about us two thousand years later? God's judgements fall on those who oppose him and his people. This has happened throughout history. Every age has had its terrorists and its tyrants, often targeting Christians. Their judgement will be our freedom. Let this hope drive out our fear!

Revelation 14:6-13   Back to earth

The sixth seal opened by the Lamb (6:12-14) had revealed a series of judgements which inspired great fear in those who had the mark of the beast but lacked the seal of God. These were not the final judgement but created great fear in mankind and corresponding joy in those with the seal of God (7:1-8). These were the 144,000 of chapter 7. Now, in chapter 14, in the thick of the battle between the Lamb and the dragon, the same 144,000 are singing their song again as they follow the Lamb wherever he goes.

For all his efforts Satan ('the dragon') has failed to destroy the church or dethrone Christ. When the final blow falls, the saints will be in glory worshipping Christ as 'the Lamb' (1). They need not fear the universal judgement. On the strength of this John turns their eyes back to earth, to the three angels with their messages.

First angel (6-7). He is proclaiming the eternal gospel to those who dwell on the earth who have his name on their foreheads. How gracious and just God is! As at the Flood, God does not strike without giving fair warning (Gen. 6:3).

Second angel (8). 'Babylon' was a code name for Rome at a time when it was dangerous to speak ill of the empire or the emperor. Ancient Babylon was the epitome of ungodliness and it fell under God's judgement. It revived in the eighth century BC as the instrument of God's judgement on Assyria, which enabled the people of Judah to be set free to return to their own land. But it was to fall finally at the last judgement (see chapter 18). To us 'Babylon' stands for the entire evil world system governed by the evil one. This will be overthrown, like 'Rome'.

Third angel (9-13). This describes the final judgement in powerful, terrifying language. This shows how it will far exceed anything that happens today. Contemporary judgements are warnings, which John's vision calls 'seals', and are insignificant when compared with the judgement to come. It will fall on those who worship the beast and his image, that is, who give to anyone or anything other than the God and Father of Jesus Christ what is due to him alone. These are distinguished from each other symbolically – one bears the mark of the beast and the other the name of God on his forehead (9). The first endure fury poured out in wrath. They know it is coming from him whom they have rejected (10) and this everlastingly (11). The knowledge of this will enable the saints to exercise patient endurance under their present sufferings (12). But lest the whole prospect alarm the Christians, let them remember what they will be doing – resting from their labours and enjoying their reward (13), particularly worshipping the Lamb in the new Jerusalem (1) and that for ever and ever while their enemies suffer (11).

Think about it: To fend off fear and anxiety and be filled with glorious hope, keep this and similar passages before you. Read hymns at home, don't just sing them in church, where they are all over in minutes! Most hymns make some reference to glory. As Richard Baxter said, 'Take a walk round New Jerusalem every day' (Saints' Everlasting Rest, and see Psalm 48:12-14).

Revelation 14:14-20   Judgement seen as a harvest

Verses 14-16: back to earth. This is God's final call to the unbelieving world to repent of its idolatry and to 'worship the Lamb' before the imminent hour of his judgement comes (6-7). Those who obey the call are assured they will 'die in the Lord' and go to their reward (13). Verse 14 brings us back to earth. First John sees a white cloud, a symbol of God's presence, for the figure on it is 'a son of man' wearing a golden crown. This is no ordinary man or even an angel, but the Messiah himself, as predicted by Daniel in Daniel 7:13. Normally this would be a message of hope, for the Messiah was the Promised One coming to the rescue. But here he is armed with a sharp sickle. What is this for? Another angel comes to tell the figure on the white cloud to reap the harvest of the earth which is ripe. This is ambiguous. Normally it would refer to the gathering of the firstfruits who are the elect of God, chosen from the people of the world and marked with his name on their foreheads, who have been promised they will be spared the final judgement because they 'die in the Lord' (13). But here they are the ones ripe for judgement!

Verses 17-20. This probably came as a surprise to the early Christians and the disciples before them, who heard Jesus in his teaching refer to his Second Coming in harvest language. If so, vv. 18-19 should say:

yet another angel, who comes and says that the ripe grapes are to be trampled in the winepress of God's wrath! Also, he is called the angel who had charge of fire (18). This explains how an angel has the authority to command 'the one like a son of man' to carry out the judgement. He has come out of the temple, the seat of God in his holiness (15), who therefore has the authority of the Father expressed through the angel.

The final proof that this is about the judgement of the wicked at the last day is in v. 20. The grapes symbolise the blood of the unbelievers crushed under the winepress of the wrath of God. That this is a universal judgement is shown by the blood flowing in all directions and deep enough for horses to swim in. The measurements are composed of four forties multiplied by ten. Four is the symbolic number of the earth and ten is the number of completeness. Finally, it all takes place in the city, that is, the new Jerusalem.

Think about it: This is how God will answer the prayers of his suffering people. We should remember this when we pray for the persecution from our enemies to cease. It will cease by their being cast into hell! What a responsibility is ours to have a part in the punishment of the wicked! God does it by casting them into hell.

Revelation 15   Seven angels with seven trumpets

With this section we come to the last of the cycles of sevens – last not only numerically but in the sense of v.1, that these are the seven last plagues because in them God's wrath is completed.

SECOND PART, SECTION 2: THE SEVEN BOWLS (chs 15–17).

Verses 1-4: At last the final judgement has come! John sees a further vision: seven angels with the seven last plagues, which John assures us are the very last – this is the sign that they will complete God's wrath. The word 'plagues' is the first of a number of words which recall God's judgement on the Egyptians when they were holding Israel captive. The sea of glass reminds us of the Red Sea which drowned the Egyptians, whose bodies Israel saw dead in the water (Exod.14). These represent the enemies of Christ and Christians, who were beginning to suffer persecution which has continued until the present day. These enemies are those who bore the mark of the beast (2). The victors carried harps and sang a song, as Israel had done at the Red Sea (Exod.15). The song ascribed the victory to the mighty power of God exercising his truth and justice (3). Who can refuse such a demonstration? Surely it must be acknowledged by people of all nations (4).

Verses 5-8. John sees a vision of the temple – not Solomon's, nor its replacement by Herod, but the spiritual counterpart of the original tabernacle or tent of Moses. This contained the ark (chest) which housed the testimony, the tablets of the law. It is from this building that the seven angels bearing the seven bowls emerge (6) and begin the process leading to the final judgement. Only priests were allowed to look into the ark, so these angels are dressed in shining linen with golden sashes; as royal priests (cf.1:13-14). The four living creatures appear and one of them gives the seven angels the seven bowls. This is ominous since these bowls are filled with the wrath of God (7). We know we are at the end because God is described as the one who lives for ever and ever. This is significant because it emphasises that this is the one true and living God and not a false god or impostor. Terrible as all this is, it is the work of the God who is holy and righteous and is doing what is right and what the saints are praying for. The smoke (8) which issues forth is the presence of God and bars any from seeing what is happening there. Judgement is a mystery, as is salvation. This continues until his work of judgement is completed. We can be sure that this is God's final act although it comprises seven acts (pouring the bowls), which are described in chapters 16 and 17 and finalised in chapter 18.

What does it all mean? Our knowledge of God's final judgement is like the smoke that filled the temple. The details are obscure, it is a great mystery. We should not be too quick to call a major disaster the final judgement or interpret God's acts. 'God is his own interpreter and he will make it plain' (Cowper).

Revelation 16:1-14　The bowls of wrath

In 15:1 John has a vision which he calls a 'marvellous sign': seven angels bearing the seven last plagues, with which God will complete his wrath. Those who were marked with God's name, exempt from the final judgement, were commemorating their victory at the sea of glass, singing to the accompaniment of harps the song of Moses and the Lamb, i.e. believers under both old (Moses) and new (the Lamb) covenants. They had survived the persecution of the beast and were victorious.

Next (15:5-6) he sees the seven angels with their seven plagues coming out of heaven. Then he sees one of the four living creatures from 4:6b giving the seven bowls of wrath to the seven angels (15:7). They are not merely serious but terminal. They are comparable to the plagues God inflicted on the Egyptians for their refusal to release the Israelites from slavery. As the judgement begins, the temple is filled with smoke; no one can see inside until the seven plagues are complete.

John hears a new voice from heaven telling the seven angels to begin pouring.

The first angel (2). In this section of the book, God is visiting judgement on the enemies of Christ and the church. These are not final but are warnings that a final one is coming. These bowls of wrath are the last warning judgements (16:1). The first angel pours out his bowl on the earth – the land.

The second angel (3) pours out his bowl on the sea. These afflict human beings in their bodies (like the plagues on Egypt).

The third angel (4-7) pours out his bowl on rivers and springs and emphasises the justice of these judgements: they are retaliation for the blood of the saints shed by their enemies.

The remaining judgements are more in the cosmic and supernatural realm.

The fourth angel (8-9) strikes the sun. This does not increase its light. The gospel does not become clearer at the end. People have heard it fully but rejected it, and so it becomes a message of judgement, symbolised by its intense heat. This does not produce repentance, but in fact only increases their anger against God.

The fifth angel (10-11) goes directly for the beast (who represents secular and religious persecution). Now, instead of too much sun, there is no sun at all. The total darkness inflicts more pain than the scorching sun! Pitch darkness can be very frightening – imagine this universally! But there is still no repentance.

The sixth angel (12-14) dries up the Euphrates – not in itself supernatural, but what it leads to is. In the Bible and history the East is the source of astrology and magic (Matt. 2:1). This is to prepare for a final gathering of the church's enemies in the demonic realm: the dragon, the beast and the false prophets in the form of frogs.

Think about it: We are all familiar with the expression 'All hell broke loose!' That is metaphorical but this is literal: the agony and cursing (10-11) describe a breakdown in civilisation caused by the emergence of the demons from hell. Satan comes into his own, all are under his reign!

Revelation 16:15-21   Christ intervenes

The way is now open for the powers of evil to come out for the final battle against the church. They are led by 'the kings from the east' (12). But this is no ordinary battle. From the mouth of the dragon (Satan, 13) along with his agents – the beast and the false prophet – come the spirits of demons who, by their miraculous signs, lure the people of God out to battle and destruction on the day of God Almighty (14).

In v. 15 comes Christ, who himself used the illustration of the thief in the night of his return to judge the world on the last day (Matt. 24:42-44) and in an earlier vision to John (Rev. 3:3). But v. 15 brings out its full significance because of the context – the final battle with the church. Christ comes as Captain of the Lord's host (Josh. 5:13-15). It is not Satan who chooses the day, for no one knows it, not even the angels, or the Son himself (Matt. 24:36). All he will tell is that they must be ready, awake and armed! This is where the thief image is so powerful. Many have thought they can work it out but none has succeeded. Neither does he tell them the place, for Armageddon is mythical. The words in Hebrew mean hill of Megiddo. There had been a town called Megiddo where battles had been fought, such as that between Israel under Deborah and Midian under Sisera (Judg. 5:19). When Megiddo was razed to the ground another town was built on the rubble, until it became a hill.

The seventh angel (17) puts it differently: a thief only affects one household, but

vv. 17-20 predict a universal destruction – the end of the world, so often described in these visions. But the mystical language is still there in the name 'Babylon'. Babylon was the first city to be built in the world (Gen. 11:4). It became wicked and defied God by building a tower ('Babel', Gen. 11:9). It disappeared for many generations until it revived in the eighth century BC and conquered the existing empires until God raised up Cyrus to defeat it and add it to Cyrus' empire. By now 'Babylon' had become a symbol of the wicked evil world system. When it fell, what the New Testament calls 'the world' fell too (19-20). This is the last judgement, the final battle, so often spoken of in these visions. Terrible as the words of v. 21 are, there is more to come in chapter 18. The seventh angel announced this when he sounded his trumpet. These judgements fall on the wicked generally, but still not on the real enemies, Babylon, the beasts and the dragon. That is still to come.

'It is done!' (17), the 'it' being Christ's return to raise the dead, destroy the present universe and replace it with the 'new heavens and earth' (2 Peter 3:13). So, forget other versions of the final day. We cannot go further than vv. 15-21 go. Instead of speculating, take heed of what Christ and his apostles tell us to do – Matthew 24:42-51; 2 Peter 3.

'Since everything will be destroyed in this way, what kind of people ought you to be?' (2 Peter 3:11).

Revelation 17:1-11 ✓ The woman riding the beast

The seventh angel's bowl has caused the great city (Babylon) to split into three parts (16:19). She is 'the great prostitute' (1) who sits on many waters – rules the earth and has seduced kings and people by her adulteries – the attractions of a fallen world (2). The vision moves to a desert place where the woman is sitting on a scarlet beast (3) with seven heads and ten horns, covered with blasphemous names (3) – the idols they have been drawn to and wicked activities they have been seduced to adopt. Her opulent garb along with the golden cup and precious stones were deceptive, for she could not drink these, only the contents of the cup! She symbolises corrupt worldly power – the beast out of the sea in chapter 13. Further, her titles (5) claim her to be both 'Babylon' and the 'mother of prostitutes' – apt symbolism of places where all sorts of abominations occur. They are also places where Christians are persecuted (6) because they bore testimony to Jesus.

When the angel sees John's astonishment at all this, he explains the mystery to him. The beast with seven heads and ten horns (7) who keeps disappearing and reappearing (8) is going to come out of the abyss to which it belongs and go to destruction, falling victim to God's final judgement. This will evoke more astonishment among Christians and will call for special wisdom (9) to explain.

Verses 6b-11: The interpretation. This combination of the powers of the beast out of the sea (anti-Christian government) and the beast out of the earth (anti-Christian religion) (ch. 13) widens the influence of evil to embrace every aspect of human life, such as human thought and philosophy, culture and leisure activities and daily work. The strange figures in v. 8 and vv. 9-11 seem to represent the fluctuating interest of the human race in the practice of these activities. There are epochs when these are good and wholesome, and other epochs when they decline into corruption and evil under the control of the beast. Some are of short duration, others longer (11). This is partly due to the rapidity with which emperors or other leaders replace each other through murder, assassination or execution. In less violent times leaders replace each other through a voting system which brings in different policies, but all were controlled by the beast whose ultimate aim is to win the war against the Lamb and break his power.

The seven hills are those on which Rome was built, and Rome herself is governed by the woman (the prostitute), which explains its corruption. This is not the city itself but the seven kings who rule it. Seven is a symbolic number meaning all. Five have fallen this way, and one is still in power. He will be followed by one who will last longer than his predecessors. He is not an eighth king but the beast himself, the corrupt spirit which controls government (he belongs to the seven). He is anti-Christian state power, responsible for the persecution of Christians. He is to be destroyed at the final judgement.

Think about it: Evidently corrupt governments and anti-Christian states plus terrorist groups will go on to the end, then cease forever! No more reports of atrocities against Christians!

Revelation 17:12-18   The ten kings

These ten kings are those who have authority in their own realm (12). To exercise this they are given power equal to that of the beast, but its time is limited. Which of these is active at a particular time depends on how much influence the beast is given, but ultimately they all serve the beast (12-13) and seek to destroy the power of the Lamb. All are united in their opposition to Christ. Lest Christians despair at this, they are promised that the Lamb will overcome (14).

For us this means the devil has power to control us through our enjoyment of these various fields. For example, he can corrupt our art, music, literature, current affairs, etc., and even our careers in the world. He tries to destroy our faith and thus bring Christ's kingdom down. This does not mean we are to give up our interest in these activities, but we must be careful not to let them take over our lives and corrupt us, separating us from Christ, as is happening to many.

Verses 15-18: Civil war among Christ's enemies. One of the means by which Christ will be victorious is when his enemies with the beast turn against the woman (16) and devour her and leave her in ruins and burn her with fire. God does not directly destroy her but simply stirs up hatred so that the enemies devour each other. He also gives the beast the superior power so that he has the victory (17). Verse 18 reminds us that the woman is the symbol of the great city, that is, Babylon, which is itself a symbol of Rome. Rome in its latter days went from being a disciplined society to a pleasure-loving one, and the beast lost out to the prostitute. Is the same thing happening in the West now?

How God will judge the world and bring it to an end. Civil war is always the worst and most destructive form of war, since the parties concerned fight and kill each other and destroy their own resources. The final judgement is much wider. Anti-Christian government turns against human pleasure (the beast against the prostitute). It is Mao's Cultural Revolution on a universal scale. The other section wants strict rules and uses severe punishments to control it. It is anarchy against despotism. In John's day it was probably the fall of Rome (the great city or Babylon).

Think about it: Don't run away with the idea that because we have examples of the principle today we are about to witness the end of the world. It will be much wider than these examples. It may be centuries ahead.

Keep your mind on v.14, take the war seriously, and believe the great promise – that Christ will win. This verse is a good key to the whole book!

Revelation 18:1-10   The fall of Babylon

SECOND PART, SECTION 3: THE FINAL STATE OF THE RIGHTEOUS (chs 18–22).

Suddenly the battle with the beast is over. This chapter continues with the fall of Babylon, the ancient city (Babel, Gen. 11) rebuilt by Nebuchadnezzar, where the Jews were imprisoned. It is used here as a symbol for Rome, itself typical of anti-Christian state power. It is the devil's instrument in his war against the church and Christ. This important matter is given a whole chapter. It was introduced in chapter 13 as the beast out of the sea. Here it becomes Babylon, the great city (16:19) and three mighty angels are sent to announce its forthcoming judgement (1,4,21).

Verses 1-3: the first angel. 'Babylon has fallen.' This is in the past tense and indicates the certainty of this prophecy, described as if it had already happened! The state is still one of the principal means used by the devil to destroy Christ and his kingdom. We continually hear of states passing anti-Christian laws and enforcing them. These states will fail and fall, some in the course of future history, others at the final judgement, announced here. She who possessed others will herself be occupied by evil forces (2).

Verses 4-10: the second angel takes the matter much further. God's people must flee the city (4). This may refer back to the time of Cyrus the Persian's conquest and his release of the Jews. Only 50,000 left (Ezra 1) and the rest remained, possibly because they had settled, since they had been born and brought up there. But it had become a place of idolatry and corruption (2-3). Whether or not the Jews participated in this, it was not safe to stay there, since the day of reckoning came, and their remaining there would have doubled what had already been inflicted on them (5-6). They may have rejoiced in this as a just revenge, but the punishment was such that it was not safe to be anywhere near it. The inhabitants had not taken it seriously, which only intensified the punishment (7-8). The later history of Babylon – its periods of rebuilding and destruction – proves the truth of this prophecy. Others, who had enjoyed her, when they saw the judgement would take it more seriously and share in the mourning, but only because they no longer enjoyed her luxuries. All nations were involved: kings and merchants, even those legitimately trading. Some used their positions, power and influence, finding loopholes in the law. But all were motivated by greed and love of luxury, and found ways to exploit the poor. How up-to-date all this is! People, however honest they are, live for money and what it will buy. Christians can get caught up in this, for money is a god – 'Mammon' – which will destroy us spiritually. See Matthew 6:19-34; 2 Timothy 3:2.

Revelation 18:11-24   Why Christians must flee the city

Verses 11-15. This is revealed in the merchants' lament. There is a complete breakdown in trade. Merchants bring their goods to Babylon, but are unable to sell them because the Babylonians are too poor to buy them. These are mostly luxuries: gold, jewels, silk, spices, etc., but there are also cattle (13) and human beings. It sounds as though a slave trade is going on there. Babylon is left in a state of utter desolation. If they could not support themselves, what is left for the Christians? All the merchants can do is to stand afar off and lament (15). Their lament (16-17) is the second of three 'woes'. The first (9) is the lament of the kings for whom the doom of Babylon would mean financial bankruptcy.

Verses 17-19. The lament of captains and crews. But it was not only the merchants and the kings who stood to lose by the fall of Babylon. There were also those who provided the ships and their crews who brought the cargoes and did the trading who would lose out. They had much to lose by the collapse of Babylon's economy. This was something unprecedented – their whole livelihood lost in one hour (19). It was worse than any before or since – no recovery! But some will benefit – the Christians, for whom their persecution would now end (24).

Verses 21-24. The third angel. Here is a preview of his judgement: violent enough to destroy, not just buildings but people: musicians and workers such as corn-grinders (22). There would be perpetual darkness without lamps and no parties such as weddings (23). Their merchants were the great men of the world, magicians who could trick people into purchasing their goods and services, but which would corrupt them. Verse 24 justifies this. It is due revenge for what they have done to the people of God down the ages, as stated in vv. 6-8. This is no idle threat, no bad-tempered retaliation, but God's way of restoring the balance of justice. It is why Christians should not fear the final judgement but rejoice in it. Christians can rejoice for they are seeing the world receiving the treatment that it has meted out to the church (18-20). All those things that make up normal life are no more. That this is their recompense for their persecution of Christians is evidenced in the bloodstains in what remains of the city (20-24). Justice has been done for the saints whose blood has been shed. It is the basis of the rest of the book, when the enemies will be dealt with as they deserve.

What do you think? Are Christians right to be glad to hear that their enemies will be destroyed? Or should they aim to convert them, and be sad if they refuse?

Revelation 19:1-10   The great 'Hallelujah Chorus'

In chapter 4 John saw a vision of heaven in which a vast number are gathered around the throne of God. He sees a similar vision at 7:9. He is invited in, but told that certain things must happen first. There are enemies seeking to prevent this – a great dragon with two beasts helping him. These are symbols of Satan and his agents – worldliness, in the form of sensual lust and political power. These are major forces which God has to destroy before he can enter his glory and reign supreme. They are corrupting the earth and shedding the blood of his saints.

The battle proceeds throughout the succeeding chapters until, in chapters 16 to 18, they are finally destroyed. Although violent, this is a just retribution for what they have done to the saints and to the whole earth (2). The evidence of their destruction is the smoke going up for ever, showing this is a final destruction (3). So now is the time for the great 'Hallelujah Chorus', which is led by the twenty-four elders of chapter 4. To this the voice from heaven (5) responds by calling all God's servants, both small and great, to join the praise.

Then John hears the great multitude (cf. 7:9) sounding God's praise like rushing water and peals of thunder (6), announcing that God is commencing his reign. There is even more to rejoice about, for as well as a coronation this is also his marriage to the church, for the bride is now ready (7). She is cleansed from the corruptions of the world and delivered from its persecutions. Now, through her union with the Lamb, her life will be one of righteous acts. For the sake of those who remain, John is told to write down an invitation to the supper of the Lamb. This was not from man, but the true words of God. It corresponds to what Jesus said in his parables (Matt. 22). John is told he must be careful how he says this, for he is so overwhelmed that he starts worshipping the angel, and has to be told that, like himself, an angel is only a creature, a fellow-servant and a witness to Jesus.

Think about it: Do we truly realise the height of our privileges under the New Covenant? Let us glory in what we, like John, have and are: servants of God, witnesses to Christ. We are only one step below the angels! Do not think too lowly of ourselves. This will make us more bold. If we are too timid, we are either ignorant of all that we are, or not really believing it.

Revelation: 19:11-21   The end of the beasts

This type of passage yields its meaning best when questions are put to it.

Who is the rider? The colour of the rider and his horses, along with his appearance at the open gate of heaven, all point to a divine figure. This and other considerations clearly indicate the figure to be the Lord Christ. In v.11 he is called 'Faithful and True'. Only one person qualifies for these titles; only one person has brought truth into the world and is faithful to his promises (John 14:6). Verse 12 resembles John's vision of Christ in 1:14, with the blazing eyes. He also wears many crowns, and has a mysterious name which turns out to be 'the Word of God', which John calls him in his Gospel (John 1:1). In Matthew 25 he is accompanied by the armies of heaven. Christ himself had declared that when he personally returns to the earth it will be with the holy angels (Matt. 25:31). All this is finally proved by the title on his thigh: 'King of kings and Lord of lords' (16). He issues one last challenge to the followers of the evil power to do their worst and show who has the greater power.

What has he come to do?

1. He exercises the authority vested in him. He judges justly (11) and makes war, for he is the Christ who returns at the end of the age to lead the church in its war against Satan and the powers of hell. His authority extends far and wide, and he signifies this by wearing many crowns. He has the means necessary for defeating and controlling them (15). His fury with the beast is that of the wrath God himself, and therefore he has power over all forces ranged against him – he is 'King of kings and Lord of lords'.

2. He has the authority to summon all who are subject to the beast and join them together to launch a final assault on the dragon, the devil himself (17-18). But the dragon's forces counter-attack and resume their war against the 'Rider', who captures both the beast and the false prophet, that is, the other beast (out of the earth), who deceived the world with his false prophecies and miracles, and casts them into the lake of fire, where they are finally destroyed (20). The rest, the people who took no part in war, did not escape by their neutrality, but were destroyed by Christ at the general resurrection by the word of Christ. So that is the end of the devil's two principal agents. But what about the devil himself?

Think about it: No more reports of Christians imprisoned by anti-Christian governments! No more of those cults claiming to cure all ills for their followers!

Revelation 20:1-6   The fate of the dragon

The beasts are defeated, but the dragon remains. Here is his end.

The scene (1-3). John sees an angel come down from heaven with the key to the abyss, into which he casts the dragon bound and for 1,000 years.

The interpretation. The angel coming down is Christ becoming incarnate to release them from their bondage to the sin which was holding them back from the knowledge of God. Hitherto only the children of Israel had heard of the Son of God coming to admit them into God's kingdom. The rest were left with their false gods. Christ commanded that this message be spread through the world (Matt. 28:19-20). It came 'to the Jew first', but many were fiercely opposed and even imprisoned as Christian evangelists. This led to evangelising Gentiles, so that churches were planted all over the Roman Empire. The Roman roads and ease of communication took the gospel far and wide. This was hindered by the corruption of biblical truth into Roman Christianity. Even after this was rectified at the Reformation, it took two more centuries before the spread of the true gospel got under way. Since then churches have sprung up all over the world. Today, the Christian faith is the largest in the world, but it will not go on for ever. 'One thousand years' is symbolic of a long period but not an endless one, for the dragon will be set free for a short time (3).

The church during the thousand years (4-6). The period between Christ's resurrection and his return is symbolised by the thousand years – a long period in which Christ is reigning spiritually. But what of his church? We reign with him, we have power to resist Satan and his evil spirits, we judge (rule over) angels (4a; 1 Cor. 6:3), that is, those angels who fell with Satan. The judges are the martyrs beheaded by the Romans in the early centuries who would not renounce Christ and worship the Roman gods. Because Satan is bound he fails to persuade them to do this. Records show how Christians even chose to die rather than yield. This happens in some countries today, but in others Christians are under pressure to adopt modern teachings and practices. Those who refuse to adopt them may lose their jobs. All the persecuted receive strength through their spiritual resurrection now, and look forward to their physical resurrection hereafter (4b). Others will not be raised in any sense until the physical resurrection at the last day (5). Only the regenerate will share the power of Christ here and hereafter.

Think about it: The devil will pay heavily for his misdeeds against Christ and us. Much can be seen in the names he is given:

1. *Adversary, enemy* – he was the author of the fall of man in Genesis 3; he opposed Jesus and tried to get him to kill himself by throwing himself off the temple wall in Matthew 4; he tried to prevent the apostles from evangelising Europe (1 Thess. 2:18).

2. *Deceiver, or liar (John 8:44)* – he lied to Eve about what God had said in Genesis 3:1,4; he uses disguises such as 'an angel of light' (2 Cor. 11:14); he falsifies the meaning of Scripture, even with Christ (Matt. 4:6).

3. *Destroyer* – he led an army against the remnant of Judah (Rev. 20:9).

Revelation 20:7-15   The devil cast out and the dead judged

At the time of Christ's return the devil is enjoying a short period of freedom. During the 'gospel age' (the one thousand years) he is unable to prevent the gospel being preached all over the world, so the world was evangelised and churches were planted in all nations as Jesus had commanded (Matt. 28:19-20). But shortly before Christ's return the devil was let loose, although we do not have the details of what this period was like. What we know is that he is brought to judgement and the judges are the Christian martyrs who are raised from the dead spiritually and share in Christ's spiritual reign, which is here called the first resurrection to distinguish it from the physical resurrection of all the dead referred to in v. 13. Because they had been faithful unto death they are given the blessing of sharing in Christ's priestly ministry, and, being promised eternal life (6), have been exempt from the second death because of their faithfulness to the gospel.

Verses 7-10: Temporary release of Satan. Satan is released from the binding that prevented him from deceiving the nations. Not knowing this was only temporary he takes the opportunity to gather his forces for a final onslaught on the saints (7). This reduces the church to a remnant (8; Luke 18:8). By the use of counterfeit miracles (16:14; 2 Thess. 2:9) he entices the church into one place (9) in order to destroy the camp of the saints, the city God loves. He refers to Ezekiel's prophecy when Gog (Antiochus) king of Magog (Syria) crushed Judah (Ezek. 38–39) after their return from Babylon (not described in the Old Testament). This was God's way of counter-attacking Satan's army who besieged the saints but were themselves surrounded, enabling God to send fire, destroying them all at once. This left Satan on his own, and God bound him again and cast him into the lake of fire with the beast and false prophet to be tormented forever (10).

Verses 11-15: The judgement of the dead. What happened to Satan now happens to his followers, that is, those who did not believe in God. The scene is set with a great white throne replacing the present universe (11). The dead of all kinds are raised, to hear their deeds, recorded in books (12) on the basis of which they will be judged. The book of life is also opened, but the dead are judged by their misdeeds recorded in the other book. There was no escape from this (13) – dying at sea, or dying before the general resurrection (14). Death itself died! For this was the second death, the first being the gift of eternal life in the work of regeneration. This is the final test determining who has a place in the eternal kingdom (15). The Christian martyrs are raised spiritually to share in this, as they shared in Christ's spiritual reign on earth in the gospel age. But what happens is that the beast, the false prophet and all their followers, and death and Hades themselves, are cast into the lake of fire. Thus the martyrs' sufferings at the hands of Christ's enemies are avenged, and they see them consigned to the second death.

Think about it: The end of the devil! Think of all he has been responsible for! That will never happen again!

Revelation 21:1-14   A vision of the new creation

The church's enemies are all gone and the way is open into the eternal kingdom. This is nothing less than an entirely new creation, for the angel uses the words of Genesis 1:1, that in the beginning God created a universe that is both spiritual ('heavens') and material ('earth'). The new creation will also be spiritual and material, though surpassing the present one, because it will be not only perfect but infallible. The first (fallible) one has passed away – past tense ('prophetic perfect'), for it is certain to happen. What is it like? John uses non-literal metaphors, but his opening words are literal – there will be an actual universe, described in picture language.

His first illustration is the city (2). This city is for sons of God to dwell in (7), so he brings in another illustration – marriage, for it will begin with the wedding. This is a frequent metaphor in Scripture (19:6-9 and elsewhere, especially Ephesians 5:22-32). God and his people live happily together as man and wife. It will be a happy relationship not ending in death, so there will be no mourning or crying or pain. This is because it is new (5), the old order has passed away (4). This was why Jesus spoke of the renewal of all things when he returns to enter his final kingdom (Matt. 19:28) and why Peter spoke of his return to restore all things (Acts 3:21). 'No longer any sea' (1) points to the prevention of the formation of dry land at the first creation

(Gen. 1:6). To describe this city further, the voice (3), clearly God's (6a) uses metaphors. This is God's own word. It is absolutely certain and is to be written down for future generations (5).

To describe the city (6-27) he uses metaphors, but these are still the words of the eternal God (1). It is a well-watered city (6b). It will be refreshing and spiritually satisfying for God's sons, but the wicked will be excluded by their second death (7-8). One of the seven angels who had the seven bowls takes up the story. He changes the metaphor to the bride of Christ, but immediately equates her with the city (9-10). Whatever the metaphor, it is the glory of God that is prominent. So another metaphor is called on – a jewel clear as crystal (11). Describing the glory of God is straining language beyond its limits!

It is a city with a great high wall (12). This embraces the inhabitants, keeping them safe and keeping them together. In heaven we shall have no divisions, unlike the present church!

The wall had twelve gates which, with the angels, give security at all times (12).

Think about it: Take a walk around the new Jerusalem every day, that is, call to mind the glories of heaven, as set out here!

'Walk about Zion, count her towers, consider well her ramparts' (Ps. 48:12-13).

Revelation 21:15 – 22:5   The vision of the heavenly glory

The theme of this passage is in 22:4 – 'They shall see his face', his essence. At present on earth we see him in his works, but in heaven we shall see him in his essential being. Our earthly language lacks suitable words to describe One who is pure Spirit. When Moses asked God to show him his glory (Exod. 33:18), God replied that he would show him his back parts but his face must not be seen. At the time Moses was leading wicked people from whom God hid his face, as he does for all who fall away. But in glory we shall be holy as he is holy. What shall we be like?

Verses 16-17. Perfect, like a square where nothing is out of place to spoil the look.

Verse 18. Strong, shown by the thickness of the walls, which are indestructible. But the angels speak more of their brightness: jasper is dazzling and gold glitters.

Verses 19-20. The foundations are unusual. They are not buried out of sight, but spectacularly visible, being twelve types of precious stone, the number corresponding to the original number of the tribes of Israel, before all their wars. This indicates that the whole description of the architecture is symbolic of spiritual things.

Verse 21. The twelve gates are also symbolic, but in their case one stone represents all twelve – a 'pearl'. In Matthew 13:45-46 some think the pearl represents Christ, others think it is the church, so precious to him that he died for it (Eph. 5:25).

Verses 22-27. The city would not be complete without its temple, which also must be symbolic – of God and the Lamb. There is no need for sunlight – God and the Lamb illuminate it (23), which enables kings and nations to bring in their splendour (24). This is why the gates are left open day and night, but nothing impure is admitted (27). It is only for the elect, whose names are written in the Lamb's book of life.

This city has two unique features (22:1-5):

Its government – 'the throne of God' (1, 3b-5). He alone rules without opposition. What we do not have here, but will have in glory, is a perfect form of government and a perfect ruler to exercise it. All give God his due – 'his servants shall serve him' (3). He has kept the promises made to John before the visions began (1:1) showing his servant 'what must take place'.

Living water (1-3a) – the river is supernatural, as predicted by Ezekiel in 47:1-12. It sustains and refreshes every part of our being. This is the gift of God through his sovereign grace (throne of God). It flows down the main street to make it available for all. Trees grow along the banks whose leaves are medicinal. This removes the curse on the tree of life (Gen. 3:22-24). The river symbolises the living water of eternal life, of which Jesus spoke to the Samaritan woman (John 4:9-15).

Think about it: Being in the flesh and in the world prevents us from having a perfect sight of God. If we contemplate this and other passages on the vision of God, we can enjoy the best of his presence to which we have access for now. Pray for it!

Revelation 22:6-21   The coming of Christ to fulfil all the promises

This book consists mainly of visions of angels and devils, with occasional glimpses of heaven, God and Christ. All through history there have been Christians claiming to have seen visions of some future event in their lives or the lives of others. Are we to take these seriously? What about those in Revelation? This final scenario deals with this matter and the whole question of the genuineness of these visions and their meaning for us. They concern supernatural matters which are easy to claim but less easy to prove. It is very important to do so. Is there an invisible God we can know, a heaven for the righteous? Do we have a soul by which we can know him and in which we can live in his heaven after we die? How can we be sure? When we invest our money in a policy about the future, we need some assurance that we can trust it. We need this assurance even more about life and death. This book closes by giving us grounds for assurance.

1. The guarantors. Who vouches for the truth of these prophecies? Who is making the promises. Are they reliable?

(a) *The angels of God.* Angels are God's special messengers commissioned by him to bring messages to his people, sometimes through a prophet. This whole book began with such a commissioning (1:1).

(b) *The apostle John.* Apostles were also special messengers and form the link between his angels and his people. They were the authors of letters to the churches and thus were well known to the early Christians. This book was one of these letters (1:1).

(c) *The Lord Jesus Christ (16,20).* He sometimes adds his own authority as the eternal One, which he does here (13,16). This confirms the words of angels, prophets and apostles.

(d) *God himself (18-19).* His is the highest authority of all, for he speaks of matters known only to him – of everlasting punishment or eternal bliss, not known to angels, prophets or apostles.

With these guarantors who can doubt the truth of these visions?

2. The guarantees. What do they cover? Everything.

(a) *The visions and prophecies of the book.* These describe the church's battle with the powers of evil, who are fighting to silence its witness to Christ. They predict the church's ultimate victory, the defeat of evil and renewal of all things. These are referred to in v. 8 as 'these things' and in v. 6 as 'the things that must soon take place', that is, what is not immediate. This is why John must not seal the book. Even today it is still not sealed and we still watch and wait.

(b) *The blessings of the righteous and the curses on the wicked who reject the promise of Christ.* Those who wash their robes are blessed with the right to go through the gates into the celestial city (14). The wicked who practise falsehood are cursed by being left outside (15).

(c) *The personal return of Christ to the earth (12,17,20).* This is the way he will fulfil his promises to defeat his enemies, raise the dead, perform the final judgement and renew all things. This is why he keeps repeating these words.

Revelation 22:6-21 (ctd) Proof of the truth of the words of the book

3. The guaranteed. For whom is the guarantee? Who benefits from the promises?

(a) *Those who are shown the visions (6)* because they are servants of Christ, and have heard or read them (1:3; 22:8).

(b) *Those who are moved to worship him (9),* as John did, because they feel unworthy, but blessed.

(c) *Those who keep them (7,9),* who believe them, keep them in their heart and put their hopes on them (4).

(d) *Those who longingly wait for him to come and implement them (17,20).* They even call on Christ to come and do so quickly (soon), as he has promised (17).

Go through these points and apply them to yourself. Do you tick all the boxes, not just some? Notice what vv. 18-19 say: do not add anything – some merely personal preference or any kind of works; do not take anything away from them because they do not appeal to you.

Hear the call of v. 17. The Holy Spirit through the church and its ministers invites you to come, just as you called on Christ to come. They call you to come and take the free gift of the water of life – salvation from the judgements and for the promise of life in heaven. Never forget: Revelation shows there are many judgements before the final one. These are warnings – opportunities to avoid the last one.

Review the book and reflect upon what you have read. The final judgement is mentioned at the end of each section, after which John returns to the beginning, and each time gets nearer the final end. In this way there is progress through the book, as in church history.

Readings on

The Messiah

by Ray Tibbs

WINDOW
ON THE
WORD

Messiah [1] Isaiah 40:1-2 The consolation and the harbinger

In 1784 the first performance of Handel's *Messiah* in a church building took place at Westminster Abbey to commemorate the composer. In that year John Newton began a series of fifty sermons drawn from the passages of Scripture on which that oratorio was based. 'The music of the 'Messiah' is but an ornament of the words, which have a very weighty sense' (Newton). These Notes will follow the same outline on Sundays. They will not follow the structure of the sermons (Vol. 4 of *The Works of John Newton* published by the Banner of Truth), but will often use the same title and occasional quotations.

God has not abandoned his people (1-2).

(a) *He speaks to them.* Despite generations of rebellion, God continued to address his people. There were times of silence so that his voice would be more earnestly sought and more clearly heard. He brought them reassurance of their continuing relationship with him and his general intention towards them before delivering the details of his message.

(b) *He pardons them.* Elsewhere in the prophecy the prospect of justifiable punishment is spoken about, but the theme of restoration is also found, once that punishment had been completed. One day their hardship would be over and their sin would be pardoned because justice would have been satisfied. God is not unjust. Although the punishment would be great, the restoration would be greater still.

God will confront his people (3-5).

(a) *By personal visitation.* God sent a message which told of his own imminent arrival. God himself would come to his people in the most unlikely of places. Preparation must be made to smooth the way for his visit. This is presented in terms of the necessary road repairs being made in anticipation of the arrival of a monarch. Bumps are flattened, pot holes are filled in and curves are straightened, but it would happen in the lives of men.

(b) *By personal revelation.* It would not be a private visit, reserved for a privileged few. It would be a public spectacle for all to see. He would be seen in all his pomp and splendour.

(c) *By personal declaration.* There was no doubt that it would happen because God had said so himself. The fact that it may be a long time coming did not in any way reduce the certainty of his arrival.

God calls upon his people.

(a) *To be comforted.* Throughout the forthcoming punishment, the people must be comforted by the expectation of even greater blessing to follow. They should not allow themselves to become dispirited but be constantly refreshed by the hope before them.

(b) *To be prepared.* God would not come until the time of preparation was complete. The call was for the people to prepare themselves and take positive action in straightening out their lives. The ministry of John the Baptist was a call to repent before the Lord appeared.

(c) *To be attentive.* If God was speaking, his people must listen to him. The voice of God is heard today. If God was coming, his people must watch for him. The glory of God is revealed today. We cannot ignore the God who has presented himself to us in such a remarkable way. Although punishment was justified, God promised to come personally and freely give even greater blessings. The pardon of God is available today.

Messiah [2]   Haggai 2:6-7; Malachi 3:1-2
The shaking of the heavens and the earth

'The "Messiah" of Handel consists of three parts. The first contains prophecies of his advent and the happy consequences, together with the angel's message to the shepherds, informing them of his birth, as related by Luke' (Newton).

An earth-shaking event.

(a) *A great disturbance.* The physical elements had been disturbed before, most notably at the flood, and at the coming of the Messiah they would be disturbed again. This was the case to a limited extent when he first came but since that cannot be separated from his Second Coming, this prophecy will have an even greater fulfilment then (2 Peter 3:7,10). The coming of the Messiah has cataclysmic implications far beyond the boundaries of the nation within which he first appeared.

(b) *A great desire.* The common desires among people of all nations are for personal satisfaction and fulfilment. It was not the Jewish Messiah that all men desired, for most would know nothing of him. But in one person alone could all the desires of all nations be finally and fully met, even though those desires might not be articulated coherently.

(c) *A great display.* Haggai was prophesying at the rebuilding of the temple in Jerusalem after the return from exile. It was rebuilt hundreds of years later by Herod. The Messiah would arrive there and his coming would render that spot glorious in a spiritual rather than a physical sense. Its very existence spoke of his coming and once his work had been completed, it was no longer required.

Although physically destroyed, the glory has not departed from its spiritual counterpart, the people of God (1 Cor. 3;16; 6:19).

A life-changing event. 'When the Lord God, who knows the human heart, would speak comfort to it, he proposes one object, and only one, as the necessary and all sufficient source of consolation. This is *Messiah*. Jesus, in his person and offices, known and received by faith, affords a balm for every wound, a cordial for every care' (Newton).

(a) *A certain coming.* The context of Malachi's prophecy is the people's doubt about the character of God (2:17). His reply speaks of his personal arrival and in that would come the revelation of his justice (3:5). They have long desired him because he has promised himself to them in the past but here he spoke of his imminent appearance. Although sudden, it would be anticipated by another figure who would be his immediate precursor. His appearance was certain because it was guaranteed by the promise of God, the character of God and the messenger of God.

(b) *A searching coming.* The existing covenant with his people would take on a new form with his arrival. Although his coming was wonderful, it would bring judgement and particularly to those who were chosen as his servants. He would come as a fire, but with the object of cleansing, not destroying. The Levites were singled out as specially called to the service of God and represented the elect. They would be purified so that their service would be rendered acceptable to him.

'Is *Messiah*, the desire of all nations, the object of your chief desire?' (Newton).

Messiah [3]   Isaiah 7:14; Matthew 1:23   Immanuel

Newton says, 'This passage expressly and exclusively refers to *Messiah*' and declares the authority of the evangelist Matthew as his warrant who 'directly applies it to him and assures us that it was accomplished in him.' On this occasion we will follow Newton's lead and not give any attention to the historical context.

How is God with us?

(a) *At a distance (Gen. 28:15)*. Consider this limited analogy. A child is taken to the playground by its parents. It could not happen without them. That is providence. The child is given instructions what to do while in the playground. Those are precepts. The parents watch but also intervene directly. That is a personal appearance.

(b) *Nearby (John 1:14)*. After Eden, there were occasions when God entered the world temporarily for a specific purpose (for example Josh. 5:13-15). But the time came when God came into our world to share our life, taking on human nature, yet without sin.

(c) *Within (John 14:18; Rom. 8:9)*. Although back in heaven, Jesus promised to stay with his people (Matt. 28:20). He does so through the indwelling Holy Spirit.

Why is God with us?

(a) *To carry out his plan*. Nobody asked God to come because no one considered it possible or necessary. Yet God has declared the reality of it and promised a greater manifestation of it (Isa. 7:14).

(b) *To save us from sin*. God and man were close in Eden (Gen. 3:8), until sin separated them. Reunion could only happen through the removal of sin. The punishment for sin had to be administered. The pollution of sin had to be removed. The power of sin had to be broken. The voluntary sacrifice of a sinless Saviour achieved it all.

(c) *To bring us to himself*. Removing the cause of separation was only part of what was required. Once that barrier had been removed, the reconciliation would be completed by the application of the righteousness found only in a man who was totally obedient to the whole law of God. The absence of a human father meant that a sinful nature was not passed on to Jesus. His perfect obedience, rendering him acceptable to God, is made over to all who put their trust in him.

When is God with us?

(a) *Before we trust Christ*. Because we are separated from him by sin, he will always be at a distance from us. But as his human creatures, we still receive the common grace he gives to all in his providential care. If we are numbered among the elect, then he is active in our awakening before we come to Christ.

(b) *When we trust Christ*. Reconciliation to God can only take place through Christ. Because he came to us in our world and died for us, then he brings us into fellowship with God forever (John 17:21-24).

(c) *After we trusted Christ*. His presence remains with us through this world and is perfected in the next (John 14:2). Because the greatest barriers to communion with him have been overcome, nothing shall separate us from him (Rom. 8:35-39).

Messiah [4]   Isaiah 40:9; 60:1
Salvation published from the mountains

Through his prophets, God has declared the remarkable truth that he shall come into the world as a man. Now that the people of God have received this stupendous message, these verses recount what they must do with it.

Responsibility is given. God's people are addressed as those who are actually involved in his coming. God does not just come to them, he comes through them – to others. Zion is charged with the task of telling others of Immanuel. Those who are close to him (Jerusalem) must tell those who are further away (the cities of Judah). The people of God are to tell each other, 'Here is your God.' Such was their ignorance, they may not realise who they are. Not only do they not know God, but they do not know themselves – in relation to him. It is only the people of God who can respond positively and receive the message.

Effort is required. This is a collective responsibility. Strenuous effort is required, for it will not be an easy task. The people of God must secure a vantage point from which their news will carry well. They must labour to find a place where they can be heard. Once such a place has been found, then they must make good use of it. There is no point in whispering. Shouting is needed. The news itself and the condition of the hearers both demand it. The speakers are not responsible for the reception of the message, only the declaration of it, so fear should not come into it.

News is delivered. The message, when faithfully given, directs the hearer away from the speaker. The subject is clear – God. They hear of his nearness. *Your* God has come to you. He is not distant, but present. They hear of his nature. He is glorious. That glory shines on you. In his greatness, he brings mercy, comfort and pardon. Those who receive his light will begin to shine themselves and convey his light to others. This theme of light will be continued in the next portion. He brings what we need, right where we are. God has become accessible so that we may become acceptable. That is the message with which we are entrusted – God, with us!

'*Messiah* establishes a new, a spiritual kingdom upon the earth, and his happy subjects are freed from the misery in which they were involved' (Newton).

'If you heard the *Messiah*, you were, perhaps, affected by the music of the passage; how much are you to be pitied, if you are hitherto unaffected by the sentiment!' (Newton).

Messiah [5]   Isaiah 60:1-3; 9:2   The sun rising upon a dark world

'As the sun is the source of light to the natural world, so is *Messiah* to the moral and spiritual world' (Newton).

Those upon whom the light of God's glory has shone must do more than tell others what has happened. They must 'walk in the light' (1 John 1:6-7).

People in darkness. Referring to the future, the first passage describes a situation of increased darkness. The darkness is both extensive, covering the earth, and intensive – it is thick or gross. Darkness may limit sight but not necessarily movement. Never having known anything else, it is possible to live without light. However, the second passage (9:2) adds another dimension to this darkness. It is 'the shadow of death'. It is a poison which needs dispersing if people are to survive. The people of God are being addressed and the implication is that they too were subjected to the same darkness. The second appeal (60:2) is to take a close look at this whole situation.

The light of God. The light has come gradually. The image is of the rising sun, which speaks of preparation and anticipation, rather than of a sudden appearance. However, it is evident that the light shines on the people of God, rather than on the whole world encompassed by the darkness. The light belonged to them. It was their light. The purpose of it, in part, was to illuminate them. Others would observe that they had

been highlighted. The light was defined as being the glory of God and indeed as the Lord himself. Thus, observers would not only see an enlightened people but God himself, because of those people. They will reveal the glory of the Lord.

Gentiles attracted. The opening appeal to the people of God in the first passage is to utilise the light. They are to be active as it shines. They must leave behind their slothful condition and take up their role as those for whom and through whom the light shines. The darkened world would not see it unless it was made manifest through them. Only when they displayed the light they had received would others – currently in darkness – seek it out. They would see for the first time what it was like to live in the light. It would appeal to them and they would approach the light for themselves, wanting to leave behind the darkness. Living in the light would have widespread appeal (Gentiles and kings), not just to those who were similar to the people of God. The sun of the glory of God would rise on the people in darkness only when it shone through the people of God. The New Testament equivalent of this truth is found in Matthew 5:14-16.

'The subjects of *Messiah*'s kingdom, the living members of his church, are so irradiated by him, that they shine likewise; as the moon shines, but with a borrowed light derived from the sun' (Newton) (2 Cor. 3:18; Eph. 5:8-14).

Messiah [6]   Isaiah 9:6   Character and names of Messiah

'Such was the triumphant exultation of the Old Testament church! Their noblest hopes were founded upon the promise of *Messiah*; their sublimest songs were derived from the prospect of his advent' (Newton).

The provision of the child.

(a) *A great change.* The first word of the passage links it with the previous verses (2-5). Darkness has become light, sorrow has become joy and defeat has become victory. The change comes through one who both possesses and exercises the power and authority of government as his right.

(b) *A great contrast.* The one who carries this government is not a king or a general but a child. The one who will achieve such super-human change will enter his destiny in the most natural way. He will be born like any other. The woeful condition of the people has been observed by God and he chooses to act. Although already in his debt, God chooses to give again rather than extract payment or impose punishment. Rather than send a servant to accomplish what was required, he sends a Son.

The character of the child.

(a) *He brings wisdom.* The first pair of words which describe him are separated and denote something exceptional – 'a wonder of a Counsellor'. None shall advise him for he has no equal. In him 'are hidden all the treasures of wisdom and knowledge' (Col. 2:3). The only way this can be is if he knows the mind of God (Isa. 11:2; John 14:24; 16:15).

That wisdom is made available to his people (John 14:26; James 1:5-7).

(b) *He brings strength.* Not only is his knowledge complete, but his power is invincible. The first term refers to a hero – a hero of a God. One who is awesome and to be worshipped and yet at the same time is not distant but has human heroic qualities – a God with us. That strength is made available to his people (Eph. 6:10; Phil. 4:13).

(c) *He brings love.* The quality of relationship is highlighted here, rather than the qualities of character. He is distinguished by a love for his own which preserves and protects them, provides for and nurtures them without hesitation, indefinitely. He gave life and will sustain that life. His people receive and know that love (1 John 3:1).

(d) *He brings peace.* The natural consequence of being in the security of a stable and lasting relationship with God is peace. He has secured peace with God. He brings peace within and among those who are his. He rules them peacefully and his peace belongs to his people (John 16:33; Phil. 4:6-7; Col. 3:15).

'When a sinner is enlightened by the Holy Spirit to understand the character and offices of *Messiah*, his ability and willingness to save those who are ready to perish, and the happiness of all who are brought into subjection to his gracious government; and when he begins to feel the cheering effects of faith in his name, then this song becomes his own and exactly suits the emotions and gratitude of his heart' (Newton).

Messiah [7]   Zechariah 9:9-10   Messiah's entrance into Jerusalem

In the oratorio, the next passage is the announcement of *Messiah*'s birth to the shepherds. We shall be considering that narrative later in these Notes and will simply quote the beginning of Newton's sermon on that portion: 'The gratification of the *great*, the *wealthy*, and the *gay*, was chiefly consulted in the late exhibition in Westminster Abbey. But, notwithstanding the expense of the preparations, and the splendid appearance of the auditory, I may take it for granted, that the shepherds who were honoured with the first information of the birth of *Messiah*, enjoyed, at free cost, a much more sublime and delightful entertainment.'

The subsequent life and ministry of *Messiah* is dealt with only briefly in four scripture passages chosen for the oratorio before our attention is concentrated on his death and resurrection. The first is the prophecy quoted in Matthew 21:5 and John 12:15 which applied to his final entry into Jerusalem. The prophet anticipated two responses to *Messiah*'s arrival.

Rejoice. A future generation of God's people is given this exhortation. Although modest in appearance, the event was so significant as to warrant *great* rejoicing and *shouting* rather than just saying. Why? God has kept his word in sending the Saviour. The fundamental problem in mankind is solved. Their darkness is past, their warfare ended and their pardon is provided. There may be little that brings us great joy in this world and what there is, soon passes. Here is something real, lasting and all embracing. 'Sinners, who, by the knowledge of *Messiah*, are delivered from going down into the pit, from the dominion of the powers of darkness, and are translated into the kingdom of God,

experience a joy far superior, in kind and degree, to any satisfaction temporal blessings can afford' (Newton).

Behold. This term means 'look carefully' or 'fix your gaze upon'. The first thing to notice is that this king is theirs. He has come for them and is one of them, raised up from among them and not a foreigner imposed upon them. That gives an immediate rapport and a sense of identity with them. His character is:

(a) *Righteous* – just, upright, fair and true. This is the factor which relates to the salvation he brings for the unrighteous (1 Peter 3:18).

(b) *Lowly* – gentle and humble, not bombastic and dictatorial. The manner of his approach indicates that. As a king he comes to rule.

In the wider context of the prophecy, God brings judgement upon the enemies of the people of God which surround them. The picture here is of God preserving this little enclave of the own people in the midst of surrounding devastation (8). So he sets a ruler over them to preserve them and maintain their identity as his people. If he were not a righteous king who could bring salvation, they would become just like those around them. The salvation he brought and the rule which arose out of it guaranteed they would not suffer the same fate as their enemies because they had become indistinguishable from them.

'If he be indeed your King, your consciences will bear you witness that you revere, imitate, and obey him. If he be your Saviour, you certainly must be sensible yourself, and others must observe, that you are different from what you once were' (Newton).

Messiah [8] Isaiah 35:5-6 Effects of Messiah's appearance

'The verses ... exhibit the effects of *Messiah*'s power and goodness ... the inhabitants of the wilderness partake of the virtue of the great Redeemer. He finds them in circumstances of great distress, which he only can relieve' (Newton).

During the earthly life of *Messiah*, the changes described in these verses occurred literally in many lives but they were symbolic of the deeper, spiritual changes which continue to take place. 'When we are made partakers of the life of God in the soul, by a new and heavenly birth, then our spiritual senses are brought into exercise ... Here are four chief effects of a work of grace upon the heart which distinguish believers from the rest of mankind' (Newton).

1. Seeing. Although previously unable to appreciate God as a living being, believers now enjoy real communion with him. They know him by experience. They see his work in the world around them and in their own lives. They are enlightened by the Word of God and approve the way of salvation it presents to them. They see their sin and understand themselves in relation to him for they grasp what *Messiah* has accomplished for them. They willingly accept their obligations as his servants and citizens.

2. Hearing. Once deaf to the voice to the voice of God, believers now receive communication directly from him. They are both attentive and submissive to his commands. The renewed faculties are linked. Clear-sightedness produces careful listening. Once the greatness and goodness of God has been perceived, then the awakened soul is willing to hear and obey his instructions.

3. Moving. Former incapacity is removed and replaced by a new vigour. Where there was weakness there is now strength and indeed an ability to perform unexpected activity. The lame are pictured as leaping, not just walking. God has worked in them not only to will but to do his good pleasure (Phil. 2:13). They have pleasure in duty and victory in warfare. There is a fresh zeal and commitment to the things of God and a desire to run with patience and perseverance the race set before them.

4. Shouting/singing. There is reference to abundant utterance here as there was to abundant movement earlier. Believers will not just speak but shout or sing. There is an exuberant gratitude at their release. There is an expansive enjoyment of their new-found liberty. There is a bold declaration of such glorious truth. There is an earnest invitation to come to Christ. 'When grace teaches the heart, then the heart teaches the mouth' (Newton).

It can be seen that the *Messiah*'s power and goodness brings about; a great change – radical not superficial, a good change – for our improvement, not our harm, and a gracious change – brought about by the mercy of God not our merit.

'May we come simply to the light, with a desire of seeing more of ourselves, and more of our Saviour; that we may be more humble and spiritual, more afraid of sin, more watchful and successful in striving against it; and in our whole conversation, more conformable to our glorious Head' (Newton).

Messiah [9] Isaiah 40:11 The great shepherd

'This character (the shepherd of his people) *Messiah*, the Saviour, condescends to bear; and happy are they who, with a pleasing consciousness, can say, 'We are his people, and the sheep of his pasture' (Ps. 100:3). He humbled himself for their sakes, submitted to partake of their nature and their sorrows, took upon him the form of a servant, and was made in the likeness of sinful flesh. If this Shepherd be our Shepherd, weak and helpless as we are, we may be of good courage' (Newton).

He will feed us. The term refers to general care. Although food and water will be supplied, he will make overall provision and neglect nothing. He will keep the sheep alive and healthy. Not only does Jesus make this provision, he is that provision in himself (John 6:51; 4:13-14). His people depend upon him for their spiritual nourishment, the preservation of their soul. It is by his word and ordinances that he communicates his own fullness to them.

He will gather us. He will draw his people to himself and keep them close to him. There, they will find protection from the hostile forces which surround them. There is not only a vulnerability to attack, there is also a tendency to wander. They are always in need of his help and he is always able to give it. He has a watchful eye, a powerful arm and a caring heart. The only place of safety for such defenceless creatures is in his presence.

He will carry us. A shepherd would carry the larger, more mature animals on his shoulders when necessary. But the small and weak animals he would carry in his arms, close to his heart. This would give them reassurance of his love and they would find the rest and security they needed. The shepherd especially gives individual attention to those little ones who are tired and find it difficult to keep up with the others.

He will lead us. The shepherd does not drive his sheep ahead of him, but goes before them. That means the sheep must always look to him to find out where they are going. The people of God need his guidance for every part of their future life and they can confidently look to him for all they need. Even though the pathway may not be straight or smooth, we must entrust ourselves to his care for everything which lies ahead of us.

Singled out for special mention here are those that have young. Newton identifies parents and pastors as two types of people who come into this category and 'feel an especial need of his compassion, tenderness and patience'. 'This is our great consolation, that he who knows us, and leads us, considers "our frame and remembers that we are but dust".'

'Such is our great Shepherd; and he is eminently the Good Shepherd also, for he laid down his life for the sheep, and has redeemed them unto God by his own blood' (Newton).

Messiah [10]   Matthew 11:28-30
Rest for the weary and Messiah's easy yoke

'The evangelist proposes him to our meditation here, in a gracious and inviting attitude, proclaiming his own sovereign authority and power, and declaring his compassionate purpose and readiness to give refreshment and rest to the weary and heavy laden' (Newton).

The time reference in v.25 is general. Luke quotes the words which precede our passage in 10:21-22. That passage therefore provides the immediate context of these words. It was when Jesus was 'full of joy through the Holy Spirit'. We shall follow the same sequence in v.28 as in vv.29-30.

The invitation. 'Come to me.' In order to respond, we must know something of the one who makes the invitation and he has already told us (27). Coming to him is the same as coming to God. That means deliberately taking steps towards him which involve leaving something else behind. The invitation presupposes a readiness to receive and so coming involves trusting (John 6:37).

The qualification. The 'weary and burdened' are those to whom the invitation is issued. If you do not recognise yourself as being in that condition, you will not hear the invitation. If you are burdened by the demands of life and religion is only wearing you down, not lifting you up, the invitation is for you. If you are exhausted by trying to fulfil the law of God, knowing you are failing, then here is relief. Self-trust has only exposed your personal inadequacy and shown you the need to look elsewhere for help.

The promise. Refreshment and renewal are promised. But although there is relief, there is no removal of the burden. The gift of rest comes from Christ. He knows our need and is able to meet it, because he possesses all things (27). Only by coming to him can we be released from the weariness of fruitless labour and be invigorated for the tasks ahead.

The invitation [2]. There is no pause, so this section develops the earlier one. 'Take my yoke.' A yoke is a means of carrying a burden. So, in order to carry a weight, you must add more weight first. It is effective because the yoke distributes the weight. A yoke is carefully designed to fit the wearer. It has come from Christ and we can be sure it will be suitable for us. 'Learn from me.' Christ provides both instruction and example on how to carry his yoke.

The qualification [2]. Because he is 'gentle and lowly', the Lord expects his followers to be like him. He came to this world and identified himself with us, while knowing the secrets of eternity. He took upon himself obedience and service and asks us to identify ourselves with him by doing the same. In becoming accessible to us, he exercised great humility and voluntarily became a dependent being, as we are. He is too sympathetic to give us something that would be too heavy to bear.

The promise [2]. Rest for the body is fleeting but rest for the soul is real. Our struggle against inner corruption is reduced when we trust his power to overcome. As we go on through life, we can increasingly trust his providence to guide and sustain us. We can trust his word that one day we shall enjoy our expected reward in glory.

Messiah [11]   John 1:29   The Lamb of God, the great atonement

Today's Bible passage begins the second part of Handel's oratorio. 'The second part describes his passion, death, resurrection and ascension; his taking possession of his kingdom of glory, the commencement of his kingdom of grace upon earth, and the certain disappointment and ruin of all who persist in opposition to his will' (Newton).

This declaration by John the Baptist seems to have been made after the baptism of Jesus (32-34). He is the only one to use this phrase but the general concept was already known. We shall look at three characteristics of the Lamb.

He is sacrificed. That is the key factor in this reference. Lambs had been used in this way from the earliest times (Gen. 4:4; 22:7-8). Later, a lamb was used at Passover (Exod. 12:21), in the daily sacrifice (Exod. 29:38) and in the guilt offering for a leper (Lev. 14:24). The lamb's life was lost so that others might benefit from its death. 'The early institution and long continued use of sacrifices, had clearly pointed out the necessity of an atonement; but the real and proper atonement could be made only by *Messiah*. The blood of slaughtered animals could not take away sin, nor display the righteousness of God in pardoning it. This was the appointed, covenanted work of *Messiah*, and he alone could perform it' (Newton).

He is sent. Not every lamb was suitable for sacrifice. It had to be a certain age and without blemish. An appropriate lamb needed to be selected. Jesus was the Lamb of God's choice. He met all the requirements. He was a man, yet sinless (1 Peter 1:19-20). We cannot choose our own Saviour, but must accept God's choice.

He is sufficient. The sacrifices were appointed for specific purposes and so the beneficiaries were clearly identified. The astounding part of this declaration is that the death of Jesus would be the sacrifice for the whole world, rather than just for the Jewish people. Only one with an infinite reservoir of righteousness could deal with a mass of human sin stretching from the beginning to the end of time.

He is seen. John called people to fix their gaze upon him. They were to take a close look, not give a cursory glance. The sacrifice was not hidden. It was publicly displayed, infallibly recorded and faithfully preached. Now we can look in wonder that God should love the world so much that he would send his Son to die for it. We can look with faith, believing that his death secures our salvation. We can look with gratitude that God should treat us with such grace and mercy.

For 'the believing pardoned sinner, the blood which frees him from distress, preserves a remembrance of the great danger and misery from which he has been delivered warm upon his heart, inspires him with gratitude to his Deliverer, and furnishes him with an abiding and constraining motive for cheerful and universal obedience' (Newton).

Messiah [12] Isaiah 53:3 Messiah despised and rejected of men

Despite his uniquely exalted status and the generations of preparation for his arrival, God's Messiah did not receive the welcome that was his due. Early in his Gospel, John identifies this as a key characteristic of his coming. He was not even recognised by the majority of people around him (John 1:10). Because of that, he was not received among them (1:11). Worse, he was not just ignored or sidelined, but actively rejected and, worse still, that rejection was total – ending in death. His whole life was marked by this attitude, a man with sorrows of his own.

He was ordinary. The previous verse in Isaiah says there was nothing distinctive about him. His appearance was not distinguished enough for him to be noticeably attractive.

He was overlooked. He was considered to be of no value and people turned away. 'When all that the human eye saw and all that the human mind apprehended was added up, the result was zero' (Motyer).

He was ostracised. Any popularity was merely transient. He was spurned by his family and his neighbours (Luke 4:29; John 7:5).

He was publicly scorned (Luke 16:14; John 10:20). 'For the seeming inconsistence between the appearance he made and the honours he assumed, they treated him as a demoniac and a madman' (Newton).

His closest friends deserted, betrayed and denied him (Mark 14:44,50,72).

He was opposed. 'They objected to the low state and former character of his followers' (John 7:48). 'They were further exasperated against him by the 'authority' and severity with which he taught' (Newton).

He was condemned by the very people he came to help (Mark 15:13,29-30).

He was unjustly accused, endured a mockery of a trial and was tortured before he died.

'The prejudices which operated so strongly against our Lord's mission and ministry were not peculiar to the people of one age or country, but such as are deeply rooted in the nature of fallen man. The same principles which influenced the Jews to oppose and despise his person still influence multitudes to slight and oppose the doctrine which he taught and which he commanded his disciples to preach and perpetuate to the end of the world' (Newton).

Newton goes on to make a telling point about the equivalence between how the Lord was treated and the way in which the gospel and its proponents have been treated subsequently. 'I have reserved to a distinct paragraph the mention of one cause why the gospel is frequently despised and reproached … I mean the scandal which arises from the miscarriages of those who profess it … It will be vain for ministers to declare that the doctrines of grace are doctrines according to godliness, unless our testimony is supported by the tempers and conduct of our people: the world will probably judge rather by what they see in you, than what they hear from us … What must the world think of our principles if they who avow them are fretful, envious, censorious, discontented, slothful or unfaithful?'

Messiah [13]   Isaiah 50:6   Voluntary suffering

This striking language describes one who is fully in control of the situation. It is not simply that men beat him, but that he put himself in the way of being beaten. The observer would not discern this truth. He would simply see someone at the mercy of those who appeared to have power greater than the victim. In fact the sufferer had the greater power and had used it to put himself at their disposal. How could one so great let himself be brought so low? This was not the surrender of power but the carefully controlled use of it. Such a radical use of power must involve a radical purpose. Such a selfless use of power must be for the good of someone very precious in the eyes of the sufferer.

'Two designs of vast importance filled his mind. These were the glory of God and the salvation of men ... For their sakes, that they might be happy, and that he might be admired in them and by them, to the glory of God, who is all in all, he voluntarily submitted himself to sufferings and death.' 'The sufferings of *Messiah* were essentially necessary to the accomplishment of his great designs, precisely determined, and present to his view beforehand; so that there was not a single circumstance that happened to him unawares. He knew that no blood but his own could make atonement for sin; that nothing less than his humiliation could expiate our pride; that if he did not *thus* suffer, sinners must inevitably perish' (Newton).

The language also suggests that this was not done in secret. 'The *strikers* or *smiters* would be those who have the public duty of beating a criminal. Beating on the back would seem to be the custom in the punishment of evil men (see Proverbs 10:13; 19:29; 26:3 and compare Psalm 129:3)' (Young). The beard was regarded as a sign of freedom and respect and so that part of the reference points to utter contempt shown through the most degrading of insults.

The victim does not recoil from or retaliate against such abuse. The implication is that he seemed to turn himself into this storm by way of welcome. His dignity and self-possession in the face of such spiteful treatment help the observer to catch a glimpse of what is really happening: it is not the sufferer who is degraded; nor is it the persecutor who is triumphant.

'It would be impossible for any sinful human being, no matter how fine a person he was, to undergo the sufferings described without a spirit of rebellion welling up within him ... Even Jeremiah complained at the way he was being used (see Jeremiah 20:9,14-18, and note Job 3). The only one who can so patiently suffer is the one who is without sin, the Christ of God' (Young).

Hebrews 12:3 invites us to 'consider him' – a mathematical term denoting the proportion between different numbers. Our Lord bore the insults of his inferiors – including ourselves, for their good. In his name, we must bear the insults of our equals that he may be glorified and we rejoice in such treatment (Matt. 5:11-12).

Messiah [14] Isaiah 53:4-5 Messiah, suffering and wounded for us

We have seen in our recent considerations of *Messiah* how, instead of being warmly welcomed, he was despised and rejected by men. We have seen how such treatment was both expected and embraced by him. Those sufferings were increased through their persistence and growing intensity and deepened by their application to one who was entirely righteous. Such evil treatment fell upon one who totally abhorred every form of evil. For One who was too pure even to look upon evil, to be the victim of some of its worst excesses must have been excruciating in the extreme.

Having looked briefly at the 'how' of these events, we now look at why they took place. 'Unless the mind be deeply penetrated with the *causes* which rendered *Messiah*'s death necessary, the most pathetic description of the *fact* will leave the will and affections unchanged' (Newton). He knew he must endure suffering *from* men because that suffering was *for* men.

The earlier verses give an assessment of the situation from a human perspective. Our passage begins (4a) with a term that suggests such appearances are deceptive. 'Surely', means 'Rather ... the truth is really this.' 'Infirmities' speak of weaknesses, the failure to achieve, our humanity. *Messiah* performed two actions in relation to this: he took up and carried – which means that he stooped down and picked up. This involved both choice and retention. He did it for us because we could not do it ourselves. The second part of the verse returns to a human assessment of these events.

The beginning of the next verse shows how mistaken that assessment is – 'but: here is the truth.' The explanation moves on and the language becomes more vivid. He did more than stand *with* us, for physical pain is specified. 'Transgressions' refers to wilful rebellion and 'iniquities' to the perversions of human nature. It is plain that he suffered extensively, not due to his own faults, but because of what others had done. He stood *instead of* us.

He did this so others would benefit from his action. The result was not simply that others would enjoy the absence of pain or death. The pain he bore was a punishment and its infliction judicial. Those for whom it was intended were free and guiltless. The law had been satisfied. Hostility had ceased and harmony restored between two warring parties. The paradox is clarified in the last phrase of v. 5. Personal renewal was secured by the damage inflicted upon another.

The underlying cause of this amazing occurrence is spelt out at the end of v. 6 and repeated at the beginning of v. 10. It was all the work of God. Such a transaction could never be of human origin and it certainly was not Satanic. Sin and its punishment are not transferable, but God made a single, all embracing exception and deliberately required the penalty for the flagrant disobedience of many from a single, willing substitute who had been perfectly obedient. Justice was satisfied and mercy demonstrated at a stroke.

'Though the death of *Messiah* is an event long since passed, yet the effects and benefits are ever new and to the eye of faith are ever present ... You who live by this medicine, speak well of it. Tell to others, as you have opportunity, what a Saviour you have found' (Newton).

Messiah [15]   Isaiah 53:6   Sin charged upon a surety

Today's verse was introduced in our reading last week but Newton's sermon concentrates on other elements and we shall summarise his points. The passage 'expresses the sentiment of those who are acquainted with the misery of our fallen state, feel their own concern in it and approve of the method which God has provided for their deliverance and recovery' (Newton).

1. It contains an expression of a guilt, common to all but variously expressed. None is free from the influence of sin and all shall suffer the same fate because of it, if it is left unchecked. *(i)* 'It is sufficient proof of our depravity that we prefer our own way to the Lord's.' We were not created that way. Designed to be dependent upon God, when we show our independence of him our life is inevitably empty and doomed. *(ii)* 'There is only one right way, but a thousand ways of being wrong.' Some false ways appear to be very close to the true way, but the true way is narrow and unique – 'I am the way,' said *Messiah*. However obvious and attractive the right way is, our natural inclination is to choose something else. Not only is the right way provided by God but also the wherewithal to follow it. *(iii)* If we are outside the fold of the good shepherd, we are liable to innumerable dangers which we can neither foresee nor prevent. Our sin blinds us to our peril and persuades us we are safe.

2. It contains an acknowledgement of mercy. Man sinned and *Messiah* suffered. 'It is a divine appointment and therefore is and must be right. It was a great design, a triumph of divine wisdom, the highest effect of the love of God. It is revealed, not to be submitted to our discussion or that we may sit in judgement upon the propriety of the measure, but it

demands our highest admiration and praise' (Newton). *(i)* 'He was thus appointed and constituted before the world began, according to the holy counsel and covenant settled from everlasting for the redemption of sinners.' The Fall did not abrogate it but anticipated it. *(ii)* 'After man had sinned, this glorious Head and Surety made known the certainty and benefit of his mediation and engagement on behalf of sinners.' The whole of Old Testament history is orientated around the eventual appearance of *Messiah*. Every part of the national life of God's people pointed to his coming. *(iii)* In the fullness of time, he veiled his glory and took upon him the form of a servant. 'The union between him and the people he came to save was completed. By virtue of this union, he is their life and they receive of his fullness.'

Newton invites us to learn three things from the substitution of *Messiah* for sinners:

1. 'How to estimate the evil of sin. That sin is a great evil is evident by its effects. After depriving Adam of the life and presence of God, it brought death and all natural evil into the world.' But amidst its many other consequences, 'in no view does the sinfulness of sin appear so striking as in the suffering and death of *Messiah*'.

2. 'The complete justification of those who believe in him. They are delivered from every condemnation … and though they are still in a state of discipline … (it is) designed to promote the work of grace in their hearts.'

3. 'The reason why believers are not wearied nor overpowered by all the difficulties of their service nor by all the arts and efforts of their enemies. They are one with Christ. He who has all power in heaven and on earth is engaged for their support.'

Messiah [16]   Psalm 22:7-8   Messiah derided upon the cross

Although not quoted in the oratorio, v. 6 is part of the same segment and our verses elaborate and explain it. That verse shows the sufferer feels he has reached the lowest point of his humiliation. The one who was infinitely exalted above man was subjected to such base treatment that he felt less than human. As if the shame of condemnation and execution were not enough, his suffering was aggravated by the scornful treatment of others when he might have expected a measure of sympathy in his dying moments.

Who derided *Messiah* in this way? *(i) The chief priests, teachers of the law and the elders.* Some of these very words were on their lips (Matt. 27:43). The religious leaders of the people were his most vociferous and persistent critics. They had rejected his claims, refused to believe both the evidence before their eyes and the testimony of Scripture and had plotted to have him silenced. They could not resist this final expression of self-congratulation. Their comment says in effect, 'We were right and you were wrong. We have done our duty and rid the world of another false Messiah.' *(ii) The people.* They had been persuaded by the chief priests and the elders (Matt. 27:20), when only a few days before they seemed to welcome him openly to their city (Matt. 21:10-11). He had lived an exemplary life before them and done nothing but good for them, having taught them and worked miracles among them, but they were fickle. *(iii) The soldiers.* This had taken place before (Matt. 27:27-31), but Luke 23:36-37 records the soldiers taking up the same words of mockery as everyone else around the cross. Mark 15:39 graphically records the impression the death of Jesus made on the centurion. *(iv) The robbers.* Matt. 27:44 records this and Luke 23:39-43 records the change of heart one of them had before his death.

The words of mockery heaped on Jesus had a common theme, anticipated by the words in this psalm. They show that Jesus had made his claims clear, for they were being thrown back in his face. This was the root of the scorn he faced – claiming so much, but apparently able to deliver so little when it really counted. There is no doubt that such words constituted a severe temptation from Satan. Satan had failed at the beginning of his ministry to deflect Jesus from his proposed course of action. Knowing there would be other opportunities (Luke 4:13), he remained active at various points in his ministry (for example Matthew 16:22-23). Now was his last opportunity before his final defeat. He could not leave Jesus alone at this critical point and there was still one way he might be able to neutralise the effect of the cross. Persuade Jesus – even at this late stage, not to go through with it. This is the tool he used: Jesus' own words, his identity. To be publicly called a failure at the very climax of the pursuit to which you have dedicated your whole life must be hard to bear. In an instant Jesus could have proved them all wrong and called on those twelve legions of angels he knew were still at his disposal (Matt. 26:52-54)! But instead, 'Bearing shame and scoffing rude, in my place condemned he stood; sealed my pardon with his blood. Hallelujah! What a Saviour!'

Pause for a moment to reflect on the response of God the Father as he witnessed what was being done to his Son. How was he able to exercise self-restraint at such diabolical treatment? He didn't. He had not restrained his love and he did not restrain his anger. It fell on his Son.

Messiah [17] Psalm 69:20 Messiah unpitied and without a comforter

The more familiar allusion to the *Messiah* from this psalm is in v.21. Our verse is the central one of the three which forms a paragraph in Hebrew. As it stands, it suggests that the scorn Messiah suffered from his oppressors had a profound, almost devastating effect upon him. This does not seem to have been part of the experience of Jesus on the cross. Apart from Gethsemane, where such heaviness is referred to (Matt. 26:37-38; Mark 14:33), the only occasion when anything similar to this emotion is recorded is found in Matthew 23:37-39. In his sermon on this passage, Newton approves of the version used in the Church of England Prayer Book, where the passage begins '*Thy* rebuke ...' In bearing the sin of many, *Messiah* suffered the rebuke of his heavenly Father. Nothing less could have produced such a feeling and it is reflected in the words he quoted from Psalm 22, 'My God, my God, why have you forsaken me?'

We cannot begin to conceive of the enormity of the burden laid upon *Messiah*. We may find ourselves shocked by the terrible sins some people have perpetrated on others, but they rarely affect us directly and so we are not usually provoked to a personal response. 'We know but little of the extreme *malignity* of sin because we have but faint views of the majesty, holiness and goodness of God against whom it is committed.' 'We have but slight thoughts of the *extent* of sin. Not only positive disobedience, but want of conformity to the law of God is sinful' (Newton). If we only have such a slight awareness of sin, how can we fathom the horrors that are encompassed in the sin of the world for which *Messiah* bore the full punishment?

The second part of our verse from the psalm again seems to have no equivalent at the time of the crucifixion itself. Indeed,

when a measure of sympathy was offered (Luke 23:26-31), Jesus gently turned it into a warning. Again, there may be a closer reflection of the sentiment expressed in the events in Gethsemane. Jesus did seek companionship and found it sadly lacking (Matt. 26:36-46). This was not weakness, but simple humanity. 'His fortitude was very different from a stoical hardness of spirit. All the affections of pure humanity, whatever does not imply sin (such as impatience under suffering, and an undue premature desire for deliverance), operated in him as it might do for us. It was no impeachment of his innocence or his willingness, that he wished, if it were possible, for some relief or alleviation of his misery' (Newton).

There is a further thought found in the totality of this verse. It is the complete aloneness of *Messiah* in achieving salvation. He had absolutely no help from heaven or earth. He alone saved. Nobody aided him in any way whatever. There is nothing in ourselves that helped him and there was nothing at the time of his death to relieve him or give him the slightest degree of assistance in what he was to accomplish.

Having briefly contemplated the terrors of eternal isolation to be suffered by unrepentant sinners at the day of judgement, Newton ends his sermon on this passage with these words: 'Should any of you hear the '*Messiah*' performed again, may God impress upon your heart the sense of this passage. Then you will understand that the sufferings of the Son of God are by no means a proper subject for the amusement of a vacant hour.' It is a sentiment with which we may be inclined to agree when we consider that there are many presentations on this subject today which are much less edifying than this oratorio.

Messiah [18]   Lamentations 1:12   No sorrow like Messiah's sorrow

Newton has some hesitation about whether this passage in a literal sense, immediately refers to *Messiah*. 'It is a pathetic exclamation by which the prophet Jeremiah expresses his grief, or rather the grief of Jerusalem, when the sins of the people had given success to the Chaldean army and the temple and city were destroyed' (Newton). The oratorio uses only the middle one of three phrases but we shall look at them all.

The aversion of the world. The most significant event in the history of the world was taking place. Day was turned into night, the earth shook and tombs were opened (Matt. 27:45,51-52). Yet for most people at the time, there was no significance in it. People passed by, ignoring just another execution. It was irrelevant and meaningless to them. These were the most favoured of people, whose whole history had led up to this momentous day. Their national consciousness eagerly awaited it because their religious ceremonies and sacred writings spoke so eloquently of it. But when the time came, the vast majority were totally unaffected by it and life went on as if nothing out of the ordinary had happened.

The world gives the same response today when the same event is presented in the preaching of the gospel. The majority are uninterested and say it has nothing to do with them. This is a conscious choice and such deliberate avoidance of a matter of such supreme importance is an expression of rejection. It is a dangerous, indeed fatal response, for it brings down the judgement of God (Acts 17:31).

The appeal of the sufferer. The one being afflicted is presented as the one who tries to arrest the attention of uninterested passers-by. He calls upon them to examine what is happening. He wants them to take a careful look and consider the significance of what they see. First they should see the extremity of his suffering – betrayal, desertion, injustice, slander, mockery, beating and death. Then they should consider the one who was suffering. He evidently had been highly favoured by God and brought nothing but good to men. Yet although he had served both God and man faithfully, neither came to his aid at the time of his greatest need. Why? The appeal is to stop and weigh up these things. It is vital to come to a conclusion about them. He is not asking for pity but faith. The one at the centre of these events knows their importance and does what he can to prevent them from being overlooked.

When the truth about Christ is faithfully declared, it is not simply man who speaks. God's Word comes from God himself. He makes a direct appeal to mankind, even though he may use a human channel to do so. To ignore the gospel is to ignore the voice of God (2 Cor. 5:20).

The anger of God. If such a state of affairs could have been prevented, then surely God would have done so, given that he possesses supreme power. But this was the only way his purposes could be accomplished and there was no feasible alternative. God's anger with *Messiah* was real and deliberate, not accidental. But he had done nothing to deserve it and his affliction was borne on behalf of others. The context speaks of the sin of the people of God and he was bearing the punishment they deserved. He suffered the anger of God in their place. 'Great is the gospel of our glorious God; where mercy met the anger of God's rod.'

Messiah [19]   Isaiah 53:8   Messiah's innocence vindicated

Newton's sermon on this passage quotes the whole verse and not just the end of it as it is found in the oratorio. As suggested by the title above, he considers the testimonies given to the innocence of *Messiah*. He briefly looks at the declarations of Judas (Matt. 27:4), Pilate (Matt. 27:24), the dying thief (Luke 23:41), and the centurion (Luke 23:47). These testimonies confirmed the innocence of his life, which is also evident on every page of the Gospels. It was, of course, an indispensable factor in the acceptability of his sacrifice (2 Cor. 5:21).

Newton also says, 'The text is not merely a repetition of what was spoken before concerning the Redeemer's sufferings; rather the declaration of what was to follow them begins here. It is the opening of a bright and glorious subject.' We shall therefore comment briefly on the whole section (7-9) and while looking finally at some of the elements of the suffering of *Messiah* referred to, we will begin the forward look to a brighter future.

His sufferings were distinguished by certain factors which are summarised here.

(a) *Fortitude (7).* Others, facing such a situation of wrongful arrest, an abuse of legal procedure and unjust condemnation, would have been very vocal in their protests. Despite all he had gone through, there was not a single word of protest. He was not ignorant of what had happened, nor of what was to come, and he was not disconnected from reality by shock. He made no objection to his treatment because he knew it to be the will of God and agreed with it. It was the silence of consent. He saw beyond the event itself (Heb. 12:2).

(b) *The process of law (8).* His death came about through a legal procedure, however abused it may have been. It was through an act of corporate, human judgement. Mankind, through its representatives, were directly responsible for his death. *Messiah* was rejected in the most complete and unmistakable manner. A death by illness, old age or accident would not have involved such rejection and therefore could not have been considered so obviously the responsibility of others. If man is culpable and God is just, the matter was not yet finished.

(c) *Overlooked (8).* The NIV does not translate the second phrase of v. 8 well and the AV is somewhat obscure. The sense seems to be: 'Who of his generation spoke in support of him?' He did not come to his own defence and neither did anyone else. To them it was a non-event. If this was so fundamental to the plan of God, it is inconceivable that it would remain so obscure. It must lead to something more.

(d) *Purposeful (8).* It was a substitutionary death. He died to take the punishment for the wrongdoing of others, for he had none of his own. If so, then the transaction was not yet complete. Those who had been released from the penalty still had to go free. New life had still to be given.

(e) *Distinctive (9).* Burial would naturally follow, but it had two contradictory associations. After a lifetime of undisputed goodness he died and was buried as a common criminal.

After a lifetime of poverty, he was buried in the tomb of a rich man. Even the burial of *Messiah* was not incidental but the subject of prophecy. Attention was drawn to his burial place, suggesting it would have some significance in future events.

Messiah [20] Psalm 16:10; Acts 2:22-32 Messiah rising from the dead

'Though *Messiah* was, for our sakes, treated as a malefactor, all who were immediately concerned in his death were constrained (as we have seen) to declare his innocence. But he was worthy of a more solemn and authoritative justification. Accordingly, 'He was declared to be the Son of God with power, by his resurrection from the dead (Rom. 1:4)' (Newton). It was the declaration of God, by his own handiwork (Acts 2:24; 3:15).

Resurrection – attested by God beforehand.

(a) *In life.* That Christ was sent from God and endowed with his power was evident from his miracles. Included among them was the power to restore life to the dead (for example John 11). God was also involved in his death, as we have seen, not only by his purpose but also in his power (John 10:17-18), and in those verses he specifically stated he would bring himself back from the dead. Jesus prophesied on other occasions that he would rise from the dead (for example Matthew 20:19).

(b) *In word.* The words in our verse were spoken by David about a thousand years before the event took place. They could not have referred to David himself for he was dead and buried. David had been promised that *Messiah* would be one of his descendants and he believed the promise of God. That scripture was fulfilled in the resurrection of Jesus Christ.

Resurrection – attested by God afterwards.

(a) *In men.* Peter and the other disciples had seen the risen Christ. They knew the resurrection was a fact and were testifying to the truth of it. Jesus had commissioned them to witness to him as crucified and risen, right across the world (Acts 1:8). The Word of God testifies to the work of God.

(b) *By the Holy Spirit.* Why should these men be believed? What makes their testimony acceptable? On this occasion it was the evident anointing, and therefore the approval of God himself as shown by their sudden ability to speak languages they had not previously learned. Soon, they would be performing miracles themselves which would help to authenticate them as genuine witnesses to the power of God revealed in the resurrected *Messiah*.

In his sermon on this passage, Newton gives three 'advantages which true Christians derive from a spiritual and enlightened knowledge of this doctrine.'

(a) 'By virtue of that union which subsists between *Messiah* as the Head of the body, the church and all his members … they know that he was 'raised again for our justification' (Rom. 4:25). 'As he by his resurrection was vindicated, justified from the reproaches of his enemies … and raised to glory; they have fellowship with him herein. They are not only pardoned but accepted in the Beloved.'

(b) 'The resurrection of Christ from the dead is a pledge and specimen of that almighty power which is engaged on their behalf to overcome all the obstacles, difficulties and enemies they are liable to meet with in their pilgrimage which threaten to disappoint their hopes and to prevent them from obtaining their heavenly inheritance.'

(c) 'His resurrection is the pledge and pattern of ours. As certainly as Christ, the first-fruits, is risen, so certainly shall they that are Christ's arise at his coming.'

Messiah [21]   Psalm 24:7-10   The ascension of Messiah to glory

Newton makes these points about the ascended Christ in his sermon on this passage:

(a) 'Messiah, who humbled himself to the death of the cross, is "the Lord of hosts". This is the title of God in the Old Testament' and it rightly belongs to Christ.

(b) 'He is conqueror of sin, Satan and death. He fought he bled, he died; but in dying he conquered. As Messiah, their king, has conquered for them, so they, in due time, shall be made more than conquerors, by faith in his blood, and in the word of his testimony.'

(c) 'As the acknowledged King of glory, in the nature of man, he ascended; the everlasting gates unfolded wide, and he entered the holy place, not made with hands, there to appear in the presence of God for his people ... as their representative and as their high priest and intercessor. He is seated upon the throne of universal dominion, and he exercises his authority and rule with a special view to their welfare.'

Having looked briefly at that understanding, let us also consider an alternative.

The title of this psalm shows David to have been its author and its subject matter leads us to think it was written to celebrate the removal of the ark from Kiriath Jearim to Jerusalem (2 Sam. 6). 'Incorporated in Israel's hymnbook, this psalm became, with a regard to its original occasion and purpose, an Old Testament Advent hymn in honour of the Lord who should come into his temple. In the New Testament consciousness the second appearing takes the place of the first, the coming of the Lord to his church, which is his spiritual temple; and in this psalm we are called upon to prepare him a worthy reception' (Delitzsch).

These verses introduce a change of mood in the psalm. The earlier section seems to speak of the Lord in his absence but now he is known to be present. Two factors are worth noting.

(a) He will wait. He has come, but he remains outside. He will not force his way in but waits for the appropriate action to be taken inside so that he can be received. It is exactly the same picture as Revelation 3:20, which is addressed to a church, not an individual. We must ask ourselves if we are keeping the Lord out of his church. It is possible for us to talk about him regularly, but not know the reality of his presence.

(b) He is identified. There is some hesitation on the part of those inside about the identity of the one outside, reminiscent of Matthew 21:10. The inhabitants did not recognise him. It is clearly the same person referred to in vv. 1, 3 but there is a new and unexpected note of supreme power and victory. He had been strong and mighty in battle and was therefore capable of making a forced entry, but he refrained. His title – awarded in view of his exploits, gives him the right of admission. The request for entry is made on the basis of this newly revealed identification. It is as if v. 10 is spoken when the bolts are drawn, the door swings open and the king is seen and welcomed. Again, we must face the possibility that we do not know the Lord as well as we think we do. New Testament people can still be guilty of Old Testament sins.

Messiah [22]   Hebrews 1:5-6
Messiah, the Son of God, worshipped by angels

The experience of *Messiah* on earth could suggest that he is no more than a man. But after the sublime introduction to his epistle, the writer to the Hebrews establishes the superiority of Christ over angels at length (1:4 to 2:4). The oratorio takes the first two of the writer's seven points to show that *Messiah* is none other than the Son of God and as such is the proper recipient of angelic worship. Newton devotes two sermons to these verses.

Jesus has a better name than angels. Angels are the highest order of created beings, superior to man (Ps. 8:5). They cannot die (Luke 20:36), do not marry (Mark 12:25), are very numerous (Matt. 26:53), are wise (2 Sam. 14:20) and powerful (2 Kings 19:35). They are spirit beings dwelling in heaven and are permanent observers of the work of God upon earth (1 Peter 1:12). But they are only angels – or messengers. *Messiah* carries a higher name: Son.

The writer quotes the Messianic Psalm 2, in which, at v. 7, the King declares the terms of his appointment: God has called him his Son. It is in the context of that relationship that he exercises his role as King. He shares the same nature and authority as the one who gave him that position. His appointment receives a formal and public recognition at a particular time. 'Today' does not refer to a twenty-four period, but is a more general time reference. The incarnation declares an established fact. He always was greater than angels, but his new appearance (as a man) could suggest otherwise. After his incarnation, he went through life, death and resurrection before being exalted back to the place he had occupied before coming to this world. So even though he was a man, he became superior to angels because his fundamental identity (revealed by his name – Son) was already superior. The use of the term 'inherited' confirms this. The name was always rightfully his, but he only entered into the fullness of it at a particular time when certain circumstances occurred.

The second quotation is the Word of God that Nathan the prophet was to give to David about Solomon (2 Sam. 7:14; 1 Chr. 17:13). The characteristics of his sonship would be seen in his obedience, the united kingdom and the building of the temple. All these factors were spiritually fulfilled in *Messiah*.

Jesus is worshipped by angels. It is clear from Scripture that one creature cannot worship another of God's creatures (Matt. 4:10; Acts 10:26), and so the second reference must also apply to the Son of God. The reference quoted is obscure in our version and our margin directs us to the Greek version of Deuteronomy 32:43 which matches the reading in the Dead Sea Scrolls. A reference to victory, it is likely to apply to the Second Coming of Christ. Angels did not openly worship him at his incarnation, nor at his death – his real moment of victory. But again the emphasis seems to be on the sudden visibility of a truth previously hidden. The victory of *Messiah* will be most clearly seen when he appears as the firstborn of many brethren – in the company of all those he has redeemed (Rom. 8:29; Col. 1:18). This does not imply he will only be worshipped then. Revelation 4 and 5 show he constantly receives angelic worship. If angels worship him, then 'humbly depending upon his promised grace, without which we can do nothing, we are resolved, that whatever others do, we must, we will, worship him with the utmost powers of our soul' (Newton).

Messiah [23]   Psalm 68:18; Ephesians 4:8
Gifts received for the rebellious

This Davidic psalm is a song of victory in which the help of God is sought, found and celebrated. Paul sees a verse from it as a prophecy concerning the ascension of Messiah and its aftermath. Three features are noted:

(a) *He ascended.* He moved from occupying a lower realm to occupying a higher realm. The context of the verse in the psalm presents an interesting contrast. The mountains of Bashan were very impressive – representing substantial human power. However, God was present on the diminutive Mount Zion – thus representing the real seat of power. The ascendancy spoken of therefore was not obvious from a human perspective. Man could not see how any greater heights were reached by it, but as far as God was concerned the heights reached were greater than those of Bashan. The emphasis is on the greatness of the heights reached, the suitability of that position for the ascended one and the reversal of human values the ascent represented.

(b) *He was victorious.* In ancient times victorious kings often returned home making a great display of the spoils of war – showing the greatness of their exploits. Conquered kings were led in procession by the victor, thereby sending a message to the welcoming crowds: 'These your enemies can terrorise you no longer for they are under my power now.' That is exactly the message of this part of the verse. The ascension of *Messiah* was a display of his conquests. Mankind's greatest enemies – who had held them captive, had themselves been vanquished. Sin, Satan and death could no longer exercise any power

over the subjects of the victorious king. The ascension was not merely the reward for a job well done or compensation for a gruelling few years of hardship. It was a demonstration of the reality and totality of the victory he had secured – even if it did not seem that way to human eyes.

(c) *He gave gifts.* The margin of the NIV says the gifts were for men, not from men as the text suggests. This is in keeping with the quotation used in Ephesians. The victor does not keep the spoils of war for himself. All his subjects benefit directly from his conquest. Newton comments: 'To bestow gifts upon the miserable is bounty but to bestow them on rebels is grace.' He identifies the primary gift as the Holy Spirit. He gives the greatest gift of all: the dwelling of God among his people. The immediacy of his presence quells any further thoughts of rebellion. They enjoy his provision personally and are eager to please him.

From this passage we can learn:

1.   Wherein lies the true glory of the church – the crucified, risen and ascended Christ.

2.   The true nature of the imposing but powerless world around us.

3.   To continue to trust in the certainty and security of the victory of Christ.

4.   To enjoy the ongoing presence of God and explain the triumphs of his Son.

'His ascension on high is the sure pledge that his servants shall follow him (John 12:26). And even at present, by faith they ascend and are seated with him in the heavenly places (Eph. 2:6)' (Newton).

Messiah [24]   Psalm 68:11   The publication of the gospel

We turn to an earlier section of this psalm of victory. Our verse begins the section which looks at the promise of victory as the conquest and its consequences are considered (11-14).

'This verse, though the particular occasion is not specified, probably refers to some season of deliverance or victory, when the women, according to the custom of the nation, assembled to praise the Lord with timbrels, songs and dances (Exod. 15; 1 Sam. 18:6-7) … It is properly introduced in the *Messiah*, and in its proper place, immediately after the view given of our Saviour's triumphant ascension, as it leads us to consider the first visible effect of that great event … If not a direct prophecy of the publication of the gospel, it is at least a fit motto to a discourse of this very important subject' (Newton).

The message is the Lord's. In context, the word was the promise of victory and so the song celebrated not only that victory but also God's faithfulness. He declared he would release those who were subject to bondage, misery and death, and it has come to pass that he has bestowed the blessings of liberty, peace and life. God has provided for the world a way of salvation which is effective. People must be informed of it and invited to respond to it. Both the provision and the pronouncement come from God and so does the power. When the gospel is accurately declared, by God's grace souls are saved. God's truth has a power of its own (Rom. 1:16).

Paul warned of perversions of the gospel (Gal. 1:6-7) and they are even more prevalent today. It was the same in Newton's day, so he defines the gospel thus: 'The gospel treats all mankind as already in a state of condemnation; it declares their utter inability to save or help themselves; and it gives assurance of pardon and salvation to all who believe in the Son of God. That they may be encouraged and enabled to believe, it describes the dignity of his person, the necessity and greatness of his sufferings, the completeness of his atonement, the prevalence of his intercession – his love, authority, power and faithfulness.'

The messengers are sent out by the Lord. In context, the number of those who proclaimed was great because a great victory had been won. There was no widespread grief at many losses suffered from heavy fighting. One man had fought and won on behalf of all. But the benefits from his conquest are shared by everyone who belongs to him – without exception and so all are involved in pronouncing his victory. This thinking is behind the phrase 'more than conquerors', which is central to Romans 8:31-39). Someone else has won the victory. We are not the conquerors, but we enter into the bounties he has secured. That means our one-time enemies have no influence over us any more. He has completely defeated them. We won without having fought. A victory that is over all and for all is pronounced by all.

However, there are some men to whom God has entrusted his 'good deposit' of the gospel in a singular way (2 Tim. 1:14). 'The Lord, by the constraining sense of his love, and by giving a deep impression of the worth of souls, and by exciting in the mind a dependence upon his all-sufficiency, can and does encourage those whom he calls and chooses, to serve him in the gospel (Matt. 9:38)' (Newton).

Messiah [25]   Isaiah 52:7-10; Romans 10:15
The gospel message, glad tidings

After *Messiah* had ascended on high, the next portion of the oratorio celebrated the publication of the gospel. Now the nature of that message is considered. There is a sense of expectancy. God's people are waiting for news. It comes as a runner seen in the distance.

There is something for us to hear.

(a) *Peace.* Peace between God and man. The intermediacy of Christ has been accepted. His sacrifice for sin has secured atonement. 'Those who believe this good report derive from it peace of conscience … It dispels their fears and forebodings and inspires them with liberty to come to God as children' (Newton).

(b) *Good* ('good tidings of good', AV). They receive blessings from the hand of God because he favours them and is concerned about their well-being.

(c) *Salvation.* The specific blessing is salvation from sin. Believers will not face punishment for it and are freed from its power over them.

The substance of the message is 'Your God reigns!' All possible enemies are defeated. His anointed one is victorious and has been received at God's side as proof. This message has come from outside and been given to the watchmen on the city walls. It is their task to declare it to the people inside the city.

There is something for us to see. Kicking up a cloud of dust as he approaches, the feet of the messenger are seen to bring welcome news. The waiting is over. Punishment is averted. Victory has been won. Safety is assured. But there is another part to the message. The victor himself is coming! If there is rejoicing about the approaching feet of the messenger, how much more about the feet of him who is the subject of the message! He is coming personally. He will not come in secret but in public. He will not come in weakness but in strength. He will not come to observe but to accomplish. God's salvation will not simply be reported, it will be seen by multitudes across the world. Part of the comfort of God's people is that, far from being a despised minority, because of their God they are the most favoured of men. When God is seen for who he is, they will be seen for who they are.

In his sermon on Romans 10:15, Newton has a section about the watchmen. 'True Christians will set a high value upon ministers who with simplicity and godly sincerity, preach the gospel of peace in such a manner as to evidence that they are influenced by a high regard to the glory of God and to the good of souls; and they give proof of their affection in more ways than by speaking well of them.

(a) By the satisfaction with which they accept a faithful ministry, as a balance to the trials they meet with in common life.

(b) By taking kindly and in good part his most searching discourses in public, or even his reproof and admonitions in private if needful.

(c) By their tenderness and sympathy with him in all his exercises; and by the care, according to their ability, to make his situation comfortable and to avoid everything that might give him just occasion for complaint or grief.'

Messiah [26]   Psalm 19:1-6; Romans 10:18
The progress of the gospel

The psalm is concerned with the glory of God. It is displayed in the created world and especially in the skies. Perhaps David chose that realm because it was the area least corrupted by man. Perhaps it was also symbolic of the revelation of God – lofty, well ordered and all embracing. Wherever men may settle on this variable terrain, all are under the same sky. In particular, the sun brings light, life, joy and cleansing heat to all. It is a fitting representation of the goodness of God to everyone and especially of his spiritual provision.

Creation was designed so that man would look beyond it – to the Creator (Acts 17:26-27; Rom. 1:19-20). But although such a search should lead to God, he will not be found in his entirety within it. He is elsewhere. Hence, in Psalm 19 there is an immediate connection between creation and the Word of God. An examination of the former leads to the latter. The beauties of the former are noted but not its benefits. However well known those benefits may be, they are far exceeded by the benefits brought by the Word of God. That is where the handiwork of God is viewed. His glory is most displayed by the effect of the Word of God upon the life of the individual.

Paul cites the psalm to highlight how widespread is the glory of God across the world. It is found in creation, it is found in his word which was given to his people and now it is found in Christ and in the proclamation of his gospel. The quotation is not saying that the prophecy had been fulfilled already and all had heard the gospel. The mercy of God was being extended further – beyond the declaration of the muted voice of creation and beyond the exclusive testimony of God to his people. The mercy of God had become incarnate and reconciled God and man. It was good news and intelligible to all. Whatever was said about the glory of God in the psalm, the gospel far exceeded it. Paul's use of the psalm anticipates the worldwide spread of the gospel because that glorifies God more than anything else.

Newton says, 'The fulfilment of the promises respecting Messiah's kingdom is progressive. So far as this prophecy has been accomplished, the arm of the Lord has been revealed. It is his doing and may justly be marvellous in our eyes. The truth of the prophecy will be proved by its final completion; which, though not likely to take place in our time, we may be assured that it cannot fail, for the mouth of the Lord hath spoken it. And besides, we have a sufficient pledge and security for the whole, in what he has already done.'

Newton explains that God has delayed its fulfilment 'so as on the one hand to display his sovereignty, wisdom and power and on the other, to afford full proof of the depravity and alienation of the heart of man'. His closing paragraph begins: 'The point I am chiefly to press upon my hearers, is, that the word of salvation is sent to you (Acts 13:26).'

Messiah [27]   Psalm 2
Opposition to Messiah unreasonable, vain and ruinous

'David, under the influence of the Holy Spirit speaks of the future as actually present. He saw the resistance that would be made to the person and kingdom of *Messiah* by the powers of the world; that they would employ their force and policy to withstand and oppress the decree and appointment of God.' '... the grounds of that dislike which the Jews manifested to *Messiah*'s personal ministry ... are deeply rooted in the nature of fallen man and therefore not peculiar to any age or nation' (Newton).

Although *Messiah* was a king and came to set up a kingdom that would last for ever, it would not interfere with the rights of human princes. They had nothing to fear from him. Their rebellion had three characteristics. It was:

(a) *Godless.* The conspirators were not those who refused to believe in God, but those who had acknowledged him and would not do so any longer. They had been under his rule but now wanted to go their own way. They had found his laws tiresome and restrictive to self-expression.

(b) *Planned.* This was not spontaneous. 'Conspire' and 'plot' show that this attitude had existed for some time. Schemes were being planned to reject God and it was not just a few leaders who were involved. This was a widespread feeling embracing many people.

(c) *Futile.* It was doomed to failure. The question 'why?' implies their opposition would be both groundless and ineffectual. They had an inflated sense of their own capabilities. How could creatures take on their Creator and expect to be victorious? Their rage would lead to a lack of self-control which would be fatal. Anyone who would not serve him would perish.

The psalm shows that God responded in three ways to this rebellion: scorn (4), anger (5), establishment (6). Only the first is found in the oratorio and the third is illustrated in it using other scriptures.

The scorn God shows is the humour of a ridiculous situation. He marvels at their stupidity. They have no hope of success at all. He is seated in heaven – where they cannot reach him. He is seated in power – which is infinitely greater than theirs. 'He has them perfectly under his control, holds them in a chain when they think themselves most at liberty, appoints the bounds beyond which they cannot pass, and can in a moment check them, and make them feel his hook and bridle, when in the height of their career' (Newton).

'The text principally respects the opposition made to his gospel and his kingdom after his ascension, which is still carrying on, but which always was and always will be, in vain.' 'Though many rise up against you, they shall not prevail; ... for the battle is not yours, but the Lord's. Your enemies are his and his cause is yours. They who associate against him shall be dashed to pieces, as the billows break and die upon a rocky shore' (Newton).

Messiah [28]   Revelation 19:6   The Lord reigns

'The impression which the performance of this passage in the oratorio usually makes upon the audience is well known. But however great the power of music may be … it cannot soften and change the heart, it cannot bend the obdurate will of man. If all the people who successively hear the *Messiah*, who are struck and astonished by this chorus, were to bring away with them the abiding sense of the importance of the sentiment it contains, the nation would soon wear a new face' (Newton).

Newton takes the opportunity provided by this passage to refer to the kingdom of providence, describing how 'his mighty arm sustains the vast fabric of the universe' and especially the kingdom of grace, '… the church, founded upon a rock and though the gates of hell continually war against it, they cannot prevail'.

This chorus came in response to an exhortation in v. 5. The exhortation came from the throne, and so it must have come from the Lord Jesus Christ because he calls his heavenly Father his God (John 20:17). The images used to describe the sound speak of great size, power and unity. In vv. 1-4, the occupants of heaven had praised God for the destruction of Babylon. The sum and substance of all enmity against him had been judged and eradicated. God alone was seen as supreme. All opposition had gone. His reign – never in doubt, was clear for all to see: the public, uncontested establishment of his universal and eternal dominion. His subjects were the ones to lift their voices in adoration.

The following verses (7-8), still in the mouth of the redeemed, expressed great joy at the immediate consequence of the establishment of the reign of God. There was nothing to stop the marriage of the Lamb taking place. Bride and groom could be united at last. There were three stages in the traditional wedding on which this image was based. First, the betrothal by which each was promised to the other. This was more binding than our engagement, for from this point the couple were considered to be married, even if they had not been united. Next there was an interval during which the bride prepared herself to receive her husband. The dowry was paid and the husband made his way to her home in order to take her to his, where the feast would be held. The marriage supper itself signified the union. That time had arrived. The Lamb and his bride had been promised to each other long before. The intervening period had come to an end. The dowry was paid in blood. His people had been made ready for this momentous day and once every enemy had been destroyed, nothing could prevent their union for all preparations had been completed. The feast – the union, would take place in his home, for he had brought his people there.

'It is impossible to make this song our own, and cordially rejoice that 'the Lord God omnipotent reigneth', unless we are the willing subjects of his government; unless we are really pleased with his appointed way of salvation, approve of his precepts, and from a view of his wisdom and goodness, can cheerfully submit and resign ourselves to the disposal of his providence' (Newton).

Messiah [29]   Revelation 11:15
The extent of Messiah's spiritual kingdom

Six trumpets have warned of judgements that will fall upon the world. Six signs have been given, each a judgement in itself, of the great and final judgement that will follow them. They are processes God has instituted in the world which are being continuously worked out until they are completed. As the seventh trumpet is sounded, a proclamation comes from heaven which will both strengthen the people of God and be a witness to others of the work of God. The element of judgement shown here is the ultimate triumph of good over evil and the establishment of God's eternal and righteous kingdom. It is a warning of God's forthcoming total victory and the utter defeat of all who have stood against him.

This passage speaks of the end of time and of the world order. This does not happen by chance but by divine decree. This is more than just a statement of fact. It is a statement of purpose. Something has changed. The kingdom of the world has 'become' under sovereignty of God, represented by Christ. The world was always under God's rule, but it was disputed. Satan sought mastery over it and history has revealed how the world has been a battleground. The outcome of the struggle has never been in doubt and indeed the struggle itself is part of the sovereign rule of God – to display both his mercy and his wrath.

The sovereignty of God has never been universally acknowledged. It has only been recognised by the church and then by special revelation. The time is coming, anticipated by this passage, when what has always been true will be made obvious to everyone. The reign of Christ will be permanently and perfectly established. It will no longer be subject to the doubt and dispute which prevailed while it was manifest in the lives of redeemed sinners within the confines of a sin-stricken world (1 Cor. 15:24-28). The next verses contain the song of the redeemed who worship God for beginning to reign with great power.

How are we to respond to this glorious prospect which lies before us?

(a) With patience and perseverance as we wait until it happens.

(b) With joy and thanksgiving because we know it is certain to happen.

(c) With adoring worship, in both the imitation of and expectation of glory.

(d) With humble service which will prove our claim to a share in that day and to hasten its coming.

Taking a rather different approach, Newton says: 'It is not necessary to suppose that every individual of mankind shall be savingly converted to the Lord in this future day of his power; but I apprehend the current language of the prophecies warrants us to hope that the prayers and desires of the church shall, in some future period, be signally answered in the following respects.

(a) That the gospel shall visit the nations which are at present involved in darkness.

(b) That this gospel shall prevail, not in word only, but in power.

(c) That animosities and disputes which prevail among Christians shall cease.

(d) That it will be a time of general peace.'

Messiah [30] Revelation 19:16 King of kings, Lord of lords

'The description of the administration and glory of the Redeemer's kingdom, in defiance of all opposition, concludes the second part of the *Messiah*. Three different passages are selected from this book to form a grand chorus, of which his title in this verse is the close' (Newton).

This title is found in 1 Timothy 6:15, Revelation 17:14 and is an echo of Deuteronomy 10:17 and Daniel 2:47. Commentators differ about the location of the inscription. For some it was on both the thigh and the clothing and for others it was on either. Some even place it on the hilt of another sword. Whatever the exact position, the reason for it is more significant. In that position the name would clearly identify the rider to anyone who was standing on the ground as it would be at eye level. No one would be left in ignorance about who he was. There are other names in the earlier part of this section: Faithful and True (11), the Word of God (13) and a secret name (12). None of these was written. The names point to the multi-faceted identity of this person. All were true, but at this time he would publicly be viewed as being the supreme ruler of all.

We cannot look only at the name, for it is part of a broader description of him. We see a combination of earlier images; the eyes (1:14), the sword (1:16), the name (3:14), the horse (6:2), the sceptre (12:5). He comes to judge and make war (11). The sword of his mouth reminds us that the truth he spoke has come to pass (for example Luke 21:27). After his conquest comes his strong rule (compare Psalm 2:9, and his execution of the justifiable anger of God upon all who opposed him). He is not alone, for the army of saints, so clearly identified with him, join him in his victory. Although his garment was dipped in blood, his resurrected body showed no permanent damage from any wound. This is a glorious picture of a triumphant *Messiah*.

Newton comments on how this name relates to the kings of the earth. 'The rage they discover, and the resistance they make, cannot weaken this truth but make it more evident.' 'They are continually disturbing the world with their schemes of ambition. They expect to carry everything before them and have seldom any higher end in view than the gratification of their own passions. But in all they do they are but servants of this great King and fulfil his purposes, as the instruments he employs to inflict prescribed punishment upon transgressors against him or to open a way for the spread of his gospel.'

Newton also comments on how this name is of comfort to believers. 'This inscription his own people read by the eye of faith in the present life and it inspires them with confidence and joy, under the many tribulations they pass through. Hereafter it shall be openly known and read by all men.' 'That he is King of kings and Governor among the nations is farther evident from the preservation of his people; for the world is against them and they have no protector but him.' 'If the Lord of lords be for us, what weapon or counsel can prosper against us?' 'How great is the dignity and privilege of true believers!'

Messiah [31]   Job 19:25-26   Job's faith and expectation

This passage gives a strong and clear testimony to Job's faith and 'forms a beautiful and well-chosen introduction to the third part of the *Messiah*, the principal subject of which is the present privileges and future prospects of those who believe in the Saviour's name' (Newton). But the passage has a context. In vv. 2-6 Job bemoans the insensitivity of his friends; in vv. 7-12 he acknowledges he is suffering at the hand of God; in vv. 13-22 he expresses his sense of desolation; and in vv. 23-29 he gives a declaration of his faith. He feels caught between man and God and in desperation has turned to him. In 17:3 he asked God for a token and it seems one was given here because Job's words are perhaps inspired beyond his understanding.

A Redeemer who lives (25a). Job had protested his innocence all along but his friends would not believe him and the evidence seemed against him. There was none to speak up for him or come to his aid. He wished that words could be permanent so they would be positive proof that when the Redeemer came, he would act on them, not the views of his friends or the physical circumstances of Job.

'There is no name of *Messiah* more significant, comprehensive or endearing than the name Redeemer. The name Saviour expresses what he does for sinners ... But the word Redeemer intimates likewise the manner in which he saves them' (Newton). There are three elements in the name:

(a) *Relationship*. It speaks of a near kinsman who is bound to act for the good of his relative.

(b) *(Revenge)*. Not the best term to use in association with the redemption by Jesus Christ, but suggesting vindication from unjust ill-treatment.

(c) *Restoration*. His work is not done until the sufferer has been safely re-established in his previous secure and prosperous circumstances.

Job knew he had a relationship with someone who could act for him in this way and, as he cannot be human (13-19), it must be God who would act on his behalf.

A Redeemer who stands (25b). Job did not expect the Redeemer to appear soon. He knew his appearing was linked to the end of everything and he was prepared to wait. The picture is of one who is raised up to stand. After a period of ignominy and distress, the Redeemer would come and intervene on his behalf. There was no question of doubt or failure in Job's mind. The coming of Christ heralds the end of everything and the certainty of vindication for all his beleaguered people.

A Redeemer who brings (26-27). The future expectation of Old Testament believers is often unclear, but here it is vivid. Job knew his body would die but, in that same body, he expected to see God. He believed that in the resurrection, his own identity would be preserved. He believed only the Redeemer could provide this because his experiences had taught him that without him it would be impossible.

Messiah [32]   1 Corinthians 15:20   The Lord is risen indeed

'The resurrection of Christ being, as a fact, the great pillar upon which the weight and importance of Christianity rests; it has pleased the Lord to put the indubitable proof of it within our power' (Newton). Yet, many people now and then doubt the proof. Let us consider the implications of such a denial of the resurrection of Christ as it is outlined in the verses immediately preceding our text.

God is a liar (15). From the beginning, the gospel message has been that God raised Jesus from the dead (Acts 2:24; 3:15; 10:40; Rom. 10:9). But that message was given to the apostles by God himself (Acts 26:22-23; 10:42). It is inconceivable that God would send them out to tell lies about him and to make them into liars. A true message was delivered by truthful messengers.

Christ is a sinner (16). If Christ is still dead, he is no better than other men and no more than a good example. Death claims the sinner (Rom. 6:23; Ezek. 18:4) and if death had the last word on his life, then he must have been a sinner and therefore unable to bring any lasting benefit to anyone. Once again, the accuracy of the biblical record is called into question because Jesus is declared to be sinless (Heb. 4:15; 1 Peter 2:22; 1 John 3:5; 2 Cor. 5:21).

Salvation is absent (17). Again the biblical record would be at fault, because it is clear that salvation comes through him alone (Acts 4:12). One sinner cannot save another eternally, and if he is discredited, there is no alternative. Salvation is only possible by the removal of sin and can be accomplished only by someone who is both willing and able to do it. We have no hope without Christ and are destined to remain in the grip of sin and evil forever.

Faith is empty (17). If Christ is not raised, Christianity is a gigantic delusion which has deceived millions of ignorant people for thousands of years. If Christianity is rejected, then a credible alternative must be presented which can demonstrably guarantee eternal life for its adherents on the basis of an irrefutable and consistent revelation of God. Christianity is the only religion in which salvation is given, not earned, and has a coherent explanation for the unfolding course of world history.

Heaven is unreal (18). Christianity claims to be a preparation for what follows this life (1 Peter 1:3-4; Rom. 8:18; 1 Cor. 2:9). It shows that the next life is more important than this one. Without the resurrection of Christ, the future is dark and foreboding. Because the promise of heaven is gone, there is no comfort when others suffer loss and no hope for ourselves. Life becomes meaningless.

'The resurrection of Christ is a doctrine that is absolutely essential to our hope and comfort' (Newton).

Messiah [33] 1 Corinthians 15:21-22 Death by Adam, life by Christ

'From Mr Handel's acknowledged abilities as a composer, and particularly from what I have heard of his great taste and success in adapting the style of his music to the subject, I judge that this passage afforded him a fair occasion of displaying his genius and powers. Two ideas, vastly important in themselves, are here represented in the strongest light, by being placed in contrast to each other' (Newton).

From Adam's disobedience (Gen. 2:17), Newton shows the three forms of death to which all are subjected because humanity traces its common ancestry to Adam:

(a) *Physical death* – 'the outward afflictions which everywhere surround and assail the sinner, and the malignant passions which, like vultures, continually gnaw his heart, all combine to accelerate the execution of this sentence of death' (Newton).

(b) *Spiritual death* – through sin, man is separated from God in this life.

(c) *Eternal death* – the final and eternal misery of the soul and body in hell.

In contrast, all who can trace their rebirth to Christ, enjoy life in two forms:

(a) *Life of grace* by which they may draw near to God, 'delivered from the condemning power of the law. Sin has no longer dominion over them' (Newton). They are still subject to various afflictions in life, but the curse and sting is taken out of them. The separation of body from soul is a deliverance from all evil.

(b) *Life of glory* – because Christ lives in them, they are spiritually united with him by faith. One day they shall live with him where he lives, in heaven. The final resurrection of the body will take place in the last day, for when united with the soul, it will be raised in power.

There are three principles at work in both of these affirmations:

(a) *Representation*. The condition of the whole company rests on the condition of its single representative. 'First fruits' (15:20) is the dedication of the first ripe grain of harvest to God as a pledge of what is to follow. In the resurrection of Christ, God has provided a guarantee of the remainder of the harvest. The rest of the same crop will be gathered in.

(b) *Union*. This could only happen if there was a genuine human connection. If death passed to all of the same kind, so life would pass to all of the same kind. There had to be a total and authentic identification of the representative with all of those who belonged to him.

(c) *Subordination*. There is a term of military precision used in this analogy. Christ has been seen to be raised first. Just because the resurrection of others is not seen, does not render it untrue. It is certain – the next event in the sequence, and so can be awaited with confidence, because it will happen in its appointed time, at the return of Christ (1 Thess. 4:13-18).

Something to think about: Am I in Adam or am I in Christ? You cannot be both.

Messiah [34] 1 Corinthians 15:51-53 The general resurrection

We cannot escape the fact of our mortality and are constantly reminded, either by personal circumstances or surrounding events, of our inevitable death. Our stay in this world is temporary, and as long as we are here we have a body which is appropriate for this environment. But our current physical condition is incompatible with the life to come. A change must come, whatever our eternal fate may be. Speaking of what will happen to all believers, Paul says we shall have a new body which will be suitable for our new environment. It will be different, but it will be better and permanent. That is only to be expected and is understandable.

Paul continues and refers to a mystery – something previously unknown but now revealed. In part, it was revealed to the world in the resurrection of Jesus Christ and is revealed to the individual soul through the indwelling Holy Spirit. Yet there was more which seems to have been revealed directly to Paul himself. First of all, sleep is denied – a continuous but unconscious maintenance of the same condition. Instead, change is spoken of. If we are to enter heaven, we cannot do so as we were. It is a wholly different place and we must be made ready to enter it. Salvation has prepared us spiritually, but our redeemed spirit must occupy a suitable body which will not resemble its earthly predecessor.

God will accomplish it himself, for as he provided our original body, so he will provide the replacement for it. We shall be entering his kingdom and he will see us suitably clothed before we do so. It will happen instantaneously, at the time he appoints. It will take place suddenly and unexpectedly when most people are going about their normal lives (Luke 17:26-30). However, remaining believers who have been watchful will be expecting it. The event will be introduced by a signal, described here as a trumpet, but that need not be taken literally. There will certainly be an unmistakable and unavoidable warning of the awesome and conclusive event that is about to begin.

'When the Lord shall come, attended by his holy angels, his redeemed people will re-assume their bodies, refined and freed from all that was corruptible; and those who shall be then living will be changed and caught up to meet him in the air. He will then own them, approve and crown them before the assembled worlds. Every charge that can be brought against them will be overruled, and their plea, that they trusted in him for salvation, be admitted and ratified. They will be accepted and justified and he will be admired in and by them that believe.'

'If these things are so, 'what manner of or persons ought we to be in all holy conversation and godliness?' (2 Peter 3:11). Should we not 'give all diligence to make our calling and election sure' that we may be found of him in peace? Examine the foundation of your hope – and do it quickly, impartially and earnestly lest you should be cut off in an hour when you are not aware, and perish with a lie in your right hand' (Newton).

Messiah [35]   1 Corinthians 15:54-57   Death, swallowed in victory

Death is only one of many enemies that were defeated (1 Cor. 15:26).

Sin is destroyed. The entrance of sin was the beginning of the downfall (Rom. 5:12). Gen. 2:17 describes both its nature and result. Sin is disobedience, rebellion against the known will of God (1 John 3:4). The destruction of sin must therefore involve obedience. The perfect righteousness of Christ cancelled it out. If the power of sin is the law (15:56), then when Christ obeyed it, it lost its power. Death was robbed of its sting by the neutralisation of sin. The greater power of righteousness had ended its dominance and has thus established itself as the new operating principle in life of the believer.

Flesh is destroyed. Within human life, sin operates in the realm of the flesh. Its selfish appetites are directed away from God to personal satisfaction. Sin is expressed through the body and so has corrupted it. But for all who belong to Christ, a new body is provided like his (22-23, 45-49). This is the new body in which the new life principle dwells.

World is destroyed. Not only are all Adam's descendants affected by sin, but the world in which they live is affected by it also (Gen. 3:17; Rom. 8:20-21). The realm occupied by man is subjected to decay and will be destroyed (Ps. 102:25-26; 2 Peter 3:7). But it will be re-created and replaced by a new heaven and a new earth (2 Peter 3:12-13; Rev. 21:3-4). It will be repopulated by a perfected people who will possess a new body designed for this new environment.

Satan is destroyed. The force behind sin is Satan. He introduced it into the world and has utilised and increased it. But he is only a created being, unable to stand against the omnipotence of God. He was beaten on his own territory and driven out (John 12:31), by one who was sent there by God for that purpose (Heb. 2:14). He attempted to overthrow Christ but failed (John 14:30), and was condemned (16:11). His final doom is as certain as the universal recognition that Christ will receive as the real ruler (Rev. 20:10).

Death is destroyed. Although still at work on the lives of saved and unsaved alike, its power is broken. Physical death – the separation of body from soul affects all, but spiritual death – the separation of the soul from God on earth and eternal death – the separation of the soul from God for ever, does not affect believers. Because death could not hold onto to Christ (Acts 2:24), it cannot hold onto those who belong to him. His victory is complete, instantaneous, personal and irreversible and they will enjoy the benefits of it.

Messiah [36]   Romans 8:31-34   Divine support and protection

Messiah has taken us to the lofty heights of heaven with the ascended Christ and will do so again before the oratorio closes. But in the midst of the joyful consideration of our future hope, we are brought down to earth and reminded that the victory of Christ brings us much comfort in our current circumstances.

God will give us all things (31-32). The reality of life is that we are obstructed in the pursuit of our Christian testimony by those who stand against us. Some will do all they can to hinder our progress and although they may seem to gain some temporary success, these verses reassure us that they can cause us no lasting harm. The resources they may use against us are nothing compared with the might God can bring to our aid. God has already parted with his Son and sent him into an alien and hostile environment, knowing that he would be mocked and killed. He gave his all out of love for us, so that we could be redeemed. Having done that, he will not withhold any lesser provision that we might need to sustain us through this life until we reach glory.

God justifies us (33-34). Satan is also at work trying to undermine our faith in Christ. Sometimes he charges us directly with wrongdoing and whispers to us that what we have thought or said or done disqualifies us from being a child of God. Job 1, Zechariah 3 and Revelation 12:10 all refer to occasions when Satan made accusations against believers directly to God. In every accusation brought against us, the charges will not stick for God has already declared us righteous in Christ. Satan sees the sin and not the righteousness, but God sees the opposite. Satan dismisses the fact that each sin has been dealt with, but God takes it into account. He has already accepted the sacrifice of Christ on our behalf. He raised Christ from the dead as proof of his acceptance.

He was given the place of supreme authority and continues to speak to God on our behalf. As our advocate, he ensures that the benefits of his death are permanently effective. His merit is continually applied to us, even though our earthly experience may suggest its absence sometimes.

'This justification is authoritative, complete and final. It is an act of God's mercy, which, because founded upon the mediation of Christ, may, with no less truth, be styled an act of his justice … The right knowledge of this doctrine is a source of abiding joy; it likewise animates love, zeal, gratitude and all the noblest powers of the soul, and produces a habit of cheerful and successful obedience to the whole will of God' (Newton).

Something to do: Make lists of:

(a) those who are against you,

(b) the accusations Satan makes against you,

(c) the resources God has given you to neutralise the effect of them.

Readings on

The Atonement

by B Ventress

WINDOW
ON THE
WORD

Atonement [1]   Luke 24:13-53

The New Testament writers always place the cross right at the heart of the gospel. Paul, in fact, sums up his preaching in these words: 'We preach Christ crucified' (1 Cor. 1:23). In all their writing or preaching this same great truth is constantly emphasised, that Christ died once, and that there is no more sacrifice for sins. We are saved, not by some fine philosophy, nor by some flash of inspiration, and certainly not by anything we ourselves can do. We are saved by Christ's atoning death.

But how does the death of Jesus bring salvation to all his people? What sense can we make of that dreadful event at a place called Calvary nearly two thousand years ago? Our best guide, as always, is the Bible itself. Like the disciples in this passage, we need to see his death in the light of all the Scriptures that were written beforehand.

Luke's narrative captures a very important phase in the ministry of the Lord Jesus. He had taught his disciples many things during his time with them, but there were certain things which he told them they 'could not yet bear' (John 16:12). The ministry of the *risen* Lord must be seen as filling in those gaps.

Note the subject on which he instructs them (25-27,44-48). He opens their understanding so that they can see the nature of his death (as a substitute), the necessity of his death (because of sin) and the achievement of his death (redemption, acceptance with God, reconciliation with God).

It was because they failed to understand these things that the two on the Emmaus road were so dispirited. Only when Christ himself appeared to them and made it plain from the Old Testament that this had all been symbolised in the sacrifices and prophesied beforehand – only then did it begin to fit together and make sense. Their understanding, gained from this and other times spent with the risen Lord, later formed the foundation of all their teaching. This was their starting point (see Acts 17:2-3). This is where we, too, will start as we seek to understand the meaning of the Atonement.

Thought: Ours is not a dry technical subject, it is the very heart of the faith. Let us pray that our hearts also may burn within us as we discover Christ in all the Scriptures (32).

Atonement [2]   Genesis 4:1-16   Sacrifice [1]

'The Law of Moses', out of which the risen Saviour taught his disciples about himself, stands for the historical books of the Old Testament. It includes the whole range of sacrifices, priestly offerings and temple services, all of which find their fulfilment in the death of the Lord Jesus as the once-for-all sacrifice for sin.

Sacrifice is a term familiar enough to us today, but our use of it differs from that of the ancient Jews. We talk of making sacrifices when we do something at a cost to ourselves, for the benefit of others – for example, the financial sacrifices parents make so that their children obtain a good education. Cost is the central idea in our understanding of sacrifice.

While it is true that cost is an important factor in any sacrifice, that is not the whole story – much more is involved. Today's passage reveals something of what God regards as an acceptable sacrifice. At first glance, we might be tempted to feel sorry for Cain. Was it just his 'bad luck' that God preferred meat to vegetables? What made the difference between them? Verses 4-5 provide the clue. 'God respected (had regard to) Abel and his offering, but he did not respect Cain *and* his offering.' Notice, it was the person whom

God accepted first, and because Abel was acceptable, so too was his offering.

The New Testament sheds further light on the subject in Hebrews 11:4. Abel offered his lamb 'by faith'. Faith made it a more excellent sacrifice than that of Cain. That is not to say that the offering itself was unimportant – far from it. On what was Abel's faith acting when he sacrificed a lamb? If 'faith comes by hearing, and hearing by the word of God' (Rom. 10:17), then we must assume that God had revealed to early man that blood sacrifice was required of him. Also, if a slaughtered lamb best expressed Abel's feelings towards God then he must have felt that he had to make amends to God. There was some recognition that death is the way by which sin is removed. Cain's offering of the fruits of the earth did not take any account of sin. It merely offered to God the results of his own labours. It was as if Genesis 3 had never happened.

Thought: Even at this early stage in mankind's history it is clear that 'without the shedding of blood there is no remission of sins' (Heb. 9:22).

Atonement [3]   Genesis 22   Sacrifice [2]

Abraham is referred to in the New Testament as the man of faith, and no wonder! His faith had been stretched to the utmost when God promised that Sarah would bear him a son in her old age. In due time Isaac, the living proof of God's faithfulness, was born.

A command from God now tested that faith even further. It seemed utterly irrational. Offer up Isaac as a burnt offering! Was he now to destroy with his own hands the promised heir? This was against all reason. What of the promise? Abraham was to be the father of many nations and Isaac was his only son, his beloved son. Was the *command* of God to destroy the *promise* of God?

We must be clear that God did not ask Abraham to murder his son, but to offer him as a sacrifice, to offer him up totally and without reserve; a burnt offering. The lives of all sinful men are forfeit before God. He can require the death of any sinner, and Isaac's death was to be that of the firstborn – a pattern of the way God was to deal with the Egyptians at a later date. One was to die in the place of many.

Hebrews 11:17-19 informs us that Abraham offered Isaac by faith, a faith that rested on the promise of God. He trusted that even though he was about to sacrifice his one and only son, God was able to raise him from the dead. See how confident he was that both he and Isaac will return (5). He trusted in God alone and found all his hope in him. He had God's promise and for him that was enough. When Isaac asked, 'Where is the lamb for a burnt offering?' Abraham flung himself on the faithfulness of God. God would choose the lamb. What God required, he would provide.

Abraham's faith does not leave us wondering at the man but rather at God. God provided the sacrifice for Abraham. God, not Abraham, paid the price for *our* redemption. He 'did not spare his own Son but gave him up for us all' (Rom. 8:32). In fact, only God *could* pay the price, not ultimately in providing a ram or a lamb, but in sending his own Son as 'the Lamb of God who takes away the sin of the world' (John 1:29). God did what Abraham did not have to do. He made his Son an offering for sin.

Thought: Consider the remarkable obedience of Isaac throughout this incident. Does it remind you of someone? (See Philippians 2:8.)

Atonement [4]   Exodus 12   Sacrifice [3]

In the rite of the Passover we are introduced to a new aspect of sacrifice. Here, the blood is not only shed but applied. It is the application of the blood which is all important.

Israel were captive in a foreign land, reduced to slavery and crying out for help. God heard their cries and remembered his covenant with their forefathers (Exod. 2:23-25). This does not imply that he could ever forget his promises, but rather that he was about to act on the basis of these promises.

God began by sending signs and wonders as judgements on Pharaoh because he obstinately refused to let God's people go. After nine plagues, Pharaoh was still holding out against Moses' demands and now God was set to carry out the threat made in Exodus 4:22-23.

None of the other plagues had touched the Israelites, but now they and the whole Egyptian nation were to be made subject to the final stroke of God's justice. Every first-born in Egypt would die (Exod. 11:4-5), and unless they believed God and followed his directions in every detail, all the firstborn of Israel would also die.

On a day chosen by God a yearling lamb without defect was to be taken for each Israelite household, kept for four days and then killed (though not a bone of its body was to be broken). The blood was to be placed on the outer doorposts while its flesh was roasted, then eaten with herbs and unleavened bread. Everybody was to be dressed and ready for a journey. The angel of death would pass over and no death would plague those inside every house where the blood was seen. Passover night came and went. In the morning every single Egyptian household mourned the loss of a firstborn, while the Israelites began the exodus with everyone safe and well.

This ritual, marking the birth of the nation of Israel, was observed annually until the coming of Christ. It is very significant that Christ chose to die at Passover time; Jesus was himself the true Passover lamb. It was he who turned the Passover into the Lord's Supper (Luke 22:19-20). Of course, the ancient ritual did not really save – no ritual does – it was merely a stay of execution until he should come who was himself the first-born of the family of God (Col. 1:15,18). For him, there was no passing over. He was the lamb without blemish and in his death not one bone of his body was broken.

Thought: 'Christ our Passover has been sacrificed for us' (1 Cor. 5:7).

Atonement [5]   Leviticus 1   Sacrifice [4]

The book of Exodus emphasises the deliverance by God of his people from their cruel bondage. It was God's miraculous intervention that sent judgements on Egypt and set Israel free. God's purpose, however, was not simply to deliver Israel from Pharaoh's yoke. It was to bring them under *his* yoke. When the people reached Mount Sinai, God had a message for them (Exod. 19:4-6). They were to be God's holy nation. Leviticus spelt out for them how they were to be restored to fellowship with him.

A specific and detailed code of sacrifice was given by Moses, covering all gifts to the Lord. Allowance was made for the differing circumstances of each offerer so that everyone was able to offer *something* to the Lord. Whatever kind of offering was made it was intended to provide a ritual cleansing of sin, and it was to be completely voluntary (3).

To save getting bogged down in the sheer number and variety of the regulations it may be helpful to trace out some general points common to all the animal sacrifices.

1. The bringing near of the animal. Drawing near to the altar with the prescribed animal was a deliberate act of preparation for worship. It implied that there was a sense of need. The term is retained in the New Testament (Heb. 10:22) to describe the believer's approach to God.

2. The laying on of hands. The offerer was to lay his hands on the animal's head and confess his sins over it, so transferring his sins, figuratively, to the animal.

3. The killing of the animal. The animal became a sin-bearer and so it was slain by the offerer. The worshipper himself performed the act, which set forth the truth that he deserved death.

4. The sprinkling of blood. This was where the work of the priest began. The sprinkled blood was evidence that a life had been given.

5. Burning on the altar. Some part of the animal was always burnt on the altar. In the case of the whole burnt offering, the whole carcase was placed on the fire.

The message these sacrifices were intended to convey was the seriousness of sin and the necessity for its removal. Enshrined in every offering made was the principle of substitution, but their continual repetition clearly showed that the only substitute who could bear the weight of sin was yet to come.

Thought:

Not all the blood of beasts
On Jewish altars slain,
Could give the guilty conscience peace
Or wash away the stain.

(Isaac Watts)

Atonement [6]   Leviticus 16   Sacrifice [5]

The annual Day of Atonement was designed by God to impress upon Israel two important truths. On the one hand, they needed to realise that their guilt and defilement because of sin separated them from God. Of course, in one sense, he was present with them at all times; he was their God and they were his people. But as to approaching him and gaining access into his holy presence, that was a different matter. In fact, as Nadab and Abihu had discovered at the cost of their lives, it was a dangerous enterprise (10:1-2). Moses even had to warn Aaron the high priest to take care (2).

On the other hand, the ceremonies of that day taught that there was a way of access into God's presence, albeit once a year, through a representative and on God's terms. This entering in was to take place in the small, dark room within the tabernacle called the Holy of Holies. Even here, thick clouds of incense had to shroud the objects in the room from Aaron's view, not so much to conceal God, but to protect Aaron (13).

The main sacrifice was of the two goats, but before he began to deal with them, Aaron had to offer a sacrifice for himself and his family. Only then was he in a fit condition to conduct the next stage of the proceedings. In fact, at every stage there was either a washing or an offering prescribed, almost as if sin was a contagious disease and all contact with it had to be cleansed away.

The fact that there were two animals involved in one sacrifice expressed the complete putting away of sin. There were death and life in the one sacrifice: one animal was killed, the other was led alive into the wilderness. Two aspects of man's sin were represented: his guilt before God and his defilement. After the first goat was offered as a sin offering, the 'scapegoat' was brought to the high priest, who made a full confession of the nation's iniquities, transgressions and sins as he laid his hands on it. Now a sin-bearer, the animal was not fit to be put back among the flock, but was led into the desert and set loose, never to be seen again.

Here, therefore, in this one offering of the two goats, there were both atonement for sin and separation from sin; deliverance from its guilt in the sight of God and from its curse in life and character.

The Day of Atonement found its complete fulfilment at Calvary. There too, there were death and life in the sacrifice. On the cross, Christ went alive into the abyss of the wrath of God to experience all that sin-bearing meant. Only when he had finished the work of atonement did he lay down his life, and only then was the curtain of the temple torn in two, signifying that the way had been opened into the holiest place.

Thought: If Christ has taken our sins out of the way, are we too apt to remember what God forgets (our sins) and forget what he remembers (the cross) and thus hang back from entering into his presence?

Atonement [7]   Numbers 16:41-50   Propitiation

So far in our studies in the doctrine of the Atonement, we have seen that the notion of sacrifice was present in man from earliest times. It expressed his felt need for the removal of the guilt of sin. The sacrifice was made at some cost to the offerer, and to be acceptable to God it had to be made in faith.

God later made it clear on what basis he would deal with Israel's sin and guilt, by giving a code of offerings and sacrifices through Moses. Sacrifice was made, a life given, to cover the guilt and thus remove the cause of offence. In other words, the sacrifice made forgiveness possible because it made amends for the sin and thus removed it from the sight of God. It was blotted out. This effect of sacrifice is referred to by theologians as making expiation for sin.

There is another word which appears in the writings of the apostles Paul and John which gives a further aspect on the effect of sacrifice – propitiation. Regrettably, this word does not appear in the main text of some modern Bible versions and is translated, 'sacrifice of atonement'. The meaning conveyed by 'propitiation' is lost in this rendering. Propitiation means the turning away of anger. It is a personal word: one propitiates a person. This is clearly seen in Numbers 16:41-50.

Moses and Aaron had been confronted by two challenges to their God-given authority. One of these was a revolt led by Korah the Levite who took exception to the priesthood being confined to the sons of Aaron (3). The other was a revolt led by Dathan and Abiram who refused to obey Moses' summons (12). No doubt these struggles over authority were typical of many such. In each case the rebels were challenged to put the matter to the test and in each case the authority of Moses and Aaron was upheld, and God visited judgement on the rebels and their families.

Following the judgement, the troubles were not yet over, for the next day the people blamed Moses and Aaron for the deaths of the rebels and, in a hostile demonstration, gathered at the Tent of Meeting. The Lord told Moses and Aaron to withdraw so that he could consume the people by means of a plague. They both fell prostrate in intercession.

Moses commanded Aaron to run to the sanctuary to bring his censer which contained the fire and incense so that he might provide an atonement (covering) for the people against the judgement (plague) that had broken out. The plague was stopped as Aaron stood between the dead and the living (a beautiful picture of the greater than Aaron who was yet to come).

Because an atonement had been made, God's anger was turned away. The very fact that the plague stopped was evidence that God had accepted the sacrifice. What we must remember, of course, is that these offerings were but shadows and patterns. Behind them lay the notion which provides the basis for understanding the death of Christ. 'If any man sins, we have an advocate with the Father, Jesus Christ the Righteous, who is the propitiation for our sins ...' (1 John 2:1-2).

Atonement [8]   Exodus 6:2-9; 13:1-16   Redemption

In an earlier study we looked at the Passover in terms of the sacrifice of the lamb in place of the firstborn. The emphasis shifts slightly in these two passages. They portray the drama of the Passover as an act of redemption.

When God told Moses that he was about to deliver Israel from Egypt, he did so by announcing that the promises made to Abraham, Isaac and Jacob were about to be fulfilled. In fulfilling them he would reveal himself not just as God Almighty, but as Yahweh, their faithful, covenant-keeping God. The covenant he had made with the fathers included the promise that the land of Canaan was to become the possession of their descendants. That promise seemed a remote possibility while they were slaves in Egypt. What greater contradiction could there be than the circumstances in which they were living!

Yet these were the ideal circumstances for God to display his power on their behalf as he undertook to redeem them with 'an outstretched arm'. We are familiar in our day with liberation movements which engage in armed struggle in order to achieve their freedom. Moses, however, did not lead a slave revolt. Israel was not delivered through guerrilla warfare; it was God's miraculous intervention that judged Egypt and set Israel free. The whole narrative of the exodus has the purpose of showing that Israel's great deliverance was God's work. 'Salvation is of the Lord.' This same emphasis is reiterated in the New Testament: 'We have redemption through his blood, the forgiveness of sins, according to the riches of his grace which he made to abound toward us in all wisdom and prudence' (Eph. 1:7-8).

In Exodus 13, God reminded Israel of the purpose for which he was about to redeem them. He would release them from an alien land and bring them to freedom so that they could live as his people according to covenant promises. Redemption makes its claims on the redeemed people. 'Consecrate to me all the firstborn', says the Lord; that is, set apart as sacred to God the life that he had spared in Egypt on the night of the Passover. God demanded the firstborn, both of people and animals, for his own special service. He requires no less of us today in that as his redeemed people we are to 'present our bodies a living sacrifice, holy, acceptable to God, which is your reasonable service' (Rom. 12:1).

The firstborn animals were dedicated in sacrifice. The Levites were given into lifetime service to God as a substitute for Israel's firstborn. The total number of Levites was 22,000; the number of the firstborn was 22,273, a shortfall in Levites of 273. We might feel that the numbers were roughly equivalent, so why worry about the difference? However, particular individuals, not an approximate number, were redeemed by God. A payment of five shekels of silver was required for each one of the 273.

The Lord Jesus, likewise, came to save particular individuals. He knows them all by name and not one of them will be lost. They were all given to him before the foundation of the world, so that, when they are finally 'delivered from the bondage of corruption into the glorious liberty of the sons of God,' (Rom. 8:21), our Redeemer will be able to declare, 'Here am I and the children whom God has given me' (Heb. 2:13).

Atonement [9]   Isaiah 52:13 – 53:12   Obedience [1]

Sacrificial language is used to describe the work of the one called the servant in this passage, but clearly it is not a dumb animal who is the victim. On the contrary, Isaiah describes the suffering and death of one who *willingly* gave his life, and in doing so fulfilled the will of the Lord who sent him.

Suffering and glory combine in the work of the servant. One is but a prelude to the other; first his humiliation, then his exaltation. There is no doubt that his work will be successful and that God will greatly honour him (13), but the prospects of success seem very unlikely from first appearances. The servant would die – but his blood would 'sprinkle many nations'. In other words, the effects of his death would be experienced worldwide. The nations of the earth would hear what they had never previously been told. They would understand what they had never before heard. But how can this be? Who could believe that myriads of the world's population would be saved through the death of one man (53:1)!

Rather than draw back from this claim, however, Isaiah spells it out even more clearly and in such language that we feel we are ourselves witnesses of events.

The prophecy, of course, concerns Messiah, the one promised for so long.

Such a wonderful person we might expect would be universally welcomed, but vv. 1-3 tell us that unbelieving hearts gave him no such reception. He came to his own but his own did not receive him. He was 'despised and rejected'. Sadly, that is still the case today. He appears to the unbeliever to have no more strength than a frail plant shrivelled in the sun. So unattractive is he, that he is deemed worthy only of casting aside; so abhorrent, that men turn their faces from him.

By way of contrast, vv. 4-9 reverse the aspect. This is the response of faith. It must have stretched the understanding of his followers to see him stricken in this way, so much so that they concluded that divine punishment was being meted out to him. They came to see, however, that it was not his own, but their griefs and sorrows he bore. All Christ's sufferings relate to our sins, not his. Consequently, the burden of them was far greater than the physical pain. He was cut off from his Father's presence while he endured the wrath of God poured out on him. Quite literally, he endured hell for us.

Never mind the verdict of foolish men, it is the verdict of the Supreme Judge that counts; he has the final word. It was the Lord who inflicted judgement upon him as he became our sin-bearer. How does he judge the willing obedience of the servant in rendering himself as a guilt offering for the sins of his people (12)? He has rewarded him in a manner commensurate with his suffering (see Phil. 2:8-11).

How does the servant himself view his work (53:10-11)? To see the blessed result of his obedience, to know his mission accomplished, brings tremendous joy and satisfaction to the Saviour (see Hebrews 12:2).

Atonement [10]   Philippians 2:1-11   Obedience [2]

It is striking to see how the apostle Paul uses the loftiest teaching concerning the incarnation of Jesus, his perfect life and atoning death, to teach the most basic of Christian graces – humility. The reason why his humility shines out so clearly in all aspects of his life and death is that it was all done in perfect, willing obedience to the Father even though he was his equal (6).

Obedience was a vital element in his work. It was his meat and drink to do his Father's will. He did nothing from any other compulsion than love to his Father and to his people. Always, he was the 'beloved Son in whom the Father was well pleased'.

Consider his baptism. There he revealed his obedient heart: 'So it becomes us to fulfil all righteousness' (Matt. 3:15). This is what he came to do, as Paul implies in Galatians 4:4 – 'In the fullness of time God sent his Son, born of a woman, born under the law, to redeem those who were under the law.' In other words, he came to fulfil the law in all its provisions and bear the penalty of a broken law on our behalf. Throughout his life, he actively fulfilled every requirement of God's law.

Consider his death. In his death he laid down his life in payment of the penalty for our sin under the same law. He was in every sense a 'lamb without blemish and without spot' – the sinless sacrifice. There was a value to his death, a worth beyond telling as the writer to the Hebrews insists (see Hebrews 9:13-14).

In the Hebrews epistle we read 'he *learned* obedience through the things which he suffered' (Heb. 5:8). But if he 'existed in the form of God and did not regard equality with God a thing to be grasped' (6, NASB), how could he *learn* anything? He learned it in that he had never before experienced suffering in a body like ours subject to the limitations of flesh and blood and supported only by that which was available to him as a man. He did not employ the divine power that was his by right. He laid that aside in order to identify fully with his sinful, suffering people. He 'emptied himself' of all the paraphernalia of glory that belonged to him as Son of God and became obedient to the point of death, even death on a cross (that is, not just death, but death as if he were a sinner himself).

It is important to realise that his obedience does not merely remove our guilt. What would be the effect if God only removed our guilt? We would be pardoned but still not restored to a right relation with God. Jesus died, 'the just for the unjust, *to bring us to God*' (1 Peter 3:18). Our Lamb of God, whose blood is far more precious than silver or gold, not only paid the penalty for our sins by his sinless sacrifice, he also purchased a righteousness for us through his obedience; a righteousness in which we can stand before God and be accepted. 'My Saviour's obedience and blood hides all my transgressions from view.'

This perfect obedience of our Saviour will not go unrewarded (9-11). It may still go unnoticed by many, but one day, in one way or another *every tongue* will be compelled to confess his glory. Even those who now oppose him will see his glory, but whereas those who await his appearing with longing will rejoice at the sight, unbelievers will want to hide from his face (Rev. 6:16). Let us be those who confess him now, and then we can be glad at his coming.

Atonement [11]   Mark 8:27-33; 9:1,30-32
Its disclosure in the life of Jesus [1]

We could study many passages in the Gospels and trace the gradual unfolding of the mission of Jesus. This particular incident, however, captures many of the points we would find in such a study.

As we read the Gospel accounts of the gradual disclosure by the Lord Jesus of his impending sufferings, death and resurrection, it becomes clear that the disciples were far from understanding the work he had come to do. We sense their frustration at his statements which, though intended to enlighten them, in fact left them bewildered. It is easy from our view of events to feel that these men were more 'slow of heart' than we would have been.

Notice that the background against which the Lord made the disclosure of v. 33 is the confession of Peter in v. 29, 'You are the Christ.' Peter was absolutely right, of course, but Jesus avoided any public acclamation of himself as Messiah in case his friends sought to have him crowned as king, or his enemies acted to silence him before God's timetable of events was fulfilled.

Instead, the emphasis that the Saviour made in his response to Peter, and then repeatedly to his disciples, was that of the suffering servant which we saw in Isaiah 53. In their hope of a coming Messiah the Jews had consistently ignored this emphasis. It was not lost, however, on a particular individual who was an unseen witness to his words. Satan would suggest an easier way, but not directly himself. It was Peter who actually insisted that Jesus should follow a way that would thwart the purpose of God to redeem sinners (33).

We are not to understand that Peter was devil-possessed; rather that the source of every error is the malicious enemy of souls. His suggestions can sound so reasonable, so humane and caring (as in this case), but at heart they are lies aimed at preventing and undoing God's work. As Jesus later revealed to the two on the road to Emmaus, 'Christ needed to have suffered.' It was an essential part of his mission. His path to glory could only be one of suffering as the sin-bearer. He, and he alone, could bear that awful load and take the sting out of death for us.

Jesus added a sombre warning to those who would follow him, that they too must be prepared for the same treatment (34). His disciples, whether then or now, must count the cost. If the price seems too high, just consider the cost of refusing to follow him – the loss of your soul. Even gaining the whole world could not compensate for that.

Atonement [12] Mark 10:32-45
Its disclosure in the life of Jesus [2]

During his last journey to Jerusalem, the Lord Jesus took his disciples to one side and again told them of the certainty of his death. While he was doing so, Salome and her sons, James and John, approached him with an ambitious request (35,37).

It was a rude interruption to his discourse, based on an entirely false notion of how the kingdom of heaven operated. Jesus did not let it go unchallenged and his response was masterful. While making it clear to them on what grounds the chief places would be decided he also skilfully led the conversation back to the subject of his death. Eminence in the kingdom of heaven is based on 'true lowliness of heart, which takes the humbler part'. Of this spirit, he is the great example. He did not come so that he could be served, but to render loving service to others, a service they could not possibly perform for themselves. He came 'to give his life a ransom for many' (45).

Almost incidentally then, Jesus unfolded something more of the significance of his sufferings and death. In Mark 8 he limited himself to stating that he would suffer and die. He now added that his death would be in the place of others. Of his own will the Son of Man came to give up his life (literally 'soul'). That life was to be the ransom price 'for many' – in the room, or place, of many. In unmistakable language Jesus was stating that his death was to be vicarious – in the place of others.

Immediately we recognise the idea of substitution, we are back with the Old Testament sacrifices. Although they may not have recognised the import of his words, Jesus was telling his disciples that he came to be a sacrifice in place of others. God would lay the guilt of their sin upon him. In his life and death he would be their substitute, paying the price demanded by divine justice to secure their release from captivity.

We do not do justice to our Lord's words in v.45 if we merely say that his death was for the good of others, in some vague, indefinite sense. The same might be said of any apostle or martyr. But if language is to mean anything, his words can only carry the meaning that in giving his life, Jesus came to provide the death which justice demanded and, in doing so, to free others by taking the punishment upon himself.

'For *many*' becomes 'for *us*' in 2 Corinthians 5:21 and Galatians 3:13, and 'for *me*' in Galatians 2:20. Can you say that?

Atonement [13]   Hebrews 10:1-25   The better sacrifice

Nowhere else in the New Testament is the superiority of Christ's sacrifice explained more clearly than in the Epistle to the Hebrews. The writer draws the contrast between the shadows of Old Testament ritual and priesthood and the reality and substance of Christ's once-for-all offering of himself. The shadows did not deal with sin in itself, nor with the guilt in the consciences of men. The offerer could never rest from making sacrifices but must repeat them over and over again (1-4).

Christ's offering fulfilled everything to which the animal sacrifices pointed. God had only ever regarded them as a foreshadowing of the sacrifice of his Son, and thus had been prepared to accept those who offered them in faith. For those who had spiritual sight to see, the psalms indicated this truth (see Psalm 40, quoted in vv. 5-7). It was always God's intention and will that believers should be 'sanctified through the offering of the body of Jesus once for all' (10). His sacrifice does take away sin and sanctifies those who come to God through him.

Just as in the annual Day of Atonement the actual act of atonement was not completed until the high priest had entered the holy place with the blood and the sacrifice was accepted, so too the Lord Jesus had to present his offering (9:24-28). As the result of his one completed offering and as evidence that his work has found complete acceptance with God, Christ is now exalted to the heavenly throne, at God's right hand. Note, he is *seated* there. His work of sacrifice is *finished* (12). There is then, no more need of offerings for sin, since God declares that the sin which Christ has dealt with is remembered no more (17).

The quotation from Jeremiah 31, setting out the terms of the New Covenant, reminds us that the new birth is also something which comes to us as a fruit of his sacrifice: a new start with God; a new heart from God; sin finally dealt with. No wonder the exhortation in v. 19 encourages believers to have boldness to enter into the very presence of God! This is not brash self-confidence, it is the full assurance of faith. The way is 'new' in contrast to the old sacrifices, and 'living' as distinct from lifeless rituals of the past. Jesus Christ is a living high priest and the effectiveness of his self-offering continues forever.

It is our own fault if we remain at a distance from our heavenly Father, and when as Christians we do so we are not only missing the joy and blessing of being in his presence, we are also showing contempt for the privilege which was bought for us at so great a cost. Access to God is linked to fellowship with God's people (25). It is our privilege as God's people to draw near to him together to enjoy the reality of a living relationship with our heavenly Father through our Lord Jesus Christ by his Holy Spirit. It is the glorious fruit of his atonement.

Readings on

Jesus:
greater than …

by Ray Tibbs

**WINDOW
ON THE
WORD**

Matthew 1:22-23; Hebrews 1:1-3

Matthew frequently quoted from the prophets and that is an indication he wrote primarily for Jewish readers.

God has spoken directly in Jesus Christ. Prophets were intermediaries, men chosen by God to convey his word primarily to their own generation. Their work was limited and preparatory, concerned mainly with what is now the past. The words of some prophets were preserved in writing and now form part of the Scriptures. They speak of God's dealings with his people and anticipated one greater than themselves (Deut. 18:18; John 1:21; 7:40; 2 Peter 1:19-21).

Jesus is no less than God himself speaking directly to his people. He came into the world to deliver his own word personally. But more than that, he personifies that word. The messenger is also the message (John 1:1,2,14). He is more than an ambassador from heaven. He said what he knew to be true and, even though on earth, he retained direct contact with his Father (John 12:49). His coming introduced a new era in which God would be in direct communication with man, without needing an intermediary (Jer. 31:33-34). Because of who he is, he addresses the present and the future and not in relation to a single nation but to the whole world order across time. He encompasses both the beginning and end of all things (Col. 1:16c). All will be rightfully his one day as he restores Adam's lost dominion.

God has spoken fully in Jesus Christ. Prophets were numerous and temporary, each

Jesus: greater than the prophets

being replaced by others. They addressed their own circumstances and received and delivered their messages in various ways.

Jesus made a single, cohesive and complete presentation of himself as the only true and glorious God. His greatness is not reflected or reduced by his incarnation. Within himself he possesses the fullness of God's complete character and is totally involved in all of life. He is not merely present within it, he actively maintains it. He provides coherence and meaning both to world events and individual lives. The constant movement in both those areas are not random, but are being purposefully directed to a glorious conclusion (Phil. 2:9-11).

God has spoken relevantly in Jesus Christ. The essential message of the prophets was to turn people back to God, but it rarely happened.

Jesus does not simply urge people to turn back to God, he accomplishes it. Because of who he is, he says and does what prophets could not. He puts away sin by the sacrifice of himself (Heb. 9:26-28), and provides cleansing from its pollution. He removes God's righteous indignation from us and makes us acceptable to him. He secures our peace with God and our place in glory. He is now seated in heaven, because he has been restored to his rightful place after his work was completed. All – including prophets – must appear before him one day (2 Cor. 5:10), and some will share the inheritance he has prepared for them (Rom. 8:17).

Hebrews 1:4 – 2:9; Matthew 1:18-25   Jesus: greater than angels

Considerable angelic activity is recorded around the birth of Jesus (Luke 1:8-20,26-38; 2:8-15). Angels are spirit beings which were created by God and cannot die (Luke 20:36). They are referred to as masculine and do not marry (Mark 12:25). They are numerous and reside in heaven (Matt. 26:53). They are wise (2 Sam. 14:20), and powerful (Acts 12:7).

Jesus has a better name than angels (4-5). He is the Son of God, not simply a messenger of God. As the second person of the Trinity, he was always greater then angels, but when he became man, he entered an order of creation that was lower than angels (Ps. 8:4-8). Then, after completing the work God gave him to do, he was raised from the dead and ascended to heaven. From that point, Jesus was declared to be the Son (Rom. 1:4), even though he retained his humanity. So as the God/man, he became superior to angels because the name he had before – Son – was still rightfully his.

Jesus is worshipped by angels (6). No creature can worship another creature. This verse may refer to the Second Coming when his final victory is seen by all. If it refers to the incarnation, angels are invited to worship him because the plan of salvation entered its final, critical stage and was therefore certain to be completed. They had been anticipating it (1 Peter 1:12).

Jesus has a higher service than angels (7-9). Angels were created by decree and could be used by God for any purpose at any time. They had a temporary function. Jesus is addressed as God and cannot change. He

has a permanent kingdom over which he exercises a righteous rule and a consistently holy character. He was rewarded for his perfect obedience by permanent exaltation to the highest place in heaven. None of that applied to angels.

Jesus has an independent existence (10-12). Jesus is dependent upon no one, but angels are dependent upon him. He remains in authority in a Creator/creature relationship.

Jesus has higher honour (13-14). Angels are called upon to serve those who are being saved, but Jesus is the author of their salvation and is exalted for that reason.

The message of Jesus is more important (2:1-4). Angelic messengers were to be heeded because they had been sent from God with an important message. The message brought by Jesus was announced by none other than the Son of God himself, and dealt with a greater subject, salvation. He was testified to directly by God (2 Peter 1:16-18), and was later confirmed by the apostolic testimony (1 John 1:1-4).

Jesus will rule the world to come (5-9). Man, not angels, was originally given dominion over the whole created order. The entrance of sin into the world rendered him incapable of fulfilling that mandate. It will be fulfilled in and through Jesus Christ. He was made a little lower than the angels temporarily and as a result will receive the supreme position of lordship as the man who is God. He will carry redeemed mankind to that position with him in the world to come (2 Tim. 2:11-12).

Hebrews 6:14 – 8:2   Jesus: greater than Melchizedek

The priesthood. The priesthood was established by God (5:4). A priest was man's representative before God. As sinners, the people of God needed, but did not have access to, God and a mediator was required. Reconciliation between man and God could only be effected through the removal of sin by punishment, so that divine justice was satisfied. This could be done by the death of a substitute, not the guilty party (Lev. 17:11). The priest offered sacrifices on behalf of others as well as for himself (Heb. 5:3). The victim was specified: a lamb free from blemish (Lev. 22:20-25), and had to be presented by the guilty party. Its blood was sprinkled on the altar. God specified not only the means of atonement but also the victim and the priest. Prayer was offered at the same time and so sacrifices were accompanied by the burning of incense signifying the expectation of a heavenly response to an earthly event (Lev. 16:12-13).

The priesthood of Melchizedek. Melchizedek appears early in biblical history (Gen. 14:18) and was appointed by God in secret. He had the unique privilege of being a royal priest, which, although expressly forbidden to the kings of Israel, was part of the Messianic expectation (Zech. 6:13). Melchizedek was greater than Abraham, for the latter gave a tithe to him (Gen. 14:19-20). His sudden brief appearance with no recorded ancestry or descendants endowed him and his office with a sense of perfection and permanence (Heb. 7:3,17-18). He was held up as a model of the priesthood, in contrast to the failures of the Aaronic line, much as David was held up as a model for kingship, in contrast to later failures in his own line.

The priesthood of Jesus Christ. God appointed Jesus to be high priest (Heb. 5:5-6) and this was confirmed by his oath (7:20-22), made public by its record in Scripture (6:13-20). Uniquely, Jesus offered himself as the sacrifice for sin (7:26-27; Eph. 5:2), which by virtue of his identity – the eternal Son of God – became a permanent offering. He was, therefore, a far greater priest than even Melchizedek (7:11-16,24). He offers prayer, as the priests did, and by the power of his indestructible life is able to do so continually (7:25). He continues to act as our priest while in heaven (1 John 2:1-2). He stands in the presence of God as the permanent guarantee of our redemption. He is our advocate against Satan's accusations (Rom. 8:34), pleading our case on the basis of his sacrifice. Because our salvation is all of grace and secured entirely by the completed work of Christ, it is perfectly secure and should be a source of great encouragement and real hope for us (6:18). God will never go back on his word and Christ can never withdraw the sacrifice he offered. It is complete and never in doubt, for nothing can be added to it (10:19-25).

John 8:31-59   Jesus: greater than Abraham

Abraham was the founding father of the Jewish nation (Gen. 12:1-3), through the covenant God established with him. His descendants enjoyed the great privileges of being the people of God. The critics of Jesus were asking what he had to offer compared with Abraham. Jesus replied:

Freedom (31-36). The Jews said even though they endured political bondage, they had retained their religious freedom. They were proud of their religious heritage which could be traced back to Abraham. They preserved their national identity and were free from destructive external influences.

Jesus said they were not free from the grip of sin. Abraham was a slave to it himself, and only the Son of God could break that yoke. Jesus is not subject to it and can bring the same freedom to others. It is not a freedom to do anything, but a freedom to live according to the Sonship of Christ – by and in his authority (Gal. 4:4-6; Rom. 6:11-12).

Obedience (37-47). Jesus continued to press his case by exposing how unlike Abraham the Jews were. Knowing their hearts, he said they were planning to kill him, even though he was God's messenger. Abraham would never have done that. If some of the tests of childhood were applied, it was evident that they belonged to Satan, rather than to Abraham. Children resemble their father in character and appearance. Children respond to the example and instructions of their father. Children have a natural bonding with their father, despite differences in age, etc. The Jews should have believed and acted upon the message from God, as Abraham did (Gal. 3:6-7). They were not obedient as he was. Jesus was not only perfectly obedient to his heavenly Father (46), but he would make over that righteousness to anyone who trusted in him (Rom. 5:19). In addition, by the power of the Holy Spirit indwelling those people, he would enable them to achieve a greater level of that obedience for themselves (1 John 3:21-24).

Life (48-53). Abraham was dead and all his descendants were subject to the same mortality. Abraham could do nothing to change that, but Jesus can. He has both the power to live beyond death (John 10:17-18), and the power to prevent death from having a permanent grip on those who trust him (John 1:4; 17:2). He is both the source and the giver of everlasting life (John 11:25-26), and it is received now by the believer through the same Holy Spirit (John 3:5-8).

Joy (54-59). Abraham looked ahead with joy at the prospect of the coming Messiah, not only for himself, but recognising in him, God's goodness to so many. Many of his descendants had the same joyful expectation. But when he came, instead of receiving him with joy, they were ready to kill him. The joy of Jesus is mentioned in Hebrews 12:2. We are told he felt it while he was on earth and it was partly that which sustained and motivated him to face death. The object of his joy is likely to be the completion of his work and the resumption of his place at his Fathers' side. There is great joy for us as we see God's promise kept, God's Son revealed and God's grace received. Our joy is in the enjoyment of Christ now and then forever (1 Peter 1:8-9).

John 4:1-26   Jesus: greater than Jacob

Jesus is a greater person. Jacob became great because he was made so by God. He was the undeserving, deceitful, younger brother, who was chosen in preference to Esau (Mal. 1:2-3). He was renamed (Gen. 32:28) and the nation of his descendants took its name from him, as God established his covenant with him (Gen. 35:10-12).

Jesus was always great. At his coming, he was announced as the Son of God (Luke 1:32-33) and although his greatness was not evident during his lifetime, it was real (Phil. 2:6-11). Even now it is not yet evident to all, but one day it will be quite unmistakable (Acts 17:31).

Jesus gives a greater gift. Jacob's well was his own possession. It was a useful, valuable and a loving gift for his posterity which had been preserved for about 1,700 years, but it had cost him nothing.

Referring to himself spiritually rather than physically, the gift of Jesus as the living water, was his own person (John 1:4; 5:26). He gave up his own life for the good of others

(John 10:11; 15:23; Gal. 2:20). Not only did he give himself for others, he gave himself to them so that they benefit from him directly and not just from his act of giving.

Jesus brings a greater benefit. Jacob's gift was limited because the well could run dry and it could not prevent a recurring thirst. Thus, it could not meet every need.

The gift of Jesus is unlimited because the life he gives is permanent and eternal. He provides a never-ending supply because he is its infinite source. The life he gives is fully satisfying because it lasts beyond the here and now. It is not temporal but all embracing; substantial rather than superficial.

The greater the giver, the greater the gift that comes from him and the greater the results that will come from the gift. The gift is valued even more when it is earmarked for us personally. Do you have a soul thirst? If so, there is only one place to find lasting satisfaction. We come to him in faith (John 6:40).

Hebrews 3:1-6   Jesus: greater than Moses

Moses was faithful in all God's house (2). A house is a dwelling place and God lived among his people. Moses led God's people out of Egypt at his command (Exod. 3:10,12). He delivered God's Word to them (Exod. 19:3-7), and ensured the national life was organised around it. His role was temporary, preparing for someone greater to come. So much of what he established pointed to Christ (John 5:46; 1 Cor. 5:7). He was declared faithful by God (Num. 12:7).

Moses was a servant in God's house (5). Moses himself was subject to God. He was part of the house he served. He served well. His appointed tasks were done correctly, at the right time and in the right spirit. He was trusted with an important job. He was not a slave and so he carried out his tasks, not with a sense of duty but affection. He willingly served, not just because God told him to but also because he knew his service would benefit his own people. But however faithful his service was, it was flawed (Num. 20:12).

Jesus was faithful to the one who appointed him (2). The faithfulness of Christ is flawless and he remains active. We are exhorted to consider him still. He is described as an apostle: one who was from God with the authority of the Sender. He is also described as a high priest: the only one able to offer an acceptable sacrifice to God on behalf of his people. From the beginning, Jesus always kept his Father in view, and that is why he was able to complete the work he was given (Luke 2:49; John 4:34; 12:49; 14:31; Matt. 26:39).

Jesus is a servant over God's house (6). The house does not just belong to God, it was actively created by him, through the death of Christ. It was built and furnished by him. Because of his relationship with the Father, Jesus has been made its Lord. Through redemption, the house is being built with living stones (1 Peter 2:4-5).

The writer was making an appeal to consider Christ rather than Moses. Why settle your attention on the lesser – one under authority – when you can fill you mind with the greater – the one in authority? We are as much a part of the house as Moses was and his example can give us inspiration in our service, as long as we remember that only Christ can give us ability, through the Holy Spirit. Only by looking in faith to the person of Christ will we find the courage to persevere in the face of the difficulties before us. A constant consideration of his accomplishments and promises will enable us to maintain a firm grasp on the hope we have of being with him in glory forever. We must not allow ourselves to be distracted by anything or anyone of lesser significance.

Hebrews 4:14 – 5:10   Jesus: greater than Aaron

Aaron was appointed by God (5:1,4). No high priest was self-appointed. The responsibility was too weighty. God chose Aaron (Exod. 28:1) and later confirmed it publicly at a time of crisis (Num. 17:8). Aaron's descendants, from the tribe of Levi, were set apart as priests.

Aaron was identified with other men (2). Aaron was chosen from among men so that he could represent them to God. He stood with them, being in as much need as everyone else. His calling did not suggest he was better than others. He was conscious of his weakness and that fellow feeling gave him a constraint to act humbly on behalf of his people. His life was devoted to standing before God on behalf of men. It was not the other way round. It was the prophets' task to stand before men on behalf of God. Aaron had no other interest. He did not own any land (Josh. 13:33), and he could not become a farmer or a merchant.

Aaron offered sacrifices for men (1,3). A primary part of his duty was to offer sacrifices on behalf of the people to atone for their sin. But first, he had to make a sacrifice for himself so a cleansed person could offer sacrifices on behalf of those who were still unclean (Lev. 9:5-7).

Jesus was appointed by God (5-6). The second person of the Trinity was given a commission before he came to earth. God had chosen his eternal Son to enter human existence through the work of the Holy Spirit in the body of Mary. Although their relationship was unchanged, it became defined by human terminology because that was the realm in which it would be experienced and understood. Melchizedek pre-dated Aaron and was not of the tribe of Levi. He also foreshadowed Jesus but in different ways from Aaron.

Jesus was identified with mankind (7-8). Having been born as a man, Jesus identified himself with humanity as fully as possible. He stood where they stood as he felt the frailty of the human body. He kept God's law and he was baptised by John. He experienced the need to be dependent upon God for his natural and spiritual life. His prayers in Gethsemane showed his need to know and yield to the will of God. He had to learn obedience, not because he was rebellious but because it was an integral part of the human experience that needed to be discovered (Luke 2:46,52).

Jesus offered one sacrifice for mankind (9). His task was to offer a sacrifice that would cleanse men from their sin. But he was not only the high priest, he was also the sacrifice. So the sinless Son of God offered himself on behalf of sinful men. 'God made him who had no sin to be sin for us, so that in him we might become the righteousness of God' (2 Cor. 5:21).

Because Jesus is our great high priest, we can 'hold firmly to the faith we profess' (14) and 'approach the throne of grace with confidence' (16).

1 Kings 10:1-13; Matthew 12:42   Jesus: greater than Solomon

The point of comparison that Jesus made was that of wisdom.

The wisdom of Jesus is complete. Solomon's wisdom was a divine gift (1 Kings 3:7-10) and was given in relation to the task of ruling God's people. Solomon had all he needed and more, as the Queen of Sheba found, but he did not have everything. His wisdom was limited by providence, capacity and need.

The wisdom of Jesus is total and innate. He possesses it because of who he is rather than because of what he did (Col. 2:3). Nothing is hidden from him: the heart of man (John 2:24-25), eternal life (John 6:68), the knowledge of God (Luke 10:22), the way to God (John 14:6).

The wisdom of Jesus is available. The Queen of Sheba covered many miles to visit Solomon on the basis of rumour. After his death some of his wisdom died with him and was lost to most people, although some remains in Scripture and continues to be of benefit.

Jesus is alive still and can communicate his wisdom directly to us through the influence of the indwelling Holy Spirit (John 14:26). We need only ask (James 1:5). The queen made a very astute observation in v. 8. Perhaps it was borne out hundreds of years later when the descendants of that group of men still retained their unique identity (Ezra 2:55). Were they distinguished and preserved because of their wisdom? Certainly, those who keep closest to the King of kings will be his wisest servants.

The wisdom of Jesus is influential. The queen had to leave, her curiosity satisfied (13). She gained materially from her visit but, having heard Solomon, hopefully she became a better ruler also. But however impressive Solomon's wisdom was, it deserted him (1 Kings 11:1-4) and its benefits were short-lived.

The wisdom of Jesus is unlimited and continues to help multitudes of people across all nations, as it has for generations. But Jesus does not simply possess wisdom. He embodies it (1 Cor. 1:24). He does more than teach it and exemplify it. He conveys it. He is the core of significance around which all of creation revolves – our lives included (Col. 1:17). He has been made over to us (1 Cor. 1:30), not so that we become infinitely wise individually, but so that we share in that great wisdom by which the universe is governed. That wisdom is found in his building of his people (Eph. 2:22) and his ruling his people (Eph. 1:22). The direct influence of that wisdom is brought to bear upon our lives personally as we live spiritually in an environment characterised by that wisdom (Eph. 5:15-17). So much human endeavour is employed in the pursuit of wisdom. Jesus warned of the just condemnation of those who sought it anywhere else apart from him (Ps. 111:10).

Jonah 1-3; Matthew 12:38-41   Jesus: greater than Jonah

There was a real experience. When Jonah was thrown out of the boat, he could not have expected anything else but death. Even in the belly of the fish, at first he expected to die. He described himself as being in the place of the dead (2:2), where the process of corruption had already begun (2:6).

The experience of Jesus was described in a similar way (Acts 2:27), but his was a real death.

There was a judicial experience. Jonah knew the storm was a result of his disobedience and that he had to be punished (Jonah 1:12,15), but the fate of sailors was bound up with his. He could have jumped overboard, but the sailors had to recognise where the guilt lay and offered up Jonah so that they would not suffer as 'innocent' bystanders. Because Jonah 'died', others were saved.

Jesus was never disobedient (Heb. 4:15). He offered himself to calm the wrath of God as a result of the sin of others (Heb. 7:27). Because Jesus died, multitudes are saved.

There was an inaugural experience. Both cases referred to the temporary nature of their state of death and the prospect of removal from it. Both men were given their life back again, although Jonah's experience was only a pale reflection of that of Jesus. Jonah entered a new life of obedience and service. For Jesus, his work was finished (John 19:30) and he entered a new position at the Father's side as Lord and Christ (Acts 2:36).

There was an influential experience. In addition to his message, Jonah's experience was a sign to the Ninevites (Luke 11:30). He was a living illustration of the mercy of God. The threat was real, but so was their hope. The experience of Jesus provided more than an illustration. It is the means by which salvation is conveyed. To experience the mercy of God, we must participate in both (Rom. 6:5).

There was a vital experience. The point Jesus made was that the people of Nineveh, who were Gentiles, repented when faced with comparatively little evidence. The Jews, when faced with the Son of God, the Messiah to whom all their history and Scriptures pointed, refused to believe. Without the ministry of Jonah there would have been no salvation for Nineveh. Without the death and resurrection of Jesus, there is no salvation for anyone in the world – Jew or Gentile.

Matthew 11:7-15   Greater than John the Baptist

Jesus is unquestionably greater than John the Baptist. The whole point of the ministry of the latter was to demonstrate that. But Jesus makes surprising statements about him.

More than a prophet (9). Prophets delivered the Word of God primarily to the people of God. They gave both promises and warnings and often predicted events to draw attention to the work of God. As well as being a prophet, John was also the fulfilment of prophecy. He was instrumental in the realisation of the coming of the Messiah. He was involved in bringing it to pass. Not only did he anticipate the ministry of Christ as others did, he shared in it, in a way that no other prophet could. He bore witness to the stupendous truth by experience, not by expectation.

None greater than John (11). Jesus declared John to be greater than Abraham, Moses and David. He was greater than Alexander, Sophocles and Julius Caesar. His greatness could be seen in various ways. We have seen that his coming was predicted and his ministry had a huge strategic significance. His birth was miraculous and his endowment with the Holy Spirit was exceptional (Luke 1:15). He was unfailingly obedient to his call from God. His ministerial influence was considerable in awakening people to their need of Christ and directing them to him. His godly character demonstrated tenacity and integrity. A man of strong convictions, he was uncompromising without being abrasive. His knowledge of Christ was unequalled and he exemplified a selflessness and other worldliness that showed the coming kingdom was not of this world.

The least in the kingdom is greater than John (11). The astounding conclusion Jesus makes at the end of his high commendation of John, is to say that his most insignificant follower is greater than John. Although John may have been great in his character, gifts and service for God, our knowledge and experience of Christ is greater than his. We know Jesus crucified, risen, ascended and glorified which he did not. We possess the completed revelation of the Word of God which he did not (1 Peter 1:10-12). By the indwelling Spirit, we can testify to our personal salvation in Christ and give evidence of his transforming power. We can share in the fellowship of the worldwide church of God and be used by him to help spread the gospel far and wide.

We have great privileges which should not be underestimated (Matt. 13:17; Luke 10:23-24). Therefore, we should not allow ourselves to be intimidated by the world or discouraged by doubts. If we are part of his kingdom, however insignificant we may feel, we can still show our allegiance to our King by our devotion to him and our obedience to his laws and help to support and defend his people.

Readings on

Encouragement

by Philip Slater

WINDOW
ON THE
WORD

1 Samuel 27:1-7; 29:1 – 30:20   Encouragement in God (30:6b)

Following Christ is not always easy. In this passage we see the difficulties experienced by David. Although the details might be different, believers are often troubled almost to the point of despair.

The context of David's despair. David, a man after God's own heart, was brought low in extreme circumstances. After David had slaughtered many Philistines (18:8), and dancing women in streets had acclaimed him superior to Saul (29:5), he felt his life in danger.

On the run from Saul (27:1-2), he fled to the Philistine king, Achish. Achish was well pleased with David and gave him Ziklag for him and troops to dwell in (27:5-6). David went to war against Israel in support of the Philistines (29:1-2) who didn't trust him. That gave him a way of escape so that he reluctantly returned to Ziklag (11). He found the city burned and families taken into captivity (30:3). David and his troops were so overwhelmed that his troops turned against him (4,6).

David the man of God in despair. David was not perfect, as well-documented failures testify. But, like Lot, he was 'just', that is, the general tenor of his life was God-ward. David panicked and took matters into own hands (27:1-2), having no divine mandate for his action. His force of 600 men had not increased. He was depressed and fearful of Saul and so he fled for his life. He failed to remember he was the designated king of Israel by divine appointment and therefore safe. By his hasty actions he became a stranger in a strange land and lost everything. By not remaining in Israel, he made things worse for himself.

The bitter medicine he had to take was made palatable by accompanying grace when later God mercifully restored him (30:18-20).

How can we be encouraged today by learning of David's recourse to God?

1. David's mistake didn't cause God to forsake him (30:7-8). We may think our failings are serious enough to be fatal, but see Hebrews 13:5b.

2. David shared Moses' lot of being threatened with stoning (Exod.17:4). Even the apostles of Christ 'forsook him and fled', as may our friends.

3. David, when in distress, was encouraged (30:6b, NIV 'found strength') in God. How?

(i) He remembered Jehovah (8a).

(ii) He drew comfort and support from God's historical dealings with the nation.

(iii) He thought about God's personal dealings with him – Goliath, Saul (6c), the Lord his God.

(iv) He recalled the promises of God. When encouraged he sought God (8a) and obeyed his word (8b,9,10a) thus proving the Word of God (8c; 18-20).

4. When we 'have no more power to weep' (4b) our encouragement must be in the living God even when we know 'fightings without and fears within'.

5. We must resist the fatalistic idea that if God allows an event it must be of him. David was allowed to flee to Gath but his rightful place was within his future kingdom. God may allow us our own way so as to discipline us in his training school.

Psalm 107   The soul's satisfaction in God (v. 9)

Job 23 tells of Job longing for God and indicating in his affliction he could not find him. However, he acknowledged God knew the way he took and would bring him to a satisfactory end. God satisfies the longing soul. God abundantly fills the souls of those who seek him in loving pursuit. He fills our soul with all the goodness laid up in Christ. These are comforting words but a challenge to the intensity of our yearnings. Often our love is weak and faint and our appetite dulled. The truth of a verse can be fixed in our mind but not experienced in our heart.

Spiritual reality. Solomon's survey of life led him to conclude that the best mercies of common grace were vanity, and only spiritual reality was of true worth. The Spirit-stirred soul realises the emptiness of everything apart from what is spiritual. Life's best pleasures are temporary, but God himself is our perpetual satisfaction. But just one manifestation of him will not suffice. The truly awakened pant, as the deer of Psalm 42:1, for regular manifestations to the soul. He longs for a closer walk with God so that he might know his cheering presence.

Passion for reality. Zeal for right ends is commendable. Lethargic people are a trial to those who are zealous in a good cause. Here we see that God fills to satisfaction those who yearn after him. Many yearn for benefits flowing from him, but here hunger is for God himself. Humanity knows natural zeal, but the regenerated soul pines with passion for God. He wants to experience the comforts of grace. Such comforts are rarely sensational but usually accord with Romans 15:4 so that we might know the comfort of the Scriptures.

What are the evidences of spiritual reality? Our text says, '*He* satisfies the *longing* soul' – he satisfies the very core of being of those who yearn for *him*. He makes happy the awakened sinner. He creates a desire for Christ and a hunger for righteousness. Spiritual longings indicate spiritual health. We must not be content with faint longings. Healthy Christians will *yearn* for nourishing ministry. Just as a diet must be balanced to be healthy, an unhealthy diet of religious 'husks' will, in time, cause spiritual weakness.

How does God satisfy the longing soul and fill the hungry soul with goodness? God makes himself of great value to believers having:

(a) shown them mercy,

(b) redeemed them,

(c) gathered them from wandering in Satan's kingdom,

(d) ordered their lives by delivering them from distress,

(e) given them security. His sheep know their times are in his hands (Ps. 31:15)

Such satisfaction is for both time and eternity.

What relevance is this verse to you today? Self-examination is difficult. Let us probe deeply to discover if we have an intensity of desire for God. We should ask ourselves, 'Where do I look for satisfaction? Do I seek it in church activity, religious books, dialogue with others on theological issues, etc., or do I seek it only in Christ?' Our encouragement is in the text.

Psalm 17; Deuteronomy 32:9-12

Spiritually, all believers are children of Abraham. Believers may take such truth to themselves for encouragement and rejoice that God brought them out of the wilderness of sin into the garden of his free grace.

Jehovah's relationship with Jacob. God is described as the portion of his people – the object of their treasure, their satisfaction in life and death. Here we look from different angles and see the people of God are his portion. He unconditionally chose Israel to be his special people (Deut. 7:6ff). He separated them from all others and figuratively regarded them as a definable territorial possession, his tract of land as measured out by cord. In the Old Testament a cord was used to measure out land to fix boundaries. It is understandable how God should be the portion of his people but it is amazing how *they* should be *his* portion. Being all-sufficient, God neither needs nor can be benefited by them.

The blessings accruing to those who dwell in God's defined territory. Those within the church *have been* found and are *being* led, instructed, kept and borne up as on eagle's wings. Deuteronomy 32:10a shows where the tribe of Jacob was found and hence where the church was found – wandering in the wilderness. Israel was taken out of Egypt and led for forty years by the pillar of fire. Having only human sight, they had no insight about the future. Enlightened

Divine dealings in grace

members of the church become increasingly aware of the dangers of their former state. Some were sensationally rescued (such as Paul) and others were gently led out (such as John the Baptist and Timothy).

Having been led out of Satan's dark forests, the regenerate must continue to live in the wilderness of this present world. For the rest of his life his Spirit-opened mind is illuminated to the truth of God and although dark forces surround him, the Lord is his diligent keeper. God likens himself to an eagle in all its strength. Having brought its young to birth and fed them, the eagle stirs up the nest and pushes the eaglets out to teach them to use their wings. As they tumble, flutter and squawk, the mother bird constantly watches and swoops to take them on her broad back so that no harm befalls them. God, in his gracious dealings, stirs up his people so as to equip them for flight in this world. He disciplines them so as to make them able to cope, and his watchful eye remains upon them. He so deals with them to equip them for the heavenly realm he has prepared for their eternal glory.

Let us never forget: While we are on earth, severe trials may cause us to murmur, but we can be confident in the God of Jacob in whom David and all true believers have found consolation, refuge and encouragement.

Psalms 121 & 125; Deuteronomy 33:12
Blessings bestowed upon Benjamin are ours in Christ

Jacob gathered his family and blessed his sons individually (Gen. 49). There, at v. 27, he made reference to Benjamin his youngest son and predicted his would be a war-like tribe. Shortly before his death, Moses spoke prophetically of the same Benjamin (Deut. 33:12). The nation of Israel was a type of the church. We can draw comfort from Moses' words. The promises of Scripture, although initially of immediate relevance to those addressed, are often relevant in principle to us today.

The status of Benjamin. Our verse says he is 'the beloved of the Lord', like all believers. This statement represents the highest value that God, who himself is love, can place upon believers. Such a declaration expresses the deep and constant love of a perfect being towards entirely unworthy objects. It is everlasting and by it people are drawn to God. It gives the Lord's people security and status in the grace they have in Christ (Rom. 5:2).

The undertakings predicted concerning Benjamin and all Lord's people.

(a) *They shall dwell in confident safety.* This does not mean difficulties will not trouble us. Psalm 32:6 promises floods of great waters shall not come near the godly (compare Isaiah 43:1-2). Psalm 91:10 promises no plague will come near us. In reality many of the godly are affected by calamities of various kinds. The meaning here is that while the trials common to man might inconvenience believers, the occasion and timing of them is only by divine permission (Rom. 8:28). Even in the 'valley of shadow of death' they will know his divine presence.

(b) *The LORD shall cover them all day long.* While angels are seen as 'ministering spirits', the ultimate protection of believers comes directly from the throne of God. As they dwell in the temporary tent of this body, they are sheltered by God (Ps. 91:4). As children of the royal household of heaven, believers are accompanied by angels who are charged to keep them in all their ways (Ps. 91:11). The consolation for believers is seen in Isaiah 54:17. The duration of this security is 'all day long' which means all the time.

(c) *He shall dwell between his shoulders.* In the original language this meant that the tribe of Benjamin would be allocated land between the sacred mountains of Zion and Moriah. Spiritually for us today it has reference to the strength of the walls of salvation which surround those who by grace are members of the city of Zion.

_____

Enjoy the benefits of your eternal security. Things which are true of us *in fact* may not necessarily be felt. We *know* we are 'kings and priests unto God', but do we *feel* it? We live by faith not feeling. Irrespective of how we *feel*, the blessing God bestowed on Benjamin by Moses is true of us if we are of spiritual Israel:

(i) We are 'holy and beloved' (Col. 3:12).

(ii) We are eternally secure in him (John 10:28).

(iii) We are covered by God's providence all day (Ps. 121:4).

(iv) Even now we dwell safely between his shoulders, and all of the blessings bestowed on Israel are ours in Christ.

Isaiah 50   Faithful God-fearers walking in darkness (vv. 10-11)

Isaiah is prophesying to Israel of the Messiah whom they would reject (4-9). That rejection would be evidenced by their contempt for him (6). Such rejection of God by Israel is likened to a divorce. In reasoning with Israel, God asks her to produce her divorce certificate to prove he had divorced her. Verses 10-11 exhort the people of God to trust him in the darkest times. There is an implied encouragement that by so doing they will *not* 'lie down in sorrow'.

An exhortation to the discouraged and bewildered people of God. The resources of God are limitless. By the parable about his creating and tending the vineyard (Isa. 5:1-7), God demonstrates his work for his people. However, hypothetically there is a sense in which he comes to the 'end' of his ability to do more. In an appeal to bystanders, he poses a question (4a). He had chosen them, liberated them from Egypt, given them the law, sent prophets to teach them, protected them, and had promised the Messiah to redeem them. That was limitless grace. In human language, he had done what he could. In response to such questions we may claim to be those who *fear*, that is, respect, stand in awe of the Lord. In fearing him, we acknowledge his person, his power and his sovereign authority. Such an acknowledgement leads to an appreciation of his capability and activity (2b,3). Those who fear also *obey* the voice of 'his servant', the Messiah. In spite of seeking a closer, holy walk with God, the believer may feel bewildered and discouraged in darkness.

One of the strategies of the devil is to seek to confuse the thinking of believers. To the bewildered and discouraged, v. 10b gives an exhortation: '*Trust* in the name of the Lord ... *stay* upon God.' The verbs 'trust' and 'stay' are in the present continuous tense. 'Trust' means to trust and *go on* trusting, *go on* putting your confidence in the *name* of God. 'Stay' means to rely upon God *and keep doing so*.

An implied encouragement for bewildered God-fearers. In God's economy, there are always two alternatives. At v. 11 we have the alternative to v. 10. If those without God-given light desire light and take matters into their own hands to create it, they will 'lie down in sorrow'. The implied encouragement to those described at v. 10 is that such sorrow will not befall *them*. Here we have the picture, not only of the ungodly but also of the *impatient godly*. Notice the *source* of that sorrow (11c): 'This you shall have from *my hand*.' It won't be because of misfortune, it will come directly from God's sovereign activity. The believer is fortified by the sovereign purposes of God, even if sometimes they cause tears. They are never needless tears, for they drive us to God. Though wearied by the fallen world in which we are called to live, the believer rejoices (40:31). The primary characteristic of the ungodly is that they have 'no fear of God before their eyes'. *No fear* leads to *no obedience*, no obedience to *darkness*, which is but the waiting room for the 'outer-darkness' which will engulf them forever.

Isaiah 51:1-16 Encouragements for the righteous (vv. 7-8)

Here is a threefold call to the people of God (1,4,7): 'Listen to me.' Living in troubled times we need support and '(our) help comes only from the Lord'. In vv. 7-8 there is an encouragement to be courageous amid pressure from the wicked, and the basis for such courage is in God. In vv. 12-13 the person and handiwork of God are set out so that his people might be fortified in the conflicts of their earthly pilgrimage.

The *character* of those called to give attention to the voice of the Lord. At v. 7 the call is to those who 'know righteousness'. In the immediate context God addresses his chosen nation. However, as the church is the 'Israel of God' (Gal. 6:16), such promises apply to all the spiritual children of Abraham. Here he addresses those who know the righteousness of God as displayed in his attributes. God said he would *put* his law in the inward parts of his people, *write* it on their hearts, *be* their God and *they would be* his people (Jer. 31:33). This Old Testament promise is valid today to those who seek after and know God. God shows that having intimate *acquaintance* with the law is insufficient (7), but those who '*follow after* righteousness' demonstrate that they really do 'seek the Lord' (1). Remembering their origins, they are to pursue godliness with the same determination as a predator would pursue its prey (1b).

The *security* of those called upon to give attention to the voice of the Lord. Even the most powerful warning will not be heeded unless the ear is listening. Security is guaranteed to those with ears attuned to his message. God gives a word of consolation. He says, if you are 'my people' and acquainted with my righteousness and revere my law (4a), you have no need to fear the reproach of men (7b). The moth will feed on mockers as if they were a garment (compare Job 4:17,19). The worm will gnaw them to destruction as it did the gourd under which Jonah sheltered (compare Acts 12:21-23). The psalmist's consolation is seen at 112:4,7,8.

The *encouragement* of those called upon to give attention to voice of Lord. God's righteousness and their salvation are everlasting. Conversely, those to whom such promises of encouragement do not apply have another promise exclusively for them (Ps. 9:17). God assures us that our consolation comes directly from himself by the Spirit (12a). In view of that, God asks: 'Who are you that you should be afraid of a man...?' He shows us the reason for any fear that might grip the souls of those who profess to be the children of the Most High (13). They forget the person and creative power of their Creator when they are afraid daily of the anger of their enemies. God asks: 'Where is the fury of the oppressor?' and infers the *impotence* of the oppressor, compared with the *omnipotence* of himself. He has given us his word of assurance, covering us in the shadow of his hand so that he might 'plant the heavens, lay the foundations of the earth, and say to Zion, "You are my people."'

Psalm 46   God our refuge in troubled times

Repeated encouragements provide inspiration to greater things and stimulus when times are difficult. Prayer for such encouragements is evidence of our need of the support of divine aid. When living in troubled times, the fact that God Omnipotent reigns is a comfort to believers, although human frailty can cause disquiet. The psalm is applicable to any time of confusion and distress. At such times those who are trusting in the Lord have no reason to be afraid.

The *stability* of the faithful.

(a) God was (by experience) their refuge and strength, the shelter in whom they trusted and fled to for cover (1). A 'refuge' was inaccessible, impregnable (Prov. 18:10) – a tower, a stronghold, a fortress. God was also their strength, for he made them firm and protected them when they ran to him. Such a God was their immediate help when trouble arose.

(b) The Lord of hosts was with them. He was with them in every situation *extending to* Immanuel. 'The Lord of hosts' (7,11) is the title of divine power.

(c) The God of Jacob was their refuge. In the 'God of Jacob' we see the covenantal relationship (7b,11b). Such factors stabilised Israel. They were confident of God's presence and speedy assistance (5c, compare 138:7-8a). This guaranteed stability gave confidence that the nation would not be moved (5b).

The *satisfaction* of the faithful. Israel was satisfied that God was competent in every situation (2-3). Natural calamities which are greater than humanity can cope with are insignificant to him. That knowledge comforted them. The ungodly raged and nations rose up against Israel, but when Jehovah spoke, the opposition melted away (6). The church's enemies will scatter when the Lord bares his arm. For encouragement to faith, they meditated upon the *historical works* of God on their behalf (8-9).

The *encouragements* for the faithful. The psalmist speaks of a river (grace) that flowed from God into the midst of his people, causing rejoicing and comfort (4-5). The secret of comfort is stillness (10), which here means be relaxed, slacken your pace, desist from anxiety, do not be disquieted and 'know' (be certain) that he is God. It refers to the people of God being at ease in God and 'standing still to see the salvation of the Lord'. This comfort stems from a proper view of his sovereignty. God sometimes allows his people to be discomforted *so that* they might become comforted, and *so that in turn* they might comfort others (2 Cor. 1:3-4). The stability of a Christian in adversity is a testimony to the grace and sovereignty of God!

God majors on the well-being of the church which is the Israel of God for whom Christ died. Each individual believer may take comfort in troubled times from this psalm. Should doubts and fears arise, remember Habakkuk 2:20 – 'The Lord is in his holy temple: let all the earth keep silence before him.' Whenever storm clouds gather, 'God is our refuge and strength, a very present help in trouble.' 'When darkness veils *his* lovely face ...' – what are we to do then? – 'Rest on his unchanging grace.' Psalm 91:1 is our encouragement and consolation: 'He who dwells in the secret place of the Most High shall abide under the shadow of the Almighty.'

Jeremiah 17:1-14 Contrasting experiences between the godly and the ungodly (vv. 5-8)

Although Jeremiah's ministry was widely rejected and resulted in his suffering hardships, such rejection didn't affect its validity. His warning of 70 years of exile in Babylon came about and his status as a true prophet was confirmed. This text sets out the alternatives of cursing upon those who trust in man and blessing for those who trust in the Lord.

The folly of those trusting in the arm of flesh. Authoritative ministry is always God-certified, and Jeremiah shows authority in speaking to Judah (5a). Men may pronounce, but the outcome is outside their control. When God speaks, it is done. God warns Judah that placing their trust in the strength of man's arm puts them under a curse because such reliance upon man indicates their failure to depend upon Jehovah their God. Their sin was not slight (1). They held the living God in contempt and worshipped dumb idols amidst trees on the mountains, and in doing so contaminated the thinking of their children. Such conduct indicated 'departing from the Lord' (5c,13). God says their conduct kindled the fire of his anger. They had looked to Egyptians and Assyrians (2:36) and so God cries out 'Cursed...!' (5a). The curse is one of misery. Man may inflict a degree of misery upon himself or others, but a God-inflicted misery is total as it brings suffering yet survival in eternal despair. He will be like a shrub which can survive in the harshness of the desert. Judah would physically survive in such appalling conditions because it was ordained that Christ would come from that tribe. However, its experience in Babylonian exile would be dry and barren even though its roots would remain alive. They would be destitute of much comfort as they squirmed under the all-seeing eye of a disciplining God.

A blessed encouragement for all who make the Lord their trust. The man who trusts in God, is 'blessed', that is, he is able to enjoy all the permanent benefits arising from that relationship. He is blessed because he places his confidence exclusively in God. All the benefits of special grace are his in Christ. The barrenness of the desert is in stark contrast with v. 8 (compare Psalm 1:3). It describes a gardener's paradise. Sometimes seeds dropped by birds fall to the ground and a vast tree results. Here, the blessed of the Lord are planted, settled in a prepared location – here by the waters of nourishment. Their roots spread out in the direction of the water. When heat comes they do not wither but their leaf remains green as they are refreshed from the roots and the sap rises to sustain them. When the period of drought is extended they continue bearing fruit because they draw from the hidden depths underground. We are sustained by the Lord in every circumstance of life. The spiritual fruit we produce (Gal. 5:22-23), will be made sweeter as God feeds us by his Word and prunes us for our own good and his glory.

John 13:33 – 14:31 The assured comfort of the Lord's presence (14:18)

When our comfort zone is threatened, anxiety often occurs. Jesus broached the subject of leaving the apostles for a place where they could not go then. Having enjoyed years of ministry and companionship, they saw the future clouded with uncertainty. Peter wanted an explanation (13:36). Jesus told them it would be a preparation for a new beginning and to their long-term advantage. He urged them *on the basis of faith*, not to be troubled (14:1). He reassured them, knowing there was to be a delay in the fulfilment of the promise.

I will not leave you comfortless. Although Jesus was addressing the apostles, 'you' is inclusive of all those who, on the basis of 'apostolic doctrine', would come to believe in Jesus and become his disciples (17:20). If we are one of them, this assurance of future security is for us today. 'Comfortless' means orphaned, parentless, abandoned, deprived of care. The apostles' dilemma was that they knew of no alternative to Jesus (see 6:66-68). Jesus assured them they would not be left to fend for themselves (Matt. 28:20b). In the absence of a visible Jesus, the unseen Holy Spirit would be their Comforter (26) and would stand alongside them as a powerful advocate.

I will come to you. Jesus said, '*I* will come to you,' and that coming implied a drawing near which would be in union with the Father (10,23) and they, *in union with the Spirit*, would be present with the Trinity. They had enjoyed blessed experiences in the past (1 John 1:1; John 1:14), but the future would bring a coming that would be to their immediate and continuing advantage.

The omnipresent Spirit would permanently *abide with them* wherever they were (16b,17; compare Psalm 139:7-10), and *abide in them* (1 Cor. 6:19). God's Spirit would comfort, reassure, and relieve them by:

(i) Teaching them (26b; 1 John 2:20,27).

(ii) Reminding them (26c), which resulted in them writing Gospels and preaching. As a consequence, we have the Spirit-inspired and inerrant word of God, which demands our reverence and obedience.

(iii) Speaking of Christ (15:26b). To testify means to give evidence of what *the Spirit had seen* of Christ from the beginning.

(iv) Guiding them into a proper understanding of the *relevance* of the birth, life, death, resurrection and ascension of Christ (16:13).

(v) Glorifying and revealing Christ (16:14-15): the Spirit would make much of Jesus so that he would be further exalted in their thinking.

(vi) Empowering them and the church for all time by the Pentecostal outpouring (Acts 1:8).

The Holy Spirit is the divine life in the regenerate soul. We should be encouraged because all his offices, as revealed in Scripture, are for our comfort today. When God makes a general address in his Word we may, *with discernment*, take it personally. We may wonder how God speaks *personally* today. We do not hear his audible voice but we may recognise his voice in Bible-based preaching or those verses marked in our Bibles which spoke to us in the past. The truth contained in some hymns can be instructive and sometimes in our prayers and witnessing he causes us to recall his Word.

Romans 8 With God on our side none can overcome us (v. 31b)

The ground of a believer's hope is their union with Christ, who is the apple of his Father's eye. Those who are in such a union are hidden in Christ with God. Every blessing recorded here is applicable to the believer and we can draw encouragement from them. Paul asks how we should react to the afflictions and blessings in this chapter and responds.

If God be for us. Here 'If' is not conditional but an assurance and means 'since' or 'because' – God is with us. In making such a statement Paul based his conviction on the covenants, promises and undertakings of the Old Testament scriptures. The writer of Hebrews assured Jewish recipients that God had promised never to leave them (13:5). It is important we encourage ourselves with the *fact* that God *is* with us, or *for us*. There is never a situation where this fact is not true. Sovereignty may baffle us and his dealings overwhelm us, but he is always loyal to us. He is on our side. If the Father punishes us for our sins, then Jesus as our advocate takes up our case on the basis of his own propitiatory work for us. This Friend 'sticks closer than a brother', befriends sinners and supports them in every circumstance. Whether we are in the right or in the wrong, he will never abandon us. If we are wrong, he does not approve, but, like the prodigal's father, he is always there for us. Having ransomed and healed us, he forgives, sanctifies and restores us. The practical effects of God being for us are:

(i) When Satan accuses us before the Lord, his accusations are shown as legally unsustainable on basis of our justification and imputed righteousness.

(ii) In life's deprivations and disciplines, he is *for us*.

(iii) In providing for our needs, he is *for us* (Phil. 4:19; compare Lam. 3:22-23).

(iv) In our eternal expectations, he is *for us* (38-39).

Who can be against us? At 31b,33-35 we have an emphatic 'Who?' When opposed by devils or men, God is *for us* (Ps. 138:7-8). When slandered we are secure (Ps. 41:5,11-12). When spiritual weapons are used to attack us, Isaiah 54:17 remains true. Our assurance is Psalm 125:2. At worst we can be distressed, but not in despair (2 Cor. 4:8). Nothing can rob us of our salvation or separate us from divine love (35).

How are we to find encouragement in view of such security?

(i) We are not condemned (1).

(ii) We are indwelt (9).

(iii) We are led (14).

(iv) We are adopted (15).

(v) We are helped (26).

(vi) The circumstances of our lives are ordered (28).

(vii) We are part of his eternal plan (29-30).

(viii) We have unrivalled security (38-39).

Our union with Christ guarantees a security that is as fixed as throne of heaven itself. There is security, both collectively, *for us*, and personally, *for me* – *my* Shepherd. Let us be encouraged in the Lord our God.

2 Corinthians 12:1-10   The sufficiency of grace (v. 9)

Sometimes blessings are costly. In Philippians 3:10, Paul associated the blessing of knowing Christ and the power of his resurrection with sharing in his sufferings and bearing his reproach with him. Paul had endured much in the service of Christ, yet he had special favours extraordinarily bestowed upon him (1-4). That elevated experience was counterbalanced in that he was buffeted and humbled by a 'thorn in the flesh'. Whatever the thorn was, it had a sanctifying effect upon him. Because of it he could glory in his infirmities (9b), and rejoice that the power of Christ rested upon him and afforded him shelter in every aspect of his life (Isa. 4:6).

An encouraging word from God. Scripture and God are inseparable. The Word was made flesh. Our verse relates a direct revelatory statement of God to Paul. The words were both a comfort and an explanation to the apostle. Paul had apostleship thrust upon him by a divine initiative and was given a unique experience. He was shown heavenly things by God which could not be detailed on earth.

An encouraging promise from God. Paul was promised he would be given grace in sufficient measure to enable him to cope. There is significance in the expression, 'My grace'. In John 14:27, the apostles were promised that his peace would be with them when Jesus had gone to heaven to prepare a place for them. Such peace was not that of a general nature involving tranquillity and calm serenity in a world in which they would know tribulation. It was the peace experienced by Jesus which came from a firm assurance of divine sovereignty. The grace promised here is the favour of being granted sufficient power to cope with a condition that would keep Paul humble and reliant upon God. From the assurance given to Paul about coping with his affliction, we can be encouraged in every circumstance of our lives. Paul was not commanded to be strong in bearing with his 'thorn in flesh' but he was promised that God's strength would suffice in his weakened situation.

An apostolic response to a word of encouragement. Paul did not doubt it, but revelled in it (9b) so that he might experience active divine interest in his *personal* situation. His response was not merely submissive, but ecstatic as he was the subject of special attention by God.

We should note that:

(i) The prayers of the apostles were not always answered in the way they desired (see Luke 18:7-8).

(ii) Paul's affliction is proof of the folly of the so-called 'prosperity gospel'.

(iii) If God gave us all we wanted, we might not count it a blessing! Have we counted the cost of being granted what we want? We pray for blessing in the church – bigger congregations, professions of faith, etc., but remember that amid the growth of the church at Corinth all was not well. There were many problems! If we pray for blessing, we must be prepared to cope with what the Lord grants.

(iv) Such thorns are sent into our lives to sanctify us. Grace is needed to endure them, but we may be encouraged by the promise that sufficient will be provided which will enable us to cope.

Philippians 4 Needs met from an abundance of divine supply (v. 19)

This chapter is full of general exhortations to the Philippian believers. Paul urged them not to worry about anything and told them to bring their concerns to Lord (6-7). He assured them that by the strengthening grace of God, he had learned to cope in every circumstance (12-13). He commended them for their generosity towards him as an expression of their fellowship in the gospel (14-18) and assured them of the trustworthiness of divine economics (19).

The source of the believer's supply. Immediately we see the personal intimacy between Paul and the source of his supply. He told the Philippians, '*My* God' would supply their need. Their need in terms of common grace would be met because Paul's God was the God who had already met their spiritual need by saving grace. The relationship between God and his people is like that of a father and his child. The Lord's people can be assured that the parent who has adopted them will provide for them. Paul was speaking from experience, for when he was forsaken by those he might have expected to be his comforters, the Lord stood by him and strengthened him.

The supply of the believer's need. The verb used here for 'supply' means 'shall make full what is lacking' (compare 1 Corinthians 16:17). Here is an assurance that the need of believers shall be supplied. Interestingly, the word 'need' is singular. Although we have plurality of *needs* yet only our *need* is mentioned. This indicates that whatever the nature of our personal requirements, all shall be met. All our plural needs (wants) are put

into singular parcel of our general 'need'. That means all aspects of our affairs are under his care and jurisdiction. It is necessary to apply two conditions to this general statement:

(i) This undertaking is given only to those to whom 1:6, etc., applies. This is the heritage of the adopted members of God's family.

(ii) What we want is not necessarily what we need. In Gethsemane Jesus *wanted* the cup of his suffering to pass from him but he knew he *needed* it in order to accomplish the eternal purpose of the Godhead.

In the outworking of Romans 8:28, our good is the aim. Requests submitted to God by faith will all be dealt with in a manner that is consistent with the divine will. Primarily Paul is speaking here about temporal rather than spiritual need, but God will supply in every aspect of his grace.

The superabundance of the supply. The well from which our needs are satisfied has an inexhaustible supply and is largely untapped! The provision for our need is according to 'riches in glory by Christ Jesus'. Riches bestowed upon God's family are according to superabundance of merit earned by the work of Christ.

Material prosperity is not necessarily a sign of spiritual prosperity. Paul's assurance was for the people of God. Demand never exceeds supply, and supply is always equal to demand. We cannot measure it by worldly possessions, but by reacting positively to the truth of 1 Timothy 1:14, 2 Corinthians 4:15 and 1 Peter1:3. If we are the objects of divine grace and mercy, let us be encouraged and enjoy the blessings of Romans 15:4.

1 Thessalonians 4:13 – 5:11   A divine appointment (5:9)

The Thessalonians were shown the importance of having an appointment and the security of it (9). They were given two important encouragements as to their security in having an appointment. While they had not been appointed to wrath, they had been appointed to obtain salvation by Christ.

God has not appointed us to wrath. The first thing to note in the text is God's involvement. God alone has the sovereign right to do as he pleases. God gives the assurance that we have not been appointed to wrath. The original word for 'appointed' means selected to any form of service (compare John 15:16). Such an appointment is at God's discretion. The inference is that while the recipients of the letter were not appointed to wrath, some people are (Rom. 9:18). To appreciate this, we need to look at the issue in the light of the attributes of God such as justice, mercy, grace, etc. A just God can mercifully withhold appropriate wrath from the guilty as an act of undeserved favour. By the exercise of original freewill in rebellion, Adam placed all without exception under condemnation. But by unconditional distinguishing favour God had, from eternity, set some aside as tokens of his benevolence and goodwill. The text is clear as to what we have not been appointed to – wrath, meaning destruction passed upon all men because of sin from which the church has been preserved by electing grace.

God has appointed us to obtain salvation. Those who believe do so only because of a divine appointment – a setting apart from before creation to obtain salvation. In the original, 'obtained' means acquired. We have, by enabling faith, laid hands upon it as one does an object. Salvation is the portion of those who are delivered from sin's power,

penalty and ultimate presence. It is eternal. Scripture knows nothing of temporary salvation.

The means by which we obtain salvation. Apart from the human responsibility to exercise the gifts of repentance and faith, salvation is unconditional. God commands man to act to obtain salvation (Acts 17:30b). The ability to act stems from repentance and faith being granted (Acts 11:18), and is the result of 'quickening' (regeneration) (Eph. 2:1). It is not man's action that brings salvation. It comes from God and is maintained by him (1 Peter 1:5). It is obtained 'by our Lord Jesus Christ', who as our substitute was raised from the dead, having delivered us 'from the wrath to come' (1 Thess. 1:10b). In his name we acknowledge him as Lord and Saviour and as the Anointed of God. In the text we see the enormity of divine energy expended to procure the salvation of the spiritually entombed (compare Ephesians 1:19-20). To achieve the salvation of his people, Christ destroyed the power of Satan.

What are some of the evidences that one has been appointed to obtain salvation by Jesus Christ? *(i)* Providence orders our circumstances to put us in the way of the preaching of the Word. *(ii)* Our spiritual interest was stimulated as our 'heart was opened'. *(iii)* The ability to exercise faith with consequent repentance and hatred of sin was granted. *(iv)* Our spiritual appetite was aroused. *(v)* Dissatisfaction with this world becomes increasingly evident (1 John 2:15-16).

Do you know anything of such evidence in your experience?

Acts 1:1-14   Jesus is coming again (v. 11)!

Of the many scriptural encouragements for the people of God, the ultimate one is the promise of the return of the Lord Jesus Christ in glory. Like the first advent, the second advent is a matter of faith. It is matter of believing what God has said in his Word through the prophets, apostles and Jesus himself. Paul was concerned that the Thessalonians knew that those who had already died in Christ and the believers who were alive at the time of his return would together 'meet Lord in the air, and so be forever with the Lord' (1 Thess. 4:17). Peter assured the recipients of his epistle that, however long the return was delayed, it was certain and would bring in 'a new heaven and a new earth in which righteousness dwells' (2 Peter 3:13). Luke, in writing Acts to Theophilus, went beyond what he wrote in the Gospel concerning the person and work of Jesus to 'the day he was taken up'. Jesus' physical ministry was concluded by his ascension but his spiritual ministry continued in the fulfilment of Acts 1:8 by the Pentecostal outpouring of the Spirit. We are encouraged to believe that certain hope that he 'shall come again'.

The ascension of the Lord Jesus Christ. The ascension of Jesus is important today because of John 16:7. Luke 24:50ff sets the scene at Bethany where, after blessing the apostles, Jesus went up into heaven. Acts 1:9 tells us he was caught up in cloud and taken out of sight. As they gazed upwards, the apostles were asked by two angels why they were gazing upwards – inferring they should instead be rushing to Jerusalem to wait. They learned that Jesus would return in a like manner, namely in a cloud (compare Mark 13:26). This was consistent with the words of Jesus (John 14:3). The necessity of the ascension is seen in that the localised presence of Jesus was replaced by his omnipresent Spirit. The benefit of the ascension was that the church was gifted and empowered to carry on Jesus' ministry (Eph. 4:8ff). Jesus was going to heaven, to his Father (John 20:17b).

The promised return of the ascended Lord Jesus Christ. The apostles were assured that 'this same Jesus' would return. That glorified, post-resurrection body would be recognisable. The wonder of his return will be universal. The church will immediately understand and know him by the 'nail-prints in his hands'. The ungodly will react as described in Revelation 1:7 and 6:15-17. Sometimes people speculate as to heaven's location. Yuri Gagarin, the first Russian cosmonaut (1961), said upon return to earth he had seen neither God nor heaven in space. Scripture suggests heaven is above, and just as the 'men of Galilee' looked up, so we look up because our 'redemption draws near'.

The encouragement produced by the certainty of the Lord's return. By such truths as 1 Corinthians 15:51-53 and 1 Thessalonians 4:14-18 we are to be encouraged and to encourage others.

Readings in

Hebrews 11

by Ray Tibbs

WINDOW
ON THE
WORD

Hebrews 11:1-3   Living by faith

A key theme in Hebrews is perseverance. All believers are frequently tempted to go back to their old ways. For many of the original readers this would mean reverting back to Judaism, and the writer shows that would be a seriously retrograde step. So it is for any who, when under pressure, feel the attractiveness of the life they have left behind. At 10:39, the writer says, 'We are not of those who shrink back and are destroyed but of those who have faith and preserve their souls.' Chapter 11 lists well-known examples of those who remained faithful, and he ends with the call of 12:1-2 directing attention to Christ. We shall look at these examples as an encouragement to 'lay aside every weight' and 'look unto Jesus'.

Faith is explained (1). Part of the attraction of the past was its appeal to the senses. For Jews it was the tangible forms of ritual and ceremonial. The Christian faith has nothing comparable to offer, so can seem empty and insubstantial. Whatever we left behind can sometimes seem to be a great loss and nothing similar has replaced it. In fact, what we have gained is far greater than anything we lost and Hebrews demonstrates that. The difficulty is to hold on to this when we are bombarded by so many sensual stimuli. That is where faith comes in. Christianity deals primarily in the realm of the spirit, not the flesh – the kingdom of Christ is not of this world. Faith is a gift of God (Eph. 2:8) and is given in measure (Rom. 12:3). Faith, not sight, is our motive power (2 Cor. 5:7). It is our life source (Gal. 2:20). It is the eyes and feet of the soul, enabling us to accept as fact what the senses cannot prove, having the capacity to see beyond the experiences of the natural world. It brings present enjoyment of a future hope. Faith is not irrational for it is based on the certainties of God and his Word.

Faith is approved (2). This faculty was possessed by Old Testament saints also. It is foundational to the life of any child of God, and out of it other things follow. It is first expressed as justifying faith, but then is subsequently exercised as a necessary consequence of its existence. There is an ongoing trust in God which follows naturally from that initial trust and is demonstrated in many actions. These records are preserved so that we can understand how faith works in practice (Rom. 15:4). The existence of faith proves their acceptance by God for they could not have done what they did apart from him.

Faith is expressed (3). Before moving on to human examples, he shows that believers already exercise this faith in relation to the creation of the world. We have not seen it, but believe it because God has told us about it. Any evidence which appears to point to the contrary is presented from a different presupposition. The evidence for creation as described by the Bible is abundant and can be accepted as easily as any other biblical truth by those who have the gift of faith. Faith does not deny reason, but puts it in its proper place – subject to the Word of God.

Are you walking by faith?

Hebrews 11:4; Genesis 4:1-10   Living by faith – Abel

By faith, Abel offered. The offering of Abel was different in form and spirit from that of Cain. It was not just according to the nature of his work. It involved selectivity. He made a choice of the best, a selfless act involving personal cost and the loss of life. It must have taken this form because it was required by God. The later stipulations about sacrifice made by God were consistent with this. The faith of Abel involved a willingness to abide by the Word of God. He could have followed the example of Cain but chose not to. The original revelation is hidden from us – as is much more, but we are told he exercised faith. He must have heard the Word of God, accepted it as his rule of life and trusted in the delivery of future promises attached to it (Rom. 10:17). The value of his action was found in the accompanying faith, not just the deed itself (Heb. 10:38). He looked beyond the action itself to God.

Do you offer worship to God by faith?

By faith, Abel was commended. Verse 4 shows that the offering was accepted because the person who made it had been accepted already. His action had been consistent with the rest of his life, just as Cain's was (1 John 3:12). Because Abel had faith, he used it on this occasion. He sought to please God (Heb. 11:6). We do not know the means whereby God showed his acceptance of Abel's sacrifice and his rejection of Cain's. The point is that Abel discerned it by faith. He knew in his spirit that both he and his offering had been accepted by God. Cain had no assurance of such acceptance.

Do you have the witness of the Spirit that God has accepted you in Christ?

By faith, Abel speaks. Both Genesis 4:10 and Hebrews 11:4 use the present tense when referring to the blood of Abel – as if it continues to be active. Once dead, Abel would no longer need faith as a resident of heaven. But he believed his blood would continue to speak for him. There was life after death for him. His God was the God of the living, not the dead. The circumstances of his death would confirm God's acceptance of him as it would confirm God's rejection of Cain. His blood would give eloquent testimony to the fate of those who were accepted by God: despised by the world but alive unto God. He believed death would not have the last word. He believed that injustice would not be allowed to prevail unpunished. He believed his blood would provide a perpetual plea which would continue to ring in God's ears and prompt his vindication at some time in the future. He believed that future generations could learn from his death. It would speak to those after him – as it does now. He committed his future to God believing God could use his silent testimony to the blessing of future generations. And so it is – because God has made it so through the Bible.

Does your faith in God extend beyond your death?

Hebrews 11:5-6; Genesis 5:16-29; Jude 14-15   Living by faith – Enoch

A life of faith: its beginning. Enoch means 'dedicated', perhaps signifying a life of faith. That life of faith seemed to have begun with the birth of his son, Methuselah (Gen. 5:22). His name must have been given by the revelation of God because it means 'when he is dead it shall be sent'. It was a prophetic name, suggesting Enoch knew he was living near the end of an era. Enoch lived 300 years after the birth of this son. Noah was born seventy years after Enoch was taken. The Flood came when Noah was 600 years old (Gen. 7:1), so Methuselah died within a year of the Flood.

A life of faith: its context. During Enoch's life Adam died, so the link with the beginning was gone. Wickedness was increasing (for example Genesis 4:23-24). Lamech was a contemporary of Enoch. Enoch's response to this wickedness was to preach against it (Jude 14-15). He could not have done that unless he was sent by God (Rom. 10:15). His message told of the coming of God in judgement upon all and the punishment of the wicked. He gave testimony to the truth amid great perversity.

A life of faith: its expression. He 'walked with God' is a phrase used only about Noah (Gen. 6:9) and Levi (Mal. 2:6). It is different to 'walking before God' (Gen. 17:1; 24:40) or 'after God' (Deut. 13:4). It suggests a closer relationship than the other terms and includes reconciliation (Amos 3:3), submission and obedience. It involves a heavenly minded, determined response to revelation (Romans 8:8; 2 Tim. 2:4).

A life of faith: its brevity. Enoch's departure from this world was somewhat similar to that of Elijah (2 Kings 2:11). The age of his relatives suggests that his departure was what we might call 'premature', but it is all the more instructive because of that. It speaks of the suddenness with which the end of life can come to anyone. It showed the reality of the continued existence of the body in the afterlife. It showed the reward for righteousness. It established that death could be overcome by faith and so prepared the way for the resurrection of Christ. The righteous would live by faith – through the power of God.

A life of faith: its testimony. Enoch gave public testimony to God and so his translation had public repercussions. He was missed. His commendation came before his departure and so was connected with it in public consciousness. As Enoch was taken by faith, it seems that he was expecting it – as a result of a prior revelation from God, and said so. His translation was a fulfilment of his own prophecy and therefore confirmed the validity of his ministry and message. His life of faith ended with proof of what it led to. A true living faith shows itself best in relation to death – and beyond. Thus, early in human history and in the biblical record we now have the accounts of two men of God whose life and death would provide inspiration for all who, in later years, would, like them, live and die by faith.

Hebrews 11:7; Genesis 6:9-22   Living by faith – Noah

By faith he built an ark. Noah built the ark because God told him to. God told Noah he would destroy the human race and Noah believed him. He believed that he could, he believed that he should and he believed that he would; but all he had to go on was the Word of God. There was no precedent for such action and no evidence of its approach. He responded with holy fear. So deep was his awed reverence that Noah continued building for one hundred years, despite the ridicule he probably faced from his neighbours. He knew why he had to build: to provide for the salvation of his family. He believed that God would use this means to preserve them all. He committed himself to the only way of salvation he knew and invested his time, energy and resources in doing all he could to give his family a future hope. What a lesson for Christian parents! Noah was not the author of their salvation. God had to move in their hearts to reject the world's opinion, trust God for themselves and go through that open door.

By faith he condemned the world. Noah would have to explain to others what he was doing. His action was a demonstration of his obedience to God. It was also a constant, visible prediction of the coming of the Flood. 2 Peter 2:5 shows that at the same time Noah was 'a preacher of righteousness'. He brought a positive message and told them how to behave in a way that would be pleasing to God. Their rejection of his message was anticipated in the building of the ark. While the ark was being built, the people were living in a day of grace (1 Peter 3:20), but, as they persisted in their godless behaviour, they were condemning themselves. Noah's faith recognised the exclusivity of it: that it was not shared by everyone. It accepted the reality of the distinctive relationship God had declared he had established with him personally (Gen. 6:18). It also accepted the just condemnation of those outside that relationship who lived wickedly.

By faith he became an heir. Noah entered into the benefits of a righteous life by his faith. An heir has expectations of what he will receive in future. He knows his status and also that he will have to wait before enjoying all that is rightfully his. The certainty of his future hope gives him a present joy. He can consider himself to be a possessor of those riches, even though he is not yet a partaker of them. For Noah, it was God who guaranteed the provision of the righteousness which would admit him into his presence for eternity. Holding on to the promises of God by faith would mean that he would receive all that God purposed to give him. The salvation of the ark was only a down payment of them, so he had no cause to doubt that everything else would follow in due time.

Are you an 'heir of the righteousness that comes by faith'?

Hebrews 11:8-10; Genesis 12:1-9   Living by faith – Abraham [1]

Abraham has more space than anyone in this chapter, as 'the man of faith' (Gal. 3:9).

By faith, Abraham obeyed and went. Joshua 24:2 shows that Abraham was from a pagan background when an unknown God suddenly entered his life. As he acted in response to the command, we see that when God calls he also enables obedience. Faith is implanted (Eph. 2:8), and action is an indispensable expression of it (James 2:26). Abraham was told to leave everything behind and go to an unknown destination. Not only was the destination unknown but the route was also unknown. Without any prior knowledge of God, Abraham uprooted his family in a life-changing experience and trusted God for his departure, his journey and his destination. He lived a life of faith almost literally step by step. God would give Abraham the land as an inheritance, that is, something he could pass on to future generations. Even the gift of land had a forward look built into it. The clear implication of the promise was that God would give Abraham a posterity of his own to whom he would pass on the land. God also promised that Abraham would be a blessing to many and have such a good reputation that it would last for generations. Abraham had to trust God for all those things, because there was no evidence that they could come about.

By faith, Abraham made his home. God had led Abraham to the promised land in fulfilment of his word. The land was promised not only to him but also to his family after him – a family represented only by his nephew at that point. There would be three features about his new life:

(a) It would always seem to be a foreign land to him, even though it was his. He and his family would always feel as if they did not belong there and be regarded with suspicion and hostility by their neighbours.

(b) Having moved from the civilised stability of city life, he was compelled to face the uncertainties of a nomadic existence. He would have no fixed abode, for tents were only a temporary dwelling place. Even though God had promised this whole land to him, the only permanent place he ever actually owned was a burial plot (Gen. 23:4).

(c) Without any form of certified ownership there appeared to be a gap between God's promise of land and its delivery. But that was the point. Abraham was not to set his sights on the land alone. There was more to come. The provision of the land was only the first part of God's promise. Having been assured by God that he had reached it, he could trust God to fulfil the rest of his promise – even if it lay outside Abraham's personal experience. He had a real home still to come, designed and prepared by God himself. It was permanent, desirable and secure – a city with prosperity, organisation and interaction, diversity and harmony. However appealing the past might have been when compared with the present, his future would be far better than anything known before. He looked forward by faith to what was then hidden from him. He had a firm conviction about things not seen. Do you? If so, how is it affecting your life now? Are you too much at home here?

Hebrews 11:11-16; Genesis 17:15-21; 21:1-7   Living by faith – Sarah

Obstacles to faith.

Personal weakness. It is understandable that Abraham's age and Sarah's barrenness led Sarah to doubt the promise of God (Gen. 18:1-15). It seems that Abraham doubted when he was first told (17:15-21), but later came to believe (Rom. 4:19). It was still early days in the revelation of God to his people. Miracles had been rare and they were still learning about who God was and what he could do. Faith faces facts but looks beyond them.

Personal strength. Self-confidence or wishful thinking can sometimes be mistaken for faith. It is easy to rely on human abilities or natural laws and think that God could work through them. That is not true faith. It is merely expectations based on means and can be dangerous because they can be flawed and fail to deliver, whereas he never fails.

The object of faith.

The person of God. It is in God alone in whom we must place our faith. Having come from a pagan background, Abraham and Sarah would have learned about him through direct revelation and experience. Almost twenty-five years had passed since Abraham's original encounter with God. His existence and authority were beyond question. His character and activities were gradually being discovered. Their faith was based on relatively little evidence, so it is not surprising that sometimes it failed.

The Word of God. The Word of God is indistinguishable from God himself and is only separated here as an explicit form of revelation through which God communicates directly with man. Because he speaks to us in terms we can understand, his word is not to be denigrated as being something less than God himself. 'In these last days he has spoken to us by his Son.' Promises made are seen to have been kept, confirming the power and integrity of the one who made them.

The outcome of faith.

Weakness is overcome. Faced with two sets of facts – human weakness and God's strength – Sarah chose to believe the latter was greater than the former. Her trust in God opened the door to experience in reality what she had only accepted in principle before. This is the direct intervention of God, not merely the sudden revitalisation of dormant faculties. She believed in what God was capable of, not what she was capable of.

Blessings are received. The reward of faith was the fulfilment of the promise. That in turn provided the ground for the fulfilment of the other promises. The exercise of faith strengthens faith. If God has done this, he can do that too. Faith always has a forward – and upward – look. God is glorified as our faith enables him to display his power. His strength is made perfect in our weakness. What God has done for his people in this life gives them confidence to expect the fulfilment of the promises he has made in relation to the next life. Because his character and therefore his word are so dependable, they can see what is unseen. The fact that God said it is true is enough for them. Do you have that kind of faith?

Hebrews 11:17-19; Genesis 22:1-19   Living by faith – Abraham [2]

The expression of his faith. Sometimes, God puts our faith to the test. Maybe we have felt that God is asking the impossible of us – and perhaps he is. His intention is not to discover whether or not our faith is up to it. He knows us better than we know ourselves and he may want to show us that our faith is stronger than we thought. That is what happened here. Abraham had proved that he had faith in God. He may not have always acted consistently with it, but it was real. God's command to Abraham to sacrifice Isaac seemed to put God's Word at odds with itself, but Abraham did not argue. He knew that God could never contradict himself. He knew he had to do what God wanted and leave the outcome to God. This is an important lesson when we are faced with what appear to be inconsistencies in the Bible. He believed the promises about Isaac were still in force and that God would find a way to fulfil them even after Abraham had performed this act of obedience. There was much about God he did not know and he was content with that. He did not put his faith in his knowledge of God, but in God himself. Abraham had surrendered all personal claims upon Isaac. Isaac had been given by God and God had a right to him. Isaac had already been offered up to God in the mind and heart of Abraham when the journey to the mountain began. Isaac had already been received back after the sacrifice in the mind of Abraham too, in some unfathomable way.

The strength of his faith. Self-denial is a key component in genuine faith. The mortification of self is required if God is to occupy the exalted position in our lives he deserves. The faith of Abraham was stronger than the constraints of parenthood. It was stronger than his understanding of the Word of God. It was stronger than his previous experience: there was no precedent for the resurrection he was expecting. It was stronger than any fear he might have felt from the reaction of those around him when they discovered what had happened. It was stronger than he expected and it took this situation to reveal its strength. Abraham unequivocally put God first and, crucially and perhaps for the first time, Isaac knew it.

The outcome of his faith. Abraham received the approval of God (Gen. 22:12), which Isaac may well have heard. He also received a fuller revelation of God (14), and a clearer view of the Messiah (John 8:56). The restoration of Isaac meant that God's covenant had been renewed. The whole incident was an early but partial symbol, illustrating elements of the future actual sacrifice and actual resurrection of Jesus Christ. Abraham saw this and was glad, and so once again faith had a forward and upward look. Once more, an early biblical record provides inspiration for many succeeding generations to 'look unto Jesus'. Is that what you are doing?

Hebrews 11:20; Genesis 27:26-40   Living by faith – Isaac

Faith looks back. Isaac had been the child of promise given to Abraham. He was the one through whom God's covenant had been fulfilled and was also the one through whom it had been renewed (Gen. 26:1-5). He had been providentially provided with a wife (Gen. 24), to whom God spoke prophetically about his sons (Gen. 25:23). Faith is strengthened by discerning the earlier words and works of God in the lives of his people which revealed his faithfulness to them. But faith is weakened when natural instincts take precedence. Despite the prophecy of 25:23, Isaac made Esau his favourite. In subsequent events before the blessing, God used the weaknesses of the various family members to establish his purposes. God is not hindered by human weakness but can circumvent or employ it.

Faith embraces the present. Faith is God-given and we see that in Isaac's blessing of his sons. Faith is given, when it is needed, even to the most unworthy. The words he spoke were against what his senses were telling him. His words were inspired by God and to a certain extent went against some of his natural inclinations. He could not help speaking them. They were prophetic. His faith overcame his reason and affection and was united with the will of God. The mistaken identity becomes irrelevant as, for this moment at least, his faith was in God, not Esau. This is confirmed in the second part of the incident when Isaac is given the opportunity to retract the first blessing and give it to the 'correct' recipient. He could not do so for his faith was strong enough not to go against what God had said through him. The real act of faith, sometimes manifest in words alone, cannot be undone because it is not a work of man. Real events cannot be made unreal by an act of will. Because they were from God, his words spoke of certainties and Isaac knew he could not change the future.

Faith looks to the future. Isaac's words spoke of things to come. There was no way in which he could have known these things apart from the revelation of God. Even though his personal hopes might have been different, he could only say and believe what he had been given. He was compelled to accept the plan of God and subdue his own inclinations. Only in that way could he see beyond his own life and death. He could see the hand of God at work in the future even though there was so little contemporary evidence for it.

It is important to acknowledge that faith does not only relate to spiritual matters. The blessings of God are varied and are applied differently to different people. Faith takes in practical affairs also. Faith in God applies to every area of life and we must not limit his reach into our everyday experiences. Are you struggling in some areas of life because you have excluded God from them?

Hebrews 11:21; Genesis 48:1-20   Living by faith – Jacob

This incident is similar to that just recorded about Isaac and its selection may seem surprising considering the events in Jacob's life. We are told:

By faith, he worshipped. Although recorded at the end of the verse, it happened first and provided the context for the blessing. Jacob knew he was dying and wanted 'to put his house in order'. But his house was not only his. He was aware of being the inheritor of some very great and precious promises. The covenant God had made with Abraham and Isaac, his grandfather and father, included him. He was the embodiment of God's faithfulness to them. His existence proved that God kept his promises. God had established with him the same relationship he had established with them. He worshipped God as his God but also as their God. He was not relying on a family tradition, for God had met with him personally. He had embraced the prospect of a good land, a great nation and extensive blessing as applying to him as much as it had applied to them. He knew they had believed it without entering into it, and he knew that with his large family its fulfilment had entered a new phase. As he came to the end of his earthly pilgrimage, he saw that the covenant community was being preserved and he believed it would enjoy all that God had in store for it. He worshipped God for what he had done, for what he was doing and for what he would do. His faith was based on the demonstrably unchanging word and work of God.

By faith, he blessed. Joseph's sons were to maintain their Hebrew lineage and reject their Egyptian upbringing. Their participation in the life of the family was to be as full as that of any other member. They had to withdraw from the world and be seen and known as what they were: part of the family of God. They could expect to receive all the future blessings promised to the rest of the family. There would be no tribe of Joseph. They would take his place in the future destiny of the family. The other children of Joseph were to be included with them. The grounds upon which this pronouncement was made was nothing less than God himself. He had proved to be faithful to Jacob's forefathers. In the physical realm, as a shepherd, Jacob knew he had been shepherded by God in the ways he had been guided and provided for. In the spiritual realm, he had been delivered from evil by the payment of a proper price. The priority of Ephraim over Manasseh would become true historically. The reversal at this point would show that their future destinies were not in the hands of men but of God. This episode gave Joseph a double portion of blessing over his brothers (1 Chr. 5:1-2); so again we see a human instinct overruled and employed by God for his greater purposes. The gift of faith is not given to accomplish our desires, but his. We do not always know when it has been given. We may also find that, although the gift is ours, others derive benefit from it.

Hebrews 11:22; Genesis 50:22-26   Living by faith – Joseph

When did Joseph show his faith? Most of the incidents chosen so far from the lives of Old Testament saints to exemplify their faithfulness have related to death. That is the case once more and it points to the theme of the letter: perseverance. A life of faith ends well after overcoming years of trials and temptations (10:39). At the time of his death, Joseph brought to mind the Word of God given to his forefathers. At that crucial point, he shared it with those closest to him, who, after his departure, would have to face its implications for themselves. None of us can predict the circumstances of our passing but we can ask God to help us to maintain a faithful testimony until, and if possible, during that time.

To whom did Joseph show his faith? Joseph was dying with his brothers around him: those who had treated him so badly in his early years. The natural bonds of family affection had been restored and remained paramount to him. Even after eighty years in Egypt, his concern was not for Egypt or himself, but for them. He made them take an oath which bound them to certain actions for posterity. In a fine example of leadership and foresight, he looked beyond the immediate generation and spoke for future generations to heed.

About what did Joseph show his faith?

An exodus from Egypt. He believed God would visit his people and come to their aid. He held on to Genesis 15:13-14 on behalf of the family. Such faith is not recorded in relation to any of his brothers. This is the man who had lived in a pagan environment for most of his life, without the traditions and support of his family. It can be done – with the help of God. Because God would eventually take them out, Egypt was not a place to get attached to. They were not to become dispirited by the hard times that would certainly come, because their stay was not permanent. There was a better life to come because God had promised it to Abraham, Isaac and Jacob. God's Word to them was sufficient for Joseph. The same promise had not been directly renewed to him personally, but he believed it as firmly as if it had been. God had spoken in the past, but until fulfilled, his word would always have relevance in the present.

Carrying his bones. His father had prophesied this (Gen. 48:21), but he used the term 'bones' rather than 'body' because he knew it would be a long time coming. He did not repeat Jacob's request of Genesis 49:29. Jacob had been a foreigner and the request was natural. Joseph was considered to be an Egyptian and so a similar request would have been offensive to Egyptians. However, he knew he did not belong there and made it known that he wanted his final resting place to be in his homeland. His request was carried out over three hundred years later (Exod. 13:19), when Moses' Egyptian background would have been useful in making it happen. The actual burial took place after years in the wilderness (Josh. 24:32). Joseph had entrusted his body and soul to God, as well as the long-term future of his family. Have you done the same?

Hebrews 11:23; Exodus 2:1-10; Acts 7:17-22
Living by faith – Moses' parents

The object of faith. It was in God, not themselves. He was at work in two ways. He had spoken. His word given to Abraham, Isaac and Jacob and believed by Joseph (Gen. 50:24), had been passed on. The parents could only have faith with the revelation of God (Rom. 10:17). Genesis 15:13 shows they knew how long their time in Egypt would last, so they would have known it was coming to an end. Also, God had given them a child. He was not their first, and somehow they knew he had a unique destiny. Although our translations do not reflect it, the term used to describe Moses in Exodus 2:2 is the same word used to describe the completed creation in Genesis 1:31. Essentially it means 'fit for purpose'. They had a God-given insight (faith) that he gave them this child for a particular reason, and so they had to keep him safe.

The expression of faith.

Boldness. They were not afraid of Pharaoh because they were accountable to a higher authority. Defiantly, they would not take away the life of the child God had given them.

Caution. They were not reckless and had to take sensible measures to preserve the child. In an act of faith, they hid him at home first, away from anyone who might have betrayed them. Perhaps it was as the child became too noisy that they had to change their plans. Faith does not deny reason.

Ingenuity. It was during this period of faith that the next phase of his preservation was worked out. Elaborate plans were carefully executed to ensure his future protection.

Confidence. The baby was taken to the place of death so it could be kept alive. The parents looked death in the face and overcame it. The word used to describe the container in which the baby was placed is the same word used to refer to Noah's ark. The actions of the Egyptian princess were unusual. She could have bathed at home. Her superstition may have explained the preservation of the baby – when all others had died there. Her contrary nature may have prompted her to care for the baby, against her father's orders.

Cooperation. This is clearly what the parents had hoped for and the providence of God was so evident that they willingly co-operated with a pagan power to preserve the life of their child. This was not compromise. Their plan, conceived and executed in faith, entrusted the baby to the care of God, not the Egyptians.

The outcome of faith. The immediate result was that they received their own child back again – legally. Their faith was rewarded. Faith always enriches and never impoverishes. God used their faith to fulfil his plans for the future of his people. Their actions were pivotal. The character of Moses was shaped in this godly home. He would grow up knowing what it meant to put faith into practice. Early in the Bible, the parents of Moses showed that even though God's people suffered affliction from authority, they were still under his providential care. Faith can conquer adversity by listening to the Word of God and looking at the hand of God, while being obedient to the constraints of God.

Hebrews 11:24-26   Living by faith – Moses [1]

By faith Moses refused. The reference to the age of Moses shows that his decision was a product of mature reflection. His upbringing had exercised a strong influence upon him through the sign of circumcision and accompanying instruction, so that he knew he did not belong in Egypt. He was prepared to deny the privileges of his position for the good of his people. He did not follow the precedent of Joseph by working from within the hierarchy of a heathen power. The circumstances were different. At that time, the welfare of God's people had depended on their entering Egypt and Joseph was divinely placed to facilitate that. Here, their welfare depended upon their leaving Egypt and Moses believed he had been divinely placed to facilitate that.

By faith Moses chose. By separating himself from the world, Moses chose suffering over sin. His loss of status would mean he would be forever identified with a nation of slaves. Although he would be despised, his union with his people was more important to him than any honours he might have surrendered. He consciously sacrificed spurious, seasonal splendours for the inevitable ill-treatment of binding himself to the people of God. There is an echo of what the second person of the Trinity did in being born as a man and it is the example the writer of Hebrews wants his readers to emulate.

By faith Moses considered. This was a reasoned choice on the part of Moses. He knew that what was truly valuable was not found in material wealth. He had a different sense of values. He chose something more precious and lasting, but unseen. The 'reproaches of Christ' could mean either:

(a) the same reproaches Christ suffered – the hardships of associating with the people of God by acts of self-denial (Phil. 3:7-8), or

(b) the actual sufferings of Christ himself on his behalf, perceived from afar by faith (John 5:46).

By faith Moses looked. Faith sees something more than present realities. It gives clear-sightedness, unclouded by the twisted perceptions of this world. It sees the future reward of a better life for God's people because it knows God will keep his promises to them. He will not break his covenant. He would bring deliverance from captivity and make suitable provision for all (Gen. 50:24). They would occupy their homeland and become established as a nation, preparing the way for the blessing that would spread out from them to the rest of the world. We entrust ourselves into the care of God because of what he has said. We are assured of a safe future because we have perceived realities which are hidden from others (1 John 5:4). Are you using the faith God has given you?

Hebrews 11:27-28; Exodus 2:11-15; Acts 7:23-29
Living by faith – Moses [2]

Faith overcomes fear. Exodus 2:14-15 says Moses fled because of a fear of being misunderstood. Acts 7:29 says he fled in order to save his life. Hebrews 11:27 says he fled in faith. Scripture cannot contradict itself, so all are correct. Moses had faith in God's plan for his future – however little he may have known about it. Aware of his destiny, he fled in order to bide his time and avoid the misunderstanding his continuing presence would produce. He fled so that his life would be spared so he could do whatever work God had planned for him. Faith is ennobling and inspires us to raise our sights above our natural instincts.

Faith sees the invisible. The second part of 11:27 refers to the whole of Moses' experience before leading the people out of Egypt. He persevered for forty years of apparently unproductive activity. After almost forty years of palace luxury, he endured the hardships of a remote, rural existence. One thing sustained him during all that time and was the source of his energy: his faith in God. Although unseen, God is real and his invisibility renders faith necessary. So God gives that gift to whomever he wants to know him. It enables people not only to discover his existence but also his character, through hearing his Word and seeing his work.

Faith is active. Outward obedience is an expression of faith in God, not a denial of it. Moses kept the Passover because he believed God would do what he said. His actions would be consistent with his character and he would act in both justice and mercy. He would act with power, having the ability to kill. He would act with perception, having the ability to preserve those who should remain alive. He would act with persuasion, having the ability to constrain the people to obey the instructions of Moses. He could plan and perform perfectly.

Faith is selfless. Because faith sees God, it does not see self in the same way as before. Moses had no personal ambition. He had no faith in himself. He needed great faith for a great undertaking. He would be leading two million puzzled, undisciplined people out of familiar surroundings into the unknown, and, in doing so, destabilising the economy of the country that had nurtured him. The route, the duration and the destination of the journey were all unknown. The demands of leadership were costly, but faith never counts the cost.

Faith is influential. By the time of the exodus, Moses' faith had grown because of his earlier experiences. He had trusted God and proved to be an inspiration which others would follow (Heb. 3:5). The institution of the Passover celebration for future generations would be a permanent reminder not only of what God had done but also of what he would still do. The exercise of our faith can be an example and a blessing to others. However, we are probably all aware that our faith is not as strong as it could be, so our constant cry should be that of Luke 17:5.

Hebrews 11:29; Exodus 14:21-31
Living by faith – crossing the Red Sea

The crossing of the Red Sea was a defining moment in the history of God's people. It was a testimony to his covenant relationship with them and a primary example of his work on their behalf. It was celebrated for generations (for example Isaiah 43:16-18). It was also illustrative of greater things to come (1 Cor. 10:2,11), and we shall consider it as a pointer to saving faith.

Saving faith is in God.

His promises. God had promised the patriarchs that their descendants would possess the land he had chosen for them (Exod. 13:5,11). That promise had yet to be fulfilled. They believed it would be, as God would ensure that no obstacles would stand in their path. God has promised salvation to all who trust in Christ (John 20:31; Rom. 10:9-11).

His command. God gave instructions about what would happen and they accepted his authority over them (Exod. 14:15-16). Saving faith acknowledges God's right to provide the way of salvation.

His presence. God was not distant from them but had become directly involved in their experience. The pillar of cloud confirmed the reality of God's companionship (Exod. 13:21). Its change of position provided protection. They had to step out in faith (Exod. 14:19-20).

His power. God was clearly at work in miraculous ways (Exod. 14:21-22). Faith is not wishful thinking. It is based on evidence (Exod. 14:31). Salvation shows the miraculous power of God.

Saving faith must be active. That first step of faith led to others. Turning back was never an option. By every step they took, they were committing themselves more deeply to the unknown future God had put before them. They had left behind their past and its bondage and, once they were on the other side of the sea, it was gone forever. This is the key message the writer of Hebrews wanted to convey: no going back. Their future, albeit hidden, was infinitely preferable to their past.

Saving faith is a gift. Faith is not given to everyone and can be falsified. The Egyptians took the same action as the Israelites but the outcome was different. This detail is easily overlooked but is salutary. The pursuing army tried to enter into the miracle provided for God's people, but it was not for them and they were destroyed by it. They could not have what was not theirs. They had no faith so they could not possess the benefits of it. The visible church has always had many such people within it. They have tried to take advantage of blessings that were reserved for others, and while their attempts may have appeared to be successful initially, ultimately, they too will perish because they lacked the crucial gift of saving faith. Their motives may have been honourable – unlike the Egyptians, but their fate will be identical. The same divine energy used to save some will destroy others.

Hebrews 11:30; Josh. 6:1-21   Living by faith – the walls of Jericho fell

The need for faith. The verse highlights what was accomplished by faith, rather than those who exercised it (cf. Matt. 17:19-21). The people of God had reached the place where God wanted them to be, but they were facing obstacles to their further progress. Again, this is fundamental to the message of the writer. There will always be hindrances in the Christian life – some of them apparently insurmountable. But look at what can be achieved by faith! Even the greatest problem can be overcome. It is worth mentioning for our encouragement that although faith was used at this point, the people did not always use it. They were – like us – inconsistent. If their failures are recorded to warn us, then their 'successes' are recorded to inspire us.

The object of faith. Outside Jericho, Joshua met the Commander of the army of the Lord (Josh. 5:13-15) and that is the basis of all that follows. Joshua's encounter with God revealed him to be supreme, separate and certain. Joshua's faith in God's rightful authority over him and the situation seems to have convinced the people to take the action they did as they shared his faith. His faith was not in his own ability or the effectiveness of the tactic, but in what God would do.

The weakness of faith. There was no direct connection between the action and the result. The apparently foolish instructions were not designed to increase the confidence of the invaders or demoralise the inhabitants of the city. It was intended to increase the expectation of what God would do for his people, as they were clearly powerless against such a strong foe. His strength is made perfect in weakness, and human strength is shown to be wholly inadequate against him.

The practice of faith. God gave detailed instructions from a military perspective. As it was a military operation, the army was to take the lead. Next came the priests and the ark to remind everyone that whatever was accomplished, would only be achieved by the power of God. Finally, the beneficiaries of the campaign also had a part to play in it. Their faith was shown in their obedience – and their perseverance. They kept on doing what was required, even though there was nothing to show for it. They were waiting on God to work in his time.

The victory of faith. The sense of anticipation came to a climax with the sound of the trumpets and the shout of the people. The trumpets were a warning of imminent activity and the shout was one of triumph – before it had actually happened. The time for Jericho to repent and surrender had passed. The strongholds of man – and Satan – can never stand against the power of God. We are engaged in a warfare of which the victory has already been won. All that awaits is its manifestation (1 John 5:4-5; Eph. 6:10-13,18). It will certainly come and everyone will see it.

Hebrews 11:31; Joshua 2; 6:25   Living by faith – Rahab

The subject of faith. The mention of Rahab is surprising and instructive. Not only was she a woman with a despised profession, she was a Gentile and a member of a tribe destined for destruction. She is an early illustration of God, in his grace, choosing to give faith to the most unlikely people (1 Tim. 1:15). She had not received a direct revelation from God but was fully persuaded about him on the basis of the available evidence (Josh. 2:10). She was convinced by the truth and acted accordingly.

Because the reference to Rahab is passive – 'did not perish', it is possible that those who acted in faith on this occasion were Joshua and the soldiers. They honoured their word to her, believing that her providential help pointed to the favour of God. Was it they who were exercising faith in a merciful way by sparing her? She had counted on the faith of the spies and the people they represented (2:12).

We shall consider Rahab here, for even if the alternative is correct, her faith was real too.

The object of faith. Rahab's words to the spies showed that although she came from a pagan background, she believed in God, accepting not only his existence but also his supremacy over all and his covenant relationship with Israel (11). She did not plead her own good deeds or appeal to the good nature of the spies or the mercy of Joshua. She was acting for the good of God's people (9), and bound herself to it (12). Her request for clemency was an afterthought and not a condition of her help.

The nature of faith.

Courage. She would stand alone, going against the whole city and its ruler. By the time the spies arrived, she had already been given the gift of faith and made her choice as a result. Their arrival – providential for both parties – gave her the opportunity to express an established conviction. Real faith has a life-transforming influence.

Self-denial. She would become a traitor by placing herself under the jurisdiction of God. If discovered, she faced death, but she surrendered her life to him, preferring to die for his name if necessary, rather than align herself with her people against him.

This would be very relevant to many of the original readers of Hebrews as they faced pressure to save their own lives and not to trust God (Heb. 10:39).

The reward of faith. Rahab had evidently persuaded her family to accept the truth about God as she had, because they did not betray her and were preserved along with her. More than that, she was integrated into the nation (Josh. 6:25) and became an honoured member (Matt. 1:5). She could not have known about that future honour, which reminds us that, unknown to us perhaps, the outcome of our faith does not relate just to our present but our future also and could impact the lives of others.

Hebrews 11:32-40   Living by faith – many conquerors

The writer of Hebrews says he has no time to continue his detailed list of faithful Old Testament saints. He suggests some he might have mentioned and identifies two groups in these verses. The first group (32-35a) are those who were enabled to accomplish great things for God. They were given great tasks which were humanly impossible. They were promised success and their faith held on to those promises of God and they achieved the divine intention. The second group (35b-38) are those who endured severe trials out of their duty to God. Their experience showed that extreme sufferings do not dim real faith but actually cause it to burn more brightly. It helps people to rise above great distress.

They were commended for their faith (39). These saints obtained a good report from God. The biblical records provide a testimony to his approval of them. He had equipped them to complete their tasks. The inner witness of the Spirit confirmed to them God's acceptance of them (Acts 15:8). They had relied upon the help of God in their difficulties and he had vindicated them – and, through them, himself.

They did not receive the promises (39). They received the fulfilment of certain temporal promises – a son to Abraham, for example. But the promises were not only temporal. There was a spiritual, future dimension to them. They received the ability to believe these promises: the assurance they would be fulfilled. They were given the ability to enjoy them – in anticipation of the certainty of their fulfilment. They were given confidence in the Word of God. The promises yet to come (13) could not be experienced before death. By faith, they could still hold on to the greatest promise of all – the coming of the Messiah and the provision of eternal salvation through him. The nature of faith meant that although the promises were still to come, they were as real as if they were present.

They will be made perfect with us (40). The writer wanted his readers to know that, however heroic those Old Testament saints were, they did not possess as many advantages as New Testament saints. We have a clearer view of Christ in the Word of God, rather than through the veiled view of types and symbols. The kingdom has been extended to include people from many nations. The Holy Spirit permanently indwells his people in a new way since Pentecost. We do not contribute to each other's perfection but we shall all receive it in full at the same time even though we leave this world at different times. This perfection will include the total elimination of sin, the resurrection of the body, the reunion of a perfected body with a perfected soul and our glorious reconciliation with God forever. These saints prepared the way for our perfection by unfolding the revelation of God through them and showing what he could do in and through his believing people. We prepare the way for their perfection by our (small) part in completing the number of God's elect. Our greater privileges involve us in greater responsibilities. If they were faithful with so little, how much more should we be faithful with all that we have? We can accomplish more and endure more than they did.

Hebrews 12:1-4   Living by faith – looking unto Jesus

In drawing his exhortations to a conclusion, the writer uses some sporting images.

We are surrounded by witnesses. At first reading this image seems to suggest an amphitheatre full of spectators watching the action in the arena: those in heaven watching those on earth. But the occupants of heaven have better things to do there than watch what is happening on earth! The witnesses are not passive spectators but active participants. Those listed in the previous chapter bear testimony to the realities of living and dying by faith. Their witness is to the nature of a faithful life – which is possible for all believers. Although a minority in their communities, believers are part of a larger group which has successfully persevered. Their assured reception into heaven gives us help and hope. They are witnessing to the faithfulness of God in keeping his people. He will continue to do so.

We must throw off every hindrance. Athletes spend a lot of time preparing for their competitions. Believers cannot do that. Their training takes place 'on the job' and takes two forms:

(a) *Getting rid of excess weight.* We must slim down: remove from our lives those things which are slowing us down. Do you struggle to fit your faith into the rest of life? We may need to take radical action if we are to put away those inconsequential, external factors which preoccupy us too much and impact our faith negatively.

(b) *Getting rid of the sin that clings to us.* The image is of closely fitting clothing which hinders progress. There may be aspects of our temperament which need dealing with, or we may be prone to particular temptations. What is holding you back in your Christian life? These things need working on if we are to 'improve our performance'.

We must run the race. We are not competing against others, but for a prize. A course has been marked out for us and we are required to adhere to certain standards. The Christian life is not a short, flat race but a marathon with hurdles! There must be forward movement, so strenuous effort is necessary. Each runner has their own race – an individual course – although the starting and finishing points are the same for everyone. We should have the determination to continue despite the hardship involved and be willing to submit to the disciples which are integral to the race. Our faith enables us to stay in the race and finish it, seeing us through the inevitable pain barrier (1 Cor. 9:24-27).

We must look to Jesus. The witnesses should only receive a passing glance from us for our gaze should be fixed permanently on Jesus Christ. We are running for and to him, not them. He is the author of our faith: the pioneer or pace-setter, without whom there would be no race at all. He is also the finisher of our faith: the champion who completes it first and becomes the one who perfects it on our behalf. He shared his victory with us. He endured and so will we. To drop out of the race is to drop out of him and lose everything. He set his sights on what he would receive afterwards and kept going to the bitter end. So must we.

Readings in

New Testament Characters

by Douglas Dawson

WINDOW
ON THE
WORD

1 Corinthians 12   Workers together: one body, many parts

Introduction to the series.

Woven into the New Testament story of the early church following Jesus' ascension are many personal stories. They are of men and women from all walks of life, drawn from different parts of the region, who became followers of Christ. Just a few, such as the apostles and their travelling companions, appear frequently. By far the majority receive much briefer mention. Some, like Cornelius and Lydia, feature just once and disappear from our view. Others are unnamed, as is the brother Paul speaks of in 2 Corinthians 8:18.

It has always been like this in the wisdom of God. Prominence or anonymity have never been the measure of importance he attaches to the work assigned to his people. This was where the Corinthian church had got it wrong. It divided over personalities (1 Cor. 1:12); failing to grasp that even the church's leaders are 'only servants' to whom the Lord has 'assigned his task' (1 Cor. 3:5). Later, in the same letter, the apostle works this out in some detail by use of the imagery of the human body. So-called weaker parts are indispensable (12:22). Some are best kept out

of sight; others can cope with the limelight (23-24). This arrangement is ordered by the Head of the church to form an effective body.

One aim of these short studies is that we might recognise what is our God-given role in the body of Christ, challenging us to be effective in it. Another is to honour all as fellow-workers, prominent or little noticed, seen or unseen, named or anonymous.

Of course, involved in every story is a testimony to the transforming power of Christ Jesus as Saviour. None started out as a disciple. All were unregenerate sinners until sovereign grace laid hold on them – cleansed, pardoned, made them new creatures and grafted them into the body. Can you say with one whose story is told in the New Testament – who described himself as 'one of the least' – 'by the grace of God I am what I am' (1 Cor. 15:9-10)? Until you can, you will never be a worker together with God.

It will be a help if you can lay hands on a Bible atlas of the Mediterranean lands in which the grand story unfolded. From time to time these Notes will identify places and routes.

Acts 6:1-15; 7:34 – 8:4   Stephen – an effective martyr

Stephen's appearance on the gospel scene was of relatively short duration. Even so it was exceptionally significant and effective. He was God's man for the hour, setting in motion the commission the Lord gave to his followers to be worldwide evangelists (Matt. 28:19-20; Acts 1:8).

His character – 'a man full of faith and the Holy Spirit' (5), 'a man full of God's grace and power' (8). He was appointed by the church along with six others to oversee the delicate task of caring for the church's widows, whether of Hebrew or Greek origin. It required men who were Spirit-led and culturally sensitive. Only the Spirit-ruled can carry out Spirit-prompted work. Though soon to be shown to be a powerful preacher and defender of the gospel, he humbly accepted the responsibility 'to wait on tables'. Often the Lord has tested those destined for prominence in his kingdom by their ability and willingness to occupy 'lesser' positions. David did not become king of Israel by family succession, but through a tough shepherding apprenticeship. Read Amos' testimony (7:14-15). Don't be too proud to fill a little corner.

His ministry. It was soon evident that the Lord had in mind a more demanding work than distributing food and money – to be an up-front fearless preacher. Stephen had equipped himself with a clear grasp of Jewish history, had powers of logical reasoning, and was God-centred in what he had to say.

Chapter 7 is an example of one who, in his address to the Jewish leaders, had a clear aim and never lost the plot. Preachers take note! He marshalled his facts systematically and powerfully. He was passionate, reaching a challenging conclusion. Either his hearers would accept what he said or hate it – and him!

The effects.

(a) The immediate outcome was Stephen's death. In the light of what followed, deeply mourned as he was, this was a minor consequence.

(b) The persecution that followed launched into reality the vision he had of a God who is not confined to man-made boundaries (49-50). The very thing the stones of the persecutors were intended to destroy, they actually precipitated. 'Those who had been scattered preached the word wherever they went' (8:4).

(c) Though the conversion of Paul is not traced to Stephen, his powerful preaching was part of the 'all things that work for the good...' (Rom. 8:28). Years later the apostle had not forgotten that day and its impact on him (Acts 22:19-21).

Ask yourself: What does it mean to be spiritually minded like Stephen?

Do I have the Scriptures at my fingertips?

Do I realise that how we face death as well as how we live can have evangelistic value?

Acts 8:1-25   Philip [1] – city evangelist

As today, Philip was not an unusual name in New Testament times. The brother of Acts 8 is not the Philip whom Jesus called to follow him, making him one of the twelve (John 1:43; Matt. 10:1-4). He is 'the evangelist, one of the seven' (Acts 21:8) and was a colleague of Stephen. Along with five others, the church appointed them to oversee the practical needs of Christian widows.

1. Like Stephen (of the other five nothing more is said), Philip served his apprenticeship in the capacity of a deacon 'serving tables'. This released the apostles to concentrate on preaching. It soon became evident, if not already recognised, that he had the gift to preach the Word, especially as an evangelist. Yet there is no hint that he felt slighted by being given a more mundane job. His motto might well have been: 'Lord, what will you have me to do?', as is confirmed by later events. Who chooses our service for the Lord?

2. The persecution of the church that followed the killing of Stephen proved to be the launch-pad for the spread of the gospel. If Satan rubbed his hands with glee at the silencing of Stephen, he was soon to wring them in anguish at the outcome. The wind that buffets us and brings the storm also carries seeds far and wide. 'Philip went down to a city in Samaria and proclaimed Christ there' (5). This was just what the Lord intended – 'my witnesses in Jerusalem, in all Judea and Samaria'. Under the mighty hand of God it was the gospel's enemies who unwittingly provoked this expansion. Whatever it was that persecution had forced Philip to leave behind in Jerusalem, it was not the gospel. That was in his heart, and he was just one of many (see 11:19-21). While not disparaging planned evangelism – churches should have a strategy – there is no substitute for the burning heart that takes the gospel wherever it goes. Both had their place in Acts as they have today.

3. Philip was the Spirit's instrument for phenomenal gospel success in Samaria. Back in Jerusalem news of this movement prompted the church to send two apostles, Peter and John, to assess the work. What Philip had begun they consolidated by praying for the anointing of the Holy Spirit (14-17). It is not often that the Lord uses one person to see a work through from beginning to end – 'Paul planted the seed, Apollos watered, but God made it grow' (1 Cor. 3:6). Was Philip's nose put out of joint by the apostles assuming the prominent role? No way! As we shall see, he was ready for the next assignment.

Think about it: Every wheel in a clock, every tooth on each wheel, is essential for the clock to work properly. What the Lord says to you, do it!

Acts 8:1-25   Philip [2] – personal evangelist

From being at the hub of a busy city gospel work, Philip was directed by God to go south-west on the desert road that ran from Jerusalem to Gaza. It was approximately 60 miles in length and was a section of the highway to Egypt. The purpose of this instruction did not become apparent to Philip until he had obeyed. Knowing how caring the Lord is for his servants (Elijah was fed by ravens and later by the widow of Zarephath, 1 Kings 17), one may wonder if a secondary reason was to enable Philip to take a breather. Our Saviour is like that (Mark 6:31). Church officers should watch out for signs in overstretched members.

1. Philip was a true servant of Christ. The master decides the venue and the work to be done. Our inclinations or intentions may be extremely honourable, yet not what the Lord has in mind. It was good, said the Lord, that David wanted to build the temple, but God had other plans (2 Sam. 7). We need to make sure that we have the master's stamp of approval on any project.

2. Apparently Philip was just God's man to approach and evangelise the high-ranking Ethiopian official. The value of the one-to-one approach can scarcely be overestimated. It does not require the planning of a meeting and publicising it, or persuading unbelievers to attend church premises where they may feel uncomfortable. Personal evangelism meets people where they are, and usually out of the public eye. This does mean, nevertheless, some thoughtful preparation:

(a) Philip was where the Lord wanted him to be. Runaway Jonah could hardly commend the Lord to the ship's crew. Be in the right spirit and in the right place.

(b) He adopted a Christlike approach. Waiting the right moment, he fastened on to the man's interest and asked: 'Do you understand what you are reading?'

(c) He possessed a competent knowledge of Scripture. Our first efforts to witness to others may be based upon our limited experience of Jesus' saving power. The Philip of John 1:45-46 had one thing he could say to Nathaniel, but it was effective. That said, all should aim to be proficient in knowing and using the Scriptures.

(d) He had a passion for the man's salvation, as from Isaiah he pointed him to Jesus. Try to avoid getting bogged down in sterile debate. Keep in mind your aim to lead the sinner to Jesus, which is the objective of all evangelism.

The results? The eunuch was converted and openly confessed Christ. Ethiopia had gained a real Christian in high places … and Philip went on to his next assignment.

Do you ask the Lord to lead you to speak to someone about their spiritual state, then look out for the opportunity?

Acts 8:26-40   The eunuch – just one desert convert

Philip might never go to Ethiopia with the gospel. There were plenty of openings for him much nearer home (40). However, in the providential ordering that typifies all that the all-wise God does, there was a better way to get the truth of God into that country – via one of its high-ranking officials.

1. A gradual work of grace. Like other converts we meet in Acts (Cornelius and Lydia) the eunuch was first drawn to the God of the Jews. Some believe he was an African Jew. So strong was the attraction that he made the long journey from his homeland to Jerusalem, the centre of Judaism. Little did he realise that the truth as yet so dimly seen would blaze with glorious light on the desert road home. How? Through the reading of the Scriptures. 'The unfolding of your words gives light; it gives understanding to the simple' (Ps. 119:130). Philip was on hand to do the unfolding, because the Lord who orders all our ways had arranged it so. There are times when the Spirit of God dispenses with human unfolders – after all, 'the word of God is living and active. Sharper than any two-edged sword, it penetrates to dividing soul and spirit' (Heb. 4:12). More often, though, God uses human means to explain the Scriptures, which is why we need to be prepared to help the seeker. Either way, keep in mind that God's Word can do what we can never do – convict and convert. In what way would you say that the eunuch was, in the word of the verse from Psalm 119, 'simple'?

2. Spirit-implanted faith is responsive to the gospel. He was eager to be taught (31). This was, and still is, evidence that the Holy Spirit is at work. He listened to Philip, asked pertinent questions, and had no difficulty in being led from Isaiah's prophecy to its fulfilment in Christ. This, he knew, was what he had been searching for: the lifting of his burden and clearing of his sight. The Holy Spirit never does half a work and is far more patient than often we are to complete the transformation. Nor does he ever say, 'God has done his bit, now it's up to you.' As Ezekiel says, 'I [the Lord] will give you a new heart and put a new spirit in you' (Ezek. 36:26). The whole operation is the work of the divine Surgeon; we are just instruments he uses.

The patient with the new heart responded: 'Why shouldn't I be baptised?' Indeed, why not? Faith must come out. Philip would certainly have explained to the convert that outward confession was part of the apostolic gospel, not an optional extra (Acts 2:38). Now the chariot carried back to Ethiopia a new chancellor of the exchequer, one that was full of joy. What did his entourage make of it? What about his family, his office staff, his queen? We can only conjecture. It only needed just one converted soul to take the gospel back to his home country and reach people that Philip could never have reached.

If you are as yet the only Christian in your circle, how privileged that circle is! Without you the darkness would be total.

'Go home and tell what great things the Lord has done for you.'

Acts 9:32-43; Mark 5:21-24,35-43   Dorcas – a busy woman

From the much publicised conversion of Saul and its effects in Damascus and Jerusalem, the narrative turns to the more rural communities. As a stone thrown into a pond sends ripples in all directions, so the gospel influence was expanding (1:8). This passage is a window on evangelism in outlying districts being consolidated by Peter (32).

Dorcas. There are no grounds for portraying her as an elderly widow, possibly physically restricted, spending most of her time knitting. If her Aramaic name, meaning 'gazelle', has any significance, she was far from confined – 'always doing good and helping the poor'. She was also to be an unwitting key player in God's worldwide plan for the gospel.

1. Dorcas – a disciple. This is the only feminine form of the word in the New Testament. It suggests a woman whose faith was clearly exhibited by her devotion to Christ and her desire to be taught about him. While we must not make too much of this slender evidence, recall that Jesus said: 'If you hold to my teaching you are really my disciples' (John 8:31-32). All who profess Christ today are expected to be learners of him.

2. A practical worker. Many a woman who is tempted to say, 'There is nothing much that I can do,' has found comfort and inspiration in Dorcas. To the poor and widows of Joppa she was the Lord's angel/messenger. Authentic Christianity has always been at the forefront of caring for the whole person. Like its master, the church is expected to exercise this all-round ministry. It has its elders and deacons to ensure a balanced ministry both spiritual and material (6:1-4).

3. Dorcas and Peter. Her death was a great blow to the church at Joppa. The apostle was 10 miles away in Lydda and so they sent for him. Joppa was inhabited by Greeks and Jews. Both of Dorcas' names imply Gentile connections. It seems that Peter's prejudices as an orthodox Jew were being challenged already. Stage by stage, the apostle was being prepared for the grand leap into the Gentile world. How carefully the Lord prepares us for his service. If Peter was unsure how to respond to an appeal for the dead, from those with Gentile connections, he had only to imitate his master. Turn to the passage in Mark, noting the similarities.

4. Many conversions (42-43). This result was entirely outside Dorcas' control. Yet what was out of her hands was firmly in the Lord's. Her death was not a disaster. It brought Peter to Joppa and led to more conversions. This is the confidence in which the believer rests. Events we would have wished otherwise, but we could not control, God works for the fulfilment of his plans and our good. New believers in Joppa meant that Peter must stay there and not return to Lydda – and all in readiness for God's next move (Cornelius, ch.10).

Consider this: It would have been kinder for the Joppa church not to be have been put through the sorrow of losing Dorcas. What is your reply?

Acts 10:1-23 Cornelius [1] – the seeker

Rome was the occupying power in Israel throughout the first century AD. To keep the peace, regiments of Roman soldiers were dispersed in the land. One garrison was stationed in Caesarea on the Mediterranean coast north of Joppa. Cornelius, in charge of a hundred men (centurion), lived there with his family and had adopted the Jewish faith. So began his journey of faith that was to lead to Jesus Christ.

1. Disillusionment. It is possible that before his posting to Judah, Cornelius had no real contact with either the Jewish or the Christian faiths. The dominant religion of Rome with its multiplicity of gods (polytheism) and idols, so often associated with corrupt and debased practices, left him empty. A divinely created discontent with life is not infrequently used by the Lord to set in motion a search for the truth. Nicodemus was first unsettled before coming to Jesus (John 3:1-2).

2. Discovery. Judaism was so different (2). It worshipped one God (monotheism). It had no idols. God is invisible. Its laws set a high ethical standard. For all its faults, laid bare by Jesus, the Jewish religion had many sincere adherents who lived to its credit.

Many students who come to the West to study, especially from the Far East, will meet Christians for the first time. How important it is that they see the genuine article. A number have done so and been converted.

3. Devotion. God-fearers like Cornelius, called proselytes by the Jews, took their new-found faith seriously. The Sabbath was diligently observed, a radical change for a Roman. God was honoured, prayed to, and his work generously supported. Luke 7:1-10 tells of another centurion highly regarded by the Jewish people – one whose faith amazed even Jesus.

Something to think about: Was Cornelius at fault in adopting Judaism and not the faith of Jesus Christ? It is probable that he had never heard the gospel. Even if he had, God does not lead all by the same path to himself. Jesus restored several who were blind, by differing procedures. On one occasion he healed in two stages: first the man saw people 'like trees walking around'; only after the Lord's second touch did he see 'everything clearly' (Mark 8:24).

Cornelius' search for the truth needed to be intensified. Faith in the God of Abraham, Isaac and Jacob laid the foundation for the coming of Christ. But faith has not arrived until it can say: 'We have found the one Moses wrote about in the law … Jesus of Nazareth' (John 1:45).

The promise still holds: 'You will seek me and find me when you seek me with all your heart' (Jer. 29:13). If you have not yet found, keep on searching until you do.

Acts 10:24-48   Cornelius [2] – the seeker finds

As always, divine providence had put every detail in place. Peter had arrived in Joppa on a mercy mission and was detained by the needs of new converts. Tired after a busy schedule he slept, fell into a trance and had a vision. Cornelius resorted to prayer, still longing for the real spiritual satisfaction that had eluded him in Judaism. He too had a divine visitation. As a result he sent men to fetch Peter, now made amenable to Gentile requests, to Caesarea.

The Holy Spirit had prepared Cornelius:

1. To receive a revelation from the Lord. It came as he prayed. Heartfelt prayer is a sure sign that the Lord is at work in the soul drawing it to himself. It was the evidence that would identify newly converted Saul to Ananias (9:11). It is not unusual for us to have a question answered or a course of action clarified while at prayer. How many of us need to take more time before the Lord awaiting his guidance?

2. To respond to what he was told – 'Send to Joppa for ... Peter' (32). More than likely news of the gospel blessings only 30 miles down the coast had reached Caesarea. Here was a test of Cornelius' earnestness: would he act on the word of the Lord? He tells us: 'So I sent for you immediately' (33). Grace in the heart does not let go the opportunity the Spirit gives to know the

truth. 'Blessed are those who hunger and thirst for righteousness, for they will be filled' (Matt. 5:6). Oh that we all really believed it!

3. To be submissive to the Word. Grace makes the hungry humble. They want the food the Lord has prepared for them. There are few Scriptures that express this more clearly than v. 33. This was a feast not to be missed by the centurion, his family and close friends. Cornelius had no doubt that they were in the presence of the Lord. Unconditionally they were ready to hear 'everything the Lord has commanded you to tell us'. Blessed indeed is the church whose minister comes with the Word of the Lord to a congregation that is eager to hear it! Read v. 33 again and again, then make it your prayer for next Sunday's gatherings.

4. To embrace wholeheartedly the good news (42-43). At last he clearly saw where his spiritual pilgrimage had been leading him – to Jesus Christ. It does not matter by which path the sinner comes, so long as it leads to Christ. Peter made no appeal. His hearers were not asked to make a decision. Peter preached ... with rapt attention the people listened ... and the Spirit gave new life.

Note the biblical pattern: Hear the gospel, believe and be baptised. Does this describe your spiritual pilgrimage?

Acts 9:1-19; 22:12-16 Ananias – a disciple

'In Damascus was a disciple named Ananias' (10). What is a disciple? Jesus left Jews who claimed to believe in him in no doubt as to the meaning: 'If you hold to my teaching you are really my disciples' (John 8:31). What followed showed an ignorance that is still widespread (John 8:33-41).

True disciples submit to their master, Jesus Christ, as Ananias did. He was chosen by the Lord as his agent to go to the aid of Saul. Not all those he uses are disciples. God sent his Son to die, and Pilate authorised his death – but not in conscious obedience to God's will. Disciples are those who want to serve the Lord. Saul, the one-time renegade, as a newly won disciple was about to receive his commission through the visit of Ananias (see Acts 22:12-16). Do you want to follow the Lord? Then learn from this disciple:

1. He was attentive to what the Lord had to say. The instructions that came to him in a vision and a voice are now conveyed to us through the completed Scriptures, which he did not have. This requires that we constantly expose ourselves to the Word of God – by reading, meditation and regular attendance at preaching sessions. Impressions and feelings are unreliable, even dangerous guides that do not spring from the Scriptures. Even the advice of others must be Bible-checked. The true disciple is a practitioner of Psalm 1:2.

2. He was responsive to the Lord. He did not initiate the move, it was the Lord that pointed the way. God makes no mistake in the choice of an individual for a special task. Ananias had already proved himself by his devotion to Scripture and the high regard in which he was held (22:12). He was just the kind of man to understand and assist a convert so steeped in Judaism as was Saul; a man who could say: 'Saul, I know the turmoil of mind you have been going through, I've been that way myself.' Your testing experience, reader, may be just the one to enable you to say to someone else: 'I know how you feel.'

3. He had courage. All he had heard about Saul depicted him as a fierce bigoted servant of the high priest – as anti-Christian as they come (13-14). Yet when the Lord said 'Go', he obeyed. The price to be paid for discipleship often sorts out the true from the would-be followers of Jesus. Sincerity is not enough. Christians have to take up the cross, unsure at times how their commission will be received. God chooses well; the visitor, Ananias, matched well the visited, Saul.

4. He was a messenger of grace. 'Brother Saul' – what a welcome to one lately the arch-persecutor of the church! Pick out the benefits Ananias brought to Saul. When we visit a fellow-disciple, what do we bring?

By the way: Did you notice someone else who rendered Saul an immense service (11)? It was just what this away-from-home new believer needed. Keep your eyes open!

Acts 4:32-37; 9:26-30; 11:19-30   Barnabas [1] – what's in a name?

Barnabas comes to the fore quite early in the church's formation. It followed the report given by Peter and John to the believers of their experience before the Jewish Council (4:23). United prayer was the reaction leading to a renewed filling by the Holy Spirit. This resulted in a greater church unity (32) and a fresh awareness of the needs of the poor. Barnabas was one who sold land, making the proceeds available to the church. His family name was Joseph, a member of a priestly family in Cyprus.

The apostles renamed him Barnabas, 'son of encouragement'. This reflected the character of his service to the Lord's people. From his gift to the poor and subsequent incidents it is easy to see how he got the name – he earned it!

1. His action in selling property and handing over all the proceeds reveals a caring spirit. One mark of genuine conversion to Christ is the re-evaluating of the worth of personal possessions. They are no longer near the top of one's scale of values. True giving is a grace, not an obligation, the outburst of grace in the heart (2 Cor. 8:1-5,7). Should we look again at our order of priorities? Generosity encourages the church in its work. But don't do it just to be in the fashion. Remember Ananias and Sapphira (ch. 5).

2. Saul of Tarsus had left Jerusalem intent on arresting any Christians he found in Damascus. Later, when he returned to Jerusalem, it was as an ardent Christian convert wanting to join the believers (9:26-30). Understandably they were more than a little suspicious. His reception was cool. Enter Barnabas – discerning, compassionate and ready to champion Saul, this one-time persecutor. Is there someone in your church whom others keep at arm's length, yet could do with a bit of encouragement? Few of us are incapable of doing a Barnabas!

3. When the news reached the apostles of blessing in Antioch, Barnabas was their choice to go, assess and assist (11:19-30). He had grown in spiritual stature and in the estimation of the church's leaders. His judgement had proved sound in backing Saul, and he had a great heart for people. Events fully justified their choice. On arrival he certainly would not have found perfectly mature converts, 'but he saw evidence of the grace of God, was glad and encouraged them ...'. Nor was that all. Here was the golden opportunity 'to do a Barnabas' and encourage his brother and friend Saul to use his undoubted gifts (25). He might have seen Antioch as the chance to build his own empire and enhance his own reputation. Not so – personal ambition was treated in the same way as personal property: all belonged to the Lord.

'Your attitude should be the same as that of Christ Jesus' (Phil. 2:5). How much of Jesus do you see in Barnabas? And what about yourself?

Acts 13:1-3; 14:21-28   Barnabas [2] – missionary and church planter

What was it about Barnabas that fitted him to be a pioneering missionary? Answering this question is as relevant today as it was in the first century.

Barnabas was:

1. Called. To this there were two parts. First, he and Saul received the internal call of the Holy Spirit: 'I have called them.' Then, this was confirmed by the God-given recognition and action of the Antioch church (3) – the external call. The church does not make ministers, it recognises the gifts and calling of the Lord to the person(s) concerned. It is a safeguard against a personal desire being mistaken for the divine call. Both individual and church are engaged in a holy exercise and must be Spirit-led. The church in sending undertakes to support its representative (14:26-28). Some time later Paul told the Philippians what their support had meant to him (4:14-18).

2. Experienced. The nature of this gospel expedition required men who had already been tested and proven. Barnabas had shown his mettle in standing by the new and unexpected convert, Saul. Both of them had shown maturity in their handling of the large number of converts in Antioch and moulding them into a healthy church. This was the kind of man, along with proven Saul, to evangelise and plant a line of Gentile churches in Asia Minor (consult your Bible map for the places named in Acts 13 and 14). Every Christian is called to be a witness and to serve the Lord, but not to run before they can walk.

Do you serve Christ to the limit of your capacity?

Do you take time to encourage and develop new converts?

The type of work described in 14:21-23 was just right for Barnabas. Can you picture him revelling in encouraging these trophies from paganism? God chooses his workers well. It was just the job for 'the son of encouragement'.

3. Compatible. To be a strong character and to work harmoniously with others is a priceless quality. Barnabas could do it. He was well-established in the church before Paul. At the beginning of their joint venture it was Barnabas and Saul. Before its completion the order was reversed – with no hint of jealousy. The progress of the kingdom of Christ is what matters, not personal kudos. 'The grace of God that brings salvation' teaches us how to live (Titus 2:11-12). Our Saviour Jesus frequently has cause to be upset by the 'worldly passions' of his disciples but is never less than gracious. Surely grace should make us easier to work with, shouldn't it?

What do you make of this? – Acts 15:36-41 is the account of 'a sharp disagreement' between Paul and Barnabas. Does this shatter the notion of their compatibility, or had the issue at stake another explanation?

Acts 13:1-12   Sergius Paulus – the devil defeated

Initially the gospel missionaries, Barnabas and Paul, went to the Cypriot synagogues, as was their practice (46). Eventually their extensive tour of the island brought them to Paphos and a confrontation with Elymas. This evil man traded in magic and the occult. He appears to have had some official attachment to the household of Sergius Paulus the island's governor. He was using his influence to keep this man from hearing the gospel. Unpromising as this confrontation appeared, the outcome was to be total victory for the truth. Who can tell how the Lord will use what, at first sight, may seem to be a hopeless situation?

1. The proconsul is described as 'intelligent' (NIV); 'prudent' (AV) is probably better: a thoughtful man wanting to sort things out, but he was confused. The wizardry of Elymas had not convinced him. Hearing of the gospel preachers, he was curious to know about the religion they brought. This alarmed the 'child of the devil'. Satan will do all he can to turn sincere seekers away from the truth. Paul was to meet this again in Philippi (16:16-17), as Jesus had before him. However, an agitated devil is an uneasy one, alarmed by the coming of the messengers of light (2 Cor. 4:4).

2. This dispute was in the hands of the all-powerful Lord, not in those of one 'full of all kinds of deceit and trickery'. As often happens, the devil overreached himself in his anxiety to silence and scare off the apostles.

Losing patience with this diabolical attempt to thwart their attempt to evangelise the governor, Paul went into action. With a Spirit-given word, the opposition was cut down to size. At the same time the mind and heart of Sergius Paulus were opened to the truth of Jesus Christ. 'Sergius Paulus' destiny was at stake, more than that, so was the very integrity of the gospel and the Saviour for Cyprus and beyond' (Keddie). Those who oppose the gospel oppose almighty God himself and must bear the consequences.

3. Elymas intended to shut out the light and keep the proconsul in soul darkness. The exact reverse happened. He experienced physical darkness, while the man he had tried to protect entered into the glorious light of salvation in Jesus Christ (2 Cor. 4:6). If the blinding of Elymas amazed him, it was the hearing of the Word of God that led him to believe. Those preachers who bamboozle their audiences by 'miracles', offering little more, are charlatans. It is the Christ of the gospel that saves. Faced as we are today by devilish opposition, do we really believe that the gospel is the power of God to salvation? To the Holy Spirit there are no insurmountable barriers.

What encouragement drawn from this passage might you:

(a) take to yourself;

(b) pass on to your minister?

Acts 15:11-40   Silas – a good companion

Silas (Silvanus) is best remembered as Paul's co-worker on his second missionary journey. The dispute with Barnabas that led to their separation left Paul in need of a replacement. Although we are not given the reasons for the apostle's choice, there are some clues.

1. Silas was no novice. He was a 'leader' in the Jerusalem church (22) – a word used at times to describe one who presided. He was also a prophet (32). New Testament prophesying was 'both a preaching of the divine counsels of grace already accomplished and the foretelling of the purposes of God in the future' (Vine). Here was a brother who could expound what God revealed to him. In no sense are missionaries to be thought of as second-rate ministers of the gospel. The work requires those able to evangelise, teach and counsel. This high standard had been required of Paul and Barnabas in their earlier venture (see Acts 14:21-25). Newly planted churches are built on a good foundation by good teachers.

2. Paul had become acquainted with Silas at the conference in Jerusalem when the ground-breaking decision was taken not to require Gentile converts to conform to the Jewish law of circumcision. The assembly had appointed Judas and Silas to accompany Barnabas and Paul on their return to Antioch. They carried the approved letter (23), aiming to deliver it and to explain the decision to the believers in the churches. This gave Paul plenty of opportunity to observe Silas using his God-given abilities. The Scriptures caution us against rushing men into prominence or office before their time (1 Tim. 3:6). The rule is 'get to know, weigh', before appointing.

Silas – the Holy Spirit's choice. We can be sure that 'commended by the brothers to the grace of the Lord' (40) included divine approval and was not dissimilar from the earlier setting apart of Barnabas and Paul (13:1-3).

The resolute quality of this brother was confirmed during the team's trials in Philippi. He knew what it was to suffer for the gospel (16:22-25). Writing later to that church, the apostle asserts: 'It has been granted to you on behalf of Christ, not only to believe on him, but to suffer for him' (Phil. 1:29). This is a price to be paid for being a witness for Christ. Nor does Scripture ever play it down for fear of putting off would-be followers. The path of the Saviour is the path his disciples must take. To suffer for Christ is an honour. It is the pathway to glory (2 Tim. 2:12). Without the willingness of God's Son to suffer and die there would be no gospel for us to believe or to proclaim.

What do you think? If Silas were a member of your church what impact might you expect him to have on it?

For further study: Using these additional passages – Acts 17:4-10,13-15; 2 Corinthians 1:19; 1 Peter 5:12 – what are the chief qualities of Silas?

Acts 16:1-10; 2 Thessalonians 3:1-6   Timothy [1] – the young recruit

Lystra and Derbe were cities of Cilicia (consult a map) evangelised by Paul and Barnabas on their first missionary journey. This was probably the time of the conversion of Timothy's grandmother and mother, Lois and Eunice (2 Tim. 1:5), and possibly of Timothy himself. All but Derbe of the places visited had a double visit from the apostles, enabling the recent converts to become established in Christ (14:21-23). With Jewish ancestry, Timothy had received a good grounding in the Old Testament Scriptures from infancy (2 Tim. 3:15). With his conversion this absorbed biblical knowledge came alive to him and relevant to his new life.

Christian parents must be diligent in teaching their children the Word of God. Do it in a lively and interesting way, making sure that is backed by prayer and undergirded by consistent Christian living. Good teaching can be negated by bad practice.

Returning to the region after about two or three years, Paul was drawn to Timothy. He was young but fast maturing in the faith. The leaders of his home church and neighbouring Iconium spoke well of him. He was just the kind of person to replace John Mark (15:38).

There is no better training for a young promising Christian than working alongside one who is mature. This was Jesus' practice. He chose twelve 'that they might be with him and that he might send them out to preach' (Mark 3:13-14). The exercising of authority in leadership is for those who are proved and approved. Church elders and other discerning members should be constantly on the lookout for young people who show spiritual promise – to help and encourage them.

Timothy's first recorded special assignment came with Paul's anxiety over the fledgling church in Thessalonica. He, Silas and Timothy had unfinished business in that city when persecution drove them out. So fierce was the opposition that it followed them to Berea, compelling Paul to hurry on to Athens (17:10-15). It was unwise for him to go back to Thessalonica, so he sent Timothy (1 Thess. 3:1-6). Wasn't this risky, even if the young man did not attract the antagonism like Paul? There are always unknown factors when God's people engage in his work. He expects us to take risks – not rash ones, but those that calculate on his infinite wisdom and power backed by his assurance, 'I will be with you.' Moses was not at all comfortable at the thought of going back to the Egypt he had left in a hurry – 'Who am I that I should go?' The Lord's reply, 'I will be with you,' was enough (Exod. 3:10-12). Both Timothy and Paul proved this, too.

Can you identify the risks that:

(a) A preacher might take in dealing with unpalatable biblical topics?

(b) A young Christian faces taking an open stand at school/college?

(c) You could encounter in speaking to your neighbours?

Now read Acts 20:22-24.

1 Timothy 1:1-7,18-20; 2:1-15   Timothy [2] – a young pastor

From a youthful assistant to Paul, Timothy graduated to exercise pastoral oversight of the church in Ephesus. As part of the apostle's team he had been well-schooled in every aspect of the Christian ministry. That he proved to be an apt pupil is clear from the assignment to Thessalonica which he seems to have fulfilled successfully. So when Paul left Ephesus he was confident enough in Timothy to leave him in charge – his first pastorate.

This provides us today with a pattern in the preparation of men for the pastoral ministry:

(a) The local church recognises a man's suitable character, temperament and gifts (Acts 16:2; 1 Tim. 4:14).

(b) He 'sits at the feet' of teachers who can instruct him.

(c) He gains experience by preaching, counselling, observing and being involved with those more mature.

The apostle's first letter to Timothy deals with the areas in which the pastor must devote his gifts and energies. These brief notes can only give an outline of the range of subjects. Try to find time to examine them in more detail. You will be rewarded with a fuller appreciation of eldership responsibilities. It should result in more specific praying for your leaders, being more responsive to their leadership, and so encouraging them.

Among matters covered are:

(a) Correcting false teaching by 'sound doctrine that conforms to the glorious gospel of the blessed God' (1:3-11). Paul knew what the truth had done for him (1:15-16).

(b) Instructing the church in the scope and manner of acceptable worship, including female attire – surely relevant to both sexes today (2:1-9).

(c) Dealing with the principles governing the appointment of elders and deacons (3:1-13).

(d) Showing the importance of relationships within the church, the family and at work (5:1 – 6:2). Failure in any of these can seriously hinder the church's testimony.

(e) Exposing the dangers of materialism and worldliness (6:3-10).

Remember, your pastor is a man 'just like us'. He, too, faces temptations and has a battle on his hands (6:11-12). He may be prone to sickness (5:23) and feel his inadequacy (4:12). Yet he has to maintain his ministry and study the Word (4:11-16).

Today's study demands more than most daily readings, but it is worth it for you and the church. The best is drawn from the minister by the best congregations.

Acts 16:11-15   Lydia – the open-hearted

Following his usual practice, on arrival in Philippi Paul sought out any known Jewish gathering. There was a small one that met by the riverside – small indeed, but to prove of great importance for church-planting in the city. Don't despise small opportunities! This one had at least one seeker, Lydia. The Lord led her, a Gentile, to Christ by the same route taken by Cornelius (Acts 10). The first step was the halfway house, from paganism to Judaism. She was 'a worshipper of God', one who had adopted the Jewish religion. But when the Holy Spirit is at work in a person he does not leave them stranded on the highway. To do so would conflict with the purpose of the cross – 'to bring us to God' (1 Peter 3:18). The Spirit of God is concerned with effectual calling, bringing to completion what he has started.

1. The Lord's moment had arrived for him to open her heart. The recorder of this event, Luke, is careful to tell us that this was more than an emotional experience. She responded to Paul's message. The Holy Spirit is the heart-opener by means of the Word of God. The Bible is the sword that penetrates, the seed that implants life, the light that illuminates and the guide that leads to Jesus.

2. The message she heard did not end with 'repent and believe the gospel'. An integral element of true faith is confession (Rom. 10:9-11). Belief must out! This was how the good news spread from Pentecost and the church in Philippi began. A businesswoman of Lydia's standing openly confessing Christ by baptism was something to talk about and to be looked into. Many reading this account will never be appointed by the church to be preachers. Disappointed? Why should you be when by your life you can tell what great things the Lord has done for you?

3. Lydia's conversion enrolled her in a new family, the people of God. What could she do to show her gratitude to the Saviour? Paul and his team were not residents of Philippi, but she was. 'Come and stay at my house.' Doubtless they would value her prayers and the money she could well afford. But they needed a secure base. Hospitality at various levels from a meal to a bed or more may be just the ministry some of us can give. Turn to 1 Peter 4:9-10. An open door to others is one of the gifts given to us. After all, we all belong to the same family.

Try this: Start where Lydia did and see how far you have travelled.

Acts 16:16-40   The gaoler – converted by chance!

To the sceptic, the meeting of the gaoler with Paul and Silas was on a par with the random occasion when, say, you bump into someone from your home town in a distant holiday resort. If the fortune-telling girl had left the preachers alone ... if Paul had not cast the evil spirit out ... if her masters had not had them arrested ... if they had not been flung into prison ... then the gaoler would not have been converted. What is our reply? Our 'ifs' are nothing more than our ignorance of what God is doing. We read of this event only after the Lord has strung its parts together. It is ever so – John 13:7; 16:12; Hebrews 12:11.

1. The Lord has planned his own timetable.

(a) The gospel Paul's team preached in Philippi was widely known (17-20). At some time, in some place, the gaoler must have heard it. Was he interested, or had he dismissed it? Who knows? Many an eventual convert was little moved by it at the first hearing.

(b) The gospel was brought to the gaoler's doorstep by the unjust treatment and imprisonment of the apostles. And while they sang the gaoler slept!

(c) It so happened, as men would say, that an earthquake hit Philippi that night, shaking the prison to its foundations and its keeper into wide-awake spiritual concern. The Lord of all seismic eruptions had ordered this one to save the souls of at least one household, possibly many more.

2. The gospel and its fruit.

(a) The good news the gaoler heard was the same that had changed Lydia and shaken the city: 'Christ died for the ungodly,' and, 'whoever calls on the name of the Lord will be saved' (Rom. 5:6; 10:13). The message remains unchanged in the twenty-first century. It makes no concessions to modern thought, which is as old as the hills. 'Men suppress the truth by their wickedness' (Rom. 1:18). As then, so now, the gospel is non-negotiable: 'Believe on the Lord Jesus Christ and you will be saved.'

(b) The good news is intelligible and reasonable: 'They spoke the word of the Lord to him and to all the others in his house.' They were not swept along on a wave of emotion or by the after-shock of the earthquake, but by gospel logic: God is holy, he hates sin, all men are sinners and destined for judgement; a merciful God has given Jesus to save his people from their sins. The gaoler and his family believed, and on God's unfailing promise were saved.

(c) The fruit of the good news is seen in transformed lives: they were 'filled with joy', 'were baptised', 'washed their wounds' and 'set a meal before them'. The grace of God produces inner peace, public confession and love for one another. How is it with you?

Philippians 2:25-30   Epaphroditus – steadfast

The church in Philippi was deeply indebted to Paul and his team for bringing the gospel to their city (Acts 16). Now their father in the faith was languishing in a prison in Rome. What could they do? Epaphroditus was the answer. He was one of their best men, a devout and able Christian. So they sent him with a gift suited to the apostle's needs.

1. Epaphroditus not only delivered the gift, he was part of it. Nothing is said as to whether sending this man represented a real sacrifice on the church's part. Yet a believer whom Paul described as 'my brother, fellow-worker and fellow-soldier' must have been greatly missed. Other churches and the mission field at home or overseas stand in need of help. The Lord requires us, individuals or churches, to give not what we can spare, but our best, as he did (Phil. 2:5-8). The Spirit of Christ, who was among us as one who serves, should be the hallmark of all who belong to him.

2. The measure of his service. The triple description of him as Paul's brother, fellow-worker and fellow-soldier is indicative of his commitment to the apostle's stance for the gospel's sake. Note the progression:

(a) *Brother* – both share the same faith, for both are part of the family of God. God's people cannot be too careful before accepting the assistance of the unconverted. This may puzzle, even offend those who offer. But the same principle applies that caused Peter to reject Simon the sorcerer: 'You have no part or share in this ministry, because your heart is not right with God' (Acts 8:21). Repentance is a prerequisite. No one can be taken into partnership whom we cannot call brother or sister.

(b) *Fellow-worker*. Those who by adoption are part of God's family are integrated into a working family. Not all will do the same work. The human body parts have different functions, but none is idle. So it is in the church (1 Cor. 12). Paul valued this brother who could work alongside him. Should a Christian ever simply do his own thing?

(c) *Fellow-soldier*. To work with Paul, the bold and fearless, was no easy option. But Epaphroditus was not looking for one. He did not pull out when the going got tough. Let us consider it an honour when the Lord puts us on the front line for the gospel's sake. Has he put you there? Then, be strong in the strength which he supplies.

3. The cost of his service. 'He was ill and almost died.' What his home church could not do for Paul, Epaphroditus 'risked his life to carry out'. The word 'risk' is like the gambler's stake that might or might not succeed. He did not know what for him might be the outcome of his 'reckless' devotion. Yet behind such seeming folly surely lay the confidence that his future was safe in the Lord's hands. Like his master, he was obedient, even if death should be the outcome. Oh, for more gamblers for God! – the final result is not in doubt – 1 Corinthians 15:58.

Epaphroditus was tough but tender. The thought that the church back home was distressed at the news of his illness speaks volumes for the high value it set on him and the close bond between them. Spend a few minutes calling to mind members of the church who, because of ill-health, age or calling, are 'out of sight'. What could you and the church do to warm their hearts and lift their spirits?

Philippians 4:1-9   Euodia and Syntyche – the contenders

Christians differ in many ways. This is to be expected. God has created individuals. So we pursue different careers, we run our homes differently, we have a variety of leisure activities. In the church, too, the Lord has spread his gifts around. Like the range of colours in a garden, the mosaic of various abilities in a church is one of its attractions. It enriches our knowledge and experience as we observe the contributions of one and another … unless any of those differences become a matter of contention. Clearly some difference had occurred between Euodia and Syntyche that could not be ignored. News of it had reached Paul in a Roman gaol who felt compelled to raise it in his short Philippian letter.

1. The dispute. Its nature was sufficiently well known that he did not need to spell it out. But surely there was another reason for not naming it. We need to know the principle, not the details. Any dispute between the Lord's people dishonours him, particularly if it is generally known. Here were two women who had been of great help and encouragement to the apostle during his time in Philippi. With him they had contended for the gospel boldly, facing the opposition. Now they were fighting each other. How gratifying to the devil! He had been humiliated by the conversion to Christ of some of his followers (see Acts 16). Now they were falling out with each other. Be warned! 'Be self-controlled and alert. Your enemy the devil prowls around … looking for someone to devour' (1 Peter 5:8).

2. The effect of the dispute. Paul sandwiches his appeal to the women between two exhortations. This is not accidental.

(a) *Stand firm (1)*. The ability to do this depends on the conscious reliance on the Lord and a wholehearted defence of the truth. Paul was grieved that those one-time contenders for the gospel had shifted their ground to contend against each other over something personal.

(b) *Rejoice in the Lord (4)*. This could hardly be achieved in an atmosphere of disagreement. The church that has to spend time sorting out internal friction will find it difficult at the same time to stand firm and to rejoice in the Lord.

3. The appeal. Euodia and Syntyche were Paul's dear friends. He had no intention of taking sides in the dispute. Even-handedly, it is as though he went to each in turn: 'I plead with (you) Euodia,' and, 'I plead with (you) Syntyche.' If they both responded to him then harmony would be re-established. Had he their dispute in mind, at least partially, in 2:1-9? It is surely impossible to be like-minded, to consider others better than yourself and to have the mind of Christ, and be at loggerheads. So pressing was the matter that Paul did not wait for the women to seek the help of a third party – 'I ask you loyal yoke-fellow, help these women.' The dispute must not be left to fester a day longer; the church must act. How could these dear but misguided women listen to the exhortation of vv. 8-9 and remain unmoved? From time to time churches need a loyal yoke-fellow to help bring together those who have started to pull apart.

Think over: How do you connect the threefold: 'stand firm', 'agree', 'rejoice in the Lord'?

Does the tension between the two women have something to say to you and your contribution to the church?

Acts 18:1-8,18-28   Aquila and Priscilla – an effective partnership

This Christian couple must have covered considerable mileage in the service of Christ and the interests of the church. Expelled from Rome (2), they went to Corinth and then to Ephesus (19). Later they were back in Rome (Rom. 16:3) and were last seen again in Ephesus (2 Tim. 4:19). Nothing is known of when or where they were converted. They first appear on the scene in Corinth as tentmakers with whom Paul stayed. The following features of their lives are worthy of our attention:

Hospitality. Little imagination is required to appreciate how spiritually profitable their lodger was to them. If they were able to put tentmaking business his way, he would certainly have enlarged their understanding of the gospel both at home and in the synagogue (4). See 1 Corinthians 15:1-8 as an example of the apostle's instruction. They benefited from Paul as Abram had from entertaining the three visitors (Gen. 18). When, some months later, the couple had moved to Ephesus, their open home policy became the school for improving the theology of Apollos (24-26). Doubtless the earlier time spent with Paul better equipped them to help Apollos. We would do well to ask ourselves if there is more that we could do in this way.

Partnership. Aquila and Priscilla were what every Christian couple should be: they were a joint enterprise in the Lord's service. What they did they did together. In Scripture they always appear as a pair – at home, on the road and around the churches. While it is true that the Lord requires that a Christian should only marry a Christian (2 Cor. 6:14), there is

more to it than that. They should be one in aims, associations and activities. Spotting that Apollos needed more help, 'they invited him to their home and (they) explained to him the way of God more adequately'. It was a joint plan to house and to instruct Apollos. They were also agreed in risking their lives to ensure the safety of Paul (Rom. 16:3-4).

Let couples reassess their oneness. It should not always be taken for granted that a partnership exists. It is something to be worked at.

Use of resources. With a trade they could follow in different places, they seemed to have made both themselves and what they had available wherever the Lord chose. More than one church was indebted to them: 'All the churches of the Gentiles are grateful to them' (Rom. 16:4). Few of us are called to this kind of roving commission, but at the back of it is the principle: 'What I have is the Lord's – home, income, skill and time.'

The word that springs to mind to describe Aquila and Priscilla is *commitment*. This in essence is what Jesus calls for in his follower: 'He must deny himself and take up his cross and follow me' (Matt. 16:24).

Could you do this? In a day when many non-believers find entering a place of worship intimidating, almost enemy territory, we should look more closely at the evangelistic value of the Christian home. It may also be the haven that a lonely, away-from-home believer needs. Do you have an open-door policy? The benefits are seldom one-sided: 1 Kings 17:7-24; 2 Kings 4:8-37.

Acts 18:18-28   Apollos – gifted and able, but…

Apollos looked to be the ideal Christian minister. Well-educated (Alexandria had a reputation for learning), thoroughly acquainted with the Old Testament Scriptures, he had a good grasp of sacred history ('the way of the Lord'). His preaching was lively and what he said about Jesus could not be faulted. He was not a man to sit back. Fired by his convictions he boldly preached in the Ephesian synagogue. What church wouldn't covet a minister with such knowledge, passion and drive! Yet when Aquila and Priscilla heard him they were uneasy. What had they spotted? Not anything he had said, it was rather what he had not said.

'He knew only the baptism of John.' John the Baptist had called for repentance. Those who responded he had baptised (Mark 1:4-5). As the herald of Jesus he had sought to prepare the way for the Lamb of God who takes away the sin of the world (John 1:29). Some who had followed John had not properly understood that fundamental to the work of Jesus Christ was the cross. In ignorance Apollos had majored on the call for repentance but not on the justifying sacrifice of Jesus at Calvary. Compare the conclusion of Paul's sermon in Pisidian Antioch (Acts 13:14-41, esp. vv. 38-39); see how he developed his sermon from John to Jesus. Then follow his reasoning in Romans 3:21-26. Any church today looking to appoint elders must seek for those who have a balanced understanding of the gospel.

Enter Aquila and Priscilla. If they were critical of his preaching it was constructive. They did not have a moan to others. In their home they explained to Apollos the way of God more adequately – the gospel of redemption through what Jesus had accomplished by his death and resurrection. Paul dealt with similar believers of imperfect understanding in 19:1-6. Apollos was a big enough man humbly to learn from this wise and devoted couple. If you are a Christian of many years' standing, don't expect all new converts to be clear on even the fundamental issues. Follow Aquila and Priscilla and help them along.

On to Corinth. It was not long before Apollos had the total confidence of the Ephesian elders. He was now a full-orbed, Christ-centred preacher. Encouraged by them and carrying a letter of commendation, he went to Corinth. There his ministry proved as valuable as Paul's, who was happy to recognise this. Unwittingly his outstanding gifts made him the object of worldly admiration, which he and the apostle deplored (1 Cor. 1:12). They were both 'only servants' – one plants, another waters, and God makes it grow (1 Cor. 3:5-9).

Therefore – treat your elders with the utmost respect. Value their gifts, but do not idolise them. It will not help them or their ministries. They are 'only servants'.

2 Corinthians 7:2-16; 8:16-24   Titus – the mediator

The evidence in Paul's letters points to Titus being his right hand man in dealing with delicate situations. Yet nowhere is he mentioned in Acts, though he must have been present on some of the occasions recorded. Despite this silence much can be gleaned about him from the epistles. He first appeared on the scene when Paul and Barnabas went to Jerusalem (Gal. 2:1-5). Most historians identify this visit with Acts 15. The issue was whether Gentile converts should be required to fulfil Jewish ritual laws, such as circumcision. Titus as a Greek was not circumcised. His presence was a kind of visible test case, given that there was still a strong Jewish element contending for the old rites. The Jerusalem council's decision not to burden Gentiles with these must have strengthened Titus, removing any lingering doubts he might have had.

The calibre of this 'partner and fellow-worker' of the apostle (8:23) became apparent in the commissions Paul assigned to him. These, until he was appointed to oversee the work in Crete (the subject of the next study), was centred upon the church in Corinth. These were:

1. Completing the collection by the church for the needy in Jerusalem. Paul did not want his boasting about Corinth's generosity to sound hollow when he and others arrived to take the gift to Jerusalem (9:1-5). Titus was not sent as a modern style fund-raiser to extract money from reluctant donors. He carried a letter from the apostle to the church in which giving to the Lord's poor is expressed

as 'an act of grace' (8:6) prompted by 'the grace of God' (8:1). What is it that moves us to give to the Lord's people – a sense of duty, 'we ought', or is it the prompting of the Holy Spirit that enables us to see giving as a privilege? The standard is set in 8:9, and 8:1-5 shows what happens when that is applied.

2. The Corinthian collection was interrupted by the pressing problem, even the crisis, that had arisen in the church over gross immorality (1 Cor. 5). Titus had been the bearer of a stern letter (now lost) from Paul, in which he took Corinth to task over its toleration of the guilty brother. The apostle had been in turmoil of spirit over the possible effects of his stricture. How had the church reacted? This lasted until Titus returned with a favourable report (7:5-16). Clearly Titus had managed the delicate mission extremely well, showing him to be made of stern stuff, yet compassionate and caring. The grace of God that moves us to give should also make us unbending when the truth is at stake, yet not harsh and unfeeling, but compassionate. Such was Titus, for when he had the opportunity to go back to Corinth to complete the collection he was enthusiastic (8:17). He was truly a skilled mediator who could resolve a ticklish situation, win the affection of those at fault, being sure they would welcome him back. Just what patience and prayer this demanded is untold – but the outcome speaks volumes.

Read Titus 1:6-9. What eldership qualities would Titus have needed to call upon in dealing with the Corinth disorder?

Titus 1   Titus in Crete

Read also chapters 2 and 3 if you have time. Apart from this letter we have no information about the visit of Paul and Titus to Crete. The apostle's interest in the island could have been sparked off by the brief contact when he was being taken to Rome (Acts 27:6-13). How long they were there together is unknown. At some point Paul left Titus in charge (5). To appreciate what this entailed we must look at the following:

1. The state of the Cretan churches. It was not an attractive picture. Considerable disorder is implied. Why should Paul feel it necessary to stipulate that elders' children must not be open to the charge of being 'wild and disobedient' and the men themselves be free from drunkenness, violence and dishonest dealing? To this must be added, 'There are many rebellious people' who were 'ruining whole households' (10-11) and who 'are detestable, disobedient and unfit for doing anything good' (16). There was also the Cretan trait (12)! Finally, in this depressing list, there is Paul's repetitive use of the need to be 'self-controlled' in 2:1-8. What a shambles! Clearly the grace of God had yet to stamp its mark on many who professed Christ in Crete. They had yet to learn that the grace which brings salvation also teaches us to say a resounding NO to all ungodliness (2:11-12). Across the centuries this uncompromising word comes to us with the same divine authority. It leaves those who profess to be Christ's with no excuse for hanging on to the baggage of their unregenerate days. Ditch it!

2. Titus's task – by any standard a daunting one. It was to appoint elders of the right calibre, and silence the false teachers, especially the Judaisers (see Acts 15:1-2). All family members had to learn to be self-disciplined and be good examples. There is much here that is as relevant for us today. The habits and attitudes of our pagan society colour many a convert's outlook. What was Titus to do? He was to:

(a) *'Teach what is in accord with sound doctrine' (2:1; see 2:15; 3:8).* The gospel of the grace of God is only truly believed by us when it results in a holy, God-pleasing life. That is the very first thing Paul says (1:1).

(b) *'Rebuke sharply' (1:13).* Correction must not be divorced from sound teaching. 'Don't do that' has to be accompanied by 'Do this.' Jesus said: 'Do not worry about your life … but seek first his [your Father's] kingdom' (Matt. 6:25,33; compare Titus 2:11-12). The rules of the kingdom of God have both 'dos' and 'don'ts'. Should parents ever say 'Don't' to a child without a positive 'Do'?

3. Titus' suitability for the Crete work. This tough assignment required proven leadership qualities which Titus had already shown he possessed at Corinth. How we would like to know whether Titus was successful! Could there be a hint in 3:12? Paul was planning to send Titus a successor, for he wanted 'his true son in our common faith' with him. He would hardly do this and put in jeopardy the welfare of the Cretan churches.

Something to bear in mind: The divine master craftsman shapes today's trainees for tomorrow's appointments. He knows what the needs of the future will be. Where do you fit into God's scheme? Do you agree that Timothy would not have been suited to Crete (see 1 Timothy 4:12; 5:23). Every workman has his work.

Acts 20:1-6; Colossians 4:7-9   Tychicus – deacon slave

In addition to the privations he suffered as a pioneer missionary constantly on the move, Paul says: 'I face daily the pressure of my concern for all the churches' (2 Cor. 11:28 – note the context). This was not a burden he could have carried alone. He had a loyal team working with him. Some travelled with him, for he seldom journeyed unaccompanied. Among these was Tychicus, probably from Ephesus. He was part of a substantial group that accompanied Paul through Macedonia and Greece. Its ultimate destination was Jerusalem to deliver the churches' gifts for the poor – dealt with at length by Paul in 2 Corinthians 8 and 9. Paul entrusted Tychicus with letters from him to Ephesus and Colosse. Towards the end of the apostle's life Tychicus was with him during his final imprisonment in Rome.

The best biographical sketch of this devoted Christian is provided by Paul's testimonial to him in Colossians 4:7-9.

1. **A dear brother** – one Paul loved deeply. The modern misuse of 'love' as a mere physical act, often of a trivial nature, must not frighten us off from speaking of great love for a brother or sister in Christ. Paul loved Tychicus because they shared the same passionate love for Christ Jesus, their Saviour and Lord; they were committed to the spread of the same precious gospel, and they looked forward to the fulfilment of the same certain hope. This is the love God has poured into our hearts by the Holy Spirit (Rom. 5:5). Such love is never sensual or temporary. The world neither knows it nor understands it.

But what to those who find? Ah this
Nor tongue nor pen can show!
The love of Jesus what it is
None but his loved ones know.

2. **'A faithful minister and a fellow servant.'** The two are closely allied. 'Minister', the word from which we get 'deacon', signifies one who has a job to do. 'Servant' or 'slave' refers to status – one who is answerable to his master; in this instance to Jesus Christ. Tychicus had the same view of life as Jesus who came 'not to be served, but to serve and to give his life a ransom for many' (Mark 10:45). Imprisoned Paul could entrust with confidence to his dear companion the carrying of letters to the churches, explain their contents and answer the recipients' questions 'that he may encourage your hearts' (Col. 4:8). This was no mere fulfilling of a duty. He set out to do all Paul in person would have done had he been free. Paul's mind was at rest. This 'dear brother' would unselfishly do all that was asked of him. What a treasure to any church are such members! Their gifts have been recognised. They have been commissioned with a work, and they get on with it. With no thought of reward they serve their master. This can only be achieved with the spirit of a servant – a slave of the best of masters. Tychicus and Paul shared this conviction. Both were Christ's slaves and both were answerable to him. The issue does not arise as to which of them was more important to the work of the gospel. Each had his role. So have we – as servants. None of us rises above this status in the service of Christ. Read Romans 12:3. Perhaps it is time to review our place in the church of Christ.

Acts 19:23-41   Aristarchus – a pillar of the church

Aristarchus was the kind of Christian who has been the backbone of the church throughout the ages. We are not told if he was a powerful preacher, a gifted evangelist, church elder or able administrator. Doubtless he had some of these and possibly other gifts. Five times he is named in Scripture. What is instructive about these allusions are the situations in which we meet him. There are times when where God's people are found can tell us much about them. Many could not understand how Jesus, who claimed to have come from God, could mix with the despised 'sinners and tax-collectors'. They failed to recognise that this very situation vindicated his incarnation (Mark 2:16-17). As those called of God, are we where the Lord wants us to be? Aristarchus was:

1. A man who had the courage of his convictions. Surrounded by a hostile and murderous crowd, he and Gaius had been singled out as representatives of a foreign religion (19:28-29). The Athenians saw their way of life to be under threat. Very probably these two were key proclaimers of the gospel. Along with Paul, their message was a direct challenge to these fanatical followers of the idol-god Artemis housed in the magnificent temple. Aristarchus was not exceptional in his courageous stand. He was but typical of what first century gospellers faced for Christ's sake, whether in Lystra (14:19-20), Philippi (16:19-24), or Thessalonica (17:5-9). Paul looked forward to visiting the Philippian church and finding them 'contending as one man for the faith of the gospel, without being frightened' (Phil. 1:27-28). As today opposition to the truth of God increases, courage is called for to take a stand for Christ where he has put us (2 Tim. 3:12).

2. A man of energetic perseverance. He was one of a number of brothers representing Greek and Asia Minor churches who were deputed to take relief to needy believers in Jerusalem. The dangers and privations which Paul endured on his journeys (2 Cor. 11:23-29), others must be ready to face as well. There was no guarantee they would return safely (on one trip Trophimus had to be left ill at Miletus). There is always the temptation to live in our 'comfort zone' – go to church, give regularly, pray faithfully but keep out of trouble. If we all do this, who will hold the hard-pressed brother's hand or answer the call, 'Come over to Macedonia and help us'? Energetic service should be a joy.

3. A man of practical compassion and loyalty. When Paul sailed for Rome to appeal to Caesar, a cryptic phrase informs us: 'Aristarchus was with us' (27:2). It has been suggested that his plan was to return home to Thessalonica. More likely, in the light of Colossians 4:10, it is that he was accompanying the apostle. In Rome he became a kind of 'voluntary prisoner' to care for and to encourage Paul. (It looks as though he shared this honour with Epaphras – Philemon 23-24). Authentic fellowship is more than Christians getting together. It is sharing others' joys and sorrows: spending an hour with a housebound saint; taking another to the clinic or providing a cup of cold water in Jesus' name.

What do you say? 'Our fellowship is with the Father and with his Son, Jesus Christ' (1 John 1:3). Since this affects all aspects of life, so should our fellowship with one another. 'Lord, give me the grace to get alongside my brothers and sisters.'

2 Timothy 1:16-18; 4:6-8,19   Onesiphorus – the encourager

Paul was imprisoned in Rome, expecting it would end in his execution. This personal letter to Timothy is the last we have from Paul. His object was to encourage the younger man to stand firm in the faith. Yet the encourager himself was just as much in need of encouragement. Christian brothers from the province of Asia (the area in which the seven churches of Revelation 2 and 3 were located) had disappointed him (1:15). Onesiphorus was the notable exception. All that we are told about him is here. His name signified one who brings profit. He certainly lived up to his name.

1. He had been of great assistance to the cause of Christ when Paul and Timothy had been in Ephesus. The inclusion of his household in the help given suggests an open home, possibly a base of operations. Itinerant preachers were very dependent on local hospitality (Acts 16:15). This is one reason why elders were to be hospitable – churches met in homes (Philem. 2). To some extent the value of the ministry of the open home has been lost sight of today.

It can benefit the householders (Gen. 18) and the guest (Acts 18:24-26). 'An Englishman's home is his castle' is not found in the Bible. Could we let the drawbridge down more often and put up 'Welcome'?

2. The arrest of the apostle reduced the number of his supporters. Imprisoned Paul was devastated. He would never have believed it of Phygelus and Hermogenes. To support the cause of Christ when things are going well is much easier than when things are difficult. The closer Jesus drew to Calvary, the fewer his followers. Onesiphorus was not put off by the risks. Probably Paul had this in mind in writing: 'If we die with him, we will also live with him. If we endure, we will also reign with him. If we disown him, he will also disown us' (2:11-13). Your Christian brother or sister may be 'imprisoned' in an ungodly home, housebound or in residential care. Could you do an 'Onesiphorus'? That is the kind of religion that God accepts as pure and faultless, according to James 1:27. What is the other element of God-pleasing religion that James includes?

3. What cheered Paul was that this dear brother 'searched hard for him'. He might have excused himself that his schedule in Rome was too tight or that officialdom was unhelpful. And no one would have blamed him, except Onesiphorus himself. He would not take 'No' for an answer. This is the stuff Christ-ruled disciples are made of. The honour of the Lord and the welfare of his people come first. In all innocence Agabus and the Christians in Caesarea had given Paul sound reasons for not obeying the Lord (Acts 21:10-14). But he could not have lived with an uneasy conscience, nor could Onesiphorus, even if no one had blamed him for not finding Paul. Recall what Jesus had to say about going the second mile (Matt. 5:41). Has that any relevance here?

Romans 16:1-2; Mark 10:35-45   Phoebe – a servant and succourer

This thumbnail sketch of Phoebe has more in it than a cursory reading might suggest. But before we look at the details, let us start with:

The overall picture. Paul had so far not been to Rome. Several times he had planned a visit to the church there but, as he told them, had been prevented (1:13). Phoebe was about to make the trip. It looks as if the apostle took the opportunity to write to the church and to use her as the carrier. Since the believers there would not know her, Paul included this commendation of her. In doing so he opened for us a window on this very useful Christian lady. He exhorted them to receive her as God's people should welcome one another.

1. Our sister Phoebe. This tells us as much about Paul as about her. Romans is doctrinally the weightiest of all Paul's letters – a truly apostolic dissertation. Yet he never thought of himself as a superior kind of Christian. Phoebe was his sister in Christ: he was the writer, she was the bearer, and the Romans the recipients; but all were equally 'loved by God and called to be saints' (1:7). Surely this is how we should view each other and all believers.

2. A servant of the church. The NIV footnote offers 'deaconess' as the alternative to servant. This is because the Greek word from which it is derived is *diakonos*. However, it is by no means certain that Paul was using it in a technical sense to depict an office – a member of the diaconate. It is better to see it as describing work carried out – a service rendered. Jesus used the verbal form of the word to teach how he viewed his own work, as the one who came 'not to be served, but to serve' (Mark 10:45). We do not have to possess a recognised status in the church to serve. The master has bestowed this privilege on all his followers.

3. A succourer of many (AV) – 'a great help to many – including me' (NIV). Paul uses a word that appears nowhere else in Scripture. It 'was the title of a citizen in Athens who had the responsibility of seeing to the welfare of resident aliens who were without civic rights. Among the Jews it signified a wealthy patron of the community' (W E Vine). Phoebe seems to have been like the women who assisted Jesus as he travelled from place to place (Luke 8:1-3). Cenchrea was a port that served Corinth and would have had many travellers passing through. Paul himself had used it (Acts 18:18).

Two aspects of service to the Lord are highlighted here:

(a) As a church in a harbour town it had the God-given opportunity to minister to travellers as well as to residents. The location of your church or mine may provide opportunity for a ministry not given to others: to a university, to migrants, to the retired and elderly, to a downtown community. Take a fresh look at where you are.

(b) As individuals, our background, culture, experience, status (single, married, widow, etc.) and resources may open a door to us that for others is more difficult.

'Lord, what will you have me to do?'

Colossians 1:7-8; 4:12-13; Philemon 23   Epaphras – the wrestler

Epaphras was a native of Colosse (4:12). It is possible that he was converted through Paul's ministry in Ephesus some one hundred miles to the west on the coast. Spurred by his new-found faith in Jesus Christ, he returned to evangelise his home district, the Lycus valley, which included the neighbouring communities of Colosse, Hierapolis and Laodicea (1:7). Paul had never visited the area (2:1). He had no need to. The seed of the gospel that had taken root in Epaphras was sufficient to open up to it a whole new territory.

This is an age when strategic planning is considered by some to be absolutely essential to world mission. Certainly we should not be haphazard in evangelism. That said, God, the master strategist, often achieves his goals by those with a burning heart for their own people. 'Go home to your family and tell them how much the Lord has done for you' (Mark 5:19).

Does the church encourage its members to be local evangelists? Do you recognise your God-given potential to be a local witness?

Epaphras was also a prayer wrestler (Col. 4:12). He had gone to Rome both to support Paul the prisoner and to carry news of church affairs back in Colosse. This prompted the apostle to write this letter to the Colossians. Did they miss Epaphras? If so, Paul assured them that their brother still carried them in his heart before the Lord: 'He is always wrestling in prayer for you ...'

1. This kind of prayer, fervent and specific, stemmed from an intimate acquaintance with the situation and a profound concern for those affected by it. Colossians 2 indicates some disturbing influences were threatening to undermine the church's life: worldly thinking (8), and meaningless rituals (16-17). Modern communications supply us with an endless stream of up-to-the-minute worldwide information that invites our prayer. This can be helpful. But it should not take the place of Epaphras-like wrestling for people and situations that are our particular care.

2. Knowing the threat as he did, Epaphras' prayer focused on the remedy, 'that you may stand firm in all the will of God, mature and fully assured'. The more detailed the knowledge, the more specific the intercession. In addition to our broad sweep of prayer for the Lord's work and his workers, there should be that costly prayer that agonises for a few. Verse 13 must mean that Epaphras' prayer for those back home required 'working hard'. That's a challenge to us to take a look at the level of our praying for the local church.

If you are looking for further examples of the effectiveness of earnest prayer, try Elijah (James 5:17); the Jerusalem church (Acts 12:5), and Jesus' illustration in Luke 11:5-13.

2 Timothy 4:9-13; James 4:4-7; 1 John 2:15-17   Demas – the deserter

The temptation to which Demas succumbed is the one known to every follower of Christ: the pull of the world. We have been delivered from the kingdom of Satan and immediately become the target of his attacks to lure us back. They are skilfully adapted to probe our individual weaknesses. What it was that enticed Demas back into the world is concealed from us, quite deliberately. While other scriptures deal with precise temptations – morals, possessions, status or pride – the departure of Demas is intended to alert us to the ever-present danger of backsliding.

1. Demas: a warning to every believer. He had been a valued co-worker with Paul in the cause of Christ. He is named as such in the same breath as Mark and Luke (Philem. 24), and joined the latter in sending greetings to Colosse (Col. 4:14-15). Yet, 'he loved this world'. To us there appear to be some stalwarts whose stand for Christ could never be shaken. Then our confidence in them is shattered: a leader disgraces his calling, a key worker resigns her position and disappears from sight. Repeatedly we are warned: 'Watch and pray that you will not fall into temptation' (Matt. 26:41). Peter did not, and fell. After he had been restored he was to tell others: 'Be self-controlled and alert. Your enemy the devil prowls around like a roaring lion looking for someone to devour' (1 Peter 5:8). However, when it suits him, he adopts the style of a crafty snake or an angel. Be warned, none of us is immune to his assaults.

2. The damage caused by Demas' departure. Just when Paul was facing possible execution, this man 'left him in the lurch'. You can sense the utter despair that swept over him: 'Demas … has deserted me.' It does not have to be a moral lapse or a fraudulent act, just a cooling off or breaking away from the church, possibly 'to think things out'. The devil's ploys are seemingly endless. The effects could not be more serious: the name of the Lord is dishonoured and he is grieved; the local church is, to put it mildly, discouraged; and the testimony of the deserter is snuffed out, inviting ridicule instead.

James says: 'The friendship of the world is hatred towards God,' to which can be added John's warning: 'If anyone loves the world, the love of the Father is not in him.' No spiritually minded person can contemplate that state and not be concerned.

3. The antidote to the love of the world. Alongside the counsel of Jesus to watch and pray, put Colossians 3:1-2. Heart and mind, affection and thoughts, are to be centred on Christ who is our life. Only when he fills us in this way will the god of this world find it well-nigh impossible to entice us back into his domain. The battle is tough. We will not win by doing nothing. What follows in Colossians 3 confirms how determined we must be: 'put to death', 'put off', 'put on', 'Let the peace of Christ rule in your hearts.' Impossible? No! We have been raised with Christ (1). He was victorious!

Something to do: Go through Colossians 3:1-17. Identify your weakness(es) and the positive things you must do.

Luke 5:1-11   James, son of Zebedee

His family. James, the son of Zebedee, is first mentioned in Mark 1:19, where he is called to be a disciple of Jesus. By comparing Mark 15:40 with Matthew 27:56, we find their mother was Salome. James and John were cousins of Jesus. As James is mentioned before John in most references, it is assumed James was the older brother.

His call to discipleship. Luke 5:1-11 gives an extended treatment of his call but it is likely this was not the first time James had met Jesus. If John 1:40-41 is one of John's references to himself, then, like Peter, James may have been introduced to Jesus by his brother. There were different stages in the disciples' attachment to Jesus. After an initial introduction came a specific summons to follow Jesus. Then, a selection was made from many followers and a particular group of twelve became closely associated with him, including James and John (Matt. 10:2). They had been with Jesus since the earliest days of his ministry (Mark 1:29). Out of that group a smaller number, in which James was included, was invited by Jesus to share some specially meaningful occasions with him. Peter, James and John were present at the raising of Jairus' daughter (Luke 8:51), the transfiguration (Luke 9:28), and in Gethsemane (Matt. 26:37). In addition to a natural desire for companionship, Jesus may have wanted those men to learn more about himself, because of the significant ministries they would exercise later.

His reputation. A distinctive feature about James is the nickname Jesus gave to him, along with his brother: 'sons of thunder' (Mark 3:17). The name may not have been given at that point in their discipleship and a later incident may have given rise to it. Soon after witnessing the transfiguration, the brothers wanted an inhospitable Samaritan village destroyed (Luke 9:54). Jesus rebuked them for their ignorant, vengeful prejudice and may have attached the name to them as a reminder of their folly. Their suggestion revealed a defensive zeal for the person of Jesus, a recognition of the seriousness of rejecting him and a willingness to submit to his will. James and John are also seen in an unfavourable light in Matthew 20:20. After Jesus had warned them of his imminent death, with the support of their mother, they selfishly sought high positions for themselves when his kingdom was established. The reply of Jesus included a prophecy they would suffer for their faithfulness to God.

His death. In John 21:2, the risen Christ appeared to the brothers as they and other disciples went fishing. Luke mentions James as witnessing the ascension of Jesus in Acts 1:13, along with the rest of the apostles. James is the only apostle of whose death we have any clear information (Acts 12:2). He was the first of the apostles to be martyred and this is the only reference to him without his brother.

The life of James may seem to have come to an abrupt, tragic and premature end, but his life and death were both in the hands of God. He was a trophy of grace, an undeserving sinner saved, blessed and used by the Saviour. Most of his service was hidden from the sight of later generations, but God alone knows how many lives were influenced by his ministry.

Acts 9:1-9   Saul of Tarsus

Saul was a Pharisee, the son of a Pharisee and educated by Gamaliel (Acts 5:34; 22:3; 23:6). His home life and education had equipped him to become an exemplary member of that religious party (Gal. 1:14; Phil. 3:6).

The date of his birth is unknown, but he grew up as a Hebrew child in a Hellenistic city before being sent to Jerusalem for further education. Promising boys were sent to such schools about 13 years of age. Before then, he learned how to make tents (Acts 18:3). Gamaliel had a good reputation among the people as being less bound by the bigotry of the sect and more open to Greek learning. Gamaliel may have helped Saul develop a candour and honesty in judgement, a willingness to study and make use of Greek writers and a keen and watchful enthusiasm for the Jewish law.

If Saul was not already a rabbi, he was on the way to becoming one. He may even have been a member of the Sanhedrin (Acts 26:10). If so, he must have been 30 or more at the time of Stephen's martyrdom. Saul may have already been involved in missionary activity among Gentiles (Gal. 5:11). Romans 7:7-11 suggests that during this period he had been plagued by a conviction of sin. He was aware of having broken the tenth commandment. He was conscious of the good he wanted to do being corrupted by the evil within him from which he could not escape. His zeal for persecution may have arisen from a misguided conscience which was attempting to do something for God to make up for the evil in his soul. Perhaps the covetousness to which he referred arose in connection with his inability to stand against Stephen's wisdom despite his learning and he envied Stephen's gifts and insight.

Knowingly and openly antagonistic to Christianity, he was the least likely person to become a Christian (1 Tim. 1:13-15). But Saul was not in control of his own destiny and Jesus broke into Saul's life dramatically without being invited. Although not a 'typical' conversion experience, it encourages us not to give up praying for and witnessing to the worst of sinners we know.

In 1 Corinthians 15:8, Paul included his conversion experience in his list of the resurrection appearances of Jesus. He had never met Jesus before as far as we know. The whole foundation of Saul's life was wiped out instantly and a new one laid at the same time. The new foundation was the very one he had sought to destroy in others. Jesus appeared to Saul in order to appoint him as his servant and his witness (Acts 26:16). In a moment of time, Saul had experienced the glory, grace, authority and omniscience of Jesus. He was blinded to the world by the brilliance of the glory of Christ. The life he had known came to an end and the change was so overwhelming that even the desire for food and drink was eclipsed by the mixture of joy and anguish, peace and pain. His meat and drink would be to do the will of the one who sent him. He had seen the Son. He knew the truth. His sins were forgiven. He was reconciled with God and his place in heaven was secure. All of grace.

More in the 365 series

365 daily readings from the Pentateuch

VARIOUS CONTRIBUTORS
EDITED BY RAY TIBBS

SKU: 365GBNPENT   £15

This 365 book of readings is taken from the Geneva Bible reading notes going through the Pentateuch, with some further readings on the Ten Commandments.

365 daily readings from the Gospels

VARIOUS CONTRIBUTORS
EDITED BY RAY TIBBS

SKU: 365GBNGOS   £15

This 365 book of readings is taken from the Geneva Bible Notes going through the Gospels, with further readings on the Beatitudes, the Lord's Prayer, and a section focusing on some of the highlights of the life and ministry of Jesus.

Available from
**Day One Publications, Ryelands Road, Leominster, Herefordshire HR6 8NZ
Telephone 01568 613740
Email: sales@dayone.co.uk   www.dayone.co.uk**

More in the 365 series

365 days of Encouragement

JOHN G ROBERTS

SKU: 365ENC   **£15**

John Roberts started writing 'Thought for the Day' messages at the start of the COVID-19 pandemic. His aim was to provide reassurance and ministry to many in his home church and more widely who were alone and struggling through lockdown.

This book arose from that and includes a year's worth of daily messages of encouragement, suitable for Christians of all ages and those who are searching. The messages in this book are, and will continue to be, relevant in any season of life long after the pandemic has ended.

'Clear, concise and encouraging. These daily meditations were prepared during a national pandemic when sickness, bereavement and isolation had become part of daily life. But they are not tied to a national crisis. Covering 366 daily readings they are meditations from the mind of a preacher with a heart of a pastor and rooted in the depth and breadth of the Bible. For all who want to begin or close the day with a vision of their God and the challenge and encouragement of His Word, these will prove a meaningful pause for thought and I warmly recommend them.'

Brian H Edwards

Available from

Day One Publications, Ryelands Road, Leominster, Herefordshire HR6 8NZ
Telephone 01568 613740
Email: sales@dayone.co.uk   www.dayone.co.uk

More in the 365 series

365 days with Wilberforce

KEVIN BELMONTE

SKU: 365WIL **£12**

William Wilberforce (1759-1833) led the twenty-year fight to abolish the British slave trade. He championed medical aid for the poor, prison rehabilitation, education for the deaf and restrictions on child labour. Wilberforce found nothing more effectual than private prayer, and the serious perusal of the New Testament. He maintained: 'All may be done through prayer, almighty prayer.' He insisted that 'in the calmness of the morning, before the mind is heated and wearied by the turmoil of the day, you have a season of unusual importance for communing with God and with yourself.' He seized upon such opportunities, believing: 'God will prosper me better if I wait on him.'

365 days with Wilberforce is a collection unlike any other. Drawing directly from Wilberforce's writings, the selections in this book illustrate how God sustained and guided him. Those who seek to walk their pilgrim's progress aright will find much to ponder, pray over and treasure.

Available from
Day One Publications, Ryelands Road, Leominster, Herefordshire HR6 8NZ
Telephone 01568 613740
Email: sales@dayone.co.uk   www.dayone.co.uk

More in the 365 series

365 days with **Newton**

MARYLYNN ROUSE

SKU: 365NEWTON   £12

John Newton was a rich and princely teacher, a sensitive and caring pastor, and a straight, outspoken guide. His whole ministry bore the marks so evident in his lovely hymns: it was consistently biblical (to share the Word of God), spiritual (to promote walking with God), simple (to make biblical truth and principles plain), and practical (to inculcate personal holiness and sound relationships in church and society). In this collection, every day bears these marks, so useful to every believer, so instructive for those called to minister.

'In Marylynn Rouse, Newton has found a true disciple, and a skilled publicist. By enormous diligence, and self-sacrificing application, she has made herself a leading 'Newton expert', and in this sensitive compilation all that expertise is put at our disposal. Come, enjoy and profit!'
—From the Foreword, **J Alec Motyer**

Available from
Day One Publications, Ryelands Road, Leominster, Herefordshire HR6 8NZ
Telephone 01568 613740
Email: sales@dayone.co.uk   www.dayone.co.uk

More in the 365 series

365 days with Spurgeon Vol 2

TERENCE CROSBY

SKU: 365 V2   **£12**

Following the warm reception to *365 days with Spurgeon Vol 1*—based on Charles Haddon Spurgeon's New Park Street Pulpit sermons—Terence Crosby has edited and selected this second volume of daily readings, which cover Spurgeon's first six years at London's Metropolitan Tabernacle.

Because Spurgeon treated every occasion as a unique opportunity for evangelism, an outstanding feature of these extracts is the diversity of the subjects covered, and their relevance to the contemporary Christian.

365 days with Spurgeon Volume 2 also contains a useful Scripture and subject index section, together with a unique guide to where and when Spurgeon preached.

If your usual daily Bible reading notes are becoming too formulaic, these pearls from the 'Prince of Preachers' will be a welcome antidote.

365 days with **Spurgeon** **Volume 2**

A unique collection of 365 daily readings from sermons preached by **Charles Haddon Spurgeon** from his Metropolitan Tabernacle Pulpit

Day One

Available from
Day One Publications, Ryelands Road, Leominster, Herefordshire HR6 8NZ
Telephone 01568 613740
Email: sales@dayone.co.uk   **www.dayone.co.uk**

Evidence for the Bible

CLIVE ANDERSON AND BRIAN EDWARDS

SKU: EFB4161   £25

This beautifully produced hardback book with over 200 full colour images reveals some of the many discoveries that either authenticate or illustrate the biblical narrative.

The text is accurate, informative and assumes no prior knowledge of the world of archaeology. It follows the biblical record from Genesis to Revelation.

Timelines of the Ancient Near East empires, articles on specific thorny issues such as the Pharaoh of the Exodus and the census of Quirinius, an assessment of fallacies in the world of biblical archaeology and a detailed bibliography, all add to the value of this unique volume.

EVIDENCE for the BIBLE

Clive Anderson and Brian Edwards   Day One

'This book will encourage your confidence in the reliability of the Bible as a historical book. In a world of scepticism and doubt, this is a formidable testament to the trustworthiness of scripture.'
—from *Evangelicals Now*, December 2014 — **Chris Sinkinson**, Moorlands College

Available from
Day One Publications, Ryelands Road, Leominster, Herefordshire HR6 8NZ
Telephone 01568 613740
Email: sales@dayone.co.uk   www.dayone.co.uk

Background to the Bible

BRIAN EDWARDS, CLIVE ANDERSON AND CHRIS SINKINSON

SKU: BTTB £25

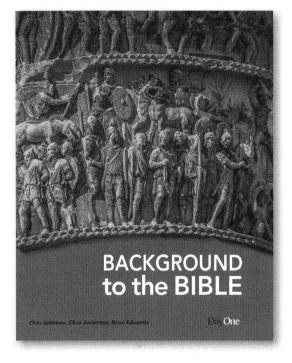

Background to the Bible is a companion to the popular *Evidence for the Bible* that was published in 2014.

That publication could not possibly cover all the evidence supporting the trustworthiness of the biblical record, and new discoveries are constantly coming to light in the vigorous and enlightening science of archaeology related to the Bible.

In *Background to the Bible* we have added new information to encourage an informed journey through the pages of the Bible.

For serious study or for relaxed and informative reading, *Background to the Bible* will prove invaluable to all who have an interest in understanding what lies behind and around the events recorded in the Bible, which is the world's most influential and widely sold, distributed and translated book.

Available from
Day One Publications, Ryelands Road, Leominster, Herefordshire HR6 8NZ
Telephone 01568 613740
Email: sales@dayone.co.uk   www.dayone.co.uk